OPIUM'S ORPHANS

OPIUM'S

THE
200-YEAR
HISTORY OF
THE WAR ON DRUGS

ORPHANS

P. E. CAQUET

REAKTION BOOKS

Published by
REAKTION BOOKS LTD
Unit 32, Waterside
44–48 Wharf Road
London N1 7UX, UK
www.reaktionbooks.co.uk

First published 2022
Copyright © P. E. Caquet 2022

Printed and bound in Great Britain by Bell & Bain, Glasgow

A catalogue record for this book is available
from the British Library

ISBN 978 1 78914 558 8

CONTENTS

A NOTE ON WEIGHTS AND CURRENCIES

This book makes frequent use of statistics. These range over a long time period and a broad geography, inevitably involving differing measures of weight and different currencies. Where applicable, the author has converted these into metric-system measures, especially kilograms and metric tons. These are the yardsticks the United Nations use, the source for many of the statistics deployed here. The main currency of reference, likewise, is the u.s. dollar, and for silver and gold the chosen unit remains the ounce. In places, for reasons of readability, original measurement units have been retained (for example the opium chest), especially the main units used by the Chinese or British in the nineteenth century. Where this is the case, their conversion value is offered in parentheses. In the days of the gold standard and metallic currencies, dollars, whether American, Spanish or Mexican, or Indochinese piasters, were often very close in value.

PROLOGUE

I n the leafy town of Taiyu, Shanxi, an inland Chinese province southwest of Beijing, the district magistrate Chen Lihe had a stele put up for public display. The date was 1817 and, four years earlier, the emperor had issued a raft of regulations against opium, including severe punishments for handling, selling or consuming it. The stele read:

> Opium is produced beyond the seas, but its poison flows into China. Those who buy it and consume it break their families, harm their own lives, and violate the law. Treachery, licentiousness, robbery, and brigandage all arise from it. Both the young and vigorous and the old and weak die from it. Wealthy and luxurious houses are impoverished by it. Brave and bright sons and younger brothers are made stupid and unfilial by it. People who dwell in peace in their houses well stocked with delicacies feel the heavy blows of the bamboo and the weight of the cangue because of it; they also suffer strangulation, exile, and banishment at the hands of the law because of it.
>
> As for its injurious effect on custom, opium destroys the five natural relationships, and its harmful effect on individual character is even more unspeakable . . . To eradicate a great scourge, its source must first be cleansed. If the district were without traffickers, from where would my people buy opium? If there were no traffickers outside its boundaries, from where would my district buy opium? . . . Henceforward,

all merchants in the district who go to Fujian, Guangdong, Jiangsu, or Zhejiang to buy goods must pledge that they will not bring a single fragment of opium back to Taiyu for sale, to the great harm of its populace. If they render respectful adherence to their oaths of abstinence, the spirits will surely reward them. If they resume trafficking, the officials will certainly punish them! And if official law cannot reach them, the spirits will surely lend assistance.[1]

By proclaiming the severest penalties against everything to do with opium, including its possession, the Chinese imperial court had in 1813 launched an all-out campaign against the drug. It sent out orders for enforcement throughout the country, including to provinces, such as Shanxi, that lay far from the coasts through which opium flowed. The stele reveals motivations that ring surprisingly modern. Opium, like modern drugs, was identified as a potentially deadly 'poison', and the text suggests it made consumers dependent (making the brave and bright 'stupid and unfilial' and having an 'unspeakable' effect on character). Socially, it threatened to make its adepts downwardly mobile ('Wealthy and luxurious houses are impoverished by it'). Beyond this, it was identified as a cause of crime and public disorder ('Treachery, licentiousness, robbery, and brigandage all arise from it'). Its lyrical language aside, the epigraphical message rings much like any statement condemning drugs today.

Qing dynasty China was the first state to ban drugs, or at least the first to do so on the basis of justifications that remain relevant today. The stele's appeal to the spirits, called on to lend a hand to officials in hunting down traffickers, sounds a quainter note. Yet religious agitation would also arise in Europe and the United States as a powerful force for drug prohibition in the nineteenth and twentieth centuries. Moral stigma and religious imagery remain part of the vocabulary for condemning drug users to this day. Our Taiyu magistrate lastly made the point that 'opium is produced beyond the seas' and that 'to eradicate a great scourge, its source must first be cleansed.' China's opium came from India and the Middle East. The belief that supply could more easily be cut off because it originated abroad was, and is, darkly seductive. States are forever prone to treat their drug problems through border policing or by placing pressure on foreign countries, avoiding the unpleasant business of confronting their own citizenry.

No nostrum would feed the long war on drugs more consistently than the idea that intoxicants can simply be eliminated at source.

The emperor's penalties for smoking opium, introduced in 1813, were a hundred blows of the bamboo cane and one month in the cangue – a type of mobile wooden pillory affixed around the head that prevented the prisoner from feeding him- or herself. Public officials caught smoking would be dismissed.[2] Under provisions that had lapsed or been allowed to fall into neglect but were now revived, traffickers were liable to the additional penalty of transportation to the frontier for service as military labourers. As to the operators of opium dens – public houses whose chief business was to dispense opium for smoking – they faced the extreme punishment of death by strangulation.[3]

It is worth highlighting that at the time of these prohibitions, the Qing empire scarcely had a rampant opium problem. China's opium smokers could not have numbered more than a few tens of thousands in 1813 – at most 10,000 to 20,000, if taken to mean addicts. This was a tiny proportion of its population of more than 300 million.[4] Per capita consumption, at around 600 grams (1.3 lb) per thousand annually, was actually lower than that of England and Wales in a comparable period, at 725 grams (1.6 lb) per thousand.[5] Opium was freely available in Britain, where it was routinely taken as a painkiller in pill or drink form.

It is from these humble origins that drug control has grown, over two centuries, to achieve the far grander proportions it has today. The war on drugs did not originate in the USA. Even less did it begin, as is sometimes believed, with Richard Nixon. Nixon was not even the first American president to declare such a war: in 1954 President Eisenhower had called for 'a new war on narcotic addiction at the local, national, and international level'.[6] Modern drug prohibition originated in China. Two Opium Wars ensued from the prohibition edicts, forcing the drug on the Qing empire. Yet the wars attracted moral censure in the United States and left a stain of guilt in Britain. At the beginning of the twentieth century, American, Chinese and European diplomats assembled at a set of conferences to reform the trade in the drug. These conferences established the norms for present-day anti-narcotics legislation, national and international. The Chinese and Americans were on the offensive, and the Europeans were eager to make amends, or at least to be seen to be doing the right thing: the result was drug prohibition. From there, controls over the narcotics trade passed on to the League of Nations and later the United Nations (UN), turning into a global endeavour.

Accompanying this process, the set of regulated drugs expanded to involve an increasingly broad array. Opium is an addictive drug derived from a plant, a white-flowered variety of poppy, whose seed pod yields the juice from which it is made. Chemically refined, it can be transformed into a range of compounds collectively known as opiates, among which are morphine and the even more potent heroin. Consumers of opiates numbered 29 million worldwide in 2017.[7] Yet patterns of drug use and the list of prohibited substances have changed out of all recognition since Qing times. According to estimates compiled by the United Nations Office on Drugs and Crime (UNODC), over a quarter of a billion people used illegal drugs of any kind in the same year, or around 5 per cent of the world's adult population.[8] The schedule now includes cocaine, a drug invented in the nineteenth century, but also a paraphernalia of stimulants and hallucinogens which, though often sold under the labels of LSD or Ecstasy, are constantly evolving in composition. Consumers of the synthetic stimulants known as amphetamines now outnumber opiate users worldwide.[9] Amphetamines have become the drug of choice in several Asian countries, including China, Japan and the Philippines.[10] Finally, the prohibited list includes the plant-based cannabis or marijuana, whose use is as ancient as opium's – though its recent legalization in a number of U.S. states and in two countries, Uruguay and Canada, suggests that it may one day leave the group of illicit drugs.

It is the story of this transformation that this book presumes to tell: how an ever larger group of mind-altering products came to be prohibited throughout the world, for what reasons, and with what effects. Why are such drugs illegal today? Should they be? Has drug prohibition worked? What have its consequences been? Two hundred years ago, the Jiaqing Emperor chose to launch a campaign against anyone among his subjects who dealt in or smoked opium. Today, the UN and its 190-plus sovereign members actively police and punish drug trafficking and use worldwide. How did one lead to the other?

Incidentally, this is a history of drug prohibition, not a history of drugs, and even less a history of intoxicants in general. It is the rise of prohibition that concerns this book, the ban on everything coming under the quaint term 'narcotics': not the drugs themselves, but the endeavour to suppress them. Nor is what ought to be considered a drug its preoccupation, and whether the list should include alcohol, tobacco, coffee or even video games. Rightly or wrongly, the legislator has made that choice. Like drugs, some of these substances or activities have been labelled addictive. But 'addiction' is a loose term whose changing meanings have themselves been part of the rise of control. All the best-known products coming under the label 'drugs' have in common that they began their modern-era careers as medicines. It is this common origin, not degrees of addictiveness, that has singled them out from other intoxicants, and it has been crucial in determining how and why they were banned.

Drug control was born of historical accident, not rational design. Colonialism, the backlash against it, and international affairs were the triggers for prohibition, interacting with often superficial beliefs about the drugs themselves. Marijuana's route to prohibition has been just as circuitous as opium's. Likewise originating in the paradoxes and mishaps of colonial interaction, it came about, in the mid-1920s, suddenly and as the afterthought to yet another anti-opium conference. But that opiates were the first drug to attract international attention was itself fateful. The drugs of abuse currently consumed throughout the world may be a diverse set, but the medical model for addiction was developed to describe opiates, substances that involve powerful habituation and withdrawal effects as well as high risks of overdose. Dumping all drugs in a common category with opiates has both fuelled the growth in the anti-narcotics system and made it especially difficult to reform. (Ask someone if marijuana should be legalized, and every so often the answer will be: what about heroin, then, should that be legal too?)

Varying cultural mores and social conditions have historically fostered differing methods for regulating drugs in different countries. There are many shades of prohibition, ranging from maximum penalties on anything drug-related, including cultivation, refining, distribution and consumption, to the tolerance or decriminalization of some of these activities, especially possession. In certain places, certain drugs are legal medically but not recreationally – and while the barrier between medical and recreational use is central to prohibition, it is sometimes as moveable as it is hard to police. Some drug regimes qualify prohibition by allowing 'maintenance': the provision of drugs to dependent users under medical supervision. The British regime as it emerged from 1916 onwards diverged from the American one. So did the French, German, Iranian and Bolivian regimes, to name but a few. To some extent these individual country frameworks continue to differ. Yet the system promoted by the community of nations and vested in the UN agency UNODC has been surprisingly successful in propagating itself, if more debatably so in its results. Drug suppression became, through its nineteenth- and twentieth-century history, a more or less uniform, internationally coherent effort. This book describes how this came about.

The story begins with the Qing edicts because it is from them that a straight line can be drawn to contemporary control. The first anti-drug laws were not actually enacted in China, and even in China they did not date from 1813. In the United States and Europe, there were no or almost no restrictions on narcotics until at least the mid-nineteenth century, and no meaningful controls until the twentieth. But earlier bans or debates have been documented in Thailand, Vietnam, Persia, on Java, and in colonial Peru. The Thai laws were probably the most intriguing. As early as 1360, King Ramathibodi I of Ayutthaya promulgated a 'Law of the Three Seals' that forbade the sale and consumption of opium. Offenders would be paraded around the city, on land and on water, for three days each, then jailed until they were detoxified.[11] Opium use was inimical to Buddhist religious practice because it was an obstacle to concentration and by extension to meditation and righteous behaviour. Among the Buddha's fundamental precepts was an injunction against intoxication.[12] Thai kingship was meanwhile steeped in Buddhist symbolism and spirituality: Thai kings traditionally claimed descent from an incarnation of Buddha, and they relied on legendary texts and rituals to underpin their legitimacy.[13] The Thai laws thus anticipated, in their condemnation of opium, the modern state's paternalistic interest in its citizens' good behaviour, combined with its concern for that behaviour's sociopolitical ramifications. At the same time, unlike the later Qing regulations, the Law of the Three Seals remained somewhat narrowly rooted in religion. It would not prove of much consequence outside Thailand.

The Vietnamese emperor Canh Tri III may have prohibited opium in 1665, calling for the eradication of crops and stores, though with what effect is not known.[14] On the island of Java (Indonesia) the seventeenth-century Sultanate of Bantam likewise banned the drug, the tentative evidence being that the law condemned addicts and even their families to slavery.[15] Dutch colonizers later respected Bantam's opium-free status, though this did not stop the drug from becoming entrenched on the rest of the island.[16] In Persia Shah Abbas I issued a decree in 1596 giving his courtiers the choice between quitting opium and exile. In 1621 he banned its use among his soldiers. Decrees of a similar nature against opium and hashish, the cannabis resin, and *bhang*, a drink made from the same plant, were promulgated by the Persian shahs in 1694, 1729 and 1796. None of these appears to have been very long-lasting, or to have found much purchase beyond court circles.[17]

The Peruvian coca leaf – the plant from which cocaine is derived – offers a rare example of an early-modern drug debate. After the Spanish conquistadors had snuffed out the Inca empire in the early sixteenth century, they quickly found the leaf a valuable commodity. Coca was both profitably farmed and taxed, and it was supplied to native Peruvians to sustain them in hard labour in the silver mines.[18] The Church, though, became offended at the leaf's association with pagan rituals and sacrifices. Missionaries asserted that coca was the invention of the Devil, and they petitioned viceregal officials to pro-scribe it. A lay criticism was that coca cultivation and chewing fostered malnutrition and disease. In the mid-century the Spanish viceroys decided to regulate and limit the expansion of coca plantations. Yet the Church itself was divided, and at the council of Lima of 1567–8, some prelates held that the leaf was only fortifying. In the end, King Philip II gave priority to his silver-mine revenues. The leaf continued as an income-generating commodity, and the debate eventually died out. The argument, in any case, had focused more on coca in its agri-cultural incidence and as an obstacle to missionary efforts than on its dangers or merits as a drug.[19]

In China, the first anti-opium edict was issued in 1729. It was at that time that traffickers and den operators became liable to military exile or death. This could not quite yet be described, though, as a declaration of war on the drug. The edict of 1729 belonged to a period of reforming zeal, triggered by a change of monarch, in which many activities deemed subversive were denounced. The opium edict was 'just one of a series of edicts in which [the emperor] condemned those who harmed public morality by seducing or confusing others – a series that also included bans on prostitution and the teaching of martial arts'.[20] Harsh penalties may have been placed on the statute books, but there is no evidence that they were applied during the rest of the century.[21] In the same year, for example, a governor of the coastal Fujian province condemned a suspected trafficker to the cangue, his torment to be followed by military exile. The culprit appealed, arguing that his opium had been for medicinal use. Not only was his condemnation overturned, but the imperial court ordered the confiscated drug to be released back to him.[22]

The foreign merchants who brought opium to China were aware of its status as an illicit article, suggesting that a degree of enforcement may have applied in coastal provinces in the late eighteenth century. The first documented prosecution under the 1729 edict nevertheless occurred in 1806. From that date, a succession of smuggling cases alerted the emperor to the drug's progress into the interior of China. An indictment was brought on smuggling and refining charges on the island of Haitan in 1806, and two more provincial prosecutions attracted Beijing's attention between 1808 and 1810. Another case, dated 1811, confronted the authorities with the practice of smoking opium in pure form, not mixed with tobacco, as had hitherto been the custom.[23] In 1810 the sentinels at one of the gates of the Forbidden City had stopped a young man trying to smuggle in a set of opium cases, and in 1813 it was the guards themselves who were caught with the pipe.[24]

At last the emperor responded with his new, draconian set of laws. Unlike earlier measures, they were wide-ranging and designed to be long-lasting. They would also have a deep foreign impact. China's opium came from colonial India, and the merchants responsible for shipping it into Canton flew the British flag. The Chinese realization that 'opium is produced beyond the seas' would prompt the emperor, all else having failed, to take the axe to the drug's foreign supply line. The merchants, though, could count on the support of the world's most powerful navy, and they depended on the aggressive reflexes of an increasingly assertive home nation. Its prohibition of opium had set Qing China on a collision course with imperial Britain.

PART I
THE RISE OF
CONTROL

1

FORBIDDEN CITIES

W hy did the Qing dynasty Chinese take to smoking opium? The question is fundamental, yet likely to remain forever shrouded in mystery. Humans have consumed opium since the dawn of historical time, and the use of the poppy's sap is thought to have been pioneered in Asia Minor or Mesopotamia. The name originates in the Greek word *opion*, the root of both the Persian word *afyun* and the Chinese *yapian*, hinting at the route the drug took eastward through conquest or trade.[1] Opium had been used in China since the Tang dynasty (seventh to ninth centuries AD), but, as in the Indian subcontinent or Europe, it served as an ingredient in medicinal preparations. In China, opium was long used for combating diarrhoea, dysentery, sunstroke, coughing, asthma, and other pains and ailments.[2] A major change took place when tobacco arrived via the Philippines or the Indonesian archipelago.[3] In Indonesia and the Malay peninsula, it had become local practice to blend opium with tobacco, forming a product known as *madat* and designed to be smoked. The custom spread to Taiwan, where local plants were thrown in to make a boiled concoction now named *madak*. After the Qing conquered Taiwan in 1683, Chinese seafarers – sailors, labourers, merchants – began to carry *madak* back home.[4]

Thus adulterated, opium entered the user's body only in small quantities. From the mid-eighteenth century, though, it began to be smoked pure. *Madak* smoking had begun as a simple affair: on Taiwan, the blend was placed in a hollow clay pot and smoked through a bamboo tube and a filter made of coir fibres produced from coconut trees. Pure opium smoking, by contrast, was the object of sophisticated rituals and even connoisseurship. Opium was typically smoked reclining. Its preparation required dexterity and training, and it was difficult to perform for a beginner. The smoker, or a servant or wait-ress in a den, would first roll and knead a small ball of opium, with the help of two needles, over the flame of a lamp. This brought it to the right temperature and to a texture much like that of caramelized sugar. Still using one of the needles, the operator would cut a conical pellet from the ball and flatten this again to fit it on top of the smok-ing bowl. The bowl itself, an often ornate china or metal globe affixed to the pipe, contained a smaller aperture through which the smoke flowed. The pellet was pierced into a doughnut shape to leave this aperture free. The fumes were now ready to seep through. The smoker leaned the pipe towards the lamp's flame, pressed his or her lips around the mouthpiece and sucked.[5] A contemporary describes the experience:

> On a miserable rainy day, or when you feel down, light up an opium lamp on a low table, recline face to face, pass the pipe around and inhale. At first there is a sudden feeling of refreshment, one's head and eyes becoming very clear. Soon afterwards, there is quietude and profound well-being. After a while, one's bones and joints become extremely relaxed and the eyes heavy. This is followed by a gradual descent into slumber, and detached from all worries, one enters a world of dreams and fantasies, completely free like a spirit: what a paradise![6]

The ostensible explanation for the spread of recreational opium, especially pure, is that it emerged as a social marker. High Qing China was exceptionally prosperous; it saw the flowering of lively consumer and leisure cultures. Among the moneyed classes, the fashion was for exotic goods: carpets, glasses, pens, pictures, musical boxes, watches . . . Opium became another article of pleasure: urban and civilized, like its consumers.[7] In an era when music halls, tea houses and other places of entertainment flourished, it joined the list of items of con-spicuous and hedonistic consumption. Urban China was endowed with quarters of river boats filled with tea or smoking shops, many of them hosting prostitutes, and their prices favoured a clientele of rich merchants, literati and mandarins. These establishments began pur-veying *madak* and, later, pure opium. From there, opium spread into the better-appointed home or the dedicated public house or 'den'.[8] Soon, rich families employed opium butlers. They collected prize versions of the utensils: items encrusted with silver mimicking flowers and leaves, ornate lamps or pipes made of precious wood, jade or tortoiseshell, or carved out of ivory in the shape of elephants' tusks. Opium even earned its own vocabulary, like oenology, with 'yellow', 'long' or 'loose' used to describe its various states, and the expression 'to light the lamp' became a euphemism for sharing the comfort of one's smoking chamber.[9]

As opium spread inland from the southern coastal provinces of Guangdong and Fujian, the volumes smoked rose slowly but surely. If one trusts the records of opium's principal carrier at the time, the Dutch East India Company, Chinese imports in the first half of the eighteenth century were in the order of two hundred chests annually.[10] (The chest, which would become a standard packaging and weight unit under the British East India Company, weighed around 60 kilograms (130 lb).) At this level, it is likely that most opium was still taken as medicine rather than mixed into *madak*. By the beginning of the nineteenth century, though, and after the emergence of pure opium smoking, imports had reached 4,000 chests.[11]

They were destined to expand by a still greater multiple in the decades to come. If demand was stimulated by opium's foreign mystique, its suppliers were eager to oblige. By the time of the Jiaqing Emperor's 1813 prohibition decree, opium had come to be cultivated commercially in China, but this was confined to remote regions such as the far western Xinjiang or southwestern Yunnan. Domestic production remained negligible.[12] The overwhelming share of China's opium came from India. Under the Mughals, opium had been traded freely and sold for export to local, Dutch, Portuguese or British traders.[13] After the conquest of Bengal, this had increasingly fallen under British control, though it was not until 1773 that Governor General Warren Hastings had placed the opium supply under the monopoly of the East India Company. The idea was simply to milk the revenues from it for the Presidency of Bengal. A contractor bought the opium from the cultivators, then sold it to the government, who auctioned it on to private traders. After 1797 the contractor was eliminated and replaced by a government agency.[14]

The scale and complexity of the operations involved should remove any doubt that the trade run by the East India Company was anything but a consciously elaborated, profit-oriented enterprise. Bengal opium was cultivated in two geographical areas. (The poppy was also grown elsewhere in India, where the product was designated as 'Malwa', but for a while the lion's share went to 'Bengal'.) The first area was centred around Patna and the second around Ghazipur, both upriver on the Ganges from Calcutta. Two Bengal agencies, one for each region, sat atop a multi-level hierarchy involving British administrators, local agents, the landed aristocracy, village leaders and poppy farmers. The farmer was legally bound to sell to the company and forbidden to sell elsewhere. Sowing was completed by November, and by late January the poppy was in bloom. Harvesting required skill: the farmer incised the plant's pod at exactly the right depth to let out its white juice while ensuring it neither hardened nor got lost. He or she then sun-dried that juice for several days, letting it coagulate and turn brown. In April or May, after the harvest, farmers and agents took the opium to rural collection centres.[15]

The Bengal agencies sold opium for distribution in India itself in the shape of rough bricks. The Chinese consumer, however, was reckoned to have finer tastes. Transportation by sea required that the product be kept in a moist state to maintain quality. It also needed to be free from adulteration and to carry proof of origin. It was accordingly processed for export in what became two vast factories in Patna and Ghazipur. After the opium had arrived and been weighed and checked for impurities, craftsmen began turning out 'cakes' or balls of opium approximately the size of a cannonball. Each ball was rolled into dried stems and poppy leaves and placed in a round, earthenware cup of the right size. This was a delicate task: each 'caker' was able to turn out no more than six cakes a day. Next, during August and September, the cakes were placed on high racks to dry out. This too was labour-intensive: to ensure that drying took place evenly, each cake was given a one-quarter turn once every six days. After that, the workers began to prepare the mango-wood chests in which the opium balls would be packed: fitted with compartments for forty balls, sealed with gum and covered in burlap, these were stamped with the East India Company's mark. At last, after another three months, the chests were ready to be shipped downriver to Calcutta for auction. At their peak, the 'Sudder' factories, as they were called, of Patna and Ghazipur would each employ more than a thousand workers. During drying season, the racks, designed to hold tens of thousands of balls, were stacked from floor to ceiling, their upper shelves reachable only with a tall ladder.[16]

Save for one ill-fated attempt in 1781, the East India Company never handled the opium trade into China directly. Rather, the chests were sold to private merchants locally licensed as 'country' traders, who shipped it out in their own name or on behalf of co-investors. The company was well aware that opium was a forbidden article at destination, and this system provided it with plausible deniability.

The Qing authorities channelled all their European trade through Canton, where it came under the supervision of the provincial and city governors and the inspector of customs or Hoppo. All authorized trade was performed through a select group of Chinese merchants named the Hong. The East India Company carried out a significant amount of business in Canton, involving both the sale of articles other than opium, such as raw cotton, and the purchase of Chinese goods, especially tea. Indeed, until 1834 it held a monopoly on the British trade with China – the India 'country' traders forming an exemption. Until that date, the company also retained control over the Canton residences, known as 'factories', where the foreigners stayed. This enabled it to discipline, if needed, the private traders on whom it relied to sell opium. In turn, the 'country' traders sought to escape that supervision, the more freely to engage in the illicit trade. They discovered, for example, the trick of registering as consuls for third-party countries in nearby Macao (then a Portuguese colony). James Matheson, for example, at one point represented Denmark and Thomas Dent Sardinia, while others allegedly stood for Prussia, Hamburg or Poland.[17]

The charade continued at payment time. Beyond Canton runs an expanding delta filled with islands of differing sizes, and it was off these islands that the opium was unloaded, not in the city itself, where it would have been too dangerous to do so. Business dealings, however, took place at the factories or in nearby streets. There, the merchants contracted opium sales with Chinese brokers. The broker paid upfront, in silver, and received a delivery order exchangeable for opium downriver. The merchant in turn took the silver to the British factory and obtained a company bill for it. The bill could be exchanged for coin or goods back in India. The company used the silver to buy tea and other articles from the Hong.[18]

The Jiaqing Emperor's anti-drug offensive began to make itself felt, in the south, from 1815. It first struck at Macao. The authorities took sixteen Chinese dealers into custody, and Portuguese ships were henceforth ordered to submit to cargo searches by local officers.[19] As to Canton, at some point the opium merchants had become so bold as to move their unloading all the way up to Whampoa, a village on a flat island close to shore a mere 20 kilometres (12 mi.) from the city. The Canton governor and the Hoppo warned the Hong about such practices, who passed the message on to the East India Company. The company's board of representatives on the ground, the 'Supercargoes Committee', seconded the warning. The merchants ignored it, declaring it a blatant attempt to extract 'squeeze' or corruption money from them. In 1821 the exasperated authorities laid charges of smuggling against the owners of four ships at Whampoa, impounded these, and told the men they could have their ships back when they moved out and pledged never to return. The smuggling trade moved further down the delta, to a more remote island named Lintin.[20]

The foreign merchants may have thought they led dangerous lives – Charles Magniac called the campaign to move them from Whampoa 'the hottest persecution we remember' – but it was their Chinese buyers who took all the risk.[21] It was they who took the opium to shore, refined it and distributed it inland. From the foreign clippers, they transferred the drug onto boats nicknamed 'fast crabs' and 'scrambling dragons': sleek craft built of bright, unpainted wood and designed for speed, combining sails and rows of oars and manned by up to sixty or seventy sailors. While evading the Chinese navy's junks was their primary purpose, these boats were equipped for combat. Scrambling dragons and fast crabs were known to fire their guns at both patrolling authorities and rivals. When cornered, their sailors were ready for hand-to-hand fighting.[22]

These buyers boiled down the opium to turn it into a more concentrated, smokeable product locally termed *chandu*.[23] Sometimes they sold the raw paste on. History does not record who the opium kingpins were on the Chinese side, but they must have existed. Some of the Hong probably participated in opium dealing, though the richest of them, a man of reputedly fabulous wealth named Howqua, is believed not to have engaged in it.[24] The evidence nevertheless attests to the role of wealthy single buyers or buyer syndicates. On its own, operating such equipment as the fast crabs and dragons required significant capital. Just one chest of opium was an expensive item, equivalent to $10,000 or more in today's money, and Jardine

Matheson's accounts show individual buyers paying for hundreds of chests over short periods.[25]

Gangs, possibly involved in other forms of crime, took the drug further inland. There, as do modern drug dealers, their members and underlings faced the risk of getting caught – and the penalty of transportation or death – and of assault from rivals or extortionists. According to a local administrator, hundreds of 'brigands' belonging to secret societies banded together to pursue the trade in the regions of Hunan, Hubei and Jiangxi, which stood on the route northward.[26] Gangs of opium dealers were reported to run the routes around Shanghai and Suzhou, off the Yangtze, their boats fitted with fire cannons to dissuade the police from investigating them.[27] At least one 'mutual aid' society dedicated to opium peddlers and dealers is known to have existed among the minority Hakka population inhabiting the key area between Fujian, Guangdong and inland Jiangxi. Members of this 'Red Society' wore little red or green woollen buttons as a mark and hid their wares in bags of salt. Reports estimated that the organization comprised between 20,000 and 30,000 men, all reputed to be 'fierce and carry daggers' and be too dangerous to arrest.[28]

Beyond the main routes, finally, distribution networks tapered into a myriad of smaller undertakings and individual dealers: small-time peddlers who, when arrested, would claim to have been offered their opium by unnamed 'Canton strangers'.[29] One of them whose record has survived was the unemployed provincial Zhang Rui. Zhang had moved to Beijing to open a fish shop just inside the city's northern gate. On a visit to his home city of Tianjin, he made the acquaintance of a boatman dealing in raw opium and 'came up with the idea of selling it in order to fish for profit'. He purchased around 1 kilogram (2.2 lb) of raw opium and carried it back to his shop in the capital. Together with an assistant, Wang Yongde, he processed the opium into smokeable paste. The men also invested in opium paraphernalia in the hope of selling it on the side. A few months later, old friends and family who were engaged in the fish and various other trades came to the shop 'to discuss the prevailing price of fish'. But just as they were sitting down, officials came for an inspection and discovered the opium, porcelain bowls and bamboo pipes. Six were arrested, though only Zhang and Wang were found guilty of opium dealing. Both men confessed and asked for mercy, insisting that they had sold the drug only this one time. They were both sentenced to strangulation.[30] It was such petty or desperate social climbers who, at most risk to themselves, stood at the end of the long chain that began in the Ganges plain around Patna and Ghazipur.

As the fishmongers' case attests, the Qing authorities again upped the penalties to the maximum for opium dealing and eventually for smoking itself.

By 1813 imported opium volumes had risen to around 5,000 chests per annum.[31] This comprised a majority of East India Company 'Bengal', a smaller quantity of opium grown elsewhere in India or 'Malwa', and a dribble from places further afield such as Turkey. As of 1820 volumes remained at approximately the same level. Thereafter, however, they began to climb steeply. Within five years, the opium imported into Canton and Macao had passed the 10,000 chest mark. By the 1830–31 trading season, this had doubled again. Volumes flattened for a few years until 1834–5, but doubled yet again in the following five years, to the unheard-of number of 40,000 chests in 1838–9.[32] At this level, consumption stood at 3.75 kilograms (8.3 lb) per thousand population.[33] For comparison, in England and Wales, per-thousand opium consumption was 1.2 kilograms (2.6 lb).[34]

Did prohibition itself contribute to this dizzying rise? By increasing the risks attendant on drug dealing, hard penalties increase the rewards demanded by those sufficiently foolhardy to engage in it. The terrible prospect of transportation or death discourages competition. The high margins inherent to smuggling in turn encourage peddlers to push drugs aggressively on customers, providing free samples and other inducements to get them hooked. Demand for addictive products being price-inelastic, margins hold up, inducing yet more participants into the trade as the user population expands. A collection of judicial cases prosecuted between 1816 and 1820 reveal that, in one province, the wholesale price of a *tael* (37.5 grams, or 1.3 oz) of crude opium was 0.86 silver *taels*. This placed the price of refined opium at 1.3 silver *taels* after accounting for the reduction in weight from boiling. The street value of a *tael* of refined opium, meanwhile, fluctuated around 1.8 silver *taels*.[35] The street dealer thus stood to make 0.5 silver *tael* for each 1.3 *tael* invested, a quick 40 per cent return.

This wholesale price itself translated into $1,800 per chest. But Pearl River estuary prices averaged just below $1,000 in that period, helping make the wholesaler $800 per chest. The total mark-up from disembarkation to end customer was thus close to 2.5 times – sizeable for such a cheaply transportable product.[36] In addition, this did not take into account the profit the foreign merchant himself was making. This is a rough extrapolation from a few cases, but the Qing judicial archives are filled with records of small traders making a quick buck, or a quick *tael*, from opium when business was too hard in their own trade. Such operations could flourish from humble origins:

> Ling Yashang of Panyu county organized an opium partner-
> ship of four men, each partner initially contributing twenty
> Mexican silver dollars. When profits began to soar, they
> expanded to thirteen partners and branched out into the
> opium den business. After a while Ling grew apprehensive,
> lest the partnership draw the attention of the authorities. So,
> as he and his partners later testified, he suggested that they
> organize 'a gang of protectors who would gather together into
> a mob to curse [and obstruct investigators] while we made a
> quick getaway. This would make it difficult for the magistrate's
> men to pursue us. We agreed that we would [pay] the protec-
> tors an average wage of one silver dollar each.' The protection
> gang numbered thirty-two local men, most of whom the
> partners 'knew very well'.[37]

Prohibition on its own nevertheless cannot be blamed for the tenfold increase in opium sales between 1815 and 1839. After all, deal-ing itself had at least nominally been forbidden since 1729 without causing such a rapid increase. It was the punishment of smokers that was the great novelty of the 1813 edict – together with a tougher en-forcement programme – and this was not likely to stimulate demand.

A second explanation is cultural and has to do with an extension of the same trends that had caused opium's original adoption in the eighteenth century. From 1800 the drug spilled further into the inte-rior and its numerous urban centres. Having achieved status through consumption by the commercial and administrative elites, it began to be picked up by the less well-off.[38] Qing China's population was exploding: from 150 million up to 300 million in 1800, and 400 million by 1840.[39] For a long while China had enjoyed a parallel economic boom, but by the early nineteenth century this was flagging, and with it the ability to feed and keep prosperous such large numbers of people. Access to the magistracy – the imperial elite – took place by examination, and the number of places, kept roughly constant, accounted for a tiny proportion of the aspiring population.[40] Improving or even keeping one's social rank, whether within the commercial or titled classes, was becoming more difficult. Addictive behaviours, including opium smoking, may well have followed from rising economic anxieties and social frustrations.

More generally, opium entrenched its position within Qing material culture and sociability. This would become more frankly discernible later in the century, but opium smoking became a part of Chinese hospitality, male companionship and celebratory rituals. Even if it were recognized as a dangerous article, opium achieved a sufficient decree of desirability to become, or almost become, a staple. That its progress was specific to Chinese culture in the period is tentatively borne out by patterns elsewhere in Southeast Asia. In places such as Cambodia, Vietnam or Burma (now Myanmar) later in the century – when surveys became available – opium smokers were proportionally far more numerous among the Chinese than among host populations.[41] This may have merely reflected greater levels of wealth and urbanization, but it is also worth noting that India had long been the site of opium-taking among a variety of social classes, yet the drug never spread there to the same extent as in China.[42]

The third culprit for opium's meteoric rise, of course, is supply. The Chinese opium market expanded because the East India Company was primed, willy-nilly, to feed increasing volumes into it. This assertion is borne out by observable price trends within the period.[43] From around $1,900 in 1820–21, when the steep increase in volumes began, the price of a chest of Bengal (at Pearl River estuary rates) fell all the way to $570 in 1834–5, remaining around that low until the end of the decade. When accused, back home, of being merchants of death, the British traders replied that they were only supplying an article the Chinese demanded. The fall in prices actually points to a glut, suggesting that the expansion in China's opium consumption was at least partly supply-led.

The chronological detail within the period is equally damning: most of the fall in prices took place in the 1820s, when volumes approximately quadrupled. When quantities delivered reached a brief plateau between 1830 and 1832, prices likewise stalled around a level of $900. They then resumed their plunge as the trade doubled again in size. Both rises in volume were thus accompanied by price declines. Had supply lagged demand, one would have expected to see rising, not falling prices. As will be seen, both the company and the 'country' traders engaged, in the 1820s and '30s, in specific actions accounting for these patterns.

The trigger for the 1813 opium decree was the emperor's discovery that opium smoking had progressed all the way into the Forbidden City itself. The edict began: 'This severely prohibits opium smoking, as recently many officials, civilians, court eunuchs and palace guards have been intoxicated with opium smoking, undermining social customs and moral norms.'[44] Another unwelcome discovery may have moved the emperor to action: Prince Minning, his son and successor, had himself experimented with opium. The evidence is a set of verses written by the prince sometime between 1799 and 1813, exalting smoking with a 'hollow pipe' mounted with a copper head and tail and sporting an 'eye', characteristics that belonged solely to the opium pipe. 'It is the first sunny day after a spring snow, the sun and the wind in the garden and the trees are beautiful. I have nothing to do except reading and studying history. Bored and tired, I ask the servant to prepare *yan* and a pipe to inhale. Each time, my mind suddenly becomes clear, my eyes and ears refreshed.'[45] We do not know whether the Jiaqing Emperor was told any of this, but twenty years later the missionary Charles Gutzlaff came across the story, in the vicinity of Tianjin, that 'in consequence of the heir of the crown having died by opium smoking, very severe edicts had been published against the use of the drug.'[46] If there was a kernel of truth to this, it would not be the last time parental fears acted as a prop to drug prohibition.

The campaign against opium nevertheless proceeded from deep-seated causes. Qing motives for fighting opium ultimately sprang from public-health concerns. Imperial rule was rooted in a long tradition of Confucian paternalism, and it was exercised primarily through a mandarinate steeped in classical ideals of good governance. This involved looking after the population's moral and material welfare.

Certainly the Qing Chinese were aware that opium put its users at risk of becoming dependent. By the early nineteenth century the word *yin* had emerged to describe the craving for opium. In 1831 a censor named Liu Guangsan described *yin* as an illness contracted from extended opium smoking that was fatal if not 'satisfied' at the proper time.[47] Earlier, the poet Yu Jiao had written: 'If one smokes regularly, it will affect the heart and spleen. If one becomes ill after not smoking for a single day, this condition is called *yin*. When the *yin* comes, the nose and eyes start to run, whereas the hands and the feet become stiff and clenched. It feels like facing a dagger while a tiger is chasing one from behind – fearful yet unable to surrender. A chronic opium smoker ends up with shrunken shoulders and neck; his face becomes wan and he is without energy, just like a sick person.'[48] Reports are that common people asked visiting doctors to wean them from opium, and mandarins listed pills and elixirs used to combat the habit, proving that it was widely recognized as such.[49] In 1810 the emperor himself exclaimed: 'Opium has a most intense effect. Those who smoke it can suddenly become excited and capable of doing whatever they want without restraint. Before long, it will steal their life and kill them.'[50]

Related to these health concerns were fears that opium use and its trafficking would rock the social order. Opium enriched criminal gangs, therefore it had to be suppressed – the court failing to see that it was prohibition that benefited the gangs. Part of Qing ideal governance was moreover that it should rest lightly on the taxpayer. The government establishment was thin on the ground: the civil bureaucracy on the statute books totalled only around 20,000 officials. These administrators employed private secretaries and hired clerks and runners locally, but they lacked a separate budget for them.[51] The police force itself, known as the Green Standard Army, was poorly equipped to deal with the well-armed syndicates of the criminal underworld. For urban surveillance, it could tap into such sources as temple keepers, harbourmasters and innkeepers, who kept tabs on travellers, recording names, professions and what they carried with them. This helped nab petty offenders. Beyond this, though, numbers were too few. Enforcement required the cooperation of local social networks and elites, the village headman or the local squire.[52] The Qing hoped to enlist such support by being seen to hold the moral high ground, and this translated, in the case of opium, into interdiction. Paradoxically, the severity of penalties compensated for weak enforcement capacity, accounting for the court's increasingly desperate measures.

The fear of drug-fuelled banditry was meanwhile no shibboleth. There was always a thin line between banditry and political rebellion.

Crime syndicates were apt to blend into the secret societies liable to foment popular uprisings. A White Lotus insurgency uniting north-eastern peasants with urban workers had defied the authorities for ten years between 1794 and 1805, and it had only been defeated after local elites were encouraged to raise their own militias. The preceding dynasty, the Ming, had fallen to just such a rebellion in the seventeenth century. In 1813 another sect carried out a daring raid on the Forbidden City in an attempt to assassinate the emperor, reaching the palace's inner sanctum before it was stopped.[53]

Complicating the court's dilemma, finally, was the issue of corruption. Beijing feared that the magistrates themselves would become addicts, further impairing an already thinly spread administration. Conversely, however, the profits from dealing risked feeding bribery, especially on the lower administrative rungs. In the 1820s and '30s higher-ranking officials proved time and again ready to enforce anti-opium legislation, no matter how much they stood to gain by not doing so. While major corruption scandals, particularly involving palace eunuchs, did shake the Qing empire in this period, it is far from clear that the mandarinate itself was corrupt as a rule. Yet these high-ranking magistrates, lacking sufficient budgets, depended on expedients to pay the salaries of their lower-level staff or on allowing them to raise their own compensation.[54] If this involved closing their eyes to opium abuse by a village headman or a squire's dependant, or taking money from a coastal syndicate rather than confront it, with all the cost in men and silver this entailed, then so be it.[55]

By 1830 the Daoguang Emperor, who had now succeeded his father, became again alarmed. 'The multitude of users expands day by day, and there are more and more people who sell it; they are like fire and smoke, destroying our resources and harming our people. Each day is worse than the last,' he wrote.[56] Two matters were judged most disturbing: the prevalence of opium smoking in the administration itself, and the news that opium was being cultivated in China, not just imported. (There had been isolated actions against domestic culti-vators in Fujian and Zhejiang in the 1820s.[57]) The emperor urged the metropolitan censorate, the mandarinate's supervisory body, to intensify operations against opium throughout the empire. Bonds cer-tifying that no drug offences had occurred in their constituency were to be filled by local officials annually. In 1831 a new decree instituted penalties against the cultivation and the decoction of crude opium into paste, making them the same as for trafficking: transportation to the military frontier.[58]

None of this stemmed the tide. On the contrary, the failures and contradictions of prohibition were starting to become apparent. The first to notice its dysfunctions were frontline officials. In 1834 a Canton scholar named Wu Lanxiu alerted his superiors to the counter-productive role of the anti-opium laws. Its illegality, not opium itself, was helping corrupt the administration. 'The stricter the laws, the larger the bribes,' Wu wrote. The imperial bureaucracy simply lacked the power to suppress opium by force of law. The obsession with punishment was misguided, he opined, and it would be better to legalize and tax the drug.[59]

Eventually, in 1836, the government invited proposals for fresh solutions, writing to a number of upper-echelon members of the provincial administration. The debate it thereby initiated ran on, through various memorials, for five months. Both sides carefully considered prohibition's impact on public health, the administration and enforcement. (China's enemies used the debate to argue that the drain in silver caused by the sizeable opium imports was the court's real concern.[60] The matter also arose, but that it was paramount is easily dismissed. If the negative trade balance had been the problem, there was a ready solution: legalize opium cultivation within China. The emperor had done the very opposite in 1831.)

Xu Naiji, a sub-director of the Court of Sacrificial Worship, was the first Beijing official to argue that it was not possible to suppress opium. Prohibition had done nothing to halt the spread of the drug. The government should focus on harm mitigation instead. Xu trod carefully around the risks presented by the suppression of opium imports. Faced with more forceful interdiction, he warned, the foreigners would simply move their ships further away from shore. They would always find customers because the locals were moved by the large profits smuggling offered. Xu admitted that 'the habit of using [opium] being inveterate, is destructive of time, injurious to property, and yet dear to one even as life.' While it was advisable to dismiss any soldiers or administrators who smoked opium, it was nevertheless best to control the trade as a whole through regulation.[61] Xu's legalization proposal was seconded by Deng Tingzhen, governor general of Guangdong and Guangxi. A local administrator, he understood from experience the costs and risks of interdiction. These were balanced by risks to public health, including to the mandarinate itself, but ultimately opium policing threatened to stretch the empire's authority more than toleration. Deng began to draft a list of regulations, thinking the court was about to change its mind.

The problem was that the case for prohibition was more simply made. It is always easier to paint intoxicants as bad, while defending them relies on complex arguments about freedom of choice, lesser evils and the self-defeating nature of bans. An example of the opposition's case is provided by Zhu Zun, a member of the Board of Rites. Opium cultivation, if legalized, would drive valuable food crops from the best lands, he began. The military would fall to the spreading habit, and the empire would become impossible to defend. But Zhu's argumentation centred on the drug, not the question of prohibition. His line was typical of Confucian tenets: 'To sum up the matter – the wide-spreading and baneful influence of opium, when regarded simply as injurious to property [that is, the silver drain], is of inferior importance; but when regarded as hurtful to the people, it demands most anxious consideration: for in the *people* lies the very foundation of the empire.'[62] Powerful figures arose on both sides of the discussion, but another notable stance is that of Lin Zexu, destined to become the empire's opium tsar three years later. Lin supported heavy penalties on users and traffickers alike, and he proposed to suppress the foreign supply. He also wished to institute a programme of public education and medical care: Richard Nixon, when he launched his own war on drugs in 1970, would devise a similar plan.[63] As the immediate upshot, nevertheless, both Zhu and Lin blamed past failures on weaknesses in enforcement.

While leaving the debate open, the emperor decided to test the waters with stricter policing in Canton. In 1837–8 anti-trafficking operations launched in that province resulted in the capture of 692 offenders. The authorities confiscated 5 tons of crude. These were not major seizures in regard to total volumes, but they looked like progress. The court reopened the debate in 1838 based on a proposal by Huang Juezi, a minister of rites, for a campaign of ruthless suppression. Opium cultivation, refining, trafficking and warehousing would all be punished by decapitation, this recommended. 'The head of the offender shall then be stuck upon a pole, and exposed upon the seacoast as a warning to all.' All those who grew opium, transported it, or paid or received opium-related bribes would be subject to the maximum penalty. As to opium smokers, they would be allowed a year to kick the habit. After that, they would face death by strangulation.[64]

The memorial was circulated for opinions within the same restricted circle. Out of 29 senior scholars, 21 came out in favour of sparing the user from the worst penalty, reserving death for traffickers only.[65] Prohibition had nevertheless come out on top. The emperor decided to go ahead with Huang's proposal in full. The regulations were promulgated in June 1839, the grace period for opium smokers to give up the drug before the death penalty applied being extended to eighteen months. Clamping down domestically, though, would not be enough. The foreign merchants would also have to be confronted.

The trade routes out of the Indian Ocean, temporarily disrupted during the Napoleonic Wars, reopened after 1815. The East India Company had absorbed another chunk of the Indian peninsula, between 1803 and 1818, in the second and third Maratha Wars. British India nevertheless remained a patchwork, with company territories bordering on nominally autonomous principalities, plus a sprinkling of Portuguese-held coastal enclaves functioning as independent exit points. Such was the background to the expansion of Malwa opium, whose exports received a dramatic impulse from 1815 into the 1820s.

The company's Bengal monopoly, by maximizing the margin between prices paid to growers, which it kept low, and the export price, which was set by auction, created an irresistible incentive to independent cultivation elsewhere. The British military forces lacked the capacity to police either Malwa poppy growers or the opium caravans that filed through the Indian states to be smuggled out of Bombay or Portuguese Daman and Diu. The company might offer a pension to the Maharana of Udaipur for clamping down on transit, or sign treaties with the Majarajahs of Indore or Holkar for restricting cultivation: they were scarcely worth more than the paper they were written on.[66] The traffic could always move elsewhere, as could the poppy fields.

Malwa exports to China, at an average of 1,100 chests in the mid-1810s, had doubled by the 1819–20 season.[67] Initially the authorities in Calcutta had merely prohibited sales out of Bombay. As it became clear that the trade had only moved as a result, and continued to expand, they decided to change tactics. Their concern was not for the Chinese customer, though there was always the fear that as smuggling into China grew, it would provoke a reaction threatening the trade in legal goods. The annoyance was rather that rising supply caused Bengal prices to fall, affecting the company's receipts. After the Maratha Wars were over, it was therefore decided to sweep up the Malwa opium, which the company itself would buy for resale. The margins on that would be low, but at least this would help push Bengal prices up again. The result, predictably, was merely another explosion in supply. By 1823–4 the company was again confronted with failure: Malwa exports now stood at 5,500 chests.[68] This was when the idea was tried of signing up the Indian princes to suppression in exchange for payment: this too only acted as an incentive, and volumes rose once more, to 7,700 chests in the 1828–9 season. It was a sorcerer's apprentice experience. From 1831 the company gave up on suppressing the trade, opening Bombay again for transit and imposing a fee instead.[69]

The opium trade remained at that time the responsibility of a few large firms plus a smattering of independent individuals (although because these firms operated on consignment, they stood at the tip of a pyramid of investors based in India and Britain). Most merchants were British-born, but there were also a number of Indian houses, the largest of them hailing from the Parsee community of Bombay. Finally, a handful of Americans were involved in the trade, selling either Turkish opium or Bengal/Malwa purchased through third-party Calcutta brokers. The main British firms were Jardine, Matheson & Co. (originally Magniac & Co.) and Dent & Co., but it is also worth mentioning the traders James Innes and Hugh Hamilton Lindsay. Key Parsee families included the Jejeebhoys and Cowasjees. Among the Americans, Russell & Co. was the largest. Several of the Americans present in Canton refused to deal in opium, notably Olyphant & Co., which was run by Charles King, and Nathan Dunn.[70]

The old city of Canton, girthed in a sandstone-and-brick crenellated wall, was encircled by sprawling suburbs. Southwards, its muddy riverfront was forever densely crowded with boats and ships of all kinds. Squeezed between that embankment and the suburbs, no more than 300 metres wide but towering over the low, wooden Chinese houses, stood a row of buildings built of granite and brick, with European-style columned verandas and terraces. The thirteen factories, run by Chinese stewards and servants, combined living quarters, warehouses and offices for the use of the foreign traders. Long reserved for the East India Company, the British factory was the most imposing. Rogues lodged elsewhere, such as the Danish factory or the Creek, at the tip of the enclave.

James Innes had always scorned authority, even the authority of the East India Company and its Select Committee of Supercargoes in Canton. When he arrived in the mid-1820s he did not even bother with the pretence of a consular commission and simply settled at the Creek factory without permission.[71] In 1835, on his way to the Hoppo's post, he was attacked by a kitchen coolie holding a chopper. Though Innes was not hurt, his reaction was to fire rockets from his veranda, setting the custom post on fire. When the committee revoked his 'country' licence in response, he simply applied for a new one in Calcutta.[72]

Relations with the Hong, through whom all the official trade passed – whether in tea, silks, porcelain, cotton or other goods – were consistently friendly. Since none of the foreign merchants spoke Chinese, business was conducted via interpreters or in Pidgin English, a local language mixing English with a few Hindi and Portuguese words set to a simple Chinese grammar. Numbering ten or so families, the Hong went by the anglicized name of their original or leading member, such as the odd-sounding Howqua, Mowqua or Puankequa. They acted as buffer between the merchants and local officials, who could be fastidious: moving up and down the river between Canton and the estuary required permits or 'chops', and there were pilotage, harbour, customs and other fees to negotiate, all of which the Hong could be counted on to facilitate. They were even known to invite their foreign partners to their river or country villas and gardens for relaxation.[73]

The unspoken agreement was that the foreigners would never go too far to provoke the authorities, in whose line of fire the Hong were the first to stand. But in 1838, at a time when enforcement was becoming increasingly serious, Innes had crates of opium unloaded from a boat moored just outside the factory, in the middle of Canton. If the 1821 experiment to set up Whampoa, 20 kilometres away, as an opium hub had been provocative, this was downright reckless. Innes's coolies were caught, but besides naming him, they wrongfully implicated an American merchant and his ship, the *Thomas Perkins*, which carried rice. Innes did nothing to clear the matter up.

The Hong merchant standing security for the *Thomas Perkins* was named Punhoyqua. The Canton governor general summoned all eleven Hong representatives and, asking for the culprits to be brought to justice, forced Punhoyqua into the humiliation of the cangue. The Hong in turn protested to Hugh Hamilton Lindsay, who was chairman of the Chamber of Commerce, but Lindsay explained that he had no authority over Innes, who was not a member. Hoping to send a message, the authorities set up a wooden cross outside the factories for strangling a convicted (Chinese) opium dealer. Innes and Lindsay, leading a group of foreigners, intervened physically to dismantle the scaffold. The incident threatened to spin out of control. The official in charge of the execution pulled back, but an angry crowd arrived from the town, and a flinging match began. The resident aliens were thrown back into the factories, which were about to be stormed. Just in time, soldiers from the Canton garrison rushed in and cleared the square. Innes eventually left for Macao.[74]

In 1834, for reasons to do with British domestic politics, the East India Company's monopoly over the China trade was terminated. This was to invite a whole host of men in the mould of James Innes. What minimal controls still existed were lifted. In 1831 there had been five British firms and a dozen individuals in China, plus the Parsees.[75] Five years later, 150 British nationals were doing business at the factories.[76]

After the regularization of Malwa, the termination of the company monopoly was the second major change in practices to boost opium deliveries. It presided over the final spurt in volumes between then and the end of the decade. Yet more inflammatory, as new entrants arrived, the established houses began to move up the Chinese coast to unauthorized landing places. In 1832 the company itself had launched an exploratory journey north with a ship full of cotton textiles under the direction of Lindsay, who at the time had yet to set himself up privately.[77] The opium clippers followed: in 1833 Jardine Matheson sent the *Colonel Young* on its own exploratory trip along Fujian, stopping off at Quanzhou and selling opium to the tune of the then fabulous sum of a third of a million dollars. By 1837 Russell had the *Rose* cruising off Namoa island, in Guangdong province, along with Jardine Matheson's *Governor Finlay* and Dent's *Omega*. They waited for an official to arrive, whom they proceeded to pay off before unloading.[78]

Like the twentieth-century drug lords Pablo Escobar or El Chapo, the opium merchants were for the most part men of modest or middling origins who turned out to do extremely well financially. William Jardine was a Scot who originally came to China in 1802 as a surgeon's mate aboard a Company ship. On the side, Jardine traded on his own account, as was common in his position. He had settled in Canton in 1817 and in 1825 joined the established firm Magniac and Co. Jardine was joined by James Matheson, another Scot who had begun in a London trading house, then moved to Calcutta. When Magniac went home, the firm was renamed Jardine, Matheson & Co.[79] By the 1830s it was the largest of the traders in opium, alongside the other goods it bought and sold, running twelve ships of varying tonnage.[80]

Thomas Dent was the third son of a well-to-do merchant from Westmoreland. After dropping out of Cambridge in 1815, he moved to Canton, where he was employed as a manager by a firm named W. S. Davidson. After Davidson's retirement, Dent became his firm's senior partner, and by 1824 he had changed its name to Thomas Dent & Co. His brother Lancelot, who replaced him in 1830, went on to build the family enterprise into the second-largest British firm in China.[81] Jamsetjee Jejeebhoy was born in 1773 to a family with a Parsee priestly background. Originally apprenticed to an uncle living in Bombay, he began his career as a hawker and peddler, collecting and selling empty bottles. Jejeebhoy made various voyages to China, on the second of which he carried borrowed goods worth up to 40,000 rupees (around $16,000). On one of these trips, he was captured alongside William Jardine by a French frigate, helping forge a long-lasting connection with the future Jardine Matheson. In 1814 he had become wealthy enough to purchase his own ship, the *Good Success*, and he acquired several more between 1818 and 1832.[82]

'We are not smugglers, gentlemen! It is the Chinese government, it is the Chinese officers who smuggle, and who connive at and encourage smuggling, not we,' proclaimed Jardine at a banquet in 1839.[83] Also like the later heroin or cocaine kings, he and his peers rarely exhibited much compunction for their actions. Jardine found the Chinese 'a people so avaricious and faithless' and 'arrogant and unjust' that they deserved only force.[84] His public writings were a compendium of the arguments exonerating the opium trade: that the Chinese ban was an excuse to extract bribes, that the government's real concern was the silver drain, and that it was the consumer who was responsible for craving opium.[85] 'Our dealings with them have been marked by the most scrupulous performance of all our engagements and a strong desire to stand well with them,' he found.[86] Matheson meanwhile saw the Chinese as 'a people characterised by a marvellous degree of imbecility, avarice, conceit, and obstinacy'.[87] By contrast, his fellow merchants were distinguished by 'a spirit of noble and persevering enterprise [that] led them to dare all dangers, to despise all difficulties'. Because China 'monopolize[d] all the advantages of their situation', moreover, the foreign community was authorized to force upon it whatever trading conditions it saw fit.[88] Nor was Jejeebhoy exempt from such belligerence: twice in the 1830s he and a group of Parsee merchants would draft petitions urging forceful action on the British government to stop Chinese interference in the opium trade.[89]

The foreign residents in Canton chafed at local restrictions – foreign women were not allowed in the factories, for example – and at the procedures in place, such as the need to ask for permits before moving in and out of the city. In Britain it was felt that the Canton system (introduced by the Qing in 1757 in replacement of freer norms) was a hindrance to commerce. The preference was for selling manufactured goods into China rather than opium, however profitable the commodity was to British India. Missions had been sent to establish equal-footing diplomatic relations with China under George Macartney (1792–3) and William Amherst (1816–17), but both had ended dismal failures. All this was fodder for the opium traders' aggressive instincts.

The presence of the vast, illegal opium trade, of course, was not calculated to encourage the Chinese authorities to loosen the rules. The opium traders were nevertheless skilled at recuperating third-party complaints to their own ends. In 1831 a set of visits to Canton by English and American ladies had triggered punishment in the form of the destruction of a shrubbery on the factories' river side: a group of British merchants had written to Calcutta to ask for the dispatch of a squadron to China.[90] Upon the termination of the East India Company monopoly, the Foreign Office appointed a delegate to act in place of the old Committee of Supercargoes: Lord William Napier. Napier, who arrived in 1834, hoped to achieve the elevated aim of gaining diplomatic recognition. This mission, too, ended badly, as Napier fell ill and died in Macao in the same year. Matheson, who briefly returned home in 1835, obtained through Napier's widow a meeting with the Foreign Secretary Lord Palmerston, again to request a punitive expedition.[91] Lindsay went further in a published pamphlet asking that terms be imposed on the Chinese and suggesting precisely what size of force was to be employed: 'one line-of-battle ship, two large frigates, six corvettes, and three or four armed steamers', plus a landing force of six hundred soldiers.[92]

Napier was briefly replaced by a succession of former company supercargoes, then in 1836 by a captain of the Royal Navy with a record of service against the slave trade: Charles Elliot. Awkwardly, the title of this representative without diplomatic status was super-intendent of trade at Canton. In a letter to his wife, Elliot described the merchants as 'a rapacious and ravenous race of wolves, each howling after their prey'.[93] As, from 1838, the Qing stepped up their fight against opium, he would become the intermediary between the wolves and the emperor's enforcers.

In New York City's Chinatown stands a statue of Commissioner Lin Zexu on a granite pedestal inscribed with the words: 'Pioneer in the war against drugs'.[94] The inscription is entirely apposite.

Lin Zexu, already a high-level mandarin at the time of the 1836–8 legalization debate, had sided with the proponents of the strictest prohibition. Lin had been born in 1785 to a Fuzhou gentry family with a once glorious but now fading pedigree. He had quickly succeeded in passing the highest of the civil service examinations, becoming a *jinshi* scholar at a notably young age and going on to join the prestigious Hanlin Academy. His career had taken him through a number of provincial posts, first as salt and judicial commissioner in various jurisdictions, then as provincial governor in Jiangsu, Hubei and Hunan. An American who witnessed Lin's arrival in Canton observed that he 'had a dignified air, rather a harsh or firm expression, as a large corpulent man, with heavy black moustache and long beard'. A contemporary portrait shows him with a thin, luminous face and piercing eyes. Among his colleagues, Lin was known for his industry and his devotion to the people's cause. But in addition to his efficiency as an administrator, he was reputed for his uprightness, his incorruptibility and, when it came to opium offenders, his inflexibility. 'Lin the clear sky' was recommended to the emperor for his probity, but also for energetic anti-opium campaigns run in Hunan and Hubei in 1838, in which he had had numerous dealers jailed and smoking implements destroyed in mass events.[95]

The emperor summoned Lin to the capital on 27 December 1838. Over the course of eight audiences, the two men locked themselves up to elaborate a new plan of suppression. Lin emerged from these meetings as China's first opium tsar: an imperial commissioner 'holding the power to act on Daoguang's behalf, answerable to none', wielding authority over Canton's officials, and having control over both the police and the naval forces stationed there.[96]

When, in the hiatus between the 1836 and 1838 debates, the emperor had ordered a renewal of enforcement, the task had paradoxically fallen to Deng Tingzhen – the Canton provincial governor but also one of the proponents of legalization. Whatever his private views, Deng had followed the emperor's instructions with vigour. Off the coast, his agents chased down Chinese smugglers and destroyed their transport ships. Inland, they went after dealers and their supply lines. By December 1837 Deng could already report that he had made thirty seizures and arrested 161 offenders, having captured 9,688 *taels* of silver and 38 chests of opium. The opium had been burned. 'Those brokerage houses found to be dealing in opium [have] been closed, while orders were issued for the apprehension of the persons who had frequented them.'[97] Chinese subjects were not the sole targets of these actions. Early on, Deng had ordered nine named foreign merchants, including Jardine, Dent and Innes, to pack up and leave Canton, giving them two weeks to do so. To drive the point home, Deng had ordered a local translator who had been caught smuggling opium to be paraded around the factories with the cangue. For good measure, he had an opium broker strangled outside St Antonio Gate before Macao.[98]

The impact soon began to be felt on the trade. Local dealers began to ask for higher fees to compensate for the danger, cutting into profits. Many left the business or went idle. The fast crabs and scrambling dragons having been burned or scared away, it became increasingly difficult to unload product. 'The drug market is becoming worse every day owing to the extreme vigilance of the Authorities,' reported Jardine in November 1837.[99] As 1837 ran into 1838, opium slowly stopped moving. The foreigners tried to push more traffic up the coast, but though prices there were higher, volumes were lacking. In desperation, they began putting opium ashore themselves. They brought the drug among their effects on the small sailing vessels for carrying passengers from Macao. Their servants secreted opium in wine bottles or pickle jars and took it ashore. But there also they ran into the police. In January 1838 the authorities searched the *Swift* and, having found three chests of opium, fined her owner several thousand dollars. The next month they seized 23 chests from the *Alpha*.[100] For now the penalties were only monetary, but how long could this last? Incidentally, Beijing's campaign also resulted in significant seizures in the distant, western region of Xinjiang, into which opium was smuggled by a land route. In 1840 the neighbouring khan of Kokand would agree to endorse the imperial ban, while itinerant traders pledged to abandon the traffic.[101]

Deng upped the pressure further in 1838. Around the Pearl River estuary that year, he had locals arrested almost every day. In December Jardine was told that the Canton prisons were holding no fewer than 2,000 opium offenders. At Whampoa, aggravated villagers arose to fight a pitched battle with soldiers sent to make arrests. Prices fell as volumes sold dwindled further. Even at $350 a chest, almost half as cheap as at the beginning of the season, Russell & Co. found that it could not move the higher-quality Turkish product.[102] Then the incident took place involving Innes's attempt to offload his opium in broad daylight by the Creek factory, followed by the affray around the dismantled scaffold. Finding his patience at an end, Deng ordered a halt to the official trade. No silk, cotton or tea would move in or out of Canton as long as smuggling went on. Elliot was compelled to tell the merchants to remove their small craft from the river, and he informed Deng that they would receive no assistance from him if caught.[103]

His conditions met, Deng reopened the trade in legal goods at the beginning of 1839. By then, though, Lin was emerging from his interviews with the emperor and heading south. As the news reached Canton, Lin's reputation having preceded him, the opium business came to a complete standstill. The police were everywhere. Passenger boats refused to carry opium. Buyers vanished. On 27 February Russell & Co. threw in the towel and announced that it was withdrawing from the opium trade. The managers ordered their ships to stop selling along the coast and come in. A few of the smaller merchants had already quit handling the drug, and several more now followed.[104]

Lin arrived in Canton on 10 March. He struck even harder. The commissioner had brought with him a list of 62 opium offenders, including local dealers, fast-crab operators and corrupt bureaucrats, and he promptly had them lined up. He would lock up six hundred examination candidates until they wrote down all they knew of the opium traffic, providing another roll call of names. Lin reproduced the eradication methods that had served him in Hubei and Hunan. He started with the mass arrest of local offenders. His men confiscated raw opium and pipes. To clamp down on the user population, he organized the city into 'security groups' of five people, each responsible for guaranteeing that none of the others were smokers. Within two months, he had arrested over 1,500 people, confiscated 230 chests (14 tons) of opium and destroyed 43,000 pipes.[105]

Simultaneously, on 18 March, Lin convoked the Hong. 'Truly I burn with shame for you,' he told them as they waited, kneeling. They had aided and abetted the foreigners in their illegal, poisonous trade, he thundered. They would be held responsible. 'The Great Minister does not want your money. I want your head,' Lin menaced Howqua. The Hong would pass on an injunction to the foreigners to surrender the opium aboard their ships – not just what might still be floating off the city of Canton, but any ship lying in or around the estuary, the full stock of what remained of the last Indian harvest. The merchants would also sign an undertaking to abandon the trade, on pain of death if it were violated. If this were not accepted within three days, Lin announced, he would execute two of the more notorious among the Hong and confiscate all their property.[106] Within the hour, the Hong had conveyed the written order to the factories. If anyone was hoping to slip away, they were disappointed. The next day, the Hoppo, who was responsible for issuing permits to foreigners for going to and from Canton, refused to authorize any departures.

It took three days for the forty-strong general meeting of the Chamber of Commerce to convene. The foreigners' first instinct was to ignore the danger in which opium had placed both their Chinese counterparts and themselves. On 21 March the merchants decided, by a vote of 25 to 14, to leave the Hong in the lurch. Their response to Lin was that they would study his proposals and provide an answer within another six days.[107] The Hong were predictably upset. Their deadline expiring, they returned that night to press their British counterparts. A second Chamber of Commerce meeting was convened two hours before midnight. It was agreed to surrender a token amount of 1,000 chests. But the next day, word came back to the factories that this would not suffice. Perhaps 4,000 chests should be proposed.[108] The foreigners still thought themselves untouchable, but amid the defiance, concern was setting in and nerves were fraying. It was dawning on everyone that the commissioner meant business.

Then Lin overplayed his hand. Victory was nigh. Perhaps this did not seem sufficient punishment at a time when Lin was finding himself forced to throw so many Chinese people into jail or even condemn them to death, but the foreign merchants were hurting where it counted: their business. Deng's measures had already brought the opium trade to a halt. Lin's campaign promised to deny it any hope of revival. Half of the last season's opium remained unsold, floating around the estuary in the merchants' ships, threatening catastrophic losses if it could not be offloaded. Jardine Matheson was finding itself forced to warehouse the drug all the way to Singapore. Prices, if they could still be computed, had fallen to 'alarm' rates of $300 for Bengal and $200 for Malwa, less than half their decade low.[109] This was also less than what had been paid in Calcutta: $497 per chest, even without accounting for transport and other costs. But the worst was that back in India, the big firms and their investors had kept buying. It had been another bumper crop, and the product of the 1838 harvest was beginning to arrive in bulk, exceeding on its own the unsold excess. Mass bankruptcies beckoned. Even the East India Company was in trouble. At the May 1839 Calcutta auction, bids collapsed to a low of $79, almost 50 per cent below its long-run manufacturing cost.[110]

The Chinese officials in Canton had learnt from experience that it was dangerous to confront the Europeans with force. It was understood, at the very least, that the Chinese navy was not equipped to chase their ships beyond the Canton river system. Lin issued around the same time a proclamation framed as a letter to the Queen of England which showed that he believed, erroneously of course, that opium was illegal in Britain. (The letter was never transmitted, but it is possible that Queen Victoria read it, as it was later published in *The Times*.[111]) This belief may have deepened his indignation. In any case, Lin at last threw caution to the wind. He resolved he must obtain satisfaction on his terms.

Faced with their procrastination, the commissioner announced that the time had come to call in the opium merchants themselves.

Jardine had departed for England a couple of months before and so had Lindsay, and Lin's choice fell on Lancelot Dent. Dent was actually not the most brazen of the merchants. He had always been respectful of the East India Company's authority. The newspaper he funded, the *Canton Press*, was perhaps surprisingly prepared to be critical of opium, acknowledging the 'evil moral and physical consequences to the habitual opium-smoker'.[112] Dent had also founded a school for Chinese boys in Macao, which in the words of his biographer 'fostered, in a modest way, greater mutual understanding between Chinese and Western cultures'.[113]

On 22 March the Scot was nevertheless ordered to come into the city for questioning. Resigned or possibly inured to his danger, he was preparing to surrender himself when a colleague pointed out that there was a precedent. In 1760 an Englishman named James Flint had been thrown into jail, on the lesser crime of having tried to learn Chinese, for a long, hard stint that had almost certainly foreshortened his life. Dent changed his mind and refused to go.[114] Nothing after that would make him budge. The next day, the two Hong leaders Howqua and Mowqua appeared at the factories wearing iron chains around their necks. They cried that they were about to be strangled. Later, three mandarins appeared in Dent's lodgings to pick him up, settling in an adjacent office. It was night-time and Dent came down to offer them, sarcastically, dinner and beds.[115] The stand-off between China and Britain, and with it two centuries of the war on drugs, hung on the will of two men.

Lin still hesitated to use force. He nevertheless gave the green light for the next, fateful step. That evening, 24 March, the Chinese servants all began to leave the factories. A cordon of soldiers deployed around the compound, encircling it. As was being made clear, the foreigners would not be allowed to leave until they had complied with Lin's demand for the opium on their ships.[116]

For several weeks, roughly 350 British, American, Dutch and Parsee merchants and sailors found themselves trapped inside the factories. The blockade never imposed any serious hardship on them. The facilities were well appointed. The British factory contained, in addition to its lavish banqueting hall, a chapel, a library and a billiard room. Howqua and other outside friends arranged for coolies to smuggle in 'a constant procession of capons, boiled hams, roast mutton, and baskets of bread and eggs'.[117] The merchants were forced to learn to do their own housework and cooking, but they still found time to play ball and leapfrog, and to organize footraces and rat hunts for amusement.

In a final twist, however, the British superintendent, Charles Elliot, who had been in Macao when the trouble began, had arrived just before the blockade was assembled. Elliot was a British official, and this would make the scene look all the more serious, in London, when it came to be reported there. He was also trapped with the others, curtailing his room for negotiation. The official trade, for which he was responsible, was shut down. Elliot decided that the situation was not tenable. On 27 March he asked the merchants to agree to deliver their opium. Each house would furnish a list, and terms would be agreed with Lin for delivery. But the novelty was this: the super-intendent assumed responsibility for the merchants' losses, in the name of the British government. The cost of all those chests floating around the estuary, unsold and effectively worthless, would be reim-bursed fully, provided they were handed in to the Chinese authorities. Ruin had been staved off. 'Our surrender is the most fortunate thing that could have happened,' commented Matheson.[118]

The blockade lasted into May, but the lists were quickly drawn up, tallied and forwarded to the commissioner. From 11 April opium clippers began tacking towards the downriver island of Chuenpi. Day after day, chests of opium were landed as Lin watched over and Elliot's deputy, Alexander Johnston, issued receipts. At last, on 21 May, the promised total was reached: 20,283 plus another eight which Innes had been found trying to smuggle at the last minute through Macao, or 20,291 chests.[119] The official trade remained closed as the British merchants still refused to sign a pledge to abandon the opium trade compliant with Lin's wording – the Americans and other Europeans would oblige in July – but the blockade was lifted. On 24 May Elliot led the last of the British merchants out of the factories, among them Dent, Matheson, his two nephews and William Jardine's nephew Andrew.[120]

In June Lin had the opium destroyed in a procedure that involved digging vast basins, 45 × 23 metres (50 × 25 yd) each, with timbered sides and flagstone bottoms, at a point further from Chuenpi where a small river met the estuary. It took three weeks to break the opium cakes into fragments, have them pushed into the basins and mixed in with fresh water, lime and salt and, after workers had stirred the whole mixture through with hoes and shovels, flush it all into the sea.[121] Lin's public performance is sometimes mocked for its ceremony, which included a prayer of apology to the sea spirit for this act of pollution.[122] Actually there were good reasons for the drama, and the ceremonial destruction of the captured opium may be dated as the first of many similarly publicized operations. The TV cameras were absent, but the publicity removed all doubt that the opium had been destroyed and not kept by Lin for resale up north. Like all similar media actions, it was intentionally dissuasive. The strict security, finally, was necessary to prevent any pilfering during the long time the operation took. At more than 1,200 tons, Lin's seizure remains the largest in the long war on drugs.

The commissioner was triumphant. The dealers, the Hong and the foreign merchants had all been cowed. To all intents and purposes, the opium trade was dead and buried. The foreigners had been forced to admit to their guilt, their opium given up and trashed. Yet unbeknown to him, thanks to Elliot's indemnity, this had only saved them from financial ruin. The British government, moreover, had by the same token become an interested party. To be able to declare victory, Lin had had to blockade the factories. Even if the siege had been non-violent, in London it would be branded an act of war.

2

OPIUM WARS

The operations of the First Opium War (1839–42) have been described elsewhere in some detail, and no more than an outline is required here. Though the British expeditionary force needed to be scrambled together from a number of locations, some of them halfway around the world – Britain itself but also the Cape and Australia, besides India – it enjoyed an insuperable advantage in armaments and tactics. The invading force was spearheaded by three 74-gun ships of the line, followed by a number of frigates, corvettes and transports. It also counted four steamers, including the massive *Nemesis*, able to navigate the Pearl River estuary's flats, land troops at coastal weak points and bombard forts at a dead angle or out of range from fixed-emplacement Chinese cannons.[1] China's armaments were wretched. On water, its war junks were unwieldy, slow and hopelessly outgunned. On land, its troops made use of rusty cannons burning coarse and ineffective gunpowder, and they sheltered in roofless forts quickly turned into killing grounds by enemy artillery. British and Indian soldiers carried breech-loading rifles capable of fast firing. Chinese muskets made use of tiny bullets triggered by a slow-burning matchlock. But even muskets were rare. Chinese and Manchu troops – much of the Qing army continued to be recruited from populations identified in speech and dress as Manchu, after the Qing home base in Manchuria – often wielded no more than bows and arrows, swords, spears or halberds, and they wore iron helmets, shields and even chain mail.[2]

An operation early on in the offensive on Canton provides an illustration of the result. The Chinese commander had entrenched his forces on two islands, named Chuenpi and Taikoktow, overlooking the passage into the Pearl River estuary's neck. A line of chained wooden rafts blocked the entry into the waterways, also protected by a fleet of war junks. On the morning of 7 January 1841, 1,400 British marines, infantry and artillery attacked the granite forts on the islands. Because they landed by steamer, the troops were able to approach the fortifications from the rear and flanks. Chuenpi fell after a 25-minute artillery barrage convinced its defenders to scatter. An hour later, Taikoktow was stormed, its men and their commander mown down by gun and rifle fire. The *Nemesis* then turned to the war junks, which had been hanging back in waters their commander judged too shallow for the British fleet to penetrate. The steamship approached and fired. Almost immediately, a Congreve rocket hit the powder store of one of the junks, causing it to blow up 'with a terrific explosion, launching into eternity every soul on board'. The sailors abandoned the rest of the fleet. On the Qing side, 280 were dead and 462 wounded. On the British side, 38 were wounded and none killed.[3] Operations were over by noon.

That the First Opium War was actually about opium has sometimes been contested, beginning with imperial apologists claiming that it was really fought to open a commercially and politically closed China, or that it represented an inevitable clash between a rising Britain and a stagnant Qing empire. At the other extreme, Britain has been accused of plotting to force opium on China with the explicit motive of weakening it for future colonization.[4] Actually the war was launched in the aim of recovering the sums Charles Elliot had promised the opium merchants and to keep a trade going that was an important fiscal prop to colonial India.[5] 'The real cause of the outbreak with China in 1839 was the prodigiously increased supply of opium from India after the Company had lost the monopoly of regular trade in the year 1834,' wrote Elliot himself.[6]

The merchants' claim was estimated, at the beginning of the war, at £2.4 million.[7] This was on its own a large sum for the government to take on: Britain's budget for 1840 amounted to no more than £53.4 million.[8] In addition, opium made an annual contribution to the East India Company of £1 million.[9] Finally there was tea, the trade in which had been halted as a result of the fight over opium. The duty on that item, imported almost entirely from China, was £3–4 million per annum, not a sum the exchequer could simply replace.[10] Leaving drugs aside, it is drug dealing that is addictive. The easy money is impossible to surrender. The wealth generated comes to be regarded as an entitlement, and violence beckons as a natural resort in safe-guarding it. It was easier to make China pay and claim that Lin's actions had affronted British honour.

The expeditionary force, approximately 3,500 strong, initially headed not for Canton but for the island of Zhoushan, strategically placed towards the mouth of the Yangtze. Arriving in July 1840, the fleet smashed the Chinese flotilla at anchor and took the island.[11] George Elliot, Charles's brother, acted as admiral, and from Zhoushan the two Elliots sailed further up the coast, before Tianjin, to deliver a message for the capital. The court agreed to open negotiations. Talks resumed in Canton and Macao in November, though they soon stalled.

From Beijing's perspective, this still looked like no more than piracy on a larger scale. The court's instructions to its plenipotentiar-ies were to bide their time while reinforcements were being gathered. In parallel, the expeditionary force fitfully renewed its advance up the Pearl estuary and took Canton at the end of May 1841. Charles Elliot had meanwhile been asking for the cession of the island of Hong Kong and an indemnity of $6 million (less than the merchants' £2.4 million). The foreign secretary, Lord Palmerston, thought these terms too modest. The Elliots were making no progress in the talks anyway. Palmerston dismissed the superintendent, and the war now entered a second, yet more brutal phase.

Elliot's successor was the 51-year-old veteran of the Anglo-Indian army Henry Pottinger. He again concentrated his forces on Zhoushan, and from there he marched them up the Yangtze. Pottinger had received significant reinforcements: another ship of the line, half a dozen frigates and no fewer than eight steamers, plus fresh British and sepoy regiments now bringing the total to 10,000 men.[12] The Qing had fortified their positions as best they could and had summoned more troops, but this remained an unequal fight. Between the winter of 1841 and the summer of 1842, the towns of Zhenhai, Ningbo, Zhapu and Zhenjiang fell to the invaders one after the other until the expe-ditionary force arrived before Nanjing. Scenes of pillage accompanied the campaign's progress up the great river.

The great opium merchants may have looked like gentlemanly figures, exempt from the violence associated with latter-day drug bosses, but there was plenty of violence now. Chinese soldiers regularly ignored or failed to understand calls to surrender and died fighting to the last man. The victorious soldiery rampaged through the towns it overran. Granville Loch, a captain of the Royal Navy, described the capture of Zhenjiang on 21 July 1842. 'Throughout the day both the Chinese and Tartar [Manchu] troops evinced a determined bravery, which commanded our respect,' writes Loch.[13] The city ramparts were soon taken in hand-to-hand combat, however, or as batteries blew their gates apart. Inside: 'I saw, what as a novice in this description of warfare shocked me much, old men, women, and children, cutting each other's throats, and drowning themselves by the dozen; and no one either attempting or apparently showing any inclination to save the poor wretches, nor in fact regarding them with more notice than they would a dead horse carried through the streets of London to the kennel.'[14] Towards evening, an advance was sounded 'towards the Tartar quarter of the town'. The invaders broke into houses and passed an official building or palace with a flying dragon painted on its walls, to which they set fire. Just beyond:

> I went with two soldiers of the 18th down a street to the right, to a large house, which I concluded belonged to a Tartar of consequence: we burst the door and entered. Never shall I forget the sight of misery that there met our view.
>
> After we had forced our way over piles of furniture, placed to barricade the door, we entered an open court strewed with rich stuffs and covered with clotted blood; and upon the steps leading to the 'hall of ancestors' there were two bodies of youthful Tartars, cold and stiff, much alike, apparently brothers. Having gained the threshold of their abode, they had died where they had fallen, from the loss of blood. Stepping over these bodies, we entered the hall, and met, face to face, three women seated, a mother and two daughters; and at their feet lay two bodies of elderly men, with their throats cut from ear to ear, their senseless heads resting upon the feet of their relations. To the right were two young girls, beautiful and delicate, crouching over, and endeavouring to conceal, a living soldier.[15]

The fall of Zhenjiang finally persuaded the emperor that the war could not be won. He despatched two Manchu aristocrats, Yilibu and Qiying, to agree terms. The result was the Treaty of Nanjing, signed on 29 August 1842. China would pay an indemnity of $21 million (in excess of £4 million). It would open to trade the five ports of Canton, Xiamen, Fuzhou, Ningbo and Shanghai, allowing consular representation at these places, and would cede the island of Hong Kong to Britain in perpetuity.[16]

What was not part of the treaty was the legalization of opium. The negotiations took place in a surprisingly jovial atmosphere. 'Young white-buttoned mandarins handed round tea, hot wine, and sweetmeats ... Numerous patties of minced meat, pork, arrow root, vermicelli soup, with meat in it, pig's ear soup and other strange dishes were served in succession,' reports Loch. 'But human nature could not support this ordeal long, and as a coup de grace, Ke-ying [Qiying] insisted upon Sir Henry [Pottinger] opening his mouth while he with great dexterity shot into it several immense sugar-plums.'[17] All the same, the British government, beholden to the fiction that the war was a reprisal for Lin's atrocities, felt that it could not force opium on China as part of the peace terms. Pottinger had only been allowed to raise opium 'as a topic of private conversation'. The Chinese commissioners asked why Britain was not prepared to put an end to the trade. 'This ... in consistency with our constitutional laws, could not be done,' replied Pottinger. 'Even if England chose to exercise so arbitrary a power over her tillers of the soil [an outrageous caveat when one recalls that this is exactly what the Company did in Bengal], it would not check the evil so far as they (the Chinese) were concerned, while the cancer remained uneradicated among themselves, but that it would merely throw the market into other hands.' He preferred to admonish the dignitaries: 'If your people are virtuous, they will desist from the evil practice; and if your officers are incorruptible, and obey their orders, no opium can enter your country.'[18]

Across China, meanwhile, even if the war ruled out any further attempts to prevent opium from being landed ashore, suppression had continued in the interior. In 1841 the grace period for the entry into force of the death penalty for possession expired. There was a rush to clear cases before this warning period ended, and it is impossible to say exactly how many people were executed, but dozens of extant capital cases are documented as having been adjudicated in Guangdong, Beijing and elsewhere. Executions petered out after 1843, with 25 offenders listed that year, but actions against trafficking continued into the 1850s.[19]

The campaign, however determined, seems to have caught few kingpins. Most offenders were of a low social profile: petty entrepreneurs and peddlers, servants, labourers, entertainers. Bosses were sometimes able to protect their hirelings by introducing 'relatives' claiming to be dependent on the culprit, a factor considered an extenuating circumstance.[20] Behind the statistics, nevertheless, hid just as many individual tragedies:

> In January 1843, a Ms Li, who was 40 *sui*, was sentenced to death by strangulation for opium smoking. She had been suffering from stomach pains and bought some 35 grams of opium paste from a neighbour as well as a pipe from an itinerant Guangdong peddler. She was cured but was subsequently ordered by her husband, Wang Er, 38 *sui*, to dispose of her paste and paraphernalia because of the prohibitions. Ms Li instead buried these items in a rear courtyard and told her husband she had destroyed them. In 1842, Wang lost his job and decided to rent out his wife as a prostitute. Wang soon became a pimp for several other women and operated a brothel out of his residence. Around this time, Ms Li experienced a relapse of her stomach pains and retrieved her opium and paraphernalia from the back courtyard. On the day she resumed smoking, officials on a vice raid entered her home and discovered her opium, pipe, and lamp.[21]

As to the holders of Elliot's receipts, they were paid out in August 1843, though at a disappointing rate averaging $300 per chest (for a total of £1.25 million).[22] The trade resumed, and the great opium merchants would all enjoy haloed, moneyed retirements. Jardine returned to Britain a rich man. He promptly obtained a seat in Parliament, that ultimate Victorian gentleman's accolade. Lindsay likewise served in the House of Commons from 1841 to 1847. Matheson succeeded in Jardine's seat after his death and continued until his retirement in 1868 at age 72. He bought extensive lands on the Scottish island of Lewis, which made him one of Britain's largest proprietors. He spent his years on committees and boards, including that of the Peninsular & Oriental shipping company. Jejeebhoy poured money into Parsee charities – famine relief, schools, hospitals – and into Indian public works. In 1842 he became the first native-born Indian to be knighted and in 1857, in recognition of his charitable activities, he was granted a hereditary baronetcy.[23]

'China, we think, is essentially right, and this country is essentially wrong.' *The Record*, Britain's leading evangelical periodical, did not agree with the war.[24] Back home, both the campaign to exact retribution on China and the trade itself were contested. The term 'Opium War' was not invented by aggrieved Chinese nationalists but by the British press. The label was popularized by such titles as the *Morning Herald* and the *Northern Star* to designate a war begun by 'opium smugglers' and 'pestiferous smuggling rascals'.[25] The years 1839–42 saw the first sustained public movement to arise, in Europe or the United States, against 'this pernicious drug'.[26] Public opposition to the war would set a marker for British repentance in the early twentieth century, with profound effects on the emerging drug-control order. Its immediate impact, though, was to quash any governmental urge to force the legalization of opium on China, and in turn set the stage for a later round of aggression.

The war was attacked in Parliament just as it was about to start, first in a long-running debate in the House of Commons on 7–9 May, then in the Lords on 12 May 1840. The cabinet almost lost the Commons vote – it would have been forced to resign if it had – which went 271 in its favour to 262 against.[27] In the Lords, public censure was avoided only after a patriotic intervention by Lord Wellington.[28] Motions were again introduced in Parliament against the war and the opium trade in July 1840 and April 1843. All this received extensive press coverage. If the opium trade had belonged to the expert's domain, it now achieved notoriety among a broad reading public.

The merchants made their own effort to sway opinion in their favour, their first aim being to ensure that the government honoured Elliot's promise of compensation. In May 1839 a group led by Jardine, Matheson & Co. despatched a deputation to London to argue its case, with £5,000 or 'any amount of expense' at its disposal to pay for lawyers and 'literary men' to perform the job.[29] Lindsay published his own pamphlet and spoke personally in the Commons on the 1843 motion.[30] Jardine had an anonymous booklet printed entitled *The Rupture with China and Its Cause*, which came out alongside a handful of similar tracts published in 1839 or 1840, most of them ostensibly to order.[31] This literature recycled old tropes blaming the

Chinese for the opium trade, or arguing that the merchants were only doing what others would do in their place. It sometimes defended opium itself, suggesting it was the Chinese equivalent of gin or dram drinking.

Against this, a broad-based campaign emerged against the trade. A group of pamphleteers took the lead in denouncing opium, themselves widely quoted in newspapers and magazines. Probably the most popular pamphlet was A. S. Thelwall's *The Iniquities of the Opium Trade with China*. Thelwall's booklet contained lurid descriptions of the effects of opium smoking on health, made all the more eye-catching by the exoticism of its Chinese vignettes. It quoted evidence to the effect that opium acted 'like the spell of a demon', causing 'emaciation, loss of appetite, sickness, vomiting' and so on, terminating in death.[32] It and its fellow publications set out the basic arguments against the opium traffic for decades to come: besides involving a dangerous substance, the opium trade relied on smuggling, crowded out legitimate manufactured goods exports to China, and hindered Christian missionary work. A set of activists formed an Anti-opium Society bringing together a number of eminent members.[33] The war and the opium trade itself were the object of campaigns by an array of press organs such as the highbrow *Eclectic Review*, the free-trade *Leeds Mercury* and *The Times*, Britain's most widely read newspaper. The campaign of *The Times* ran, between 1839 and 1842, into tens of articles, letters and editorials. The editors, in the name of 'honour' and 'humanity', called for Parliament to 'put down this abominable traffic' and free China from 'this poisonous pest'.[34]

This literature would in due time enter the canon on drugs in Britain and beyond. More immediately, it placed the government and war party on the defensive. The *Morning Chronicle*, for example, the chief Whig newspaper at the time and an unconditional supporter of Palmerston, found itself forced to deny that the war was about opium at all: 'Fearful would be the responsibility of the Government, and deep-dyed the guilt with which they would have sullied and degraded our national character, had they permitted the battle flag of England to be unfurled in favour of a trade which bears, wrapped up in every case and bale it carries to the shores of China, delirium and death, and a moral plague more baneful than ever borne to a doomed people by "the pestilence which walketh in darkness". The Chinese war has no such aims.'[35]

The government was forced to disown the trade even while it pursued the war it had caused. This, plus the change of cabinet that took place by 1842, explains why the Treaty of Nanjing included no condition that China should legalize opium. It would prove no help, though, to the Chinese. On the contrary, as would soon become apparent, the resulting limbo only paved the way for achieving the same end through a second war.

Deliveries of Indian opium, having resumed as soon as the war began, continued to climb in the 1840s and '50s. Chinese imports reached a new peak of 78,000 chests in 1855, or approximately twice as much as before the war.[36] Hong Kong now provided a safe distribution platform for the drug, and newly introduced steamships shortened the journey. Hopes for a surge in British manufactured exports were meanwhile disappointed. On the contrary, from the 1850s China's trade balance turned positive again in spite of the opium purchases.[37] The silver drain had reversed.

From that time, the Foreign Office began to angle for a renegotiation. In 1854 it appointed the political economist John Bowring as superintendent. The post, among other things, now involved acting as governor of Hong Kong, but Bowring was also given the mission of renegotiating the Nanjing terms. The British were hoping to get various new clauses agreed to, such as changes to tariffs and better access to the interior of China, but on their agenda was also the legalization of opium.

Bowring took his proposal to Tianjin, where he met with high-ranking officials. In 1856 he approached Ye Mingchen, the provincial governor in Canton. He was rebuffed both times. Upon hearing of Bowring's failure, Palmerston, who was now prime minister but continued to have a hand in foreign affairs, contacted the Paris Quai d'Orsay. His proposal was for a joint military demonstration in China – the French being preoccupied with the fate of the Catholic missions there. The French responded cautiously but positively.[38] The necessary forces were available. The powder keg was packed, and all that remained was to wait for the spark.

On the morning of 8 October, a young Irish captain named Thomas Kennedy was sitting at breakfast with some friends in Canton harbour when he espied his ship, the *Arrow*, being boarded by Chinese soldiers. The ship – a 'lorcha', a ship with a European-type hull but Chinese sails – had served as a pirate vessel before it had been resold and eventually registered in Hong Kong. Three of its sailors were known associates of pirates. They had just been identified by one of their old victims, who had alerted the authorities. As the Irishman sat looking on, a war junk boarded the *Arrow*, took prisoner twelve men out of her crew of fourteen, all of them Chinese subjects, and marched them out.[39]

Kennedy walked off to report the incident to the consul, Harry Parkes. He made much of the Hong Kong registration. As he told the story, upon boarding the *Arrow*, the soldiers had lowered the Union Jack that had been hanging from its mast. Parkes proceeded aboard the offending war junk, and on his visit behaved in such a peremptory manner that a Chinese officer slapped him. Incensed even further, the consul brought the matter all the way up to Governor Ye Mingchen. Ye, seeing his danger, promptly released the nine innocent men. Parkes demanded that all twelve be freed. The whole matter was intolerable, and he expected a public apology from Ye.

The *Arrow* was Chinese-owned. As Parkes soon discovered, even its Hong Kong registration had recently expired. It had been invalid at the time of the incident. Kennedy, besides, who had minimal seafaring experience, was only its captain on paper. He was almost certainly lying when he said the Union Jack had been hauled down – it would have been against nautical practice for it to have been up in the first place. Parkes nevertheless had the commander of a Royal Navy frigate cruising in the vicinity seize a Chinese war junk in reprisal – only for the two of them to realize that they had mistakenly boarded a private trading vessel. Ye, shrugging off this misstep, eventually agreed to release the three suspected criminals as well. He regretted he could not issue a public apology, however, as this would undermine his own authority. Parkes was irate. The governor's conduct was clearly beyond the pale of civilized behaviour. Bowring wrote to London. On 27 October the British fleet began bombarding Canton.

The *Arrow* incident and the incipient war were the occasion for another heated debate in Britain in which a number of political luminaries – Richard Cobden, Benjamin Disraeli, Lord John Russell and William Ewart Gladstone among them – lined up on China's side. In the House of Lords, critics found Parkes's behaviour 'grotesque' and Bowring's 'unworthy'. This time the cabinet was actually forced to resign, in Parliament. Around the country, though, it was a classic triumph of the simplicity of untruths over factual argumentation.

All the public heard was that Ye had hauled down the Union Jack and was therefore a monster. Palmerston crushed his opponents in the 'Chinese' general election that followed.[40] The *Arrow* had not been carrying opium, and the affray around it had nothing to do with the opium trade. It may thus seem odd to call the war that ensued a Second Opium War. The Arrow War, however, would achieve the goal Palmerston and Bowring had beforehand established: the legalization of opium imports into China.

This time the Chinese were better prepared, and though the outcome was never in doubt, the war was more hard-fought. The Qing, separately, were locked in a mortal struggle with a rebel army known as the Taiping, hobbling what resistance they could put up to the European invaders. British forces were meanwhile supplemented by a French contingent of nine hundred marines and several gunboats.[41]

The assault began, under the joint leadership of Lord James Elgin and Baron Jean-Baptiste Gros, on Canton in December 1857. After a long bombardment, the attackers scaled the walls and entered the old city in force. They seized Ye Mingchen's treasury and his archives, and they took him prisoner – he would die in exile. There were 450 Chinese casualties to some 130 French and British. As in the First Opium War, however, taking Canton was not enough to force the emperor to yield. In the spring of 1858 the invading army therefore sailed north and disembarked before Tianjin. In May, outgunning and outmanoeuvring the Chinese artillery, it took the forts guarding the Hai River. The road to the capital stood open. Qing emissaries were dispatched to the scene and, on 3 and 4 July, a treaty was signed, known as the Treaty of Tianjin.

The treaty provided for the opening of embassies in Beijing by Britain and France – as well as by Russia and the United States. When a year later the British and French ambassadors arrived, however, they decided to sail to the capital under guard from a military flotilla. The Chinese objected to the show of force, and a battle ensued in which, for once, the Europeans were bested. The Qing caught the enemy marines in a crossfire, inflicting more than 1,000 casualties. Elgin and Gros were sent out on a second invasion, this time with a much larger force of 7,500 men on the French side and as many as 13,000 British troops. In July–August 1860 a revenge assault was launched on the Hai River forts, leading to another bloody battle won by superior artillery power. Tianjin was occupied and negotiations opened once again.

In a final theatrical action that September, the Qing forces captured 39 of the European party in a dawn raid, taking them into harsh prison conditions in Beijing. This was the prompt for a final advance, taking the British and French through fields, suburban gardens and imperial tombs to the capital's northern edge. After a last rout of the Qing cavalry, Beijing came in sight of enemy guns. Eventually it surrendered, though not before the occurrence of the Second Opium War's most notorious episode: the sack of the summer palace and the destruction of its priceless artefacts by an out-of-control French and British soldiery, in an orgy of looting that lasted several days. The emperor, who was in flight, could do no more than mourn the desecration of his collections and the torching of his favourite residence. His brother was left to negotiate. Multiple treaties were signed in Beijing between 23 and 25 October 1860, confirming the Tianjin terms with a higher indemnity.[42]

The Treaty of Tianjin, or rather a follow-on conference pursuant to one of its clauses, legalized opium imports. The drug would be subject to a tariff of thirty silver *taels* per chest, approximately 8 per cent by value.[43] The irony is that this would make little difference to the volumes imported, and in the long term would even pave the way for the Indian trade's decline. Though imports initially continued to expand, eventually domestic cultivation took off as enforcement slackened to nil. Domestic developments opened the floodgates: first as a knock-on effect of the legalization of imports, second as the product of emergency measures taken by the Qing themselves in their struggle against the Taiping.

The Taiping Rebellion had proved right the Qing administration's fears tying together the social peace, malign foreign influence and political stability. The revolt began at the instigation of a failed mandarin examination candidate named Hong Xiuquan who had half-absorbed Protestant missionary ideas in Canton. His movement, preached amid famine conditions, was a hotchpotch of social and moral reforms, including the communal ownership of property, the segregation of the sexes and the proscription of intoxicants. It quickly grew into an out-of-control military threat. Hong, having linked up with underworld figures, initially established a mountain redoubt in his native southern region of Guangxi. Breaking through surrounding imperial troops, his embryo force marched out in 1851 and, plundering weapons and stores and recruiting the dispossessed everywhere, began slashing its way north. Within barely more than a year, Taiping ranks had swelled to 500,000 and their columns had reached the Yangtze. In 1853 they took the great city of Nanjing. They would plague China for two decades. The Taiping launched raids as far as Beijing itself and in 1860–61, just as the Qing were dealing with the Anglo-French assault, they rampaged through the Yangtze valley to the edges of Shanghai. The Qing took Nanjing back in 1864, but Taiping remnants spread south again towards Canton. Their last forces were defeated only in 1871. Through violence, famine and associated diseases, estimates are that they left 20 million dead.[44]

The Qing survived, but just barely, and their administration fell under maximum strain. A number of provinces, cut off from Beijing, were forced to fend for themselves. They soon discovered that, if money needed to be raised, opium offered a solution. During 1856–8, before the Treaty of Tianjin still, the Shanghai authorities decided they might as well tax the drug. The rate was set at twelve silver *taels* per chest. Boats patrolled the harbour, flying flags with the inscription 'Public Committee for Patriotic Collections'. Duty was collected from local dealers. The procedure radiated such an official atmosphere that the *North China Herald* told its readers that 'an Imperial duty upon opium has at least been imposed at this port.'[45] The governor in Fuzhou implemented a similar system. The Ningbo authorities did likewise, farming out collection rights to local financiers. In 1858 the city of Xiamen, which had been levying $2 per chest, raised this to $50.[46]

The expedient that saved the Qing from the Taiping was that they allowed provincial governors to raise their own armies. In the mid-1850s an official named Zeng Guofan set up a Hunan Army on the south bank of the Yangtze. It was he who recovered Nanjing in 1864. Zeng also sponsored the formation of parallel military bodies in neighbouring regions. His troops, however, professionally raised and highly paid, were expensive to train and maintain. They made use of modern weapons bought from the Europeans or manufactured in arsenals set up with their help, and this, too, needed to be paid for. The solution was a new tax: *likin*. An internal duty levied on goods passing through certain fixed stations – waystations on water and land routes, market towns – *likin* would notably come to be raised on that highly portable and valuable item: opium.[47]

Making the best out of a situation that had been forced on it, the Qing state began after the signature of the Treaty of Nanjing to raise significant revenue on the drug. A new tariff was agreed with Britain in 1885, under the Chefoo Convention, setting import duty plus *likin* at a total of 110 *taels* per chest, or around $150.[48] Within three years, the total tax take from opium would reach 9 million silver *taels*, or approximately $12.5 million.[49] Between 1885 and 1905 opium would bring between 6 and 7 per cent of the annual imperial tax revenues, and as much as 14 per cent in 1906.[50]

Officially, opium remained a prohibited article: it was only imports that had been legalized. Penalties on possession were lifted in 1859, but sentencing continued to apply on smoking by officials, soldiers and eunuchs. It remained forbidden to open or operate opium dens, and only merchants licensed to deal in foreign goods were theoretically allowed to handle the drug.[51] Cases published in the *Peking Gazette* during the 1870s and '80s provide examples of the offences prosecuted: an imperial clan member was punished for operating an opium den in Beijing; a Jiangsu magistrate was banished for selling opium; a eunuch was beheaded for smoking opium in the palace and operating a den; a boy was condemned to death by slicing for providing his mother with opium – he had thought she wanted to smoke but she had used it to commit suicide.[52]

In 1865 the imperial court even issued a fresh ban on cultivation, repeating it three years later.[53] Why go through such pretences, however, after the foreigners had forced China to agree to take in imports? In practice, the laws were rarely enforced. The result was that domestic opium, cheaper to produce, began to substitute for the foreign variety. Poppy cultivation had already attracted notice in the 1840s, but was then mostly restricted to tribal settlements in the southwestern provinces of Yunnan, Guizhou and Sichuan.[54] During the second half of the century, though this core area remained the largest by acreage, the poppy spread to all Chinese provinces. Statistics were imprecise, but domestically grown opium probably overtook imports sometime in the 1880s.[55] These had by then peaked at a level of 83,000 chests. By the early twentieth century the Chinese opium output would swell well beyond these bounds, yielding several hundred thousand chests annually.[56]

By then, opium's social trajectory had undergone a full arc, from sailors and migrants to the titled and moneyed classes, and back to the simple cart-pusher. People of every station smoked opium: men and women, urban and rural dwellers. From the riverboat inn and the gentleman's private smoking-room, opium had found its way into the cultivator's cottage and to the roadside stop. From the courtesan, the pipe had passed on to the housewife. Women of middle-class families, often confined to the home, had time to spare and space to share, and they escaped their boredom with recreations such as playing chess, tasting tea and now smoking opium.[57] (Foot binding may also have contributed to the spread of opium among women. Foot binding was painful, and opium is a sedative.) Labourers of all walks of life took it before or after work. A traveller observed: 'The men always worked harder after they had smoked, and obviously took a pipe before doing a strenuous job.'[58] Sedan-chair bearers, boatmen and porters or 'coolies' used it to soothe the strain of their effort or to deal with hunger pangs.

Upper-class smoking remained extensive, all the more so when it ceased to be surreptitious. Among the highest ranks, Grand Secretary Ju Hongji and Imperial Censor-in-Chief Lu Baozhong were known to be big smokers. So were the governors of Jiangsu, Chen Qitai, and of Kaifeng, Wen Ti. The boy genius Jiang Jianren sold his literary works for opium, and the artist Ren Bonian did likewise with his paintings. Liu Kunyi, governor general of Guangdong and Guangxi and as such the successor to Deng Tingzhen and Lin Zexu, smoked opium 'as frequently as others ate rice'. An associate wrote: 'Liu's capacity to smoke is unusual ... Every morning, his servants would prepare about ten mouthfuls of opium paste ... Then they would wake him up. He would continuously suck about ten mouthfuls before he started to wash and eat breakfast, then he worked. He would not smoke until the evening. After dinner and dessert he would smoke until the early hours of the morning.'[59]

Good-quality opium came to be aged as a syrup in ceramic or clay jars, triggering a process of fermentation. In Shanghai, the better opium houses seasoned their opium for three years in porcelain jars inscribed with the auspicious characters for longevity, good fortune or happiness. Matured high-quality Bengal was prized much as rare wine vintages were in Europe. Opium of a good season and vintage, twenty or twenty-five years old, could command soaring prices.[60] Conversely, at the lower end, consumers were given dross recycled from ashes, sometimes mixed into paste to make it smoother – dross may have accounted for a third of the opium smoked by weight during the second half of the nineteenth century. There were numerous product classes, tailored to popular demand and priced based on market segmentation:

> Opium from Yunnan, for instance, was turned into four varieties before being transported to the markets. 'Horseshit' was made of raw opium from the southeast of Yunnan; blackish and wrapped in bamboo leaves, it had the distinct appearance of horse manure [though] it was considered the best of all domestic opium and was custom-made for the Guangdong market. 'Buns' came second, consisting of raw opium from the west of Yunnan. Wrapped into characteristic oil paper, 'bun opium' was mainly sold in Sichuan, Hubei and Shanghai. 'Opium cakes' resembled home-baked cakes and were dark in colour. This third type reached its target markets of Guangdong, Hunan and Guangxi and retailed in bamboo containers padded with bamboo leaves. The most affordable category was 'brick opium', red or yellow, wrapped into rough paper and particularly popular in Hubei and Guangxi.[61]

The opium den, finally, became the symbol of the drug's ubiquitous progress. Whether a humble shop with a few beds catering to men of the lower orders or an opulent hall sporting the best furniture and accessories and passing on its dross for reuse, the den became the proof that the drug had conquered China. In Chongqing, a city of 120,000, there were thought to be 1,230 dens in 1878.[62] The newspaper *Shen Bao* counted more than 1,700 of them in Shanghai in 1872.[63] The ethnographer Justus Doolittle wrote that in Fuzhou there were 'several thousand' and that the locals described them as being 'more numerous than rice shops'.[64] An activist reported of Hunan province: 'There are about 1,000 opium dens in the cities and towns near here, irrespective of the private arrangements provided in places of business and guest halls, and he thinks the average number who visit each of these dens daily would be 30.'[65]

Opium bestrode China like a fifth horseman of the apocalypse. The plague had overrun the country. Opium was everywhere, and it held its elites and populace alike in a perpetual smoke-induced stupor. Or did it? Such, increasingly, was the stereotype, but was it accurate? Shanghai was China's main platform of opium commerce and consumption, and it was not representative of the rest of the country. Fuzhou was another treaty port and transit point. Foreign observers were more likely to find opium dens in the conspicuous locations where they landed. Activists wishing to rouse opinions against the drug, whether Chinese or foreign, had a motive to exaggerate its spread. By contrast, some travellers, even though they made detailed notes on Chinese social customs, failed to find opium even worthy of mention.[66]

Opium enjoyed a certain level of acceptability, no doubt. It had come to be served in certain social settings. Opium might be deployed on a festive occasion. Younger people smoked to imitate their peers, or to see if it lived up to its reputation as an aphrodisiac. It might help clinch a business deal, and hosts in commercial settings sometimes offered a welcome smoke to visitors, alongside tea and refreshments.[67] A foreign doctor practising in China noted: 'In the large mercantile hongs, in Swatow, it is becoming more and more the custom . . . to keep the opium pipe for the use of friends and visitors.'[68] Another observer remarked that Chinese doctors themselves expected to be invited to a smoke at the houses of their patients, and that even policemen and constables partook of the pleasure.[69]

At the same time, enough people evidently feared addiction sufficiently to ensure they steered clear of the drug. One indicator is the prevalence of anti-opium cures, whose popularity became widespread. The newspaper *Shen Bao*, for example, ran advertisements for 'the foreign white powder that helps one quit smoking'. There were 'white pearls' and 'red pearls', smokeable from a short pipe.[70] Remedies such as astringents, tonics and camphor pills, or withdrawal aids including strychnine, quinine, capsicum and gentian, were eagerly sought.[71] Popular brands in the 1900s included the 'Resurrection pill', 'Awakening China anti-opium pill', 'Heaven-made cure', 'Universal salvation', 'Benefit of Heaven' and 'Race-protecting pill'.[72] One problem was that many of these cures actually contained opium. Missionaries sometimes unknowingly dispensed them in the refuges they ran, and the pills became known as 'Jesus opium', much to the horror of those who had given them out.[73]

Transcripts of court cases tell of parents brawling with local addicts who were trying to lead their sons into opium use.[74] Opium was rarely given to children – even to quieten them when they cried, as was done, for example, in Britain.[75] Manual workers may have taken the odd pipe to help them through the day, but examples abound of light use kept prudently short of addictive behaviour. As to the wealthy, 'the opium habit is universally regarded by the Chinese as injurious and degrading,' wrote a social commentator, even as he noticed 'some discrepancy between their precepts and practice'.[76] Contemporary novels and guidebooks testify to the same ambivalence. In certain settings, opium remained a mark of fine taste, but beyond certain levels of use it was frowned upon. The drug remained a glamorous product, but only if consumed in socially acceptable ways. There was a polarity between those who should smoke – especially the rich and educated, who could afford and appreciate opium – and those who should not: the poor, who faced destitution if they became dependent, and anyone who did not have the strength of will or self-knowledge to smoke it in the right way.[77]

The main objection, however, to the claim that opium had become ubiquitous in turn-of-the-century China is in the data. The volumes were large, but they do not support the vision of an entire nation lying stupefied.

How many people took opium, on how many days a week and in what quantity is not knowable exactly. What is known approximately is the total volume of opium consumed in China at the time. Also available are surveys attempting to establish how much various categories of users may have smoked. These have allowed contemporary observers and historians alike to establish probable numbers of opium smokers.[78]

At its peak in 1905–6, based on official statistics, China's domestically cultivated opium totalled around 480,000 chests, as the average of a given range.[79] To this must be added net imports of 29,000 chests. The number must also be reduced for boiling and adjusted for the recuperation of dross. A plausible end-volume was 414,000 chests, or 25,000 metric tons. Previously, China's imperial customs service had performed a survey to establish how much opium the average smoker consumed. The tentative answer was 4 grams per day for a 'beginner', 11 grams for an 'average' smoker, and 33 grams for a 'heavy' smoker.[80] Dividing the total volume (25,000 mt) by the annualized dose for the average smoker (4 kg, or 8.8 lb) yields a possible number of users: 6.2 million, or 1.4 per cent of the population.

The result is only as good as the data inputs (for a discussion, see Appendix 1). The volume of raw opium may have been as high as

613,917 chests. The daily dose of 11 grams is probably too high, as comparable surveys from other Far Eastern countries suggest. Using the higher total number of chests and a daily dose of 5.5 grams, one obtains a perhaps more realistic number of 15 million smokers, or 3.3 per cent of the population. Such an assessment puts the Chinese opium epidemic at a far from negligible level. At the same time, it is nowhere near impressionistic notions of an entire country held in drug slavery.

What is certain, moreover, is that one cannot have it both ways. Mathematically, the higher the number of opium smokers one assumes, the smaller his or her average use had to be, and therefore the less he or she conformed to the stereotype of the heavy user, the addict. Perhaps there were 50 million opium smokers in 1905 China, but then they cannot each have taken more than a light couple of pipes a day. (There is no set threshold for opium addiction, just as there is no threshold for alcoholism, but 1–2 grams of smoked opium per day is a fraction of what a modern-day opiate addict typically injects.) Conversely, if all smokers are believed to have been hopelessly tied to their drug, then based on the same total volume they can have numbered no more than 2 to 2.5 million, or 0.5 per cent of the population.

In 2015 in the United States an estimated 13 million people abused opiates or synthetic opioids.[81] This was 4 per cent of the population, more than the plausible 3.3 per cent for China in 1905–6. Worldwide, according to the most recent UN statistics, a quarter of a billion people use drugs, or also 3.3 per cent of the total population – though this mixes a broad range of drugs, not all comparable to opiates.[82] The Chinese opium plague, then, was in all likelihood comparable to the modern American opioid epidemic: acute, but not quite cataclysmic. The lamentable episode that was the Opium Wars has stood in the way of sober analysis. Because the wars did so much, in official Chinese iconography, to shape the country's fate, it became a commonplace that China was the victim of a drug apocalypse.[83] This, though not entirely without basis, is inaccurate.

A tragic feature of the modern American opioid epidemic has been the number of deaths by overdose: on average 40,000 per year between 2014 and 2018.[84] It is unlikely that opium produced the same casualty rate in turn-of-the-century China. Smoked opium, much less concentrated than heroin or prescription opioids, is less prone to induce overdosing. The social nature of smoking, practised mostly in shops or dens, moreover, defended against secretive, addictive behaviours. The evidence is widespread of casual use unlikely to have led to dependence. The manager of a tannery in Shanghai employing three hundred men, for example, reported that though many were opium smokers, none was ever incapacitated for work.[85] The manual worker who took opium to help take him through the strain can only have smoked so many pipes without becoming inapt to his job, and so can the businessman who treated his clients to a smoke.

At the same time, it is clear that a sizeable proportion became addicted. The same tannery manager said of a business relation: 'All the merchants that I spoke to and knew intimately, agreed that there was no straighter broker than Fong-kee. I said to him "why for smoke so much opium; your teeth are black?" His face was so wasted that you might almost have made your hands meet in the hollow of his cheeks … He told me: "Suppose I do not smoke one day, I must die."'[86] The missionaries who opened opium refuges, treating dependent users, found that it was not an easy task. Frederick Gough, of the Church Missionary Society in Ningbo, caught his patients lowering baskets through the windows to accomplices who supplied them with opium. When he placed bars on the windows, they were broken and removed. Inside, 'violent quarrels took place, tempers being irritated by restraint and by the sight of some securing the longed-for drug.'[87]

It is, moreover, likely that, more than in twenty-first-century America, in China the drug wrought significant damage through its social side effects. An economically exposed and often underfed population, lacking modern safety nets, was always more vulnerable when it came to basic health and family structures. The porter who allocated ten cents every day to his pipe was more likely to go hungry. The farmer who smoked half his harvest might lose his land in a bad year, leaving his dependents destitute. A witness recalls the following scene:

> I saw that *eight little girls*, ranging from seven to twelve years of age, were placed in a cart … 'These children have been bought cheaply in Ta-t'ong Fu [a town in the northern part of Hunan province], by the man you see with them, who is going to sell them at T'ai-ku for a high price.' … By way of explanation he said the people in the north of the province

being poorer, the opium habit reduced the victims to extremities more rapidly, and that selling their daughters was one resource to get money in order to procure the drug.[88]

The Qing had failed to tame opium. Foreign bullying forbade them to do so. Yet their policies, however well-meaning, had also been too ambitious from the start. Opium prohibition swam against a tide of negative demographic, economic and material circumstances pushing the state towards internal decomposition, as the Taiping revolt confirmed. The pre-modern Qing state, for all its tradition of good governance, utterly lacked the means to police something like opium. Its paternalistic tenets proved wrong-footed and even counter-productive. They paid no heed to the juggernaut that was China's rising opium culture, whatever the malign, supply-side role of the foreign dealers may have been. The paradoxical outcome was that the drug ended up funding resistance against the Taiping and, in part, China's industrial and military modernization, but only after the damage had been done.

A second consequence was that opium became tied, in China's emerging national consciousness, to foreign defeat and humiliation. While its drug epidemic looks merely comparable in gravity to latter-day scares, it was the first of its kind. It made an all the deeper impression that it was something new. The shock itself would help the dying Qing state stage one last, surprisingly successful push against the drug. By then, though, opium had acquired a heft and reputation that went far beyond Chinese shores. Indeed, it had been spreading abroad for a while already.

Indian opium had never only been bound for China. Even before the Europeans appeared on the scene, the drug had been a staple of Southeast Asian trade. As, in the seventeenth century, smoking became fashionable, the colonizers had identified opium as a profitable article. Gradually, they began to carry it everywhere on the Indochinese peninsula and in the Indonesian archipelago, where they distributed it via increasingly structured networks.

The Dutch East India Company had been a pioneer. In the mid-seventeenth century it had begun shipping Bengal opium down to the Malabar coast – still in India – having wrested that trade from the Portuguese. In 1642 it obtained a monopoly from the sultan of

Palembang, on the island of Sumatra, on the importation of textiles and opium. It also began selling the paste at Batavia, its outpost on Java. Total quantities handled remained modest, a few hundred chests annually by the late eighteenth century, but slowly the company acquired the right – usually by force – to distribute the drug through-out the rest of the island.[89] (On Java, opium was mostly consumed as *candu*, or pure smoking paste, but unlike in China it also continued to be mixed in or soaked into tobacco or maize leaves for rolling into cigars. Some Javanese also ate opium, spiked their coffee with it or mixed it with betel.[90])

The Dutch were the first to adopt a distribution model destined to become popular throughout the region: the farm. An opium 'farm' was not an agricultural undertaking, and it had nothing to do with growing poppies. Rather, it was a licence to distribute opium within a certain territorial unit, ranging from a district to an entire colonial state. Models varied, but the licence was typically sold for a fee and for a period of one to a few years. The Dutch East India Company handled the opium's purchase in India and its transportation. On arrival, it sold the product wholesale to a licensee or licensees. Prices were fixed, as sometimes was the volume the 'farmer' was expected to purchase.

The farming-out system was inaugurated on Java in 1809. The Dutch divided the island into 22 residencies. In two of these, opium had traditionally been forbidden, and it remained banned under Dutch rule. By 1832 the other twenty all possessed opium farms.[91] The number of stores within each farm was set by the administration and stipulated by contract; by 1851 there were more than 2,600 opium shops on the island, though that number fluctuated downwards in the ensuing decades.[92] The system was not unique to the drug. The farming out of excise collection, such as on salt or tobacco, in one guise or another was typical of administrations in the Far East, and it had long been practised in Europe itself. The opium franchises would nevertheless turn out to be particularly rich sources of fiscal income.

The British Indian administration adopted the same model within the territories it controlled, closely behind the Dutch. Briefly, the Bengal authorities had flirted with banning the smokeable mixture of opium and betel leaves known as *madat*.[93] In India, though, opium was chiefly eaten. In 1813 the government introduced a farming system. The terms varied across the subcontinent and as time went by, but the government fixed the number of retail shops in each district, where it sold individual or group licences. In the 1890s excise shops totalled just over 10,000, dispensing opium in pill form, as pharmacies in Europe did. The only difference to the Dutch system was that the government also monopolized cultivation and manufacturing.[94]

British ships and administrators later pushed opium farms further into the region: Hong Kong, Singapore, Malaya, Sri Lanka, Burma. The regime varied in the detail: in the Straits Settlements and Malaya, dens were restricted to adult Chinese males, though Chinese women and Malays were allowed to consume the drug at home. By the 1900s the opium farm accounted for almost half the fiscal revenues of the Straits Settlements colony.[95] In Burma, the first opium farm was introduced in 1826, spreading thereafter as each Burmese kingdom fell. The exception was Upper Burma, where Shan and Kachin tribal populations traditionally grew poppies. There, opium licences were freely granted at a set fee, with sales allowed to ethnic Chinese, Indians, Shan or Kachin, though not to other native Burmese.[96]

The British example even persuaded the independent Kingdom of Thailand to legalize opium. It will be recalled that Thailand had issued the first recorded ban on the drug, in the fourteenth century. King Rama II renewed this prohibition in 1811. In 1833, when Thailand signed a trade treaty with the United States, this specifically excluded opium. Another interdiction was issued in 1839, with penalties that were strictly enforced. Persistent smuggling from Singapore, however, and the ominous example of the First Opium War convinced King Rama IV that it was more prudent to allow the drug in after all. In 1852 Thailand set up its first opium farm: the farmer, later a government agency, bought the imported product, processed it in a factory and sold it on to licensees.[97] From 1893 it also fixed retail prices. There were two main varieties: superior, which was Bengal opium, and lower-grade, which was a mixture of Indian and Chinese opium.[98]

As this last detail hints, Chinese merchants were also involved in the trade, and they remained active agents within the structures set up by the Europeans. On Java, for example, a hybrid Chinese–Indonesian community dominated commerce, also operating monopolies such as ports or salt production. This community continued to be granted substantial economic power under the Dutch, and its members won all the opium farms.[99] There would be Chinese opium farmers in Singapore, Malaya, Thailand, Cambodia and Burma. In Vietnam, where opium remained prohibited, Qing merchants played the role of the smugglers. A Chinese oligarchy controlled most foreign trade, and the authorities found it accordingly difficult to discipline. As the merchants soon noticed, moreover, the Vietnamese tax inspectors did not board visiting junks at the river mouth but in Hanoi itself. The traders got their ships to unload their merchandise downriver, in the countryside, for taking into the interior, just as Jardine Matheson and others did in the Pearl River estuary.[100]

It was the French, however, who would impose the drug whole-sale on the Vietnamese as they gobbled up their kingdoms between 1862 and 1884. No time was lost: as early as 1862, Messrs Ségassié and Télésio became the proud owners, for eighteen months, of the opium farm for Cochin-China – or southern Vietnam. They paid the tidy sum of $91,000 for the privilege, though theirs was not an auspicious start. The company quickly became embroiled in mismanagement and fraud: the Frenchmen asked for a reduction on their licence pay-ment, then it was revealed that they had been skimming profits into their own trading enterprises. The operation was liquidated and the principals were thrown into jail. The next opium farmer was a pre-sumably more honest Chinese merchant named Wangtai.[101] France had at the same time imposed an indemnity on the neighbouring kingdom of Annam which it was unable to pay. The kingdom con-ceded, as a means to raise money, its first opium farm to a private (Chinese) group.[102]

In Vietnamese Indochina, each region initially remained under a separately run but similar regime: Cochin-China, Annam and Tonkin. Cambodia, which became a French protectorate in 1867, itself established an opium farm shortly before colonization.[103] As opium became more embedded in Indochina's colonial administrative struc-tures, though, the French sought to establish greater uniformity and control. In Tonkin, smuggling remained rife, especially from the adjacent Chinese province of Yunnan. Laos, which became part of French Indochina in 1893, was an opium-growing region in its own right. Both the challenges this represented and the drive to maxim-ize a valuable fiscal resource led to the creation of a new system into which these regions were progressively assimilated. In 1882 France established the first integrated opium monopoly, known as the *Régie de l'opium*. Originally only an import monopoly, the *Régie* took over wholesale distribution in 1890 and manufacturing in 1892. From

1895 it began selling individual licences to retailers.[104] Importing both Bengal and Yunnan opium, from 1900 it concentrated all manufacturing in Saigon.[105]

Following the French example, *Régie*-style integrated monopolies – whereby every link in the chain was government-run except for the last, the individual shop – in turn replaced farming systems in most of the region. In 1893 the Dutch parliament approved the formation of an *Opiumregie* for Indonesia, rolled out the next year in its first trial residency. All opium affairs were concentrated in Batavia, where a government plant, employing hundreds of workers, churned out products of uniform quality sold in standardized and marked packaging. A Java-wide bureaucracy replaced the farms and sub-farms; it even ran its own network of stores.[106] In Burma arrangements for selling licences were altered in 1902–3, with retail now tightly controlled based on fixed margins.[107] In Thailand the royal government instituted an *Opium Régie* in 1907.[108] In Sri Lanka a centrally run system was put in place in 1909.[109] In Singapore and most of British Malaya, a government-run monopoly replaced the old farms in 1910–11.[110]

With the exception of the Straits Settlements and Malaya, per capita consumption of processed opium remained, in all of these territories, well below Chinese levels. On Java, by 1900, it had flattened at just above 1 gram per annum. On Sri Lanka this was 2 grams. In Burma as in French Indochina, official consumption was just under 6 grams (though this ignored substantial smuggling), and in Thailand 11 grams. China, by comparison, stood at 56 grams.[111]

In India, the number was around 2.5 grams, less than in Britain itself, where it was above 4 grams. Dr Kailash Chandra Bose of the Calcutta Medical Society testified: 'Opium does not have any deleterious influences upon the health of habitual consumers. On the contrary, it is a prop to old age, and elderly men pull well under its influences.'[112] In India, most consumption was medicinal. The problem, however, was that everywhere else opium was smoked. This, making it impossible to hide beneath the cloak of medical use, exposed the drug and its distribution networks to growing criticism. The *Régies* themselves had only become popular because the principle of unbridled fiscal profiting from opium was coming under attack.

The *Courrier de Saigon* wrote in 1864: 'France has not come to this country to force people to poison themselves. It found opium spread widely already among all classes.'[113] While it was still possible to make such patently false statements in the 1860s, around the end of the century it was becoming more difficult.

The colonial administration in The Hague was the first to begin departing from blithely self-serving views. Revisions made to opium farm regulations in 1853, 1874 and 1890 comprised commitments to restrain consumption as well as maintain revenues. From 1853 the Dutch reduced the number of retail outlets in Indonesia, also creating new opium-free enclaves.[114] Such initiatives acquired fresh momentum as Charles Te Mechelen, a Eurasian Javanese, became chief inspector of opium affairs. Mechelen was charged in the 1880s with investigating the opium habit. Alongside anti-smuggling measures, he recommended that the government take over manufacturing and deepen its control of the farms, which were reproached for sharp promotional practices and a structural bias towards expanding consumption.[115]

In the 1880s the MP Willem van Dedem had already attacked the colonial opium administration in the Dutch parliament. Like-minded politicians and administrators criticized the Mechelen report, published in 1888, for not going far enough. Ex-East Indies men such as Pieter Brooshooft, the editor of a Javanese newspaper; Isaac Groneman, a long-time Yogyakarta resident and royal physician; and the activist Elout van Soeterwoude upped the pressure by forming an Anti-opium Bond, comprising newspaper editors, jurists and academics as well as several prominent churchmen and MPs. The bond obtained promises that the new regime, the *Opiumregie*, would be able to check and, over time, reduce opium's reach.[116]

In Burma, likewise, Chief Commissioner Charles Aitchison took on indiscriminate opium sales from 1881. In his opinion, it was one thing to sell opium to ethnic Chinese or Indians, who had a culture of opium consumption (or were, in contemporary racial discourse, constitutionally better equipped to resist the habit), but to push opium on native Burmese people was immoral.[117] Restrictions on sales introduced in Upper Burma in 1888 reflected his views. In 1893 they were extended to Lower Burma, where existing users were to register if they wanted to continue receiving supplies.[118] In 1907 the Straits Settlements commissioned an inquiry into opium. The inquiry recommended ending the farming system and instituting the monopoly that was established in 1910–11 as well as putting in place a preventive service.[119]

In other places, local opposition was able to push for tighter controls. In Sri Lanka and in Thailand, as in Burma, the Buddhist interdiction against intoxication was taken seriously. In Sri Lanka public gatherings took place in the 1890s demanding restrictions on opium imports and sales, gathering tens of thousands of signatures. Eventually, the colonial government introduced a monopoly combined with a smoker registration system designed to stop opium use from spreading.[120] In Thailand the *Opium Régie*, when it was established, proclaimed that it had the aim to 'ultimately suppress the use of opium', to be accomplished by reducing the number of shops and eventually establishing a registration system for 'habitual smokers'.[121]

Alongside Thailand, finally, another independent country had watched the Opium Wars with mounting apprehension: Japan. The Japanese, rather than legalization, had opted for strict prohibition. This fitted both the archipelago's isolated geography and its almost total absence of an opium-smoking culture. The region around Osaka was the site of poppy cultivation on a small scale, but there was no smuggling, whether by Chinese or European merchants. In the 1840s the shogunate received both Dutch and Chinese accounts of the First Opium War, including the mistaken information that the drug was a forbidden article in Britain itself. The defeat of the Chinese behemoth came as a shock. If opium became an item of trade, it would crack the door open to colonization, the Japanese concluded. In 1855 and 1856, as it inaugurated or upgraded commercial relations with Russia and the Netherlands respectively, Japan was able to incorporate anti-opium clauses into its treaties. Its luck was that it was American and not British gunboats that, under Commodore Perry, forced it to open its ports. When in 1858 the United States and Japan signed a Treaty of Amity and Commerce, this likewise explicitly forbade the importation of opium, and an accord with Britain replicated the same terms soon thereafter.[122]

Japan's first domestic prohibition was enacted in Meiji times, in 1868. Smoking opium was forbidden, and anyone who sold the drug for the purpose or who induced others to smoke risked maximum penalties.[123] In 1870 the government introduced regulations on medicinal opium requiring druggists and physicians to report sales to the authorities. This was followed by legislation dated 1878 allowing the Sanitary Bureau to purchase opium on a monopoly basis for pharmaceutical resale. In typical Meiji fashion, this imitated or reinvented conditions observed in European countries such as France and Germany. The bureau processed the raw opium into paste and distributed the output through a network of offices in Japan's main cities. Pharmacists could only sell the drug on prescription. Between 1880 and 1907, finally, the penal code was rewritten, including penalties for the illicit importation, manufacture, sale, possession and use of opium and smoking paraphernalia. Smokers faced up to three years of penal servitude, and dealers up to ten years.[124]

China served as a scarecrow, fostering a national consensus that helped sustain what at the time was the strictest regulatory regime. Japanese resolve was nevertheless tested when in 1895 the country acquired Taiwan. The island possessed a large community of opium smokers, estimated at 170,000 or 6–7 per cent of the total population.[125] Milking Taiwan through opium farms, as the Europeans were doing with their Asian colonies, was out of the question: the island was to be treated as part of the mother country, and the Taiwanese to become Japanese citizens. At the same time, enforcing sudden and complete prohibition was going to be difficult.

The government ordered a survey of the land and customs, including opium use. Goto Shinpei, the head of civilian affairs in the Taiwan governorate and as such the official in charge of assimilation, proposed pursuing gradual suppression by means of a monopoly. The *Régies* recently instituted by European colonial administrations were the right model, he argued. Back home, the Sanitation Bureau objected. An official called upon Japan to 'proclaim to the world our government's disinterest in profit' and 'follow the path of humanitarianism and righteousness'. Allowing opium smoking to continue even temporarily would sap the 'racial' strength of the Taiwanese.[126] The chief inspector for the imperial army in Taiwan, Ishiguro Tadanori, responded with a pitch, aired in a series of newspaper editorials, for gradual interdiction. Though he upheld the ideal of a ban, Ishiguro warned that sudden prohibition would cause people to die from the agonies of withdrawal.[127]

The resulting compromise system was destined to be much emulated. As of 1901 the governor general took over the opium supply. Manufacturing was centralized. A newly set up bureau authorized retail distributors to sell the drug on its behalf. But the bureau also issued permits to users: these permit holders, of a minimum of twenty years of age, required prior vetting by a doctor as 'habitual smokers'. Without a permit, it was not legally possible to procure opium. The idea was that as smokers quit or died out, their total number would fall over time. Prices were set at a voluntarily low level to discourage smuggling.[128]

Although contraband no doubt began to make its way onto the island, the Taiwanese regime appeared to be successful. The law was enforced vigorously, with around 2,000 prosecutions every year.[129] The bureau aggressively reduced the number of licensed merchants from 3,339 in 1899 to 1,039 in 1907.[130] Smoker numbers slowly fell. From around 170,000 officially, they were down to 109,955 in 1909. They would keep falling, to 10,788 in 1938.[131] Volumes of opium paste sold onto the retail market declined from 212 metric tons in 1899 to 142 tons in 1907 – on a per capita basis, below the Chinese level.[132]

A new dynamic was taking hold in the region. The French Indochinese *Régie* had been little more than a fiscal prop. The Dutch version aimed to put an end to abusive sale practices and limit opium's progress among the population. In Burma, informed by racial notions associating opium with Chinese ethnicity, the system put in place in the 1880s and '90s sought to prevent access to Burmese natives. In Taiwan and afterwards in Thailand, opium monopolies explicitly aimed to reduce the number of users, tending towards extinction.

The Taiwanese model would attract the attention of yet another player eager for an influence in the region: the United States. As the Americans took over the Philippines in 1898, they found an opium farm in place, set up by the Spanish authorities in 1843.[133] At a loss as to how to deal with their newly acquired population of opium smokers, the American authorities assembled an investigating commission. This commission observed: 'What has been done during the past eight years by the quick-witted, enterprising nation for the benefit of the [Taiwanese] has resulted in a state of peace such as probably the history of the island has never before known, even temporarily. Not least in the Japanese campaign of progress has been the attempt to grapple with the opium problem and solve it so far as it touches [Taiwanese] life.'[134]

As the United States became interested in opium and the drug's East Asian role, it would turn to China, imparting to its policies an even franker prohibitionist twist. Setting the seal on the Opium Wars and their legacy, this would pave the way, tentatively at first but at last durably, for a new international regime. For this to happen, though, a parallel transformation needed to have taken place in Europe and the United States themselves.

3

PARADISE LOST?

On a dark and damp evening in December 1845 the novelist and poet Théophile Gautier arrived in front of the stone mansion known as the Hôtel Pimodan on the Ile Saint-Louis, one of two islands at the heart of Paris. A thick fog rose from the Seine, blurring everything save the reddish stains made by the occasional lantern – or so the author's fictionalized account has it. Having tumbled out of his carriage, Gautier banged the gate's sculpted knocker, and the solid, wooden panel opened. An old concierge pointed towards the back of the grass-grown courtyard beyond, and the poet waddled across the irregular paving. He found himself at the bottom of a curving staircase in the style of Louis xiv, an Egyptian chimera, holding a candle between its curved talons, gazing at him.

Gautier was on a call to a 'mysterious convocation, drafted in enigmatic terms, understandable to those in the know, unintelligible to others', an assignment that made the island look like 'a distant place, a solitary oasis in the middle of Paris, isolated by the river from invading civilization'.[1] On the walls hung Italian and Spanish old masters, and from the ceiling a mythological scene shone through the penumbra. The caller, having ascended, felt pulled two centuries back in time. At last: 'I stepped towards the better-lit part of a hall, where a group of human forms appeared to busy themselves around a table. As the light, engulfing me, disclosed who I was, a vigorous hurrah arose, shaking the old building to its foundations. It is he! It is he! several voices cried at once; let him have his share!'

Presiding over them, the 'doctor' was waiting:

He stood by a sideboard on which had been placed a tray arranged with Japanese porcelain saucers. With the help of a spatula, he drew lumps of a green paste or jam, each about the size of a thumb, out of a crystal vase, and tossed them onto the saucers. The tiny plates were equipped with vermeil teaspoons. The doctor's face beamed with glee ... This will be deducted from your slice of heaven, he told me as he handed me my allocated dose. Everyone having eaten their share, coffee was served in the Arab style, sweet and half-filled with residue. We sat down to dinner.

The Hôtel Pimodan belonged to the Romantic painter Fernand Boissard de Boisdenier, but it was frequented by a bohemian population that included such leading literary lights as Honoré de Balzac and Charles Baudelaire, as well as the better-known artists Ernest Meissonnier and Eugène Delacroix.[2] The doctor, on the night Gautier describes, was almost certainly Jacques-Joseph Moreau de Tours. Moreau had travelled to North Africa and the Levant, and he knew where to procure the green 'jam': hashish. A Paris alienist, he held as his principal interest the investigation of the causes of madness.

'An honest philistine might have had a fright at the site of these long-haired, bearded or moustachioed guests, or shaved in singular fashion, flourishing sixteenth-century daggers, Malay Kris-knives, and Navajas, and bent over foods that, in the vacillating glow of the lamps, took on suspect appearances,' continues the poet. Some struggled to bring a glass to their lips while others laughed with vacant eyes or cried out at nothing. Gautier himself began to feel warm, his brain addled.

'An armchair beckoned to me by the mantelpiece, and I abandoned myself without resistance to the effects of the fantastic drug.' Suddenly it was as if the lights shone anew, and the whole room, a panelled lounge with sculpted gilding and plaster friezes of satyrs pursuing nymphs, took on a splendid appearance. 'An enigmatic figure appeared to me in a flash ... It had a crooked nose much as a bird's beak, green eyes circled three times in brown ... As to its legs, they seemed made of mandrake root, bifurcated, black, rough and full of warts and nodes ... The strange creature burst into tears and, briskly rubbing its eyes, told me in a doleful voice: "Today we must die of laughter!"' A merry dance began, cherubs cackling in a circle around a troupe of half-human, half-animal creatures. One of the few guests not to have sampled the green paste began to play the piano, and Gautier enjoyed the finest musical sensations he had ever known.

Predictably, the dream turned to nightmare. The strange man reappeared, telling the poet he had an elephant's head. Gautier promptly verified the fact in a mirror. 'One could have taken me for a Hindu or a Javanese idol: my forehead had grown, my nose, elongated into a trunk, fell onto my chest, my ears beat at my shoulders, and to make things even more unpleasant, I had turned an indigo hue, like Shiva, the blue god.' He recovered his head, only to find that the half-human master of ceremony was at the same time holding it in a handkerchief. Gautier tried to leave, but his legs felt as of marble. The house's stairwell turned into an abyss. A demon barred the way beyond, growling and green-eyed, egged on by the host to bite Gautier. At last our poet made it into the courtyard. 'The odious fiend entwined me within the net of its legs and, its hands clinging at me like clamps, pulled me back up and, to my despair, plunked me back into the lounge from which I had only escaped with so much anguish.' Gautier lost consciousness. 'Your carriage is waiting downstairs,' he next remembered being told. Returning home, utterly lucid, he was surprised to find that the evening had barely begun.

Hashish, at the time of Gautier's escapade, was a barely known, obscure product in Europe. The paste is derived from the cannabis plant, also known as hemp. It is obtained from the same bush as marijuana, the difference being that marijuana consists of the dried flowers and upper leaves, whereas hashish is a resin extracted by rubbing the plant, or specifically the tiny hairs (trichomes) found on it. While Europeans had long cultivated hemp, until the nineteenth century they had only known it as a source of fibre for cordage.

A contemporary horticultural journal describes how, in India, it was cultivated in a different manner: 'Instead of being sown thick as it ought to be when intended for cordages, it is sown thin by the natives who afterwards transplant the young plants and place them at distances of 9 or 10 feet from each other. The effect of this is to expose them more freely to light, heat and air, by the agency of which the plant is enabled to perfect its secretions in a more complete manner.'[3] The Indians understood that only the female plant was a source of intoxicant. Their variety, *Cannabis indica*, was also more potent than the European *Cannabis sativa*. Planting began in March or April. The peasants ploughed and ridged the field multiple times to place the saplings. They pruned the bushes of their lower shoots. In November an expert came to identify the male plants, which were weeded out. Female shoots were moved into the empty spots created, further spacing out the plants. Flowers sprouted in January. When they turned yellow or brown, the field was harvested.[4]

Though the first-century Greek botanist Pedanius Dioscorides listed cannabis in his medical classic *De materia medica*, it was the Indian variety that had entered European pharmacopoeias in the 1700s.[5] In the United States the medical journals confirm it was used against such ailments as venereal disease, chorea, strychnine poisoning, insomnia and migraine.[6] A British pharmaceutical manual dated 1813 wrote that cannabis leaves 'are also sometimes given in cases of Diarrhoea and, in conjunction with Turmeric, Onions and Warm Ginglie oil, are made into an application for painful, swelled and protruded Piles'.[7] In the 1840s the Irish doctor and inventor William Brooke O'Shaughnessy, based in India, found that it could be useful for treating menstrual pains and hydrophobia in rabies patients, as well as 'cholera, delirium tremens, tetanus and other convulsive diseases'.[8]

As an intoxicant, nevertheless, cannabis remained something foreign. Hashish had come to French attention when Napoleon had invaded Egypt in 1798. The French, in the few years that they spent there, noticed that the locals had a secret for working hemp leaves into 'marvellous compositions, prone to procure, during sleep, diverse imaginary pleasures and the dreams one desires'.[9] The Egyptians ate it as a jam or smoked it mixed with tobacco.[10] They even sold it in special shops: 'All these preparations, of which both city and country dwellers made great consumption, are not to be found among druggists, like simple medicines; they are retailed in specialized shops, widespread among the Egyptian towns.'[11] Even so, as of the early nineteenth century, Western knowledge of the hemp drug remained minimal, basically limited to the medieval legend of the Old Man of the Mountain and his hashish-eating assassins – a story set in the Middle East and popularized by Marco Polo and John Mandeville. Gautier's hosts at the Hôtel Pimodan had baptized their little society the Club des hachichins, and he eagerly explained that the green paste he had been handed by the 'doctor' was the same drug the medieval sage had once given to his faithful.[12]

More so than cannabis, opium was a widely used medicine in Europe, and it could even be described as a popular product. As early as the fourteenth century, Raymond Chalmel de Viviers is on record for having prescribed theriac, an opium-based preparation, to Pope Clement VII.[13] In the 1660s the English physician Thomas Sydenham had invented an alcoholic opium tincture that became known as laudanum. By the early nineteenth century opium pills and laudanum were widely used as painkillers throughout Europe and the United States. Just as in China, opium was employed to treat a broad variety of ailments, including the catch-all categories that were fevers, inflammations and neuralgias, plus a long list of more specific conditions ranging from rheumatism to lockjaw.[14]

In Britain and the United States opium and its preparations were available everywhere, not just in pharmacies. Drugstores and even grocers sold opium, whose distribution, at the beginning of the century, remained unregulated. There were opium pills, lozenges, powders, plasters, enemas and liniments. Opium entered into a number of branded preparations, the precursors to modern pharmaceutical products, known as 'patent medicines'. Long-famous preparations such as Dover's Powder and Bateman's Drops were joined from the mid-century by Collis Browne's Chlorodyne, Godfrey's Cordial, Dalby's Carminative and Mrs Winslow's Soothing Syrup, the last three explicitly aimed at the market for children.[15]

Nor were opiates an elixir for the rich. A Nottingham chemist reckoned that in 1808, upwards of 200 lb (91 kg) of opium and above 600 pints (340 l) of Godfrey's Cordial were retailed to the poorer classes in his town. In the marshy region north of Cambridge known as the Fens, opium was widely consumed by people of limited means, who took it to deal with swamp fever.[16] Some of this opiate consumption even stood at the border between medical and recreational: the housewife who gave Mrs Winslow's Soothing Syrup to her infants to put them to sleep, the sufferer from toothache who had become accustomed to his or her daily draught of laudanum, the Fenland boatman who took opium pills to cure hangovers. The writer and chemist William Howitt observed, speaking of Lancashire mill workers:

I have contemplated with horror the rapid increase of the consumption of opium, and its spirituous laudanum, within the last ten years. The ravenous fierceness, with which opium-eaters enter the druggists' shops, when want of money has kept them from their dose beyond their accustomed time of using it, and the trembling impatience with which they watch the weighing of the drug (every moment appearing to them an age), and the avidity with which they will seize and tear off their wonted dose, and swallow it – are frightful to be seen.[17]

Yet there was a difference between self-medication, even of the compulsive kind, and recreational drug taking. Perhaps some continued to eat their pills after the medical need had passed: taken for leisure, the perception was that drugs belonged in traveller's tales from the Levant or the Far East. There had been attempts to cultivate the poppy in Britain and in parts of the United States, but in Europe as in North America, raw opium was essentially an Asian import. The vast majority of it arrived from Turkey, with smaller volumes coming from Persia and India.[18] The drug retained a foreign identification, specifically an Oriental identification. The Baron de Tott described Turkish opium eaters in the eighteenth century: 'The most experienced swallow four of these, larger than olives; and every one drinking a large glass of cold water upon it, waits in some particular attitude for an agreeable reverie, which, at the end of three quarters of an hour, or an hour at most, never fails to animate these machines, and make them gesticulate in a hundred different manners, but they are always very extraordinary and very gay.'[19] While Turks might be known to chew opium for pleasure and Chinese people to smoke it in large volumes, such behaviour was not believed to involve Europeans or Americans.

The same could be said of hashish, and Gautier's text was in this sense revolutionary. So was another, more substantial work destined to become a classic: Thomas de Quincey's *Confessions of an English Opium-Eater*. A handful of personalities are known to have been opium devotees before the publication of De Quincey's *Confessions* in 1821: the conqueror of Bengal Robert Clive, for example, and the anti-slavery campaigner William Wilberforce. So, notoriously, was the poet Samuel Taylor Coleridge. But what De Quincey did for opium, and after him Gautier for hashish, was different: they explicitly engaged with the use of drugs as intoxicants.

De Quincey's *Confessions*, of novel length but written in autobiographical style, was a literary work, not a treatise. In many respects, including its allegiance to the confessions genre, it was a typically Romantic piece. Yet it delved in unprecedented detail into the relation between opium intoxication, the senses and the self. Physical bliss, inner exploration, an incomparable elevation of his artistic spirits: numerous were the pleasures of opium as De Quincey described them. Even the book's section on the unavoidable pains associated with managing and eventually shaking his habit contained much to make the drug look beguiling, the source of intense poetic visions. The very title, with its mention of not just any opium eater but an English opium eater, itself highlighted the incongruousness of using opium for pleasure under a northern clime. De Quincey repeatedly played on the difference:

Under the connecting feeling of tropical heat and vertical sunlights, I brought together all creatures, birds, beasts, reptiles, all trees and plants, usages and appearances, that are found in all tropical regions, and assembled them together in China or Hindostan. From kindred feelings, I soon brought Egypt and her gods under the same law. I was stared at, hooted at, grinned at, chattered at, by monkeys, by paroquets, by cockatoos. I ran into pagodas, and was fixed for centuries at the summit, or in secret rooms; I was the idol; I was the priest; I was worshipped; I was sacrificed. I fled from the wrath of Brama through all the forests of Asia; Vishnu hated me; Seeva lay in wait for me. I came suddenly upon Isis and Osiris; I had done a deed, they said, which the ibis and the crocodile trembled at. Thousands of years I lived and was buried in stone coffins, with mummies and sphinxes, in narrow chambers at the heart of eternal pyramids. I was kissed, with cancerous kisses, by crocodiles, and was laid, confounded with all unutterable abortions, amongst reeds and Nilotic mud.[20]

The book's reception, often quizzical, bore testimony to the novelty of its topic. *The Lady's Monthly Museum* explained that until the publication of De Quincey's work, the effects of opium were known only from reports out of Turkey and other Eastern countries. 'Opium, however, neither brutalizes the faculties, nor injures the constitution, like vinous liquors or spirits. [Nevertheless] the philanthropic object of the author of these Confessions is to supply motives to avoid the habit of taking this inebriating drug: and this he has done by a forcible and vivid description of the complicated sufferings which he has incurred.'[21] The *British Review and London Critical Journal* cautiously praised as proofs of the power of opium 'the sublime pictures of ideal combinations which have been drawn upon his fancy, and engraved upon his pages'.[22] The *Eclectic Review*'s appraisal was more double-edged: 'The work is written throughout in the tone of apology for a secret, selfish, suicidal debauchery: it is the physical suffering consequent upon it, that alone excites in the Writer a moment's regret. In a medical point of view, the work is quite worthless: in a moral point of view, it is truly affecting.'[23]

Whatever the critics grasped or failed to grasp, the *Confessions* were a runaway publishing success. At first anonymously serialized in the *London Magazine* in 1821, they came out in book form within a year. They were soon reprinted and translated into multiple languages – into French, for example, in 1828.[24] They brought De Quincey overnight fame. His book had set the Western world alight with the idea, whether it was to be emulated or loathed, that drugs were to be taken recreationally.

Perpetuating its influence, the work would find many imitators. It even pioneered an entire genre, running from Gautier's Club des hachichins all the way to William S. Burroughs's *Junky* and the 1996 film *Trainspotting*. After De Quincey, the idea of drugs as intoxicants became established. There was a *Hasheesh Eater*, published in 1857 by an American.[25] George Eliot's *Middlemarch* had one of its characters become dependent on opium, and so had Anne Brontë's *The Tenant of Wildfell Hall*.[26] Dickens's *The Mystery of Edwin Drood* featured opium smoking in the heart of London, and Wilkie Collins's detective novel *The Moonstone* used opium's intoxicating properties to drive the plot. Though for now confined to literary tradition and bohemian types, drug taking for pleasure was at last recognized as a practice liable to be taken up in Europe and America.

So far there was nothing fundamentally disruptive to the development. Characters who fell prone to the opium habit were rarely completely innocent, but their problems were their own. De Quincey's and Gautier's own texts were at heart Gothic fantasies, harmless and even comic in parts. Another landmark in the genre was Charles Baudelaire's *Les Paradis artificiels*. Baudelaire's text comprised, as its second half, a palimpsest of De Quincey's ode, but its first part was an original appraisal of hashish – which the poet, an inveterate opium habitué, rated the more dangerous of the two drugs.[27] (Of the hashish eater: '*He wanted to be as an angel, he became a beast.*'[28]) Baudelaire's text, at least in France, would, like De Quincey's, enter the canon. This would prove significant, as the French literature in turn became influential in causing cannabis to be banned under the twentieth-century drug-control system. But Baudelaire's book also anticipated, by a decade, another major shift. Like *The Mystery of Edwin Drood* (1870) and Collins's novel (1868), it stood on the cusp of a second, yet more important tectonic change. Doctors were about to become involved, with quite a different outlook.

In 1872 the Berlin psychiatrist and pioneer of the German asylum system Heinrich Laehr published the case of a patient, a lady he had taken in at the sanatorium Asyl Schweizerhof, who had begun injecting herself with morphine regularly after an operation.[29] Deprived of her drug, Mrs H. began to behave very peculiarly.

> She began to experience anxiety attacks. She turned on those around her, she shouted, she vomited blocks of a chocolate colour. Her stools thinned out. Her face turned bluish, her eyes sinking in their orbits. Her hands were cold, and she complained of chills and pains in the knees. Her pulse was barely to be felt ... She abused her carer. She stood up to walk around at night, ran away from the nurse, and refused to be brought back. She managed to secret a knife into her room concealed in a pencil case, and she lacerated her wrists with it. Only the prospect of an upcoming injection could bring any calm.[30]

After three weeks of treatment Mrs H. began to recover, and she was released after a few months. But this was not the only case Laehr had seen. Patients were increasingly taking morphine on their own. They administered themselves higher doses as the medicine's effect dulled, with the risk of a resulting accident. It was correspondingly harder to wean them off the drug.

Morphine was invented sometime between 1803 and 1805 by the Hanover pharmacist Frederick William Sertürner, who, having isolated the white, crystalline substance from opium, called it 'morphium' after Morpheus, the god of sleep.[31] It began to be produced on a commercial scale in the mid-1820s in Germany and Britain and in the 1830s in the United States. An alkaloid of opium, morphine is as a rule of thumb ten times stronger than the raw product, though morphine contents vary according to provenance (at the time, Turkish opium boasted a morphine content in the low to mid-teens, whereas Indian and Chinese opiums typically contained less than 10 per cent morphine). Though, like opium, it began to be employed to treat a wide variety of ailments – it was so powerful, and its range so great, that it came to be referred to as 'God's own medicine' or even 'GOM' – morphine was particularly useful in appeasing acute pain, especially during or after surgery.[32]

Morphine was at first administered orally or applied locally after the removal of a patch of skin where treatment was needed. A more effective method of administration suggested itself, however, with the invention of the hypodermic syringe in the 1850s. Crude forms of hypodermic administration had existed since at least the seventeenth century, but the syringe was effectively the invention of three men: Dr Francis Rynd of Dublin, Dr Alexander Wood of Edinburgh and Dr Charles Hunter of London. Rynd was the first to record making an injection by means of a hollow needle, in 1845; Wood was the first to use both syringe and needle, in 1853; and Hunter both improved the instrument's design and demonstrated, in 1859, that the hypodermic method could have a systemic, not just a local, effect.[33] By the 1870s the hypodermic syringe had become a staple of the doctor's bag. It could also be procured by patients, some of whom soon learned to use it on their own.

A whole corpus of research into drug dependence followed in the groove set by Laehr. The first key publications were also by German doctors. Eduard Levinstein, the director of the well-known Schoenberg-Berlin clinic, came out with a book-length study in 1877, complete with case analyses and suggestions for treatment. His book was translated into English the next year under the title *Morbid Craving for Morphia*. The neurologist, psychiatrist and journal editor Albrecht Erlenmeyer followed with another work in 1883. Their observations were picked up and added to by French, British and American researchers. Books and journal articles on the topic flourished. As more morphine cases fell under the lens, a new concept began to take shape: addiction.

This is not quite to say that doctors discovered such a thing as addiction in the 1870s, or that they coined the concept *ex nihilo* from that date. Observers had remarked on opium dependence before, and there can even be said to have existed, among those so aware, a layman's notion of addiction. Travellers to Turkey and Persia had noticed that opium devotees took huge doses, and that they became restless when in need of the drug. The French traveller to Persia Jean Chardin thus wrote, in 1686: 'It is certain, that if one should leave off Opium suddenly, he would die for Want of it . . . they dare only appear when the Drug affects them.'[34] China was another example. The pamphlet campaign around the First Opium War evinced awareness of the addictive properties of opium. The term 'addiction' was itself rarely used, and it meant something different, akin to being dedicated to a thing or an activity, but commentators compared the opium habit to slavery.[35] The *Foreign Quarterly Review* observed: 'Any one who is once enslaved by it, cannot, it is true, give it up without great difficulty . . . In this state they eagerly return to the cause of their suffering, and strive to drown the extent of their pain by increasing their daily quantum of the fatal drug.'[36]

Some medical treatises touched on the basics of opiate dependence: tolerance, or the need for increasing doses, and the pains of withdrawal. John Jones, for example, in *The Mysteries of Opium Reveal'd* provided a list of 'The Effects of sudden Leaving off the Use of Opium, after a long, and lavish Use thereof', though nowhere does the book go into opium tolerance.[37] Samuel Crumpe observed in 1793 that 'these doses, however, it generally becomes necessary to augment, and sometimes to very considerable quantities,' though he showed no awareness of the dangers of withdrawal.[38] Doctors, however, had been reluctant to probe their own panaceas too critically, and such examples were the exception more than the rule.[39]

Layman's notions moreover lacked the vocabulary and authority of medical fact. The difference was that between folk wisdom and scientific dogma. Medical researchers, having set out to subject opiate dependence to experimental scrutiny, came to classify addiction as a disease.[40] A disease category opened the door to calls for treatment, voluntary or not, and for control of the drug's distribution by or through doctors and pharmacists. Limiting drugs to the medical sphere in turn implied prohibiting recreational use.

Addiction research focused initially on morphine and accessorily on anaesthetics such as ether and chloral. Opium and morphine were almost interchangeable, since the second was but a purer version of the first. (Heroin, a yet more potent derivate of morphine, was first commercialized by the German pharmaceutical company Bayer in 1898, but it did not come under scrutiny until later. Amazingly, doctors were at first unaware that it might be addictive, but in any case heroin taking did not take off until the 1910s.[41])

Views and information circulated between the various national medical bodies, helping addiction theory quickly spread across borders. American and British journals kept close tabs on what appeared in German or French publications, and vice versa. The first pieces by Laehr, Levinstein and Erlenmeyer were followed by a flurry of comparable surveys in France and, with a small delay, in the United States and Britain. The volume of French addiction research was notably large, led by figures such as the Paris alienist Benjamin Ball and by Oscar Jennings, a British surgeon who practised in France. (If only for reasons of size, these four countries appear to have led the charge into the new discipline. Sweden had seen the first use of the term 'alcoholism', coined in 1849 by a doctor named Magnus Huss, yet it saw little professional discussion of drug addiction until the interwar period.[42] In countries such as Italy, Austria or Poland, the topic attracted only minimal attention – though Austrian and Swiss medical men were known to air their data in German medical journals.[43])

The classic statement of addiction as disease was made by Erlenmeyer, who distinguished 'chronic morphine poisoning' from 'morphine addiction' as 'two concepts which in no way overlap'.[44] Erlenmeyer defined the affliction as follows: 'I understand under the disease "morphine addiction", alongside the clinical symptoms which through chronic morphine poisoning gradually build up, the pathologically defined, unmotivated addiction of the individual to morphine taken as a pleasurable stimulant, not a medicine.'[45] Chronic morphine poisoning led to certain observable negative health effects, such as loss of appetite, pallor and so on, but compulsive morphine taking was something else, a disease in its own right.

Addiction theory was destined to live a long, influential life. From the 1880s the concept had integrated the mechanisms of opiate dependence that were tolerance and withdrawal.[46] A single term was emerging in each language to designate the condition. In Germany this was *Sucht* and in France *toxicomanie*. In English 'inebriety', a term encompassing both alcohol and drug dependence, was the more common for a while, but in the early twentieth century it began to yield to 'addiction'. Everywhere, crucially, addiction was accepted as a condition possessing identifiable symptoms and requiring that doctors interest themselves in its treatment.

What addiction was precisely, how it worked and what it meant to call it a disease was another matter. Addiction's ultimate nature remained a point of debate, as it continues to be to this day. Was it, crucially, a form of chronic intoxication or a more deep-seated condition? Not everyone agreed with Erlenmeyer. For Levinstein, morphine addiction did not belong to the list of mental diseases, which were 'caused by changes of the central nervous organs', while chronic morphine poisoning 'only causes functional derangements'.[47] A follower stated: 'In my opinion, morphine addiction is only a symptom, a consequence of morphine poisoning.'[48] In France a group of Paris alienists around Benjamin Ball theorized addiction as a mental illness. The cornerstone of their work was to distinguish 'morphinism', namely the sum of the symptoms produced by prolonged morphine use, from 'morphinomania', a disease. The morphine habit brought 'a paralysis of the will'. The 'morphinomaniac' was sick, and he or she needed to be treated, preferably indoors.[49] Ernest Chambard, another alienist and a student of the great Jean-Martin Charcot, was doubtful: 'Why change the name of the morphine habit, whose symptoms, when craving awakens, amount to a veritable mania in the common but so telling sense of the term, in favour of another term describing only an extremely rare form of intoxication?'[50]

One problem was how to explain why some patients seemed to become addicted and not others. Erlenmeyer describes the case of a lady who for fifteen years had suffered from paraplegia. She lay in bed and every day at 6 p.m. suffered a hysterical fit accompanied by acute pain. She was given morphine intravenously to ease the pain, daily, in the same dose of 0.5 grams. She never became addicted.[51] Precisely because he observed such cases, Levinstein's opinion was that 'for this reason, the description "morphine disease" is not acceptable and even less so "morphiomania".'[52] Going further, the samples on which addiction theory was based contained an inherent selection bias. It relied on cases reported by doctors concerning patients admitted to the asylums they ran or treated within their private practices. By definition, these were people who had developed health problems. If others elsewhere took morphine over long periods of time without suffering from it, they were much less likely to come to attention. There was no control group.

In Britain and the United States, the waters were further muddied by the competing concept of 'inebriety' and the influence of temperance. Norman Kerr, a Scottish doctor and the president of a Society for the Study and Cure of Inebriety, wished to establish inebriety as a disease in opposition to notions of 'moral vice'.[53] This could lead into convoluted formulations: 'If we try inebriety by Dr. Bristowe's comprehensive and philosophical definition of disease there can be no doubt of the disease element, his definition being "a complex of some deleterious agency acting on the body, and of the phenomena (actual or potential) due to the operation of that agency".'[54] Neither could Kerr quite adjudicate on the disease's nature as a mental disorder: according to him, opium addiction involved both 'mental prostration and moral perversion'.[55] Thomas Crothers, editor of the *Journal of Inebriety* on the other side of the Atlantic, criticized temperance moralists who saw inebriety as 'a vice from a sin, the only treatment of which is prayer and conversion'.[56] He nevertheless thought that addicts suffered from a 'double personality', sometimes developing criminal tendencies.[57] According to a *Journal of the American Medical Association* contributor, finally, morphine addicts should be classified into three groups. The first comprised 'normal individuals' who had contracted the habit from pain treatment, but there were also 'a second larger group of moral degenerates who indulge in the vice of morphinism, and a third, and much the largest group, recruited from among the neuropathic weaklings, from the victims of improper training and lack of early discipline; from the vast army of defectives, who, beginning to lose ground in the race of life, resort to drugs as a spur.'[58]

A meta-study of 1,000 cases of morphine addiction came out in 1897. Everyone agreed on the phenomena of tolerance and withdrawal pains, and on the symptoms enabling diagnosis.[59] Doctors preferred treating opiate addicts in the hospital or clinic rather than at home, because this enabled them to control the supply of morphine under gradual withdrawal or the symptoms if the sudden method was employed.[60] Another shared concern was that so many of the addicts they identified came from their own profession: originating in data from multiple countries, the study showed that 50 per cent of male morphine users came from the medical or pharmaceutical profession, and that among women, 15 per cent were nurses, midwives or doctor's wives.[61] The caveat remained, the study recognized, that the nature of the disease itself remained disputed.

At the heart of the question was the extent and point at which the addict surrendered his or her free will. Was it from the outset, past a certain point, or never? Did it depend on the person and on his or her heredity? Was it permanent, or limited to times of withdrawal?[62]

The stakes could be dramatic. In 1882 the prosecution of the young American doctor George Henry Lamson became an international press sensation. Lamson practised medicine in a seaside English resort. Married, he had a brother-in-law who had been paralysed for several years and who was also the owner of a fortune which, upon his death, his sister would inherit. Lamson had one day visited the invalid at the boarding school where he lived and administered to him a powder which he said was sugar. Half an hour later, the victim was shaken with spasms and bouts of vomiting, and he expired in the evening. Within a week Lamson was charged with murder. The inquiry revealed that he had administered aconite, a deadly vegetable poison, to his helpless relative. The evidence was overwhelming, and the court sentenced him to execution.[63]

The case took a controversial turn when letters arrived from America testifying to the defendant's addiction. Lamson had been injecting himself with large doses of morphine for some time, having begun to do so to treat neuralgias. He was known to take the drug up to sixteen times a day and had been seen handling his needle in the street. His behaviour had long been erratic, both during his time as an army doctor in Turkey and back home, where he had previously prescribed aconite in dangerous doses. One day, without motive or explanation, he shot a gun from his window. Lamson had returned from a trip to Paris to give himself up after having committed his crime, suggesting he did not quite realize what he had done. The American Secretary of State wrote in person to ask that his compatriot be allowed to plead insanity. Lamson's fate fell hostage to medical controversy. The *British Medical Journal*, for one, found against him. The journal accepted that Lamson 'was addicted to the use of narcotics' but opined that 'irresponsibility for criminal conduct cannot be admitted in anyone addicted to such drugs, unless a continuous state of mental disorder, abolishing the knowledge of right and wrong at the time of committing the act, has been set up by them ... It is only when a mental state analogous to delirium tremens [arises] that insanity of such nature as to exempt from punishment can be said to exist.'[64] The appeal failed. Lamson hanged. English justice was more severe than the French, commented Benjamin Ball. According to him, Lamson's morphine habit 'had perverted [his] moral sense while having left his intelligence sufficiently intact to conceive and execute a crime whose gravity and consequences he could not understand ... It is regrettable that certain English medical press organs found it their duty to intervene and proclaim the defendant's full responsibility, shutting the mouth to those who would have spoken up for him.'[65]

More generally, questions of free will and addiction were fundamental to the long-term regulatory prospects of opiates and other drugs. If drugs deprived the user of his or her free will, there was a rationale for intervention by a higher power, be it a medical authority or the state itself. Robbing someone of their free will by selling them drugs might be construed as a crime. Deprivation from his or her capacity for choice potentially qualified the patient for medical confinement, though not, under the same logic, for imprisonment. Whether addiction was a 'disease of the will' was not a mere question of theory.

In the space of the last few decades of the nineteenth century, the medical bodies on either side of the Atlantic had coined a new term to characterize the drug habit: 'addiction', which they categorized as a disease. Modelled on the effects of opiates, especially morphine, this conceptualized the key mechanisms that were increased tolerance and acute withdrawal pains. The doctors also agreed on the symptoms on which to base their diagnosis and on the necessity for treatment. At the same time, the concept remained half-baked: it rested on incomplete and therefore skewed samples, it mixed unprovable moral assumptions together with its science, and it failed to reflect any agreement on the fundamental nature of the disease, if this was what it was. None of this would prevent it from becoming yet more firmly entrenched as another drug came under medical scrutiny: cocaine.

For centuries, the coca leaf had remained confined to the Andes, where the locals had chewed it for strength, endurance and enjoyment. Then, in 1859, a naturalist returning from Peru delivered a sheaf of it to the Göttingen chemistry professor Friedrich Wöhler. Wöhler passed this on to a student, Albert Niemann, thinking that it would be interesting if he could isolate its principal active agent as part of his doctoral thesis. The next year, Niemann announced that he had invented cocaine.[66]

Cocaine is a radically different substance from opiates. Rather than drowsiness, it induces wakefulness. A stimulant, it creates a sense of euphoria and energy that tends to peak rapidly. It nevertheless possesses the ability to dull pain locally. The Darmstadt-based company Merck, a pharmaceutical firm that also made morphine, began producing it a year after Niemann's discovery. There was at first little uptake but this changed when in 1884 the Austrian ophthalmologist Karl Koller used it as an anaesthetic while performing eye surgery. Koller's innovation immediately made medical news. The excitement was that local anaesthesia made accessible operations that had previously been hard or impossible to perform, such as on the eye but also the nose and throat. Before that, surgeons could either choose general anaesthetics such as chloroform or ether or use no anaesthetics at all. Cocaine enabled them to perform delicate operations, or operations in which the patient needed to be awake. By the end of the year, it was being adopted by doctors around the world.[67]

The attention generated soon ensured that cocaine was taken up in other therapeutic areas. In November 1884 the American *Medical Record* described the contraction in the mucous membrane that followed an application of solutions of cocaine. Doctors began to use the drug against hay fever, asthma, catarrh and colds.[68] Its virtues as a stimulant were also discovered, and it became popular for treating nervous diseases such as neurasthenia. Another area where it appeared promising was in treating morphine addiction.

Notoriously, an early experimenter in this application was Sigmund Freud, a colleague of Koller at the same Vienna hospital. Freud was ambitious and eager to make a name for himself. He had befriended the pathologist Ernst von Fleischl-Marxow, who had taken to morphine after an operation. Freud decided to test cocaine on Fleischl-Marxow following morphine withdrawal, and he began to give the drug to his friend in 1884. 'I expect it will win its place in therapeutics, by the side of morphine, but superior to it,' Freud wrote. Without waiting for the results of his experiment, he published a piece entitled 'Über Coca', proposing the product as a stimulant as well as a remedy for indigestion, anaemia and depression. He also proceeded to try his panacea himself. 'I am as strong as a lion, gay and cheerful,' he announced. 'I am very stubborn and reckless and need great challenges; I have done a number of things which any sensible person would be bound to consider very rash.' Freud's enthusiasm did not earn him the glory he expected. He soon became involved in a controversy with Erlenmeyer, who sounded the alarm over the risks of using cocaine to treat morphine dependence. Meanwhile Fleischl-Marxow, far from quitting morphine, began taking both drugs simultaneously. He died in 1891, his health probably not bettered by the experiment.[69]

At some stage, Freud had protested to Erlenmeyer that cocaine was not addictive and that the symptoms he observed and objected to were due to morphine. Freud had a point. A number of doctors tried cocaine on morphine addicts around that time. The data on cocaine were tainted, marred by the presence of so many morphine users within the samples. In 1886 Erlenmeyer published observations on thirteen patients who had been treated in this way: 'He thus climbs onto ever higher doses. Now he wants to separate himself from cocaine of his own will, but it is not possible anymore . . . He needs cocaine in order to be able to work, he desires cocaine – he is a cocaine addict.'[70] Actually cocaine differs from opiates in that it involves sharply rising tolerance, but far less marked and more short-lived withdrawal symptoms.[71] The case against it is probably in the far-from-negligible risk of overdose rather than in its addictive properties. But doctors looking for generalizations insisted on the hallucinations that sometimes characterized withdrawal, including the illusion that one had ants crawling under the skin, or 'formication'. It was not the last time that a drug quite dissimilar to opiates would be made to fit an addiction model originally devised for them.

Paradoxically, the poor data only helped cocaine gain a reputation as an addictive drug more quickly and surely. *The Lancet* warned of the danger as early as 1887: 'To summarise. Cocaine may be toxic, sometimes deadly, in large doses. It may give rise to dangerous, or even fatal, symptoms in doses usually deemed safe. The danger, near and remote, is greatest when given under the skin. It may produce a diseased condition, in which the will is prostrate and the patient powerless – a true toxic neurosis, more marked and less hopeful than that from alcohol or opium.'[72] According to the Philadelphia-based *Medical and Surgical Reporter*, the cocaine habit was already 'one of the three scourges of mankind'. Borrowing information from the *Therapeutische Monatshefte*, it explained: 'General mental weakness may set in rather early, to be observed in a loss of memory and unusual prolixity in conversation and correspondence. When the drug is withdrawn, besides the vaso-motor symptoms there may be seen depression, impairment of will-power, weeping, etc. The chronic form does not protect from acute intoxication.'[73]

As with opiates, doctors were alarmed to find that many cocaine addicts came from among their own. The case of Dr Charles Bradley of Chicago made a strong impression. Bradley had begun experimenting with cocaine in 1885, having been led to believe that it was harmless. The drug 'gave him such a sense of well-being as he had never experienced before, the sense of complete repose and self-satisfaction it produced being much more marked than that derived from opium', according to a friend. Bradley increased his dose until he reached 1 gram per day, injected hypodermically. He gave cocaine to his family, much like Freud declaring that he would 'revolutionize medicine generally, and become the world's benefactor'. But he only ended up mortgaging his house, reducing his children to poverty. He began to decline physically, and an acquaintance persuaded a judge to commit him to an asylum. Bradley interrupted his stay and fled to Canada. In 1887 the police arrested him, back in Chicago, after he had turned on a gas jet at a drugstore where he had been refused the drug. According to a newspaper account, he was 'suffering from acute mania, convulsions, and every distressing phase of violent insanity [and was] reduced to a skeleton'.[74]

Cocaine had meanwhile found a profitable home within the unregulated, unsupervised patent medicines. Their range was broad: from low-concentration toothache drops, haemorrhoid remedies, habit cures for inebriety and lozenges for throat aid all the way to asthma and catarrh cures exhibiting a much higher pure cocaine content. There were Cocarettes, produced by a St Louis firm, Coca-Bola, a chewing paste with cocaine, and Lloyd's Cocaine Toothache Drops. Catarrh cures – Agnew's Catarrhal Powder, Birney's Catarrh

Powder, Coles' Catarrh Cure – were to be taken by sniffing.[75] All these products were widely advertised, as was pure cocaine, though in this case the target was not the end user but the doctor. The principal American producer of cocaine, Parke, Davis, & Co., used sales and marketing tactics prefiguring those deployed by Purdue Pharma and the opioid manufacturers at the turn of the twenty-first century. Parke, Davis owned a pharmacological laboratory whose researchers placed papers in the medical press. The firm had established a publishing enterprise to disseminate favourable information on its products, among which was cocaine. Its publications, the *Medical Age*, *New Preparations*, *Bulletin of Pharmacy* and *Therapeutic Gazette*, reprinted articles from New York and Philadelphia medical journals, but negative findings were less likely to make the cut.[76] How gullible the consumer was may be debated. In Chicago, 'the proprietor of a large downtown drug store noticed several years ago that at noon numbers of the shop girls from a great department store purchased certain catarrh powders over his counter. He had his clerk warn them that the powders contained deleterious drugs. The girls continued to purchase in increasing numbers and quantity. He sent word to the superintendent of the store. "That accounts for the number of our girls that have gone wrong of late," was the superintendent's comment.'[77]

All this would in due time badly harm cocaine's reputation. Also responsible for the drug's shooting-star trajectory from wonder cure to Devil's dust was that coca itself had been enjoying a parallel turbulent career. Wöhler and Niemann's interest in the coca leaf had not been entirely random. European botanists having catalogued the plant in the eighteenth century, from the 1820s travellers had been remarking on its Andean use as a stimulant.[78] In the 1860s such reports came to the attention of an enterprising chemist from Corsica, Angelo Mariani. Mariani was excited by the leaf's potential as the basis for a consumer product. In 1871 he began commercializing a tonic made from Bordeaux wine and coca named Vin Mariani.[79] From France, Angelo Mariani sent his brother-in-law Julius Jaros to New York to open an American branch, and his Americanized version was an immediate success.[80] The firm also sold a Pâté Mariani, Pastilles Mariani and a non-alcoholic Thé Mariani. Mariani published lavish testimonies from personalities including famous writers, European kings and even the Pope. The fad for tonics based on coca, and therefore containing small amounts of its cocaine alkaloid, followed in his footsteps: Lambert Company's Wine of Coca, with Peptonate Iron and Extract of Cod Liver Oil, and the Sutliff and Case Company's Beef, Wine, and Coca were two examples of popular me-too products.[81]

Both the demand for tonics and patent remedies of various kinds and the medical appeal of pure cocaine induced a manufacturing boom. In Germany Merck was followed by Gehe, Knoll & Co., and by Böhringer.[82] German and American firms alike suffered from quality problems because the leaf tended to decay in transit. In response, they began to move refining facilities to Peru. Skyrocketing demand fed a fast expansion in cultivation. Peruvian cocaine exports sextupled between 1890 and 1900 alone. The bonanza in turn encouraged a local pharmacist, Alfred Bignon, to develop a simplified method for producing cocaine using fewer and more readily available chemicals – namely kerosene and soda ash. In the twentieth century Bignon's more easily portable method would become popular with Andean *narcos*; for now, it fed a Peruvian coca pride that manifested itself in a flurry of publications vaunting the drug.[83] Yet even the Peruvians were compelled to look over their shoulders: from 1883 the Dutch, finding the soil and climate propitious, began cultivating coca in Indonesia. Indonesian coca leaf exports took off in the early 1900s, and they briefly displaced the Andean variety, achieving a volume of 800 tons shortly before the outbreak of the First World War.[84] All this was purchased by the Nederlandsche Cocainefabriek, established in 1900 and by 1910 the largest single cocaine manufacturer in the world.[85]

The most successful of the coca-based tonics, of course, was Coca-Cola. The future world-famous drink, too, may have originated in a case of morphine addiction. Its inventor, the druggist John Pemberton, had been shot and slashed with a sabre during the Civil War, and he suffered from various ailments. Pemberton is known to have become dependent on morphine. Though his interest in coca was long-standing, judging from the timing of his invention it is almost certain that he read of cocaine's ability to relieve his condition. In 1885, taking his cue from Mariani, Pemberton advertised a Coca Wine as 'infallible in curing all who are afflicted with any nerve trouble, dyspepsia, mental and physical exhaustion, all chronic and wasting diseases, gastric irritability, constipation, sick headache, neuralgia . . .'.

His new drink was recommended to all 'who require a nerve tonic and a pure, delightful, diffusible stimulant . . . a sure restorer to health and happiness'.[86]

Pemberton never got rich from the brand he created: he sold it in 1888, having removed wine from the formula two years before. By 1900 Coca-Cola had become a phenomenon in the hands of its new owner, the Coca-Cola Company, and its main shareholder and director, Asa Candler.[87] The cocaine content, though, attracted controversy. In 1898 a zealous evangelist named Lindsay arrived in nearby Marietta, Georgia, and became the minister of the local Baptist church. From the pulpit, Lindsay launched a virulent attack on Coca-Cola, the ingredients of which, he was certain, were two-thirds cocaine. Imbibing it, he asserted, was tantamount to 'morphine eating'.[88] This being the post-Civil War South, the *Atlanta Constitution* wrote: 'Use of the drug among negroes is growing to an alarming extent . . . It is stated that quite a number of the soft drinks dispensed at soda fountains contain cocaine, and that these drinks serve to unconsciously cultivate the habit.'[89] The Internal Revenue Service sued Coca-Cola based on its health claims, in a trial that lasted until 1902. This and the negative publicity convinced the company to remove the alkaloid from its drink: in 1903 Candler contracted with the Schaefer Alkaloid Works of Maywood, New Jersey, to de-cocainize the leaves before sending on 'Merchandise No. 5' to Atlanta.[90] In the long term at least, the controversy did not harm the drink. Alongside the boom in cocaine-based patent medicines and the other coca tonics, however, it confirmed cocaine's reputation as a ubiquitous drug with an insidious reach.

How many drug users there may have been in the United States or the larger European countries at the time is difficult to ascertain, but the numbers are unlikely to have been very high. Some doctors blamed Germany's 1860s wars of unification for having spread morphine use there. Soldiers given morphine to relieve the pain of battle wounds would have remained addicted as veterans. The evidence for this, though, is poor. Germany's overall rate of opiate consumption remained low as of the turn of the century: between 225 grams and 545 grams (0.5 and 1.2 lb) raw-opium equivalent per 1,000 population, compared to 4.8 and 5.2 kilograms (10.5 and 11.5 lb) respectively for Britain and the United States.[91] The overwhelming concern in the German literature was the spread of morphine addiction by doctors, whether among themselves or their patients. One survey found some military men among its sample of morphine users, but 46 per cent were doctors.[92] Another reported that there were no known cases of opium overdose in the country.[93]

This in turn sheds doubt on the notion that the Civil War was responsible for spreading morphine use in the United States.[94] Enthusiastic prescribing and straightforward availability are likely to have done much more. As most addiction was ostensibly iatrogenic (of medical origin), trying to calculate addict numbers is almost meaningless: most opiate-dependent users may well have been palliating chronic pain. Contemporaries nevertheless bandied around numbers varying from 80,000 to 200,000. The *New York Times* offered a number of 200,000 in 1878, while the specialist Thomas Crothers thought 100,000 approximately right in 1902.[95] The most serious attempt at an estimate has been made by the historian David Courtwright. Courtwright collated and compared information from different sources, including ratios of total opium imports to average use, surveys of doctors and pharmacists performed at various dates, and army enlistment data. His conclusion was that the u.s. addict population peaked in the 1890s, and that it cannot have exceeded 313,000.[96] Courtwright's concern, however, has been to establish a conceivable maximum, not a probable mean. His data purposely assume nil medical consumption. Using the same basis to arrive at a reasonable average yields a total of perhaps 120,000, or 0.2 per cent of the country's population – a number, incidentally, that is consistent with doctor and pharmacist surveys.[97] Courtwright's point, moreover, stands that this population peaked well before the establishment of federal drug prohibition.

Estimates of the number of recreational cocaine users are even more tentative, but the total may have been around 25,000 at its maximum, around 1903.[98] Most of this consumption is likely to have come in the form of patent powders and catarrh cures, though there is tentative evidence of employers having distributed cocaine, with the goal of enhancing workforce performance, to stevedores and other dock labourers on the Mississippi River, in road construction and among Ohio mining communities.[99] This would place the total number of American recreational drug users, opiates plus cocaine, at just under 150,000 out of a population of 76 million. The combined peak would have occurred around 1900.

The legislator had by then taken steps to tighten availability. Britain passed a Poisons and Pharmacy Act in 1868 limiting the sale of a list of substances to pharmacies – though the law made no demand for medical prescriptions and left patent medicines out.[100] Another Act dated 1908 placed cocaine on the list and asked that the buyer be known to the druggist. In the u.s. federal legislation would have to wait until 1909, but a number of states and municipalities began regulating opiates and, later, cocaine. Pennsylvania enacted the first anti-morphine law in 1860, and Illinois the first measures against cocaine in 1897. The District of Columbia caught up on both in 1906. (State anti-morphine laws differed, but they typically left patent medicines untouched while requiring that pure drugs be purchased at a pharmacy and with a prescription to be retained for inspection for a period of time.[101] Cocaine laws likewise varied: Louisiana required affidavits that retailers were not selling to 'any habitual user', while Chicago merely limited packaging to small sizes.[102])

In France and in Prussia, opiates had from the early nineteenth century only been allowed for sale on prescription and at pharmacies, including the relevant patent medicines.[103] In 1872 the principle of the pharmacist's monopoly on sales of opiates was extended to the whole of the German empire, and in 1890 this was expanded to include cocaine.[104] From 1896 the need for a prescription likewise became law throughout Germany.[105] The French rate of opiate consumption was even lower than the German: 240 grams (0.5 lb) per 1,000 population as of the early 1900s, or something like one-twentieth of the British and American rates.[106] The far higher levels of opium use observable in the UK and USA confirm that letting pharmaceutical manufacturers and distributors run wild does spread addiction, a lesson the USA would have to learn again with the twenty-first-century opioid epidemic.

The main point, however, is that incipient prohibition was not motivated by rising addict populations. Public concern and/or agitation spurred regulation, yet activism itself did not reflect growing drug use. The correlation between spreading anti-narcotic fears and user numbers was nil. International comparison confirms it. Britain, with a rate of opiate use that approached that of the United States and in all likelihood comparable addiction rates, saw remarkably few drug-related press cuttings. The odd affair in which drugs were involved appeared in the newspapers, such as the Lamson story, but any coverage of drug use as such, sensationalist or not, was extremely rare.[107] By contrast, France, with its basically non-existent addict population, was the scene of a boisterous drug literature and feverish press interest.

The French literature grew around 1900 to remarkable proportions, to include both novels – Marcel-Jacques Mallat de Bassilan's *La Comtesse morphine* (1885), Jean-Louis Dubut de Laforest's *Morphine* (1891), Jules Boissière's *Fumeurs d'opium* (1896), Pierre Custot's *Midship* (1901), M. D. Borys' *Le Royaume de l'oubli* (1909) – and non-fiction: Maurice Talmeyr's *Les Possédés de la morphine* (1892), Fabrice Delphi's *L'Opium à Paris* (1907) and Richard Millant's *La Drogue* (1910), to list but a few.[108] Such interest seeped into the press, which developed a prurient attention to drug-related stories. 'If you love life, fear morphine,' *Le Matin* splashed on its front page in 1912. 'Craving for morphine can push people to the worst expedients and the most shameful manoeuvres . . . A factor of depopulation and degeneracy, the morphine mania is a hateful vice destroying the best minds and degrading the strongest and most generous natures, especially as every morphine manic seeks to makes proselytes.'[109] For *Le Petit Parisien*, '"coco" [cocaine], as all night establishments have baptized it, is of every party, every orgy, and is master of all. Its victims have become innumerable.'[110] The daily ran the story of Simone Floch, twenty years old, a former maid and 'a pretty girl'. A victim of heartbreak, Floch had launched into 'the world of gallantry' and started to take morphine, then cocaine. Her discovery one morning, dead from an overdose, had led the police to her purveyor, Henri Jarzuel, aka 'the coco merchant', who in turn had been found, upon arrest, with three young women sleeping next to him . . .

Rather than France's scarcely more than anecdotal prevalence rates, this intense interest reflected established anxieties. It was the imagined threat, seen through the prism of pre-existing dislikes, that made drugs seem dangerous. France had lost a war to Germany in 1871, and the perspective of *revanche* was slipping ever further as German demographic growth outran the French. Drugs were seen as a hindrance to national recovery. In 1907 a scandal had erupted over a blackmail and spying affair involving a young naval lieutenant, Charles Benjamin Ullmo, who had taken up opium smoking and had been prepared to sell military secrets to the Germans.[111] Another obsession was that the Indochinese colony's reliance on opium was sullying France's civilizing mission. In Paul Bonnetain's *L'Opium*, the hero begins the novel by accepting a junior post as an administrator in Cochinchina. In Hanoi he is lured by a Chinese den keeper into trying the drug. His is a downward path of idleness and vice until he dies.[112] French writers described opiates as a 'social poisons' whose spread threatened to reach Europe from Asia, one author even seeing in this process of contamination a form of revenge from the colonized on the colonizers.[113]

Racial prejudice likewise classically informed drug-related fears in the United States. Perceptions that Blacks were predominant among cocaine users, especially in the South, were common. In an article entitled 'Negro Cocaine Evil', the *New York Times* described how from a 'dreamy state' resembling an opium trance, the cocaine user passed to 'one of wild frenzy'.[114] In 1901 the *Journal of the American Medical Association* connected cocaine and the 'coke habit' with 'negroes' in a blatantly racist call for control.[115] (Actually African Americans were unlikely to be proportionately large users of cocaine, if only for economic reasons. In 1914 the medical director of a Georgia asylum reported on 2,100 Black patients admitted in the past five years. Only two had been cocaine users, and they had not even been admitted for cocaine-related afflictions. The director explained that they generally were too poor to buy cocaine, and that reports of 'cocainomania' among Blacks published by the newspapers were myths.[116]) Chinese immigrants were otherwise blamed for the spread of opiate use. One newspaper suggested that Chinese people living in American cities were all 'addicted more or less to the habit of smoking opium'.[117] In 1875 San Francisco passed an ordinance against Chinatown opium dens.[118] A magazine commented: 'Dr. Anderson has witnessed the sickening sight of young white girls from sixteen to twenty years of age lying half-undressed on the floor or couches, smoking with their "lovers". Men and women, Chinese and white people, mix indiscriminately in Chinatown smoking houses.'[119]

This newfound vocabulary for commenting on drugs in turn owed to the shifting medical discourse on them. It was addiction theory, and the scientific stamp of disapproval that accompanied it, that made the supposed progression of drug use so frightening and that enabled its resonance with racial bigotry. Both *Six années de morphinomanie* (1910), by Comte D'Almond, and Léon Daudet's *La Lutte* (1907) purported to be based on medical research. The press was apt to quote doctors in distorted, sometimes extreme language: 'Dr. Graeme Monroe Hammond, the neurologist, says that it is absolutely impossible to cure the cocaine fiend, once the habit has become fixed upon him. "There is nothing that we can do for the confirmed user of the drug," says he."The best thing for the cocaine fiend is to let him die. He is of no use either to himself or to the community."'[120] Both addiction disease theory and the compendiums of symptoms listed in medical journals made their way into the popular press, such as the magazine *Current Literature*:

> The habit seems more a disease than a vice, for the whole nature of the victim undergoes a complete revolution, moral, mental, and physical ... The flesh begins to fall away and the space around the eye becomes dark from being surcharged with blood; the skin loses its normal color and changes to a sodden gray, a blotched brown, or an unhealthy yellow. And then the victim shivers and perspires at the same time, and is easily moved to tears. When this stage is reached there is little hope of a cure. They must and will have the drug, and will resort to any device to procure it.[121]

Medical professionals themselves made public statements running far ahead of actual drug-user numbers. In the *New York Times*, a Dr Catherine Townsend claimed in 1897: 'A word of warning must be sounded against the use and abuse of opium and its preparations, and of cocaine and chloral. In the United States alone there are 1,500,000 men and women who habitually use opium in some of its forms. The vice is increasing.'[122] The doctor George Pichon, in an 1893 article, quoted a supposed authority to the effect that France possessed 100,000 morphine addicts. The incredible statistic that Paris hosted 1,200 opium dens somehow became common currency.[123]

Gone were the highbrow effusions of De Quincey and Baudelaire. Calculated to shock polite society without offending it, these now looked quaint. William Rosser Cobbe complained in *Doctor Judas*, published in 1895: 'The evils of the fascinating "Confessions of an English Opium-eater" have been beyond estimate and are daily luring innocents to eternal ruin.'[124] He warned: 'The first work of the Judas drug is to double-lock the prison door of the will, so that success-ful struggle against the demoniac possession is impossible. During the subjection I fought nine times three hundred and sixty-five days against the diabolical master."[125] *La Comtesse morphine*, by Mallat de Bassilan, was prepared to be even more lurid:

> A fresh access had just seized the countess. Plunged into an attack of erotic delirium, she rolled violently around her bed, calling in a pleading voice Hugues, Gontran, baron Slavini, all the men she had loved. She passionately begged for their kisses, fainting under the caresses of these invisible lovers.
>
> Suddenly, pushing her bedding away and tearing off her shirt, she appeared to the assembled domestic staff, who had rushed in at the sound of her cries, stark naked, the decrepitude of her limp body visible to all, her sickeningly wan flesh stained by the blood of her ulcers and the taint of unconsciously loosened excrement.[126]

The nineteenth century had seen opiates transformed, in Western consciousness, from something mysterious and remote into a terrible threat. The patchwork of beliefs that characterized them had coalesced and in the process taken a negative turn. From something chewed on Levantine shores or smoked in Chinese boudoirs, they had travelled, in the public imagination, to become menaces brewing in the heart of the European or American home.

The first step had been the revelation, under the Romantics, that recreational drug use need not be confined to oriental settings. The second had seen medical researchers assume authority over the drug habit. The isolation of morphine and the adoption of the hypodermic syringe had modified opiate use to suit it to the scientific age. This and the interest of an increasingly confident medical profession made it look all the more malign. From being cures, opium, morphine and their derivatives turned into the sources of a disease baptized 'addiction'. Cocaine joined them into this new club of fallen medicines, or 'drugs', which also included such minor concoctions as ether and chloral. In part thanks to a brief boom in coca-based drinks, it helped them all morph from shadowy presence to clear and present danger.

The notion that indulging in intoxicants was a matter of private choice looked increasingly tenuous. Disease concepts of addiction encouraged the idea that the drug user ought to be made the doctor's charge. In distorted form, they entered the public discourse, where they were found to be of useful service to racial prejudice and associated nostrums about contamination and miscegenation. Opiates, cocaine and other drugs had seen their reputations comprehensively trashed. Calls for official involvement were not far off. For that, nevertheless, a trigger was required. It would come, once again, from the Far East.

4

SHANGHAI AND THE HAGUE

C hina had lost another catastrophic war, this time to Japan. In 1894–5 the Qing empire confronted its island neighbour over the control of Korea, and it lost. China was forced to relinquish Taiwan and a string of Pacific islands, and to pay a large indemnity. Worse, a scramble by foreign powers for fresh concessions followed. New treaty ports and enclaves opened where foreign residents could operate beyond the reach of Chinese law, and more railways and other economic monopolies were sold off. The defeat, which involved the destruction of China's modernized fleet, prompted a renewed bout of soul-searching. The court, now run by the formidable Empress Dowager Cixi, wavered over the need for radical reform. In 1900 the empress made the mistake of endorsing the Boxer Rebellion, a movement of militias practising martial arts that for a year attacked resident foreigners, their religious missions and their Chinese employees and friends. After another iron-fisted response from the combined great powers, China hit rock bottom. The Qing understood that they must adapt or die.[1]

'There is no prospect of defeating enemies as soldiers have taken to the pipe, while neither workers nor merchants who smoke can expect to prosper,' wrote the Shanghai daily *Shenbao*. 'After opium is eliminated there will be a new China.'[2] In the aftermath of the Sino-Japanese War, as more and more Chinese people came to realize that their country required a deep political, economic, military and social transformation, opium began to be singled out. New opium critics arose, including high-level officials, scholars and journalists. The drug, as they saw it, was a source of national weakness and humiliation.

Zhang Zhidong, the army reformer, administrator and member of the Grand Council, the de facto government, dedicated a chapter of his book *Learn* to the denunciation of opium.[3] Yan Fu, the first scholar to introduce Darwin and the social Darwinist Herbert Spencer to a Chinese readership, felt the same: if China was to be strong again it needed to tackle its opium problem.[4] Reforms begun after the failed Boxer uprising included the abolition of the Confucian canon as the basis for education and administrative recruitment, the recasting of legal codes and an ambitious programme of political innovation reliant on elected assemblies. Along with these, the government launched a campaign against customs perceived to be holding the country back, including bans on certain interracial marriages, foot binding and opium smoking.[5]

The difficulty with opium was that it could not be stamped out without putting an end to imports. By then, the vast majority of the opium consumed in China was grown domestically, but were this to be eradicated, imports would certainly rise again in substitute. British support had to be tested first. On 21 July 1906 the foreign ministry official Tang Shaoyi approached Lancelot Carnegie, British legation secretary in Beijing, and announced his government's intention to 'introduce some regulations with the view of diminishing the consumption of opium'. Carnegie did not even bother to write home for guidance. 'His Majesty's Government would meet the Chinese Government half-way if they showed that they were really in earnest,' he assured Tang.[6]

This stunning change of stance was actually the end point of a hard-fought process. In Britain opposition to the trade had been making its own comeback. It will be recalled that the First Opium War had attracted lively criticism domestically in the 1840s. The Second Opium War, however, had occasioned a parliamentary dissolution followed by an election, which the prime minister, Palmerston, had won by running an explicitly nationalistic, anti-Chinese campaign. For a while, this had doomed agitation against the opium trade. But opposition had revived in 1874 with the foundation of a Society for the Suppression of the Opium Trade (SSOT).

The SSOT had quickly grown to a position of influence by recruiting philanthropists and MPs to its cause. In 1875 it had received the backing of the wealthy railway family scion and politician Joseph Pease. Within another year, it could count seventeen MPs on its general council. In 1880 Lord Shaftesbury, a high-profile social activist who had been an early campaigner against opium, agreed to serve as its president. The society's leadership also included a large bloc of religious figures, especially Quakers and Baptists though also a few Anglicans: it could tap into the growing network of the Protestant missions in China, collecting testimonies and producing statements on the drug's deleterious physical and social effects. The SSOT published books and pamphlets denouncing the trade. It organized mass rallies and printed a periodical entitled *The Friend of China* (masthead: 'Righteousness exalteth a nation, but sin is a reproach to any people'). It recruited figures such as the missionary Frederick Storrs Turner and the former ambassador in Beijing Sir Rutherford Alcock to speak on public tours. Most directly, it sought to force a change in government behaviour by submitting resolutions against the trade in the House of Commons.[7]

In 1875 the SSOT proposed: 'This House is of the opinion that the Imperial policy regulating the Opium traffic between India and China should be carefully considered by Her Majesty's Government with a view to the gradual withdrawal of the Government of India from the cultivation and manufacture of Opium.'[8] This lost by 94 to 57 votes. During its long career, the SSOT would bring seven motions against the opium trade.[9] In 1889 the Commons were asked to agree that 'the traffic in that drug [is] repugnant to the true interests of that country,' and that the government should initiate talks with China to extinguish it. This was opposed by 165 to 88.[10] In 1891 Joseph Pease called 'the system by which the Indian Opium Revenue is raised ... morally indefensible'. Pease overtly attacked the government for not just allowing but participating in the trade at every step from cultivation to manufacturing.[11] For once, this drew more than a perfunctory response. The Scottish MP and doctor Robert Farquharson objected: 'Some time ago I heard of the case of an old woman living in a low district who died at the age of 90, and who had been in the habit of taking some 200 or 300 ounces of opium per diem (*laughter*) of course I mean grains. Yet she carried on a laborious life, and died in the full odour of sanctity at the age of 90 years.' More convincingly, Farquharson rebutted the SSOT's numbers for opium addicts, opposing statistics from the Chinese Maritime Customs service.[12] This time, nevertheless, the resolution actually passed, by 160 to 130 votes. To no avail. An amendment was immediately voted that Britain should compensate the Indian government for the fiscal loss, burying the decree.[13]

Success beckoned again in 1893. The great Gladstone was prime minister. Like Shaftesbury, he had been a youthful opponent of the First Opium War. Though Pease and his supporters were unlikely to know this, Gladstone's sister Helen had been a lifelong laudanum addict. This time the ssot attacked Indian opium cultivation while asking that the government examine fiscal retrenchment measures that would enable the colony to make up for its losses.[14] Gladstone replied in person. 'So far as I have been able to hear the speech of the Mover ... I sympathise wholly with the general tone of his remarks, which, I think, tended to elevate and purify the atmosphere of this House.' But the prime minister was worried about the ability of the Indian administration to stamp out opium. He also pointed out that, while he was proud of having opposed the Opium Wars, conditions had changed, with China now a major poppy cultivator: 'We have ceased that operation of forcing the trade upon China. We have left that matter to China herself.'[15] In attacking opium's cultivation in India instead of the trade, the ssot had made a tactical mistake: its motion contained the request that the government set up a Royal Commission to look for substitute revenues. The house agreed to appoint a commission, but to a different purpose: 'to report as to ... whether the growth of the poppy and manufacture and sale of opium in British India should be prohibited except for medical purposes'. There was no opium epidemic in India ...

The ssot was not the only lobby group to militate against opium. There was also a Christian Union for the Severance of the Connection of the British Empire with the Opium Traffic, formed in 1888 and endowed with a journal named *National Righteousness*, and a Women's Anti-opium Urgency League, established in 1891.[16] These were not without opponents. The naturalist and Indian official George Birdwood defended opium in *The Times*, the deputy surgeon general of the Bombay Presidency William Moore published a pamphlet around the same time entitled *The Other Side of the Opium Question*, and the Hong Kong solicitor William Henry Brereton printed another, named *The Truth about Opium* – though none of them was a disinterested party.[17] The debate, however, died with the publication of the Royal Commission report. Having safely avoided China and confined itself to India, where there prevailed a long culture of controlled opium consumption, the commission was able to recommend that nothing should be undertaken. The SSOT's claims about opium were not grounded in serious medical evidence, it wrote, and India was an example of the 'temperate' use of opium, comparable to that of alcohol in England. The British authorities could not 'deal experimentally' with their innumerable Indian subjects, and the financial arguments were strongly against prohibition.[18] The SSOT published a rebuttal, and in 1895 Pease intervened again in the Commons to condemn the report, but this met yet another defeat.[19]

Matters might have remained there had it not been for the return of another Liberal government with a large parliamentary majority in 1906. Sir Edward Grey was now Foreign Secretary and John Morley Secretary of State for India. Morley had supported the society's efforts since becoming an MP in 1883, and both men had been associated with anti-opium factions in the 1890s. So had a good number of the MPs now belonging to the majority.[20] Pease was dead, but on 30 May 1906 the long-time anti-opium activist Theodore Taylor introduced the motion that: 'This House reaffirms its conviction that the Indo-Chinese opium trade was morally indefensible and requested His Majesty's Government to take such steps as might be necessary for bringing it to a speedy close.'[21] In a moving speech, Taylor went through the long history of British bullying and Chinese resistance, even quoting Lin Zexu's 1840 letter to Queen Victoria. The doctor and MP Vickerman Rutherford spoke next, incidentally showing that the debate had internalized the modern medical discourse on opiates: 'Opium was after all a narcotic poison . . . The outstanding scientific fact about this drug was the terrible craving that was rapidly developed in those who indulged in its use.'[22] Then Morley took the floor. As befitted his post, he was circumspect. Morley first confirmed that what was being discussed was the China trade, not opium in India, perhaps drawing the lessons from the last great debate. The opium revenue, he explained, was now £3 million, or 7 per cent of the budget. He warned that the matter would need to be managed carefully on the Indian side. Yet he could not hide his pride: 'In that great task, in that civilising mission of the regeneration of the East, whatever our attempts might give us, or might fail in giving us, do not let us fall behind,' he concluded.[23] Thirty years of efforts had paid off. The motion passed without a division.

Though the British and Chinese anti-opium movements ran separate campaigns, there was always a degree of cross-fertilization.

Educated Chinese people, some of whom now travelled outside the country, were horrified by their stupefied image abroad. As they understood it, they were called 'the sick men of Asia' because opium had made them physically weak. At a time when it looked as though China was in danger of being carved up and colonized, threatening its very existence, social Darwinism segued into tropes about a national body weakened by drugs. Evolutionary theory seemed to imply that each individual was as a cell in the body of society; if one cell was weak or sick, it affected the whole entity. After the war of 1894–5 these activists also held up the example of Japan. A contemporary text wrote: 'People who smoke opium have weak endurance and cannot bestir or cheer themselves up. Their degraded minds make them able to contemplate only short-term matters, destroying their willpower . . . The Japanese prohibited opium severely, and as a result, their national power has grown. A large number of Chinese citizens smoke opium, and China's power has consequently decreased.'[24]

Prominent anti-opium reformers included Yuan Shikai, provincial governor and future president of the republic, and Tang Shaoyi, the diplomat who approached Carnegie in 1906 and a future prime minister. The SSOT interviewed these figures, aiming to prove that the Chinese were sincere in their desire to stamp out opium, and that they only awaited a signal from Britain. In 1894 a delegation visited the Qing foreign affairs council, where it collected encouragements. 'Your Society has long been known to me and many of my countrymen, and I am sure that all – save victims to the Opium habit and those who have not a spark of right feeling – would unite with me in expressing a sense of gratitude for the philanthropic motives and efforts of the Society in behalf of China,' they were told by a high-level official. The Chinese government remained opposed to opium, these officials said, but its treaties committed it to keep the trade going. China was ready to eradicate opium domestically if Britain moved to end the trade.[25]

Also active was China's small Christian community. A Shanghai congregation, for example, met in 1890 to call for new drug-prohibition policies, passing resolutions for the diffusion of anti-opium material and asking that its members militate against the sale of hack cures.[26] The Shanghai clergyman Yen Yungking, educated in the United States and ordained by the American Protestant Episcopal Missionary Society, journeyed to Britain on a speaking tour in 1894. Yen visited

52 cities and addressed 112 meetings, of which 49 were on opium. He testified before the Royal Commission and was considered a star of the anti-opium movement.[27] News and information also flowed back into Britain and the United States thanks to the movement of missionaries to and from the country. Church publications, eager for stories from China, were willing to print pieces about opium and their correspondents' good works. The missions also made use of medical testimonies, many missionaries having been educated as doctors, and of periodicals such as the *Chinese Recorder*, published at the Presbyterian Mission in Shanghai from 1868.[28]

All this was rewarded with official action in 1906. On 20 September, having received the right assurances from Britain, Beijing issued a new edict prohibiting opium. This time, suppression was to follow a carefully elaborated plan. A ban on cultivation was to be phased in over ten years, beginning in 1908. Acreage dedicated to the poppy was to be registered and reduced by a set percentage each year. Violators would forfeit their land, while anyone who achieved a faster reduction was to be rewarded. Shops would operate under strict controls and dens and other outlets cease to sell opium altogether. Opium smokers were to register in person, and the amount they were allowed to buy would gradually taper. The plan had two more facets. The first was a treatment programme involving the production of cures for addicts, to be provided for free to the poor. The second was a propaganda campaign that enlisted both the magistracy and civil society, encouraging citizens to associate, disseminate information on the ban, and urge everyone to participate.[29]

In parallel, the Chinese government approached Britain on the subject of the Indian trade. In November 1906 it proposed entering into a bilateral agreement to reduce Indian opium exports to China in equal instalments over ten years.[30] An agreement was signed in 1907, coming into force in January 1908. Reductions were to match the pace of domestic eradication, sloping down to zero by 1917. The parties would take stock of the situation after three years, and if China could show it was upholding the domestic side of the bargain, Indian export reductions would continue. By 1912 the Patna factory had closed. The agreement was duly renewed in 1911, and the last consignment of Indian opium actually left in February 1913, four years ahead of schedule.[31] Through a system of import permits which China imposed unilaterally, from 1909 it was able to enforce matching reductions in deliveries from the other two main opium exporters: Turkey and Persia.[32]

The matter might have ended there had another power not taken notice. Between the Commons vote of May and the Chinese approach of November 1906, Edward Grey received another proposal, this time from the American ambassador. The idea was to set up a 'Joint Commission or a Joint Investigation of the Opium Trade and the Opium Habit in the Far East', putting together the USA, Britain, France, the Netherlands, Germany, Japan and China.[33] The news from Beijing had not only made an impression in Britain but had inspired another international actor keen to establish itself as a friend of China.

Notwithstanding the involvement of American firms such as Russell & Co. prior to the First Opium War and, more discreetly, of a few others afterwards, the opium trade had never been popular in the USA. The American press had roundly condemned the war. The *Christian Examiner*, for example, had lambasted Britain for introducing the drug into the 'great nation' of China, and such publications as *Hunt's Merchant's Magazine* and the *American Farmer* had done likewise.[34] A writer for the *Boston Recorder* had asked: 'When has a Christian and civilized nation been engaged in a more disgraceful enterprise!'[35] Nor had the war been popular in political circles. Senator John Calhoun had publicly charged the British with waging a war to 'force a poisonous drug down the throats of an entire nation'. Congressman John Quincy Adams, when he attempted to blame the conflict on Chinese arrogance rather than opium, had only attracted obloquy.[36]

In the middle of the hostilities, the American government had dispatched a squadron of two warships to the region. Its commodore carried instructions to 'impress upon the Chinese and their authorities that one great object of your visit is to prevent and punish the smuggling of opium into China.'[37] The result was the 1844 Treaty of Wanghia, granting the USA the same privileges as Britain except that the American government accepted that any of its citizens who dealt in opium would be fully liable to Chinese laws. In 1880, likewise, as part of a new commercial treaty, the United States and China had agreed to prohibit their nationals from bringing opium into each other's ports.[38]

Beyond their aversion to opium, American governments had long been hostile to imperialist encroachment on China. Achieving America's manifest destiny involved opposing European colonial practices, from which the USA was meant to distance itself and which it was even expected to combat. From 1862, when the United States opened an embassy in Beijing, its representatives had been active in formulating the vision of a special national stake in helping China reform and secure itself against foreign aggression. This found application, in the 1900s, in the articulation of an 'open-door' policy in China to demarcate itself from and to forestall European and Japanese intrusion. The idea was that free markets and American capital would transform China, while American friendship would help curb great-power belligerence. The alternative, that the United States should partake in annexations, had briefly been considered, but had publicly been ruled out by President McKinley.[39]

Cooperation on opium offered an obvious avenue for furthering the Sino-American relationship. The American initiative of 1906 was all the more timely because for a while the two countries had been at odds over immigration. Throughout the 1880s and '90s a movement had been building support in the United States for keeping Chinese immigrants out, a policy named 'exclusion'. Legislation introduced in 1882 had suspended the admittance of Chinese workers for ten years and introduced a system of certificates for residents. This had been renewed in 1892, and in 1902 exclusion had been extended to Hawaii and the Philippines. There were 90,000 Chinese people in the USA at the time, and the policy was unambiguously racist. Predictably, the Chinese authorities were unhappy with it. They made their dissatisfaction clear by refusing to roll over an immigration treaty in 1904 and letting run a popular boycott of American goods in 1905.[40]

A second motive for action was that the USA had acquired its own population of opium smokers as it took over the Philippines, after its victory in the Spanish–American war of 1898. The next year, the American administration terminated the opium-farm system that had been instituted by the Spanish and ordered all dens to be shut down. The governor, William Taft, imposed an import duty on the drug. As it had been under the Spanish, opium remained forbidden to Filipinos, being effectively reserved to the 70,000 or so residents of Chinese origin in the archipelago. In 1903, though, a change was discussed: the colony's governing body proposed setting up an opium monopoly, as was being done in many places in the region. The idea was that it would help defray the costs for young locals to be educated in American-run schools.[41]

At this stage, the evangelical lobbies made their presence known. The Methodist Bishop of Manila, Homer Stuntz, mobilized the Protestant missionary network in China, which in turn enlisted its extensive anti-opium associations back home. Stuntz scored a coup when he convinced the Presbyterian minister and agitator Wilbur Crafts to take up his cause. Crafts was a lifelong activist who opposed alcohol, cigarettes, gambling, narcotics, divorce, close dancing and so on. His crusades against the spread of alcohol and opium among the 'native races' betrayed a strong belief in America's moral responsibility to the rest of the world.[42] He ran an International Reform Bureau with considerable clout and reach. The bureau arranged for 2,000 petitions against the proposed monopoly to be printed on telegraphic blanks and sent to persons of influence. Crafts channelled thousands of letters from businessmen, church groups, women's clubs, Christian Endeavour chapters, the Women's Christian Temperance Union and so on to President Theodore Roosevelt and Elihu Root, the Secretary of War.[43]

As Roosevelt knew, the International Reform Bureau was quite able to get its way: it had just run successful campaigns against the supply of alcohol to soldiers and the medical inspection of prostitutes in the Philippines. The president, in the lead-up to the 1904 election, was not about to alienate a reform/missionary coalition that claimed 30 million supporters. He asked for a report from Root, who had the bill postponed. Crafts and his allies upped their protests, with more petitions and complaints arriving from churches, educational institutions and temperance societies urging prohibition pure and simple. Roosevelt decided to instruct the Philippine authorities, who remained doubtful and were counting on their opium revenues, to set up a committee to study the various regulatory systems available.[44]

On this committee was appointed one of the big beasts of the long war on drugs, alongside Lin Zexu and a few figures yet to appear in this book: Bishop Charles Brent. Brent was at once a deeply spiritual and an energetic figure. Born in Ontario, Canada, he had spent several years in a monastery in Boston before taking over an abandoned church among the city's slums, where he had preached and performed social work. In the Philippines Brent had once volunteered to act as emissary to a group of Muslim 'pirates' based on one of the islands, which he approached on a small craft named the *Peril*. As one of them threatened to massacre his crew, the bishop pulled out a pocket knife and laughed that this was his only weapon, showing that he was also capable of courage – though perhaps on this occasion his bravery was overshadowed by that of the two ladies who accompanied him, one of whom, in a copycat gesture, pulled out a hat pin.[45] Brent served as Episcopal bishop in Manila from 1901, and he acted as the 'moral conscience' for the commission that had responsibility, under the War Department, for managing the American colony.[46] He had the further advantage that he was not associated with the evangelical wing of his church, helping to make him look like a neutral party.

Bishop Brent was nevertheless no partisan of opium. In 1903 he had urged Taft not to fall in line with the rest of the discreditable East. 'We would be educating men in vice in order that we might educate their children intellectually,' wrote Brent.[47] The Opium Committee of which he formed part – also including Edward Carter, an army surgeon, and José Albert, a Filipino doctor – performed its job earnestly. The committee set out on its travels in August 1903 and went through Japan, Taiwan, Shanghai, Hong Kong, Saigon, Singapore, Burma and Java, collecting information on opium legislation and conducting meetings with officials and other parties, returning to Manila in the following year.[48] For all this thoroughness, though, it was sometimes ready to take the anti-opiumists' views at face value, for example that 'a man who uses habitually even a small quantity of opium becomes as thoroughly dependent on the drug as if he used to excess, and that he is as miserable, useless, and hopeless when deprived of his usual dose of opium as he would be in such cases were he a user of considerable quantities of the drug.'[49] Of the various models it surveyed, it was most impressed by the Japanese system of opium management in Taiwan, combining a government monopoly with centralized manufacturing and the issue of permits to registered users. The committee recommended the adoption of a similar system for the Philippines, though it also thought this should be replaced, when practicable, with absolute prohibition.[50]

These recommendations actually won out in even stricter form. The continued pressure from Stuntz, Crafts and their friends had borne fruit. In 1905 Congress accepted the principle of issuing permits to smokers, but as a short phase-in for full prohibition. Adult smokers of Chinese but not Filipino origin were allowed to keep receiving opium for three years. From March 1908 the drug would be banned outright save for medical use.[51]

Prohibition was satisfactory to Brent, who saw it as a victory of virtue over vice. Anti-opiumism was in the air anyway, the context one of public ferment and mutual emulation between the USA, Britain and China. Beyond the Philippines, Crafts had set his sights on the opium trade. International Reform Bureau branches now opened in Canada, Japan, China, Australia and Britain. Levering the 'open-door' policy, Crafts persuaded chambers of commerce in New York, Pittsburgh and other locations to write to the president to the effect that 'the pauperizing of more than one hundred millions [*sic*] of people by opium' was 'one of the largest of the obstacles to the development of that largest market in the world'.[52] He also pestered Grey. In January 1906, for example, Crafts wrote to the British Foreign Secretary to ask that Britain allow China to 'take the same course which Japan has wisely taken', enclosing the Philippine Opium Committee report for information.[53] The report enjoyed wide circulation besides, including in China.[54] Both Theodore Taylor and John Morley cited it when they spoke in the House of Commons that year.[55] Crafts was, moreover, far from alone: the anti-opium Commons resolution passed amid the year-long badgering of key politicians by domestic associations – by an association named the Christian Union for the Severance of the Connection of the British Empire with the Opium Traffic, for example – or by such personalities as the Archbishop of Canterbury.[56]

It was in this context that Brent had been inspired to write, in July 1906, to Roosevelt to propose calling an international conference on opium. The idea was to repeat the Philippine exercise, but with applicability to the whole region, and indeed the world. The conference, exploratory at first, would if successful lead to an end to opium smoking, or any opium abuse. The project, from a foreign-policy perspective, offered the twin benefits of setting American policy as an example for others to follow and of establishing a new field of cooperation with China. Roosevelt was enthusiastic.[57]

Grey reacted to the American invitation that November by consulting the India Office. There was some hesitation due to fears this might derail negotiations on the Anglo-Chinese reduction agreement, which remained in process in 1907. The response was nevertheless positive, providing the project covered domestic Chinese opium as well as the trade.[58] The American State Department proceeded to issue the invitations, and the main colonial powers all agreed to attend. They were to be joined by China, Persia, Thailand and, as late additions,

Italy and Austria–Hungary. On 1 February 1909 the delegates of these thirteen countries met at the Palace Hotel in Shanghai.[59]

Even though the Shanghai conference was no more than an informal gathering without the power to produce a treaty – indeed for this reason it was not even called a conference, but only a commission – it stands out as probably the single most important moment in the long war on drugs.

Multi-lateral organizations and agreements possess normative power often well exceeding what coercive strength they can mobilize. The need for a commonality of rules in international trade, the desire to form part of the community of nations and be seen to do so, and the authority of internationally sanctioned technical and scientific standards have all, in the twentieth century, guaranteed the influence of such initially informal gatherings. The resolutions of the Shanghai International Opium Commission would come to form the basis, through the League and the United Nations, of the world's drug regime as it exists today. As well as acquiring direct power via trade and cross-border policing, they would inspire drug laws throughout the world. The Shanghai commission and its successor gathering, the Hague conference, would set the tone on drug control for the next hundred years and counting.

The commission, having assembled, was off to an inauspicious start. The Shanghai governor, Tuan Fang, welcomed the guests by putting forward China's opium prohibition edict and its successes.[60] The delegations had beforehand been asked to arrive with reports detailing their respective legal frameworks and the levels of opiate use in their home countries and colonies. China had come up with incredibly high estimates for the period before the edict. The British consul Alexander Hosie disputed these. Hosie observed that the Chinese statistics for 1906 were only based on scattered observations for 1907–8, upped by a set percentage to account for success in the eradication programme. He also thought that estimated average use per smoker was too low, leading to an overstatement of the extent of China's addict population.[61] A spat ensued. France, which seemed to have different priorities, moved that French should be adopted as the commission's official language.[62]

Yet the confrontation properly began when the American delegation took the stand. The commission had established Bishop Brent as its president. Alongside him sat two other Americans: Charles Tenney, a consular official in Beijing who, having gone to China as a missionary, had learned Mandarin Chinese and risen to become president of the Tianjin university, and Hamilton Wright. Wright was a doctor with a speciality in tropical medicine, especially beriberi, the plague and malaria. He had worked in laboratories in Germany and Britain before returning to the United States in 1903, where he performed research at Johns Hopkins University. He was passionately engaged on the side of prohibition. To Brent's moral figure, he would play the role of the scientist with an edge.[63]

The American team had mapped out its game in advance, drafting a number of mock resolutions ahead of the conference. Procedural matters over, Wright introduced these at the first session of substance, on 23 February 1909. They came as a bombshell. Wright's opening shot was to propose no less than the complete prohibition of all opiates, except as confined to medical practice: 'Be it Resolved, therefore, that in the judgment of the International Opium Commission a uniform effort should be made by the countries represented at once or in the near future to confine the use of opium, its alkaloids, derivatives and preparations to legitimate medical practice in their respective territories.'[64] At one stroke, the use of opiates as intoxicants or as self-medication were to be ruled out. This was the Philippine model writ large, or rather, the as yet unproven, newly adopted Chinese model. It was a model at odds with practice not just throughout the region, but in Europe and the United States themselves, with their loose regulation of opiate manufacturing and distribution and their complete absence of sanctions on non-medical use.

If this were not enough, Wright moved as his next proposal to dismantle the opium monopolies that prevailed throughout Southeast Asia: 'No Government should, as a matter of principle or necessity, continue to depend upon the production of opium, its alkaloids, derivatives and preparations for an essential part of its revenue' and 'no system for the manufacture, distribution or use of smoking opium should continue to exist.' As a supporting, practical measure, Wright also proposed to clamp down on the trade, suggesting that 'all countries which continue to produce opium, its alkaloids, and derivatives and preparations . . . prevent at ports of departure the shipment of opium, its alkaloids [etc.] to any country which prohibits the entry of opium.'[65]

The British delegate, Sir Cecil Clementi Smith, flabbergasted, immediately moved that each resolution be discussed as it was brought forward, rather than all of them at once. He added: 'It is . . . with extreme regret that we find ourselves unable to give the conveners of the Commission our entire support in all the proposals which they put forward. Misunderstanding and misapprehension, we believe, can only result from a vote in favour of prohibition in the unqualified form in which it is presented in these resolutions.' Restriction to medical use, Clementi Smith understood, equalled drug prohibition. 'We object to the construction in the first place because it unquestionably puts an erroneous construction on some of [the country] reports, when it lays down in its preamble that they recognize that the use of opium should be confined to medical practice.'[66]

Clementi Smith contrasted the United States and China with India, where the opium habit 'had been known for centuries' and yet consumption remained subdued, as the reports showed, proving 'that the system of regulation built up in India is in fact, in a large measure, an efficient instrument in the prevention of abuse'. Opium was 'one of the main household remedies' in India, and there were strong, practical objections to the possibility of enforcement there or anywhere. Faced with this barrage, Wright proposed changing his wording to read '*medical practice or Government Regulation*'. The German delegate Walther Rössler offered to add the caveat 'as far as practicable'. British opposition, Clementi Smith insisted, was a matter of principle. 'To put it perfectly plainly, and to be entirely frank, the British Delegation is not able to accept the view that opium should be confined simply and solely to medical uses.'[67]

Clementi Smith found that, by contrast, he could back the Wright resolution promising controls over the export of opiates to countries that prohibited them, namely China. This was what Britain already did under the Anglo-Chinese Agreement of 1907. Neither did any of the other delegates object. With a couple of minor changes of wording, this was approved.[68] The clause found its way among the nine resolutions eventually adopted by the commission, taking its place among a short list that also mentioned the dangers of morphine, the closure of opium dens in China's international settlements and the regulation of anti-opium remedies.[69] Trade was an important tool around which the powers first assembled in Shanghai and later at the League of Nations would elaborate the architecture of drug control, and this modest, original idea would have a significant practical future.

The first Wright resolution, however, had not been voted down, but merely sent into committee. This committee hammered out a compromise text, producing a modified draft that was again put to the delegates on 24 February. In session, Wright and his colleagues wore down their opposition. The Shanghai commission was about being seen to stand on the moral high ground, and the proposal could not be thrown out entirely. The delegates eventually accepted the idea 'that the Commission finds that the use of opium in any form other-wise than for medical purposes is held by almost every participating country to be a matter for prohibition or for careful regulation'.[70] In qualified wording, the prohibition of drug use except under medical control had found its way onto the list after all.

Its importance was not just in what the principle aspired to, but in what it excluded. To embrace Wright's philosophy was also to rule out alternative formulas. Prohibition in its strictest formulation – the Chinese and the American formulations, at least as implemented in the Philippines – prevailed, and to the detriment of other policy ori-entations. The ideas that intoxicants were something to be managed rather than combated, that their non-medical use might be acceptable under certain circumstances, or that addiction might more easily and usefully be treated than stamped out all died in Shanghai.

When Clementi Smith lauded the Indian culture of opiate use over the Chinese, this was of course self-serving. India's opium culture had benefited the colonizer. His speech made a valid point nonethe-less. India's per capita opium consumption was far lower than China's, or indeed than that of Britain itself. Too little was known as to why opiates were prone to spread like wildfire within one culture and at one point in time, such as nineteenth-century China, and not in another place or period. British imperialism was partly responsible for China's problem, admittedly, but then India also lay under the imperial boot. India's light regulation of the drug had arguably worked better than either the drastic, pre-Opium War Qing policies or the complete tolerance that had been forced on China afterwards.

The French delegate likewise defended his country's Indochina policy: 'It must not be imagined that a growing revenue derived from opium means any relaxation of the policy of regulation. On the contrary the result would be reduced consumption. In such countries as Java, and French Indo-China, the fact that the tax on opium is regularly increased practically takes the drug out of reach of the native population.'[71] France had anticipated the Shanghai conference with restrictive measures. In 1907 it had closed down the opium dens in Tonkin and Annam. Existing dens remained tolerated in Cochinchina and Cambodia, but it was forbidden to open new ones. This protected the most vulnerable: poor smokers unable to invest in the smoking equipment that the dens provided. In parallel, the colonial government had tasked a commission with studying how opium consumption could be reduced and the fiscal shortfall made up. This had ushered in public education measures and a ban on the sale of dross, alongside the rise in prices.[72] In similar vein, the Dutch spokesman proposed a plan by which, alongside intrusive restrictions on domestic operations, 'henceforth the wholesale trade in opium be allowed only between the Governments of opium-producing and opium-consuming countries and be forbidden to any private persons'.[73] (Wright, his free-market reflexes suddenly awakened, was horrified.) The Dutch genuinely believed, based on experience with the *Opiumregie*, that prohibition was counterproductive, and that it only created opportunities for smuggling and brought misery to addicts.[74]

None of this was given a serious hearing. The colonialists, whether British, French or Dutch, were on the back foot. The legacy of the Opium Wars and the cynicism of the old farm systems worked against them. China, the aggrieved party, and the USA, the righteous party, prevailed over the guilty parties that were the imperialists. Those who defended other options were discredited, therefore prohibition pure and simple prevailed. This dynamic determined, inescapably, the direction drug regulation took in Shanghai and, through the commission's standard-setting, beyond it.

Wright's second proposal, his attack on the monopolies, was temporarily deflected. This, though, was only after Japan pointed out that its Taiwanese scheme aimed at an eventual nil consumption.[75] There also, the final wording was merely modified. The argument was ignored that prohibiting drug use was impractical and dangerously difficult to police. Warnings that bans led to smuggling and its host of associated evils, once raised by Qing mandarins and now made by the British and the Dutch, were brushed off. While it was recognized that the opium monopolies would continue to operate for the foreseeable future, the commission recommended 'that each Delegation concerned move its own Government to take measures for the gradual suppression of the practice of Opium smoking'.[76] The end aspiration was the same: to forbid rather than to tax, with all the latent implications in terms of policing, incarceration and crime.

As the delegates filed out of the Palace Hotel, they congratulated themselves on a job well done. Perhaps not all of them understood the significance of what they had just agreed. Overnight, prohibition in its strictest expression had become the guiding principle of an international system in the making. The long war on drugs had received its most vital boost since the original Qing edicts of 1813.

On 12 October 1915 the British doctor Sir William Collins delivered a lecture on the subject of 'the ethics and law of drug and alcohol addiction'.[77] Collins discussed John Stuart Mill, liberty and the appropriateness of state intervention, defending, in Victorian fashion, the sanctity of individual choice. He did not like social reformers, especially the then popular medical reformers who were the eugenists. 'If a mere majority ... is arbitrarily to decide what they may consider to be socially right in opinion and action and to enforce it against whatever they are pleased to deem anti-social in thought or deed, then the days of Liberty will verily be numbered ... We might live in a benevolent despotism, a community of well-conducted and well-cared-for slaves, a menagerie of well-regulated animals, but it would be despotism and slavery all the same.'

At the same time, Collins argued, the question was whether addiction left the drug user with any ability to exercise his or her freedom in the first place. 'Alcohol and drug addiction are to be regarded as examples of the surrender of self-control in favour of self-indulgence,' he thought. What this came down to was Mill's principle that one should not be allowed to surrender one's own liberty voluntarily – Mill's point having been made in regard to slavery. ('The principle of freedom cannot require that he should be free not to be free.') State intervention, therefore, was not tyranny if it protected the user from surrendering his or her freedom to the drug. 'It is the restraint of liberty to secure a larger and truer liberty. It is the limitation of self-will in the interests of free-will and self-control.' Collins praised the principle that drugs 'should be restricted to medical and legitimate purposes only', and he agreed that 'not only national but international control of the traffic in these noxious agents is required in order to be successful.'

Doctors, as a collective, were not calling for the punishment or criminalization of the drug user. If addiction is a disease, the drug user belongs in hospital, not prison. The British Society for the Study and Cure of Inebriety and its American cousin, the Association for the Cure of Inebriety, actually hoped to rescue addicts and drunks from incarceration. In Britain, under a seventeenth-century Act that remained on the statute books, public drunkenness was an offence, and disorderly drunks or people found publicly intoxicated and unable to make it home were routinely jailed.[78] (The number of those sanctioned on this charge was high: 23,000 in 1876.[79]) The Society for the Study and Cure of Inebriety pushed for the alternative: to commit inebriates, who included not just habitual drunkards but inebriates in opium, morphine, ether, chloral and cocaine, to treatment facilities. It had successfully pressed for the legislation contained in the Inebriates Act of 1888, which provided for the detention of drunkards in government-licensed retreats. In 1908 an administrative ruling extended inebriety to drug-taking, though confinement remained voluntary, expensive and in practice rare.[80]

Doctors, however, were divided. They could not quite agree on the moving cause of addiction, whose very nature remained ambiguous, or on the question of the patient's free will and legal responsibility. Many of them continued to treat drug use as a mere vice. They also differed on the issue of compulsory versus voluntary commitment. This created the irony that the disease theory of addiction, itself the keystone to the notion that drug use should be confined to the medical sphere, was left to be recuperated by others when it came to action.

Among these were investigative journalists, with their nose for scandal and taste for juicy anecdotes. An example was the series of *Harper's Weekly* articles published by Samuel Hopkins Adams under the title *The Great American Fraud*. 'Gullible America will spend this year some seventy-five millions of dollars in the purchase of patent medicines,' began Adams. 'In consideration of this sum it will swallow huge quantities of alcohol, an appalling amount of opiates and narcotics, a wide assortment of varied drugs ranging from powerful and dangerous heart depressants to insidious liver stimulants; and, far in excess of all other ingredients, undiluted fraud.'[81] The role of the press as pressure group in another country, France, has already been noted.

Britain, and even more so the USA, also had to contend with powerful temperance movements. In the USA an anti-saloon league had from 1895 been harassing state legislatures to pass laws allowing local governments to abolish saloons. Its campaign was phenomenally successful, and by the 1910s vast swathes of America, especially rural, had become saloon-free. The league followed up with a national drive for alcohol prohibition that would culminate in the Volstead Act of 1919.[82] Temperance was a bugbear of the societies for the cure of inebriety because it emphasized sin and vice, and therefore established the drunkard or addict as a guilty party, not a patient deserving of care. Its chosen cause moreover easily shifted from alcohol to drugs: Wilbur Crafts's role in promoting the unforgiving Philippine opium regime was the best illustration.

Governments were meanwhile increasingly prepared to set down norms for public hygiene. In the USA the American Pure Food and Drug Act, passed in 1906, enforced the accurate labelling of food and drugs and forbade misbranding or adulteration, creating the Food and Drug Administration. In Britain the 1911 National Insurance Act established compulsory health insurance for workers for the first time. Legislators, in Europe as in the USA, were increasingly primed to accept that public health was part of their remit, and it had become at least conceivable that this remit should include drug control.[83]

After Shanghai, the only questions became when and how such controls might be enacted: answers were provided at The Hague in 1911–12. Less than eight months after the dissolution of the Shanghai commission, in September 1909, the American State Department began to solicit the participants for a follow-up, this time with the aim of coming up with a legally binding agreement. Wright drafted the invitations. He was able to persuade the new Secretary of State, Philander Knox, to take up the idea by once again pointing out the advantages to American prestige in China.[84] Up for discussion would be the control of the production, manufacture and distribution of opium, national drug regulations, governmental oversight of imports and exports, and reciprocal search rights on vessels suspected of smuggling. Among the American proposals was also the creation of an international commission for supervising the future agreement.

Faced with this ambitious agenda, the Shanghai powers were at first reluctant to participate. The British did not reply for a year. The Foreign Office was infuriated by a report Wright had published on the Shanghai commission aggrandizing the American role and portraying

Britain as obstructionist.[85] The British nevertheless eventually consented conditionally, with among other dilutive counter-proposals that cocaine also be discussed. Eventually the principal states concerned agreed to meet in The Hague in December 1911.[86]

In spite of this unpromising start, the Hague discussions were friendly and uncontroversial, congratulatory in tone, even, compared to Shanghai. Brent was once again appointed to the president's chair. The French and Dutch delegates paraded recent measures taken in Indochina and Indonesia to reduce the scope of opium smoking, and the head of the Chinese delegation reported favourably on the progress of eradication in his country. The Persian representative, Mirza Mahmoud Khan, announced a new law aiming to eliminate opium smoking within eight years, on the Philippine model. Even a typically less-than-gracious aside by Wright on malaria failed to spoil the mood. ('They all know now that opium was not a specific cure for malaria, yet in certain parts of England and America laudanum was still regarded as a cure for certain ills, and often its use was attended by serious results, and that the conclusions reached by the Royal Opium Commission in 1896 on this subject are held by the medical profession to be entirely erroneous.'[87])

As a first measure, the assembled powers soon agreed to 'prevent the export of raw opium to countries which shall have prohibited its entry'.[88] The Hague Opium Conference continued likewise along the lines of the agenda set two years before, with cocaine added to the list and with the aim of making binding resolutions. Another significant step was taken with an agreement to pursue 'the gradual and effective suppression of the manufacture of, internal trade in, and use of [smoking] opium, with due regard to the varying circumstances of each country concerned'.[89] The pious wish that the Southeast Asian opium monopolies should tend towards extinguishing consumption had acquired treaty sanction.

Friendly emulation, however, encouraged the delegates to do more than simply bestow legality on the various clauses agreed on in Shanghai. The conference reiterated the principle that the manufacture, sale and use of opiates, and now cocaine, should be restricted to 'medical and legitimate purposes'.[90] Expanding on this principle, however, the conference now took it upon itself to make the user, rather than just the manufacturer or seller, penally responsible. It was Clementi Smith himself who introduced the idea that 'each participating Government undertakes to examine the possibility of introducing legislation to prohibit the unlawful possession of morphine, cocaine, and their respective salts.'[91] For the first time, someone had mentioned possession explicitly and proposed to make it illegal.

That it was the British delegate who came up with the proposal may be found surprising, in light of the ideas he had professed in Shanghai. But Clementi Smith was a colonial administrator with long experience gained in India and Hong Kong.[92] That he should defend the opium user, as he had done in Shanghai, was nothing unexpected. It was by the same token equally natural that he should oppose the 'unlawful possession' of intoxicants, which in the colonies meant smuggled goods, something that it was the administrator's vocation to fight. Clementi Smith, besides, had more reason to be familiar with Chinese than with European norms when it came to drugs – and the new Qing prohibition edict, with its punishment of unauthorzed use, looked by the time of The Hague conference to be succeeding. Meanwhile with Britain in the lead, none of the other colonial powers were likely to oppose the point, and neither, of course, was the prohibitionist camp. The treaty read, in final form: 'The contracting Powers shall examine the possibility of enacting laws or regulations making it a penal offence to be in illegal possession of raw opium, prepared opium, morphine, cocaine, and their respective salts.'[93]

The criminalization of the drug user was a far from inevitable feature of The Hague Opium Convention. The conference might just as well have confined itself to conferring legality on the Shanghai norms. Ostensibly the new norms fitted with the double influence, in evidence in Shanghai, of colonial and late Qing practices – as Clementi Smith's conspicuous role confirmed. But they also owed to Western ideas as better embodied by Wright. Medicine served as an alibi. It provided the scientific patina to a programme originally made topical by the anti-opium edict passed in China and the American desire to cooperate with it. Addiction, loosely interpreted, provided the excuse that drug users were by nature unfree. User criminalization internalized medical findings (that addicts were sick) while at the same time discarding their logical upshot (that they should not be criminalized but treated). By this sleight of hand, what already applied in the Far East, or part of it, was made valid everywhere else.

One final piece of obfuscation emerged from the conference, or rather its immediate aftermath: the resurrection of the idea, once an important Qing tenet, of supply suppression. The notion arose, or rather re-emerged, during the follow-on sessions arranged to ensure ratification.

The treaty, The Hague Opium Convention, concluded with legally innovative clauses concerning its entry into force. The aim was also to broaden membership beyond the original list of twelve signatories. A protocol was drafted for adhesion by newcomers. The Dutch government was tasked with collecting these adhesions and ratifications, and it was agreed that the convention would go into effect three months after all had been duly obtained. This was a slower process than anticipated, however, and another meeting was accordingly called in The Hague, convening in July 1913. Twenty-four states had now signed, but not necessarily ratified, the convention, and a number of key states remained outsiders, including Austria–Hungary, Turkey and Peru – the first a great power and the other two significant producers of opium and coca respectively.[94]

At issue was whether the participating powers might put the convention into force even though the states on this second list remained non-signatories. Germany, followed willy-nilly by a few others, declined to do so. It was agreed to urge non-signatories again and that, should these efforts prove unsuccessful by the end of the year, yet another conference would be convoked. This third and final Hague opium conference convened in June 1914. The countries represented now also included Guatemala, Montenegro, Romania, Sweden, Uruguay and Venezuela, but key states continued to be missing. Britain announced that it was ready to ratify anyway, and so did the Netherlands, Argentina, Chile and Ecuador.

Germany, however, reiterated its opposition. The reason was simple: the convention would remain ineffective if outsiders were able to take advantage and pick up the slack created by it. 'An international Convention regulating the production and sale of opium, morphine, and cocaine, cannot achieve the desired result as long as it will be possible for citizens of non-signatory states to produce these drugs and circulate them without restraint . . . As long as a flourishing drug trade is capable of developing in these countries [Turkey, Greece, and Serbia, who had refused to sign], the Imperial Government will expect these states also, to accede to the Convention.'[95] Faced with this obduracy, Charles Denby, one of the American representatives, read out a report vaunting anti-drug measures in the USA and the Philippines.

The problem was that there was some smuggling. 'It is fairly to be presumed that with a worldwide control of the traffic under the terms of the Convention which is under consideration even this small extent of smuggling could be stopped. The laws of the United States as to the Philippines leave little to be desired in control of the opium and drug traffic, but to make those laws perfectly effective, the United States Government does depend on the cooperation of the other powers.' Denby urged the existing signatories to put the convention into effect whether or not others had done so.[96]

The German delegate had raised the valid point that an incomplete system of drug suppression was likely to prove leaky and ineffective. Denby's answer was to strike farther and harder. Senator Joe Biden explained of the war on drugs in 1994: 'The drug war overseas has always been an important element of u.s. counter-narcotics policy. America must be ready to look beyond its border for opportunities to combat the drug trade. Fighting the drug war overseas – where the most dangerous drugs used in the u.s., cocaine, heroin, originate – is the first line in defense in combating the scourge of drugs.'[97] The panacea of supply suppression would prove as powerful as it was tenacious, influencing international action for decades to come.

Notwithstanding its difficult ratification process, The Hague Opium Convention promptly set the ball rolling on anti-narcotics legislation in a number of national jurisdictions.

In the usa Wright led the assault. The ring was tightening around the drug user even before the passage of the keystone in federal drug legislation: the 1914 Harrison Act. Cocaine and morphine users were already liable to find themselves on the wrong side of state or local laws if simply by association with public disorder. States and cities were reinforcing control over the main outlets – pharmacies and druggists – and clamping down on infringement. In New Orleans, for example, drug arrests for 1911 totalled seventy, but reached 316 in 1914, the first year of the city's Poisonous Drug Act.[98] The drug industry, smarting from the bad publicity, was voluntarily abandoning cocaine. By 1914 nearly all of the coca and cocaine products were gone, including dozens of wines, tonics and snuffs. There only remained the increasingly suspect catarrh cures, still on sale because their manufacturers depended on them for economic survival.[99]

The USA possessed no national anti-drug legislation, except for the new Philippine regime, to show for itself as its delegation made its way to Shanghai. The State Department agreed that a gesture was in order. At its behest, Congress passed an Act forbidding the importation of smoking opium on 9 February 1909. This was in the middle of the conference, and Wright was able to announce the measure with a flourish.[100]

The next step was the passage of federal legislation. Wright drew from the data-collection exercise performed ahead of the conference to publish panic-inducing estimates of American opiate addiction. 'Of all the nations of the world . . . the United States consumes most habit-forming drugs per capita,' he announced, rather incredibly, in the *New York Times Magazine* in 1911. Americans, he said, consumed more opium than Russia, Austria–Hungary, Germany, the Netherlands and Italy put together. Massaging data that actually showed a downward trend in the last decade, Wright revealed that: 'Since 1800 the population of this country has grown 133 per cent, while the amazing fact is plainly on the records that our opium consumption has increased 351 per cent.'[101] The press scarcely needed this kind of encouragement, but Wright's tactics were popular. The *New York Times*, for example, agreed that the American people were at risk of 'degenerating back to something worse than monkeydom'.[102]

Passing legislation was trickier, and Wright initially overreached. President Taft presented the American delegation's report on the Shanghai Opium Commission to Congress in 1910: this concluded that 'habit-forming drugs' should be regulated federally, through the Treasury Department.[103] With this backing, Wright arranged for representative David Foster of Vermont, chairman of the House Committee on Foreign Affairs, to introduce a measure for eliminating the non-medical use of key drugs. The bill imposed meticulous record-keeping, labelling and reporting obligations on drug distributors, with stiff penalties for violators.[104]

The hearings, carried out in December 1910 and January 1911, were chaotic. A representative of the National Wholesale Druggists Association, Charles West, attacked the use of stamps and labels and the financial burden it would entail. He felt the law's provisions were too severe, though he did acquiesce to a simpler law, 'one that can be enforced and will not inflict too much hardship on the trade'. West was meanwhile questioned by Francis Harrison, who asked: 'What about this material they call Coca-Cola? . . . Isn't it a habit-forming drink?' West agreed that it was, and so was Pepsi-Cola. Harrison then proposed that coca leaves be included in the bill as an ingredient of 'Coca-Cola and Pepsi-Cola and all those things that are sold to Negroes all over the South'.[105]

Another witness, Charles Towns, operator of a drug and alcohol hospital in New York, thought that the most dangerous substances were codeine and cannabis, opining that 'there is no drug in the *Pharmacopoeia* today that would produce the pleasurable sensations you would get from cannabis . . . and of all the drugs on earth I would certainly put that on the list.' Charles Woodruff and William Muir spoke on behalf of the drug manufacturers and the New York Pharmaceutical Association respectively: both denied that the trade associations opposed legislation, but they warned that they were against the painstaking registration of infinitesimal doses. They incidentally disputed Wright's numbers on the prevalence of drug abuse. Finally, Henry Wiley, the architect of the Pure Food and Drug Act, arrived from the Bureau of Chemistry with samples of narcotic-containing proprietary medicines, including addiction remedies and infants' soothing syrups. Wiley wanted a prohibitory law, but he thought caffeine should be added to the list, as well as the major drugs of abuse that were acetanilid, antipyrene and phenacetin.[106]

The bill failed. Its control provisions were too onerous and scared off the trade associations. Both the American Medical Association and the American Pharmaceutical Association were favourable to a properly framed drug law. They did not necessarily support measures such as the denial of opiates to dependent users, though, or, in the pharmacists' case, the removal of exemptions on patent medicines. They were also weary of being asked to carry the burden of control, with all the costs it involved.[107]

Wright resumed his campaign in June 1912, after the success of The Hague conference. His new sponsor, after Foster had died, was the New Yorker Francis Burton Harrison. Again, the bill at first failed to pass the House Ways and Means Committee, the cantankerous Wright having abstained from incorporating changes demanded by the drug trade. The manufacturing and distributing interests had formed a National Drug Trade Conference (NDTC) to keep tabs on narcotic legislation. Harrison sat Wright across from the NDTC and had them agree a compromise. Harrison introduced his revised bill in the House in June 1913 and, anti-climactically when compared to the failed Foster Bill, it passed within a week.[108] With special interests out of the way, its sponsors were able to invoke on the one hand The Hague Convention and on the other the dangers of drugs in the abstract, achieving a swift consensus.

The bill languished in the Senate for a year, but on 17 December 1914 it was signed into law. The Harrison Act established registration requirements for anyone importing, manufacturing or distributing opium or coca and their derivatives. It relied on the purchase of stamps from the Bureau of Internal Revenue of the Treasury Department, which was thereby established as the regulatory authority. It made it illegal, finally, for anyone to either sell or be in possession of these drugs except 'in pursuance of a written prescription issued by a physician, dentist, or veterinary surgeon'. Penalties consisted of fines up to $2,000 and five years of imprisonment.[109] Drug prohibition had come to America.

In China the anti-opium campaign was proceeding apace, or at least it did so until a revolution overthrew the Qing in 1911. Its success rested, aside from poppy eradication, on two innovations. The first was to enlist local anti-opium societies or create new ones when necessary. The Fuzhou Anti-opium Society, for example, standing at the heart of a regional branch network, organized rallies and parades, burned smoking implements, leaned on scholars to make public statements and lectures against opium, and so on. The Fujian Anti-opium Society went further, running treatment centres and sometimes participating in uprooting poppy plants. It helped with the organization of the smoker census and the allocation of user licences. It even became involved in the investigation of illegal smokers and opium dens, its inspectors patrolling the local wards alongside police, searching premises and looking for violators.[110]

The campaign's second original idea was to develop a new language and visual imagery designed to attack opium's popularity. The smoker was portrayed as lazy and neglectful of his family and national duties. His figure (the stereotypes used were male) was associated with crime and indolence. Rather than fashionable, he was portrayed as enslaved by his drug. But what was new was that the opium smoker was increasingly shown as frail, thin and poor. Associating its use with poverty and low social standing stripped opium of the glamour it had hitherto possessed. Chinese people had tended to hold ambivalent views of the drug, believing that responsible use was possible and even socially useful while condemning excess. The new iconography banged home the opium rake's progress as he slid down the path to physical and financial ruin. This, over time, would curb opium use more effectively than any other measure.[111] Though opium smoking became resurgent in the interwar republican and warlord period, it would never recapture the heights seen in the late Qing.

The eradication programme was meanwhile pursued with force. Lands were confiscated, houses burned, farmers imprisoned on long sentences or even shot. Local gentry were jailed or flogged, and failing to inform could be punished just as severely. A 1922 magazine article retrospectively wrote: 'Crops were uprooted and trampled on; men were beaten senseless by the roadside in the midst of their ruined fields; the job was done with a savage thoroughness which defies parallel.'[112]

Alexander Hosie, the same British consular official who had criticized China's opium statistics at the Shanghai conference, was tasked with investigating the extent of poppy eradication in 1910 and 1911. Hosie's report was laudatory. If he saw any violence, incidentally, his account glossed over it: 'Towards the end of November of last year it was discovered that at a place called Yün-t'ai-p'u or Yün-t'ai-ch'ang ... the farmers had sown the poppy, and when the magistrate of Ch'ang-shou proceeded to uproot the young plants, resistance was offered, and the magistrate obliged to beat a retreat. The matter was reported to the viceroy, who dismissed the magistrate, and instructed the Prefect of Chungking to proceed to destroy the crop. This was done, and Yün-t'ai-ch'ang is believed to be the only place in which cultivation was attempted throughout the whole province in 1910.'[113]

Hosie reported that, in the few key provinces where most of the opium was grown, drastic reductions had been achieved, ranging from 70 to 100 per cent. In his own words, this was 'a notable achievement', and well ahead of schedule. A sign of things to come, Hosie only noted that after the revolution began 'the Central and Provincial Governments lost control, and were unable, for the time being, to prevent a recrudescence of poppy cultivation'.[114]

The Paris professor of medicine Paul Brouardel recounts, in his multi-volume lectures, the following anecdote:

A well-heeled lady was arrested in the act of stealing from a store. After her arrest, it was discovered that she was a morphine addict. Her husband, seeking to find where she obtained the money to buy the drug, discovered that she had sold the second row of the books on her bookshelves, and even her grandfather's field marshal's baton. Thereupon, a pharmacist had the audacity of presenting the husband with an invoice of FRF 1,650 for the provision of morphine. Within the space of 516 days, he had supplied 6,930 g of morphine in deliveries of 10, 15, 20, 40, 60, and 100 parcels, for a total of 3,465 parcels of 2 g each. To begin with, the pharmacist had merely fulfilled the order contained in two medical prescriptions, but he had proceeded to replenish the same amount, then sell more without prescription, even agreeing to post his wares to the lady while she was travelling.

The husband refused to pay and sued the pharmacist who, on the strength of my testimony, was condemned to eight days' incarceration. In addition, he was ordered to pay for the lady's treatment in a clinic ... Fortunately for the pharmacist, she died after six weeks.[115]

As this shows, in France, too, the drug trade was not without restrictions, though they continued to fall lightly on dishonest dealers. As in the USA, the Shanghai conference coincided with the first French measures targeted at opium smoking. In 1908 the authorities tightened registration procedures on opium imports and wholesaling, reiterating that retail sales were restricted to pharmacies and required prescriptions.[116] This was followed by more aggressive enforcement of the law on 'poisonous substances', the pharmacy law as it applied to opiates. Whereas prior to that date, no more than a handful of people had been indicted annually for violation, the number climbed, in the five years to 1913, to a total of 182 indictments.[117]

The Hague conference acted as the prompt for the preparation of a comprehensive drug law, as it did in Britain. In 1913 three French MPs separately drafted acts governing the sale, transport and possession of cocaine, ether, hashish, morphine and opium outside medical channels.[118] In Britain a governmental committee was put together to consider how to make good the resolutions of the Shanghai and Hague conferences. At a set of meetings running from March 1913 to May 1914, this committee established the British version of their requirements.[119]

The French government hesitated. For one thing, it still balked at penalizing possession. Did the means exist to police drug users? Perhaps forbidding drug use in public places would suffice, a draft decree suggested. As an experimental measure, the vice squad was reorganized to include a section for combating the narcotics traffic.[120] In Britain pharmaceutical representatives signified that they were unhappy at the low thresholds established at The Hague – 0.2 grams of morphine, for example – though they did not object to the law itself.[121] In both countries, reform was delayed by the declarations of war.

It was no more than a hiatus. Wartime conditions actually favoured the passage of the proposed laws. The French parliamentary chambers debated the governmental text in 1915 and 1916. Worries over the French population's physical condition compared to the enemy's had not disappeared; on the contrary. Nor had journalistic enthusiasm. The senators who introduced the law thanked the newspapers for having whipped up the right level of enthusiasm: 'The press has widely honoured itself, by putting a red-hot iron to the wound, by pursuing opium and cocaine addicts into the underworld.'[122] The Shanghai commission and Hague conference finally set a model for the world which France was honour-bound to champion: 'They were the starting point for legislative and humanitarian measures which, if faithfully applied, would soon have put an end to poppy cultivation and the opium trade: the new era began of a crusade among nations against an evil whose ravages remain incalculable, an international impulse set to put an end, to mutual benefit, to the degeneration of both Eastern races and Western peoples.'[123] The law passed, having met no opposition, on 12 July 1916. Its penalties involved imprisonment of up to two years, whether for illegal sales or for possession. Unlike the Harrison Act, it listed hashish alongside the drugs of addiction that were opiates and cocaine.

Britain enacted its own restrictions by administrative fiat reliant on emergency wartime powers. Unlike France, the role of the press and public were minimal, even if the cases of a London prostitute and an ex-convict arrested for selling cocaine to Canadian soldiers caused a minor sensation in February 1916.[124] In May 1916 the Army Council moved to forbid the sale or supply of cocaine, opiates and other drugs to members of the forces. Yet it was an under-secretary at the Home Office, Malcolm Delevingne, who took the initiative of using the

Defence of the Realm Act (DORA) and its emergency provisions to pass Britain's first comprehensive anti-drug measures. Under DORA regulation 40b, it became an offence to sell or be in possession of cocaine or opium except based on a medical prescription.[125] These provisions became the basis for a Dangerous Drugs Act, passed in 1920, which also applied to morphine. Contravention was punishable by a fine of £200 and up to six months' imprisonment.[126]

When asked, years later, why Britain had passed its first Drugs Acts, Delevingne observed that 'Great Britain has been fortunate in that the vice or disease of drug addiction has not spread to any serious extent among its population.' He was sometimes asked why Acts were therefore necessary: 'The answer is that the Dangerous Drugs Acts are the outcome of a profound international public opinion which for many years had been steadily growing, and which has culminated in international action – an action which it is steadily believed is for the benefit of the whole human race.'[127] The Acts 'sprang directly out of International Agreements arrived at after prolonged consideration by official conferences in which Great Britain took part'.[128]

The drug laws – the Harrison Act, the Loi du 12 juillet, DORA 40b – all passed with varying degrees of public pressure and involvement from medical and pharmaceutical lobbies. None of them met any opposition other than technical. They all had in common two things. The first was a background by which drugs, namely opiates and cocaine, had acquired a uniformly sinister reputation. Ultimately this reputation sprang from disease notions of addiction as defined by the medical body, though only as mediated and embellished by other voices and lobby groups. This background made drug laws conceivable in the first place, and helped ensure the absence of opposition. The second commonality these laws shared was that they took their inspiration from the conferences initially called to deal with the continued struggles over opium in China and the Far East or, in other words, to amend the damage done by the Opium Wars. The conflicts of the Far East reacted with the template of Western science, giving birth to the anti-narcotics order we still possess.

Germany had yet to ratify the Opium Convention. Nevertheless, by the close of the last sitting in The Hague eleven states had done so, including the United States, Thailand and China, and four had announced that they were prepared to oblige: the UK, Japan, the Netherlands and Persia. A provision now allowed ratifying powers to put the convention into force among themselves, regardless of what other states did, after the end of 1914.[129]

At the war's close, the victors insisted that the defeated powers – in particular Germany and Turkey – adhere to the convention. Article 295 of the 1919 Versailles Treaty specified that accession to it was equivalent to automatic ratification of the Opium Convention. Signatories had twelve months to enact the necessary legislation.[130] Within a few years, a flood of national drug laws followed, among the Versailles Treaty signatories but also among neutral states. In 1919, for example, the Dutch Opium Act restricted the sale of opiates and cocaine and any patent medicines containing them to medical purposes – possession would be criminalized in 1928.[131] Canada implemented its own set of drug laws between 1911 and 1921, with illegal possession punishable by up to several years' imprisonment.[132] Spain passed its first narcotics law in 1918, and Colombia in 1920.[133] It was not just that the Versailles Treaty bound its signatories to enact the Hague Convention. It had also placed a new body in charge: the League of Nations. The war on drugs had enlisted its first global institution.

PART II
PROHIBITION
TRIUMPHANT

5

GANGSTERS

On 15 October 1929 a consignment of 1,000 cold lime powder tins arrived in Alexandria and was opened by the Egyptian customs. Upon inspection, it was revealed that 980 of the tins did indeed contain lime powder. The remaining twenty, though, were filled with heroin to the tune of 10 kilograms (22 lb). Heroin having recently been declared illegal in Egypt, the police promptly nabbed the consignee, a certain Moritz Grünberg, alias Georges Cassab, a Romanian printer living in Cairo. The Egyptian counter-narcotics unit decided to find out more and, alerted by the package's Swiss provenance, dispatched an officer to Basle. With that officer's cooperation, the Basle police discovered that the heroin had come from the laboratories of a Dr Fritz Müller, who was promptly arrested along with his wife. The investigators were on to a heroin-smuggling ring that had been active since at least 1924.[1]

The inquiry led to another purchaser named Frederic Cohn, a British subject living in Chatenoy, France. The French police took Cohn into custody early in the following year. The evidence gathered in Switzerland meanwhile pointed to ramifications extending to Geneva, Lugano, Milan, Genoa, Trieste, Vienna, Constantinople, Freiburg im Breisgau and Hamburg. An intercepted letter led to the arrest of a Mrs Metzendorff, from Vienna, at the Jura Hotel in Basle. Metzendorff had been travelling to Basle to take heroin deliveries in double-bottomed suitcases. But she was only a mule, as she revealed, for two male associates named Altmann and Hussein, both based in the Austrian capital. The men ran a business under the fictitious name of 'The Isihi Egypt Company in Kobe', whose speciality was the smuggling of narcotic drugs into Egypt and France. The double-bottomed trunk device was a trademark of theirs, and they employed at least five carriers other than Metzendorff.

Müller, the manufacturer, had other clients: one of these was a Dr Rauch of Vernier, in Switzerland, dealing through a Geneva-based firm called Farma SA. Rauch in turn sold heroin to a Tamara Handelgesellschaft in Hamburg, an S. Kajima & Co. in Tokyo and a C. A. Lejeune in Buenos Aires, all fronts for illegal distribution. In one delivery to Germany, Rauch had shipped heroin as 'Alipogal', a children's milk preparation. As luck would have it, the Swiss customs had opened the tins, not in search of drugs but because they wanted to know whether they contained sweetened or unsweetened milk, which attracted different tariffs. A test had revealed that the powder was heroin, but Rauch had managed to convince the officers that the product was a perfectly legal morphine derivative named morphine hydrochloricum. This would react yellow rather than red to nitric acid, Rauch helpfully explained. He was only caught in the backwash of the Müller affair.

The Müller–Rauch connection also trailed into Italy. An individual named Regli and his associate, Piatti, of Milan, had been buying regularly from Müller. The drugs were smuggled through the border by an Italian-Swiss accomplice who kept a little inn near Lugano. Still more scandalous, the inspection of Dr Müller's books showed that he had delivered large quantities of narcotics to a man called Borella. This may have been Müller's biggest client, with purchases in the hundreds of kilograms for hundreds of thousands of Swiss francs. Dr Müller refused to release the particulars of the mysterious Borella, but the police had reason to believe he was a foreign diplomat who came to Geneva for the meetings of the League of Nations.

Arrests cascaded one after the other. The trial of the Swiss culprits in Basle made sensational press headlines. The inquiry had been a feat of international police cooperation. The results were nevertheless underwhelming. Grünberg, in Cairo, got a month's imprisonment plus a fine. Metzendorff spent five weeks in jail. Altmann and Hussein, in Vienna, were condemned to one and four months respectively. The Lugano innkeeper got six weeks plus a fine. Müller was sentenced to nine months' imprisonment plus a fine of 20,000 Swiss francs, and

Rauch to four months plus 10,000 francs. Müller's wife and their two Swiss mules all received 'not guilty' verdicts. Because Cohn's offence had been committed on French territory, extradition proceedings could not be carried out, and he was set free by the police. During the trial, the court called on the expert testimony of a Professor Hermann Emde, director of the pharmaceutical-chemical institute of the University of Königsberg. Emde stated that the control of narcotic drugs in Switzerland 'was defective from A to Z'. Then he added that actually controls were deficient not only in Switzerland, but in most countries.

Traffickers lost no time moving into the gap created by drug prohibition. As drugs became forbidden articles in one country after another after the end of the First World War, illicit dealers arose to take advantage of the profit-making opportunities. The system founded in The Hague was meanwhile far from complete. International monitoring, licensing, policing: all this remained to be put in place. There was still, besides, the challenge represented by the smoking-opium franchises of the Far East – prohibition may have won out in principle, but in practice they continued to a form a significant exception, potentially even a competing model. The coming couple of decades would make or break the newly installed prohibition system.

The League of Nations was responsible, based on its founding covenant, for enforcing The Hague Opium Convention. The articles dealing with domestic drug legislation were non-binding (however successful they had proved, by the 1920s, in prompting the passage of drug-control laws in a number of countries). The League did not have the power to push for more on that front. It was in charge, however, of the more actionable clauses to do with the international drug trade. Building from this base, the League would, in its twenty years of activity, put in place a system of oversight and policing that remains at the core of the global drug-control architecture today.

At its first assembly in 1920, the League set up an Opium Advisory Committee (OAC). Composed of seven delegates from designated countries (originally China, France, India, Portugal, Japan, Thailand, the UK and the Netherlands) plus three non-country experts, this oversaw the licit trade and, by extension, the traffic in opium and other regulated drugs. Meeting annually for sessions of a few weeks, the committee had access to a special administrative section of the League in Geneva that would collect data and information and act as a secretariat, and it was empowered to come up with new drug-control initiatives.[2]

The OAC immediately faced the problem of enforcement. States had promised to prevent the export of opium and other regulated drugs, except for medical purposes, to countries where they were forbidden. Yet this was precisely where openings had been created for traffickers. Drugs ostensibly produced for the medical sector, such as morphine, were being smuggled abroad and resold for street use. The OAC could only act through League-member governments: the question was how to ensure state actors did what they had promised to do, and that they did it effectively.

The committee adopted a two-pronged approach. First, it proposed to implement a paper trace on imports and exports to prevent producers from leaking drugs into the smuggling trade. Second, it volunteered to monitor the trade directly in order to identify traffickers and, when leakage did take place, set the competent authorities on them.

Malcolm Delevingne, the author of the 1916 DORA regulation 40b, was Britain's representative on the OAC and for a while he acted as its de facto leader. As early as the committee's first session, in 1921, he proposed to subject the international trade in drugs to a double-certificate system. Exporters would first obtain a certificate 'from the Government of the importing country [proving] that the import of the consignment in question is approved by that Government and is required for legitimate purposes'. Equipped with this document, they would proceed to request an export permission from their own home authorities. The exporter would release the goods only after this was obtained.[3] If this procedure was duly followed, theoretically no drug could be diverted from licensed manufacturing facilities into illegal sales. The mechanism would apply both to manufactured drugs such as morphine and cocaine and to the smoking opium that was still being shipped from India to territories such as Indochina, the Malay States or Dutch Indonesia where, unlike in China, it remained legal.

The certificates system was also designed to facilitate the collection of data on production, imports and exports. A request of the OAC was that governments submit annual reports on the new legislation they had passed plus statistics pertaining to their national production, manufacture and trade in regulated drugs.[4] This made it possible to compare production with legitimate needs – the task of estimating licit needs being assigned to a separate body named the Permanent Central Opium Board, or PCOB. Comparing production with needs, the OAC intended, would reveal how much was entering the black market.[5]

Even more precisely, the certificates and the data they provided could point to the countries where smuggling originated and even to individual infringement. Discrepancies in reporting would tip the OAC off as to where and when diversion had occurred. Data from 1927, for example, showed Germany had received 440 kilograms (970 lb) of morphine from France which had not been cleared with the German Ministry of Health: Germany wanted the French to supply details of their exports and consignees in that year. The committee thus assumed the role of patrolling the system where it was breached. Assuming such consignments had fallen into criminal hands, it took up these matters, often energetically, with the authorities in each country.[6]

The OAC even took to examining individual trafficking cases, becoming a clearing house for unsolved international drug-dealing inquiries. It was often Delevingne who led the charge on these matters. A dutiful, career-long civil servant who never married and would eventually retire to tend his roses, Delevingne was dedicated to the cause. For a while he turned into the world's first flying anti-narcotics cop.[7] In 1927, for example, the Danish police reported that it had caught a Mr Ruben in possession of a kilogram of cocaine, in the Copenhagen harbour, whose provenance was the Chemische Fabrik Naarden, the Netherlands. An explanation was demanded from the Dutch government. (It denied everything.) Cocaine had been seized in Hong Kong on the steamer *Fook Sang* bearing the brand Fujitsuru: Delevingne pushed the Japanese authorities to identify the manufacturer. (They thought the originator might be a Wai Kee from Kobe and were trying to locate him.[8]) In 1928 the Dutch government seized a case of 60 kilograms (133 lb) of illicit heroin aboard the steamer *Gemma*, headed for the Far East. A search warrant led to the discovery of sales, over the past couple of years, to China but also to France and Germany. Based on the tips obtained, more heroin was seized in Rotterdam and Marseilles. This in turn helped to identify a Viennese trafficker named Wilhelm Stuber, for whom the Austrian police were looking.[9]

By 1923 a few states had put the certificates system in place of their own volition, including the UK, South Africa, Spain, Mexico, Thailand, Japan and Czechoslovakia.[10] For the mechanism to become general procedure, however, a treaty was required. A conference was accordingly called, in Geneva, in 1924–5. This eventually produced a new International Opium Convention: the 1925 Geneva Convention, which put more flesh on The Hague terms and institutionalized the international control system revolving around information sharing and the issuance of import/export permits championed by Delevingne.[11]

Member states also needed to be encouraged to develop their own drug-fighting capabilities. In parallel to these innovations, state actors established their own specialized anti-narcotics units. In Britain, after the passage of the 1920 Dangerous Drugs Acts, the Home Office appointed an inspector, an assistant and a pair of clerks to support police officers around the country. This increased to four inspectors and five clerks in 1937 and expanded again in 1939 by absorbing the staff and responsibility for policing 'obscene publications'.[12] In 1927 the Berlin police set up a specialized anti-narcotics unit named the Rauschgiftpolizei, which was expanded on a countrywide basis in 1935, with a dozen policemen and administrators at headquarters and nineteen local intelligence-gathering stations.[13] In Egypt the colonial administrator Thomas Russell created a Central Narcotics Intelligence Bureau in 1929. Russell Pasha, as he was known, a 'hard-bitten Briton in charge of Cairo police', chased desert caravans carrying opiates and patrolled Egypt's long coast for night-time smuggling on fishing boats.[14] His bureau would have the honour of pioneering the use of sniffer dogs in drug searches, a practice soon borrowed by his American counterparts.[15]

Drug enforcement most quickly acquired significant means in the United States. As early as 1920, the Treasury Department, which had been made responsible for narcotics control under the Harrison Act, could deploy 170 agents working out of various district offices.[16] This remained for a while the adjunct to a larger Prohibition Unit in charge of chasing down bootleggers and busting speakeasies. After a corruption scandal engulfed the narcotics division chief, though, and as alcohol prohibition started to become less popular, the authorities spun off drug control into an independent bureau. In 1930 a Federal Bureau of Narcotics (FBN) was born under the leadership of the formidable Harry J. Anslinger, a self-taught investigator and law enforcer who combined the toughness of a former breaker of navvy gangs and the talent for intrigue of an ex-consular official. By the close of fiscal 1931, the FBN counted 426 employees, among whom were 271 agents, and possessed a budget of $1.7 million.[17]

The OAC lauded the 'exemplary punishment' meted out to drug traffickers by American agencies.[18] It encouraged the formation of specialized anti-narcotics forces and in 1931 managed to make their creation mandatory under a new treaty.[19] It also tackled weaknesses and loopholes in multi-jurisdictional law enforcement, which it was essential to close if cross-border smuggling was to be stopped. At another conference in Geneva in 1936, the League managed to establish a number of drug offences as extraditable. Exchanges of information on illicit transactions, trafficker identities and drug sources would boost police cooperation.[20] The resulting treaty finally committed signatories to 'make the necessary legislative provisions for severely punishing, particularly by imprisonment or other penalties of deprivation of liberty', a long list of drug-related acts ranging from illicit manufacturing or sale to possession.[21]

Police cooperation, nevertheless, could only achieve so much. The field was vast, and domestic forces, even the American FBN, were stretched. The gangsters, as the OAC was well aware, were often one step ahead. Even the certificates system was insufficient. It was a useful tool, but it was imperfectly applied, and as soon as it was adopted it became subject to fraud. The committee, even driven on by the indefatigable Delevingne, could only accomplish so much – there were too many cases in which national authorities were unable or unwilling to follow up. Therefore, with the ink on the 1925 Geneva Convention barely dry, the shibboleth of supply suppression began again to rear its head.

The brothers George, Nassos and Elie Eliopoulos were glittering socialites. They frequented fashionable resorts and hotels. They entertained lavishly. Elie, the leader of the three, was on a first-name basis with 'more crowned and uncrowned royalty than anyone else on the French or Italian Rivieras'.[22] Originally hailing from Greece, where he claimed to have been an arms merchant during the First World War, he had later moved to Paris. There, 'he was the bon vivant, a frequenter of boulevard cafés, impeccable, always carrying his gold-topped cane which was a kind of trademark, splashing his money around for champagne parties, race tracks, opera and dinners, and an assortment of women.'[23] Ostensibly the Eliopoulos were bankers and industrialists. In reality, their fortune came from drugs, and in their heyday they were probably the biggest drug dealers in the world.

Their rise had been meteoric, reflecting the extraordinary opportunities created by the post-war drug regime. Sometime in or shortly before 1927, finding himself in 'low waters' financially, Elie had sat down in an Athens café with David Gourievidis, a Russian native who had fled his country during the civil war and taken Greek citizenship. Gourievidis told Eliopoulos of the vast profits to be made in narcotics in China. He claimed to have good contacts there. The two men flew to Tianjin to get the lie of the land, and on their second trip they met another compatriot, Jean Voyatzis, the boss of a gang of smugglers established in that city's French Concession.[24] Eliopoulos's value was that he could procure manufactured drugs, namely heroin and morphine. He established himself in Paris, where he was able to convince two major manufacturers, the Comptoir des alcaloïdes and the Société industrielle de chimie organique, both licensed businesses, to become his suppliers. From 1928 Eliopoulos had been importing opium from China into France – most of the time legally but sometimes in crates marked 'tea' – which he sold to his industrial partners below market prices. The finished goods were smuggled back to Tianjin or shipped elsewhere, the United States soon becoming another important destination.

At its height, Eliopoulos's business was sending a monthly average of 300 kilograms (660 lb) of white drugs to China alone, for which he received $50,000 per month from Tianjin via American Express.[25] 'Within one year, Elie had agents working for him not only in China, France and America but in Egypt, Turkey, Greece, England, Germany, the Netherlands and Italy.'[26] Sealing his mastery, Eliopoulos gained the protection of Inspector Martin from the Paris Préfecture de police, also known as 'Zani', whom he bribed to the tune of first FRF5,000, then 10,000 French francs per month. Eliopoulos promised not to sell drugs in France and to expose competing dealers to Zani.[27] His activities eventually reached such proportions that they came to the attention of the OAC. Delevingne passed a complaint from Anslinger to the French, who would later apologize to the FBN commissioner for the whole affair. For now, though, Eliopoulos remained beyond the reach of the law.[28]

It was only in 1931 that a series of mishaps brought his operation down, forcing him to go on the run. First, Elie fell out with Gourievidis, either after some private spat or because Gourievidis became nervous knowing that he was under suspicion of narcotics trafficking. Gourievidis went to the Paris police and noise got out in the press, causing Eliopoulos to lose his protection.[29] Around the same time, an American gangster who was a buyer from the Eliopoulos network, August Del Gracio, or 'Little Augie', was caught in Hamburg taking consignment of 250 kilograms (550 lb) of morphine cubes. The affair was murky, involving double dealing and a mistimed delivery concealed within crates of machinery parts. (Del Gracio had been swindled, his delivery diverted and reported stolen, but then an intermediary unwittingly approached him as the seller of the exact same quantity of morphine from the same provenance.) The police connected Augie to a woman living in Berlin, and from her to an Afghan national who was tied to the Eliopoulos operation.[30]

But what brought the whole business down was the capture of Jean Voyatzis himself, or rather of a thinly encoded notebook holding the key to the entire network. At this stage, Voyatzis was under watch. When he left China for a trip to Athens, the British consular authorities sent a cable to Cairo warning that he would be passing through Port Said en route. From Port Said, Voyatzis continued his journey by train to Alexandria, but he left his heavy baggage in bond to follow by goods train: there, Russell Pasha's bureau conducted a complete search of it. 'More valuable ... than gold or rubies', its agents found a pocket-book that was 'a perfect "Who's Who" to the contraband trade and gave the key to the code which he was using in his telegrams to the Paris group and others'.[31]

Several deliveries were promptly seized. The notebook listed the members of the Voyatzis gangs in China and Japan, the Eliopoulos brothers, Gourievidis, their buyers, their transports and their industrial suppliers. The ring was suddenly closing around Elie. He had already been arrested on his way through Mannheim on suspicion of involvement in the Del Gracio affair, although, the Voyatzis notebook not yet having been found, he was released for lack of evidence. Having taken flight to Athens, he made a bold move: he contacted Russell Pasha and asked that he send over an agent, to whom he would reveal all.[32]

The Eliopoulos operation was typical of the style of drug-trafficking venture prevalent in the 1920s, or perhaps it represented its apex. These ventures sourced drugs from legally established manufacturers and sold them into the black market. It was the simplest method of procurement. Manufacturers were unused to the new drug regime and enough of them were corruptible. Export/import permits could be falsified or circumvented altogether. Long before Elie's cable to Cairo, the OAC knew this much: illegal drugs came overwhelmingly from legal producers. Its solution, therefore, was to shut down this line of supply.

The idea was to impose a production-quota system on the main manufactured drugs: morphine, heroin and cocaine (plus a few related alkaloids). The Italian delegate on the OAC, Stefano Cavazzoni, was the first to introduce it in 1927. Cavazzoni noted that worldwide production exceeded medical needs by a good margin, leaving large quantities of drugs to be diverted. Worried by his own country's position, he asked for direct limits to be placed on manufacturing.[33] Cavazzoni was at first forced to water down his proposal because other committee members told him that imposing quotas could not be done without a new treaty.[34] A while later, however, a private initiative landed on the OAC's desk: a proposal by the American businessman and philanthropist Charles Crane to do exactly what the Italian delegate had suggested. This also attracted scepticism at first, including from Delevingne and from the French, Swiss and German representatives. But Cavazzoni supported the plan. France became concerned, meanwhile, at having been identified as a major source of smuggled drugs. The OAC also knew that the idea was likely to be viewed favourably in the United States. Changing his mind, Delevingne went to the League Council, which agreed to call a conference.[35]

The conference met in May–June 1931, and it gave rise to a Convention for Limiting the Manufacture and Regulating the Distribution of Narcotic Drugs, also known as the 1931 Geneva Convention. The treaty applied solely to manufactured drugs, not the raw materials that were opium and the coca leaf. Each year, countries would make estimates of the amount they expected to need for home consumption and of what volumes they planned to export or import. These estimates would be collected and vetted by a newly created supervisory body, which would assign annual quotas to producers. Each designated state would only allow its manufacturers to produce up to its approved amount.[36]

The new system of double controls, cleared with a central authority, curtailed the bogus imports/exports that had still been possible based solely on the certificates. Before 1931 the volumes allowed under import/export permits had been unlimited, providing scope for issuing fakes. Drugs could also be diverted from production theoretically earmarked for domestic markets. Now manufacturing itself was constrained, and in each country it became subject to direct inspection, drastically reducing opportunities for leakage.

The League enthused over the results. The OAC struck a buoyant tone in its 1933 report to the Council. The illicit traffic's European sources were fast drying up thanks to the 1931 Geneva Convention, it wrote.[37] The Eliopoulos brothers, Gourievidis, Del Gracio and a few notorious others had been 'pulled from the shadows where they were complacently hiding'.[38] France, meanwhile, had withdrawn the licences of three of its largest morphine producers, retaining only three more authorized manufacturers.[39] The volume of morphine officially produced worldwide fell sharply: it shrank from a high of just under 60 metric tons in 1929 to 27 tons in 1934.[40] The Permanent Central Opium Board estimated that by the mid-1930s the legal manufacture of morphine, heroin and cocaine had dropped to the level of legitimate, medical demand.[41] For the rest of the decade, the OAC minutes would be far less concerned with illicit trafficking cases.

The question, nevertheless, is whether this was any more than a pyrrhic victory. The evidence is that production merely moved underground, typically ending up in more violent hands. Perhaps there was a hiatus, but traffickers today refine heroin or cocaine in their own labs, and for higher margins. They began to do so in the 1930s. The Eliopoulos affair provided a hint of what was to come. When, a year or so before he was caught, the French authorities closed down his French suppliers, Elie had persuaded them to move to Turkey. 'At his urging, the factories supplying him with drugs in France packed up their equipment, their machines and trained personnel and shipped them off to Istanbul. Here – backed by Devineau of Paris – Elie convinced his clients that the production would not only continue but increase.'[42]

Morphine refining spread to the weakly policed Near East and Balkans, to Turkey, Albania and Bulgaria, where the poppy was also cultivated. An example is provided by Georges Bakladjoglou. A Turk who had moved to Athens, Bakladjoglou established a pharmacy there, which he used as a front for selling heroin. By 1934 he was running an extensive narcotics business from illicit factories in Bulgaria and Turkey. He boasted to an informant that he received most of his heroin from 'hundreds' of small factories working in Turkey. For a while he also operated his own facility in Tirana, though apparently Albania's lawlessness was too much even for a heroin dealer, and the place was plundered by his own partners. Bakladjoglou dealt with Turks, Greeks, Bulgarians and Italians. Eschewing riskier bulk deliveries, he shipped heroin to the United States in 1-kilogram packages carried by stewards on Italian steamer lines.[43]

Production also moved farther afield. As Elioupolos confided to Russell's agent: 'Recent measures in France, Germany, and Turkey make it practically impossible to obtain for other than legitimate needs any considerable quantities of narcotic drugs in Europe ... The situation in China has entirely changed ... As a result the Far Eastern traffickers have turned to Chinese opium for their raw material and many factories have been established in China for the manufacture of narcotic drugs.'[44] An example of this reversal of flows is provided by the fortunes of the Ezra family of San Francisco. Under its patriarch, Isaac Ezra, the family had long dealt in opium in Shanghai, dominating the legitimate business around the turn of the century. It had only profited from the return of Chinese prohibition in 1906. After a hiatus in which they lost the fortune bequeathed them by their father, the brothers Isaac and Judah began again smuggling narcotics from Europe to Shanghai in 1927. But by 1931 European manufactured drugs were growing scarce, and they decided to move the same product from Shanghai to San Francisco instead. Using a wood-oil-importing company as a front, they packed opium, cocaine, morphine and heroin inside oil drums and shipped the drugs to California. They distributed narcotics throughout the West Coast through such local underworld figures as John Rose, Leong Chung and 'Black Tony' Parmagini. The FBN finally arrested the Ezras in 1933. The San Francisco district attorney estimated that they had moved a total of $1.5 million in drugs, at street value, into the United States.[45]

In New York, the principal American point of importation for drugs, distribution was just beginning to shift, in the 1930s, from the Jewish to the equally violent Italian gangs. During the 1930s bureau officials believed that one of the 'most powerful operations in narcotics traffic was that of the Newman brothers.' The brothers George,

Charles and Harry Newman would have distributed narcotics worth $25 million on the streets between 1934 and 1938. With their head-quarters in Manhattan, they were believed to be the source for drugs distributed by 'Big' Bill Hildebrandt in Minneapolis, the Kayne–Gordon gang in Chicago, Louis Ginsburg in Dallas and Arthur Flegenheimer ('Dutch Schultz') in New York.[46] Internationally they were or had once been connected to the Eliopoulos operation.

Other kingpins included Meyer Lansky, who would enjoy an extended career after the Second World War, Yasha 'Jack' Katzenberg and Louis 'Lepke' Buchalter, all of whom cooperated as much as they competed with each other. Some of these gangsters were caught (we often know of them only because they were caught). Katzenberg used another Greek supply source in China to move opiates to New York. His network relied on a corrupt American Express agent to ship goods via France to the United States, and on two New York customs officers whom he bribed to let the drugs through.[47] Pursued by the FBN, Katzenberg eventually fled the country, but he was apprehended in Romania and deported. He was convicted and sentenced to ten years in jail.

Lepke, the son of Russian immigrants, had by the 1930s become the 'nemesis' of the Federal Bureau of Narcotics.[48] Lepke imported heroin from China into New York to the tune of $10 million between 1935 and 1937. He was also known to run various racketeering operations in the garment and baking sectors. Lepke was well connected, and the FBN only moved against him at the end of 1937. At first he went into hiding, but he surrendered himself two years later, hoping for a lighter sentence. Lepke was condemned to twelve years. In a final twist, the Justice Department managed to tie him to a contract-killing syndicate infamously known as 'Murder Inc.', run by gangster Emanuel 'Mendy' Weiss. In 1940 the bureau arrested Weiss after it uncovered a morphine plant he operated. Both Lepke and Weiss were convicted for their roles in Murder Inc., and Lepke died in the electric chair in 1944.[49]

As to Eliopoulos, his gamble to appeal to Russell Pasha paid off. To the Egyptian envoy and the FBN agent who came to participate in the interviews, he spun wild tales. He threw overboard one of his mules, a naive but high-profile Peruvian diplomat named Carlos Bacula. He managed to disassociate himself from the Hamburg seizure and from Del Gracio, who unlike him had been caught red-handed. The rest of the evidence was too circumstantial. Or perhaps Eliopoulos managed to intimidate his antagonists, threatening to make public his deal with Zani of the Paris police, and cause major embarrassment to the French government.[50] Eliopoulos remained in Greece. Ostensibly his trafficking activities ended, but it is possible they moved underground in a smaller format. During the war, after the German invasion, he briefly collaborated with the Nazis but was eventually forced to flee, escaping first to South America and later to New York. Commissioner Anslinger was waiting for him, a thick file at the ready. ('We knew he was coming; our men were at the pier waiting when the ship came up the harbor past the Statue of Liberty . . . We picked him up as he came down the gangway.'[51]) In 1943, after a lengthy investigation, the Eliopoulos brothers were duly convicted of narcotic trafficking by a Brooklyn jury. Three months later, however, this was overturned on the grounds that the statute of limitations excluded most of the evidence. Elie walked. The war over, the FBN managed to have him deported to Greece, where he spent his last years as a mining entrepreneur.[52]

The United States was not a member of the League of Nations. As such, it could not participate directly in running its institutions. At the same time, it was too passionately engaged on the side of drug prohibition not to try to influence what they did. The resulting policy confusion, though mostly self-defeating, had an unforeseen impact on the second major domain the League set itself to govern: that of the forever contested Southeast Asian smoking-opium franchises.

League members realized that they could not leave the United States out altogether. When the first members of the Opium Advisory Committee were appointed, they took care to nominate an American among its three non-country assessors: no less than Mrs Elizabeth Wright, the widow of Hamilton Wright of Hague Opium Convention and Harrison Act fame. At the very first meeting of the OAC, which was concerned with the teething problems of procedure and reporting and obtaining the ratifications of remaining treaty outsiders, Mrs Wright was already asking for a new conference.[53] Meanwhile the State Department itself sent an observer, the former surgeon general Rupert Blue, to the first of the 1923 meetings. In these early sessions, the committee was preoccupied with measuring how large the illicit drug problem was. The simplest yardstick was to compare reported worldwide narcotics production to legitimate global needs. But what constituted legitimate needs? Did drugs handed out for the maintenance of existing users count as legitimate? If so, in particular, the countless regular customers of the Asian opium monopolies counted towards legal needs. The American visitor would have none of it. Blue hectored the committee members. At his insistence, the Mixed [medical] Sub-committee agreed to its report, redefining drug abuse to include all non-medical use and declaring quasi-medical use 'not legitimate'.[54] Running far ahead of the committee's agenda, Blue went on to advocate restrictions on cultivation, forcing the baffled OAC to postpone its vote on the question originally asked.

During the interwar period, there would be three phases to U.S. interaction with the League: a period of exhortation during which the Americans stood belligerently outside the door through to 1925, an empty-chair policy that lasted until 1931, and a tentative resumption of cooperation starting from the time of the 1931 Geneva conference. (The Americans were able to make formal appointments to the supervisory body created by that conference as well as to the Permanent Central Opium Board, which, as the products of self-standing treaties, were both technically independent from the League.[55]) Ironically, the United States was probably the most dutiful country in reporting high-quality data, including production, trade, seizures and so on, to the OAC and PCOB. At the same time, it made little contribution to the drug-control apparatus built by the League. Incapable of compromise, it kept pushing for treaties and devices it subsequently refused to ratify. There was nevertheless a caveat: the Americans acted as the League's guilty conscience, forever urging the total prohibition which they held as the only valid goal. The result of this pressure, perversely, was that the League and through it the opium monopolies ended up successfully taming opiate use in East Asia.

The Americans returned with an even more muscular delegation for a special visit to the OAC's next session: Rupert Blue; Stephen Porter, who was chairman of the House Foreign Affairs Committee; and the patriarch of the Shanghai and Hague conferences, Bishop Brent. They brought with them a list of five resolutions. Three of these merely had to do with the more stringent implementation of the Hague Opium Convention, but the other two were squarely aimed at Far Eastern opium: that all use of opium products other than medical constituted abuse, and that raw-opium cultivation must urgently be controlled 'in such a manner that there will be no surplus available for non-medical and non-scientific purposes'.[56]

Smoking opium remained, as before the First World War, the wedge by which America would push for an ever stricter drug regime, as well as a tool by which to maintain influence in China and the region. (At the same session, the Chinese representative, Chao-Hsin Chu, complained that the colonial monopolies had failed to produce the reductions in consumption promised before the First World War.[57]) More broadly, the action of the United States was fed by the conviction that its norms were superior and deserved to prevail over those of the immoral colonialists. Brent made a speech to the OAC, complete with quotes from the Lord's Prayer, urging it simply to put an end to opium use. Porter was a self-appointed champion of the cause who would later become responsible for the creation of the Federal Bureau of Narcotics. Quoting Cicero, he brandished the Harrison Act at the committee.[58] Meanwhile both had their hands tied: when Porter asked the Senate for funding to participate in the 1924–5 Geneva conference, it responded by attaching strings to the effect that the delegation could not sign an agreement that did not both limit narcotics to medical use and place controls on raw materials.[59]

But the lakeside Swiss city actually hosted two narcotics conferences in 1924–5, not one. The first dealt with the adoption of Delevingne's import/export certificate system described above. But the League also called up a parallel set of proceedings, on the back of the original intervention by the Porter team, to debate the opium monopolies. The main conference, involving a wide set of participants, began on 17 November 1924. The second, parallel conference on opium opened just before that with representatives nominated by eight countries only (the UK, China, France, India, Japan, the Netherlands, Portugal and Thailand, but not the United States). It was actually Delevingne who had thought up the tactic of splitting the proceedings. The main conference, for adopting the certificates scheme, was successfully in planning. But American insistence, seconded by China, on placing Far Eastern opium on the agenda could not be ignored. His solution was to separate the issues.[60] Delevingne, however, had not allowed for American wrecking tactics through their participation in the main proceedings.

At first the talks on the Far East went smoothly. The opening address reiterated the goal formulated in The Hague: the long-term suppression of opium smoking.[61] The Japanese delegate found that the solution was to treat addicts as sick people: the model to follow was Taiwan, which allowed users to function with maintenance doses while denying opium to potential converts.[62] The Chinese delegation, whose main speaker was the former government minister and ambassador to Washington Sze Sao-Ke, complained that no progress had been made in eradicating opium in the region. But China was isolated: warlordism had caused a recrudescence of poppy cultivation and opium smuggling. The Chinese republican government's own anti-opium regime was regarded as ineffective at best. From mid-November the conference therefore moved on. The Japanese delegate volunteered an expression of goodwill towards China, looking forward to future cooperation. Then the session turned to prepared points, the first of which was the generalization of opium monopolies.[63] By mid-December a text was even ready for signature, recommending the adoption throughout the region of government-run opium *Régies* alongside a list of constraining measures.[64]

By then, however, Porter and his team, which once again included Brent and Blue plus Mrs Wright, had managed to throw a spanner into the works of the main conference. Brent, in a grand speech taking for its axiom that 'moral considerations must determine practical measures,' set the scene. The certificates system under discussion must apply to raw and smoking ('prepared') opium as well as to manufactured drugs, he insisted. This was nothing controversial, but Brent also introduced the proposal that the opium monopolies adopt a ten-year reduction plan, sloping down to zero.[65] Porter went even further. He wanted to establish the principle that opium and coca could be grown only for medical use.[66] An acrimonious discussion ensued between Sir John Campbell, who represented India on the OAC and at the conference, and Porter and Brent.[67] The conference was being wilfully derailed, as several delegates noted with dismay. The bickering only ceased when the Spanish representative proposed that everyone refer back to their governments.[68] The conference broke up. But so did the parallel proceeds actually meant to debate the Far East, with their now completed draft treaty.

Brent, disgusted, decided to return home. He was invited to London, where he met Foreign Secretary Austen Chamberlain.

Chamberlain managed to persuade him of the reasonableness of the British position: the civil war in China precluded a solution to the Far Eastern opium question, he explained, and restricting domestic production in India was therefore useless. Brent passed on the request to drop the smoking-opium ban to Porter.[69] Talks nevertheless remained gridlocked when they resumed in January 1925. The assembly agreed to form a joint commission to work out a compromise: Delevingne, Sze and Porter all sat on this committee. Porter proposed to extend the termination period for smoking opium to fifteen years. The French and British countered that this would be nullified and indeed made worse by smuggling from China. The deadlock was only broken as the main conference convened for its next session, in early February: the Porter delegation theatrically announced that it was pulling out. China soon followed. With them gone, both sets of proceedings could conclude without obstruction.[70]

Paradoxically, however, the American tactics did bear fruit. The final treaty mandated its signatories to institute government opium monopolies, if they had not already done so, in the territories they administered. Sales to minors would be prohibited. Opium-den numbers would be curtailed, and the recycling of dross forbidden. Materials warning against opium would be disseminated in schools and public places. None of this was revolutionary, but along with the treaty came a protocol: this enshrined the Porter proposal to end the production of smoking opium within fifteen years.

Admittedly, the countdown was only to kick in once China's domestic situation had improved and smuggling ceased to be a threat, putting off the final deadline.[71] Notwithstanding this loophole, the Geneva conference would end up having a major impact on the Far Eastern opium markets. In the same year, the Indian government donned the mantle of virtue and decided to end opium exports to states acting as centres of illicit traffic – even if they produced valid import certificates – such as the Portuguese-owned Macao and Persia. In 1926, dropping the precondition that China curtail its own illicit poppy cultivation, it announced a gradual reduction in exports of non-medical (or, as it was euphemistically called, 'quasi-medical') opium, to slope down to nil over ten years.[72] The government discontinued its opium auctions. The maximum volume of smoking opium allowed for export to each country would be reduced by 10 per cent per year.[73] By 1930 the poppy acreage of British India, the source for the overwhelming majority of the opium smoked in Southeast Asia, had fallen to 25 per cent of its 1923 total.[74] This was slightly less radical than it sounds: the reduction in acreage applied only to territories directly under Crown rule ('Bengal' opium), not the nominally autonomous principalities ('Malwa'). Yet Malwa sufficed to meet little more than domestic needs. Between 1925 and 1935 total Indian opium output would fall by 75 per cent.[75] The rest of the region, willy-nilly, was by then moving along the same path.

It was not quite true, as the Chinese complained, that the colonial monopolies had failed to preside over reductions in opium smoking. In Indonesia, compared to 1900, opium consumption per capita had remained approximately flat. In French Indochina, however, it had roughly halved between 1900 and 1922, from 6 to 3 grams per capita per annum. In Burma it had done likewise, and the percentage fall was comparable in Thailand. In the Federated Malay States opium consumption had fallen by two-thirds between 1911 and 1922, and in the Straits Settlements by a quarter.[76] The data, which did not always include smuggling, were necessarily imprecise, but the magnitude of these falls was sufficient to be conclusive.

More was to come in the 1920s and '30s. In Taiwan the number of opium smokers, who were all registered, had fallen from 169,064, or 6.3 per cent of the population, in 1900 to 26,942, or 0.6 per cent, in 1928. By then, the authorities recognized that this probably failed to account for a substantial amount of unofficial consumption, especially in rural areas. They launched a fresh registration drive, netting 25,527 applicants. This doubled the number of opium smokers, but the total still stood at less than a third of the 1900 number, and even less in terms of the percentage of the population.[77]

In 1924 the government of British Malaya (the Malay States plus the Straits Settlements, or most of present-day Malaysia and Singapore) published the results of an inquiry into opium smoking. This rejected prohibition: 'We feel impelled to utter a warning that Government cannot rely on the active and continuous support of the Chinese community in carrying out measures which will be distasteful to an appreciable portion of that community,' the report warned.[78] Anti-opium societies only enjoyed limited support locally. A ban, besides, would bring smuggling, corruption and police malpractice in its wake. (Perhaps this may be regarded as cynical advice, yet around the same time, in 1926, Britain itself adopted policies allowing for the maintenance of existing opiate users, something similar to what was being proposed for the colony.[79]) The authors recommended the introduction of smoker licensing, with for the first steps the takeover of the retail trade by the monopoly in place, a reduction in the number of shops and stricter packaging rules.

By this date, government monopolies or *Régies* had become ubiquitous throughout the region. A growing number of regimes were also becoming closed to new entrants through registration systems. Smokers were now asked to register in Taiwan, Burma and Dutch Indonesia and from 1929 in British Malaya.[80] India remained a patchwork, but an Act dated 1930 let provincial authorities adopt smoker licensing or even prohibit opium smoking.[81]

Governments were also bringing restraining measures to bear through control of the retail trade. In British Malaya retail was now directly government-operated. In Burma it remained in private hands but it was mandatory for an official supervisor to be present in each retail establishment. In Taiwan retailers were licensed but tightly inspected. The system varied in both Indonesia and Thailand, with a mix of government-operated and licensed shops, but it was trending towards direct control. In French Indochina, finally, they remained under license, but retailers were only allocated a fixed quantity of opium each.[82]

The system began to produce lower user numbers. Gone were the days of the opium farms. In the 1920s and '30s the volumes of opium smoked fell in every territory, in some places drastically. (See Appendix II for tables.) In Burma total opium use fell from 31 metric tons in 1922 (the year the OAC began to collate statistics) to 19 tons in 1937 (the last interwar year for which reliable data are available). For the Malay States and Straits Settlements, volumes declined even more steeply, from 108 to 59 tons. For Thailand this was 50 tons in 1922 and 30 in 1937, and for Indonesia 64 and 21 tons.[83]

Since populations were rising, these falls were even more pronounced when expressed on a per capita basis. Thai opium use, for example, fell from 5.3 grams to 2.1 grams per capita, or by 60 per cent. Registered smoker numbers tell the same story: while Indonesia had 142,730 registered opium users in 1923, by 1937 there remained only 41,260. The Malay States had recorded 107,906 opium smokers in 1930 after they completed their registration drive, but by 1937 this had fallen to 52,097. In Taiwan, in spite of the update given to the registers in the late 1920s, smoker numbers declined from 42,923 in 1922 to 12,063 in 1937.

There is no reason to believe these falls reflected shifts towards contraband. The amount of smuggled opium went by definition unreported, but it can be approached tangentially through seizures. In Indonesia seizures remained small, at 540 kilograms in the mid-1930s. In Thailand they were higher, at over 3,000 kilograms, but this did not necessarily point to a black-market shift: the country's geography makes it certain that smuggling had already been significant in the 1920s.[84] As to the Straits Settlements and the Malay States, they reported that 'the illicit traffic is insignificant or non-existent.'[85]

In French Indochina the *Régie* distributed 68 metric tons of smoking opium in 1922, and 51 tons in 1937. This last data point was an outlier, however, possibly due to an influx of Chinese refugees. In 1935–6 the average volume had been 34 tons, half of what it had been in the early 1920s. Trafficking was sizable, helped by the colony's lengthy jungle border and proximity to Yunnan, one of China's prime poppy-growing provinces. The French reported that a typical annual number was 8 to 9 metric tons.[86] Again, however, smuggling is likely to have been just as prevalent in the previous decade. Opium seizures actually peaked in 1928, at 15 tons.[87] Even allowing for contraband, total consumption was sure to have fallen materially between the early 1920s and late 1930s, perhaps even more sharply than the official fall of 50 per cent suggested.

As to the *Régie*'s income, higher prices compensated for a while for the falling volumes. Net receipts nevertheless fell sharply through the 1920s and '30s. While the opium monopoly contributed, on a net basis, 19 per cent of Indochina's budgetary receipts in 1920, this was down to 4.7 per cent in 1929. For 1937, the number was 12.9 per cent, but this was only because the *Régie*, burdened with unsold inventory, was able to cease importing that year, bringing its material costs down to zero. In 1933 and 1934 its net receipts were actually nil, and the average for 1932–7 was no higher than 5 per cent.[88]

This is where any argument that the Southeast Asian regimes were not sincere in their reduction programmes or that they merely regarded opium as a cash cow ceases to be tenable. Throughout the region, fiscal receipts from opium collapsed. In the Straits Settlements these fell from 43.6 per cent of total budgetary income to 20.6 per cent between 1923 and 1937, and in the Malay States from 16.9 to 5.2 per cent. Hong Kong saw a reduction from 23.3 per cent to zero. The contribution from the Indonesian Opiumregie was 7.1 per cent of the colony's budget in 1923, and 1.4 per cent in 1937. For Thailand the same number fell from 20 to 7.8 per cent, and for Taiwan from 3.8 to 1 per cent.[89] Opium ceased to be a significant budget contributor anywhere except for the Straits Settlements, where its importance had even so fallen by half.

The situation was more chaotic in China. The republic had initially stuck to the Qing's prohibition of opium, though with great difficulty in enforcing it. In 1916, after the death of the dictator Yuan Shikai, the country began to fall apart. Army-generals-turned-warlords took entire regions under their own rule. Amid economic and social breakdown and under the pressures of military competition, opium turned once again into a ready and easy source of cash. In 1924 the Kuomintang regime, at the time based only around Canton, established an opium monopoly. This was a departure from the nominal prohibition of the Qing and early republic. It was also a sham. In practice, there was no control, and various phases in the production and sale process – purchase, wholesale, boiling and so on – were farmed out to the highest bidder. The practice persisted under various permutations after the Kuomintang, having defeated its rivals in 1927 and moved its capital to Nanjing, achieved at least nominal control over the rest of the country.[90]

The problem was made worse by Japanese intrusion, especially after it morphed into full-scale invasion in the 1930s. Japan had taken over the Kwantung Leased Territory, a peninsula on the gulf east of Beijing, in 1905. This became the site of an opium farm, then in 1912 a Taiwan-style registration scheme, and finally a monopoly run by an 'Opium Prohibition Office', but none of this was serious. The peninsula functioned as a major smuggling centre, channelling drugs through Tianjin and other Chinese cities. The office was beset by a major scandal implicating high-level Japanese political figures in 1921.[91] Korea served as another trafficking platform. After its 1910 annexation, Korea had been made to adopt Japanese anti-opium laws, but the Japanese had also begun to grow opium there for use by their pharmaceutical industry. In the mid-1930s the country entered the club of significant producers with an output of 20 metric tons, not all of it for licit use.[92]

Japan even had its own version of Elie Eliopoulos, though in this case he possessed his own legally established pharmaceutical firm: Hoshi Pharmaceutical. Hoshi Hajime had long pushed for the development of a native Japanese opium supply, and he had been rewarded during the First World War when this had been allowed. Alongside his Japanese business, he owned a morphine-manufacturing concession in Taiwan, and this became the base for more questionable transactions. Hoshi imported crude morphine into Taiwan, then arranged for it to disappear from the records. He stored excess opium in bonded warehouses, a legally valid practice with the advantage that the product was not registered as imported. Both were discreetly taken to China. No one checked how much actually remained in the warehouses. Hoshi bribed the Monopoly Bureau chief, Kaku Sagataro, to keep his eyes shut to the vanishing opiates. Between 1915 and 1924 Hoshi is estimated to have trafficked in excess of 28 metric tons of morphine, or something approximating the medical needs of the entire world for one year, into China.[93]

Hoshi was more successful than Eliopoulos. In 1924 a new prime minister began to make changes to the personnel of the Taiwanese Government-General. One by one, Hoshi's friends in the colonial bureaucracy departed. Their successors revoked his crude morphine concession. An inquiry followed, and in 1925 he was convicted of narcotics trafficking. The next year, however, he managed to have this overturned on a technicality. Hoshi published press accounts portraying himself as an upstanding businessman and the victim of chicanery. He set up Hoshi Pharmaceutical anew after it had gone bankrupt: by 1927 it was once again processing morphine in Taiwan, though it now shared the licence with two other firms. (Kaku Sagataro managed to avoid prosecution altogether and was even promoted. In 1924–5 he represented Japan at the Geneva conference.[94]) During Japan's ultra-nationalist phase, in 1937, Hoshi was elected to the lower house of the Diet, and he again became a member of parliament in 1948. He died some time thereafter while en route to inspect a coca plantation in Peru, where he had set up an operation.[95]

After Japan invaded Manchuria in 1931 and, from 1937, began overrunning the rest of China, its opium dealings spiralled out of control. Japan set up an opium monopoly in the Manchurian puppet state of Manchukuo, complete with centralized purchase from cultivators, registration of smokers and prison sentences for breach. The organization had registered 500,000 smokers by the end of 1936. In 1938 it introduced a ten-year reduction plan. But the region was a significant poppy grower – the Manchukuo coins even bore an image of a poppy in bloom.[96] The regime's grasp on rural areas was tenuous, and smuggling, a precious source of funding for the Japanese military, remained rife. Neither output nor the number of addicts fell, and large amounts were diverted into China proper.[97]

As to the rest of occupied China, the Japanese imposed various nominally Chinese-run governments in the areas they conquered after their 1937 offensive. Knowing they lacked the reach and authority to make them function, these did not even try to put opium monopolies in place. The occupier merely slapped opium farms or taxes on these areas, milking imports and dens. The invasion itself disrupted both local cultivation and imports. Both Manchukuo and Japanese-controlled China, however, began ordering large shipments of opium from Persia, one of the last few exporting countries that remained open for business.[98]

Nor were the Japanese alone in abetting the traffic. The International Settlement and French Concession in Shanghai long acted as platforms for distribution beyond the reach of Chinese law. The Settlement was thick with grandiose opium dens. An American journalist noted: 'Shanghai was not only far and away the largest consumer of narcotics in the country, it was the reservoir for the stream of poison that flowed through China's veins. Incalculable quantities of mind- and body-wrecking poppy juice and its crystalline laboratory progeny, morphine and heroin, found their way into the city.'[99]

The separate French Concession went one further. It was for a long time the base of Shanghai's opium king, a gangster named Du Yuesheng. Du had a particular eye for opportunity. A small-town youth, he had initially pursued an indifferent career of small jobs and petty crime, then later joined the Green Gang, an organization half answering to the description of Chinese secret society and half to that of modern mob. At the time, a crime boss named Huang Jinrong ran or co-ran the gang. Since 1918 Huang had also been doubling as chief superintendent of police in the French Concession – French policy being to turn poacher into gamekeeper, or rather to let the gamekeeper continue to poach for himself while imposing a semblance of order on the rest. In 1924 Huang clashed with the local warlord in a spat over a Beijing opera actress. Du, who had risen to become his confidant, took his place.[100]

From 1925 the French extended their agreement with Huang to Du Yuesheng. The gangster ran opium shops and trafficking operations from the concession and paid off the French, who as a side benefit harassed his competition. The sums were significant and helped meet a large share of the administrative costs of the French Concession. In 1927, when the concession authorities became concerned about the disorder mounting in and around Shanghai, they extended the bargain to include internal security and strike-breaking. They distributed rifles and revolvers to Du's men, who helped execute the anti-Communist coup that took place that year. The arrangement lasted until 1932, when the French, wishing to avoid provoking the Japanese, decided to clean house.[101]

Yet Du's expulsion from the French Concession did not mean that his opium career was at an end. On the contrary, it flourished as the Kuomintang took over. In a bewildering double game, Du was sequentially appointed as the head, or to the boards, of various drug-control structures set up by the nationalist regime in Shanghai and Jiangsu province between 1933 and 1935. Du paid large bribes and was allowed to operate what amounted to opium farms under the names of Special Tax General Bureau or Shanghai Municipal Opium Suppression Committee.[102] Like drug barons before and after him, he even played the philanthropist. Du provided disaster relief to areas hit by floods; made gifts to hospitals, orphanages and schools; and sponsored a model farming community. Bolstering his mediocre pedigree, Du had a temple to his ancestors built in his home town, Gaoqiao, in 1931.[103]

As Du Yuesheng's ability to reinvent himself proves, the nationalist regime struggled, for the decade or so it managed to hold China together, between the urge to suppress opium and the temptation to use it for firming up its fragile grip on the country. Sun Yat-sen, the Kuomintang founder, had always proclaimed his hostility to the drug. Opium smoking did not sit well with the party programme of national strengthening and modernization.[104] Once the nationalist government became established in Nanjing in 1927, it began to pass fresh opium-control regulations, emulating the Qing edict of 1906. 'All cultivation of opium was prohibited forthwith. The import of, and wholesale traffic in, the drug was placed in the hands of the Opium Suppression Bureau ... All dealers and smokers would be licensed, and no license would be granted to any person under the age of 25 years ... An annual reduction of one-third of that quantity was to be effected so that the trade should be exterminated at the end of 1930.'[105] There was a repressive side to the laws passed. In 1931 the sale or use of opium became the most common criminal offence in China, with 27,000 out of 70,000 reported convictions throughout the country.[106] The government also opened addiction centres – numbering around six hundred by 1934 – housing patients in often rough conditions.[107] Yet the need for funds proved more pressing. There was a catch in the form of a stamp tax on the product. This made it overwhelmingly tempting to keep the system in place without the planned reductions. Fiscal shortages battled the official anti-opium stance in the years that followed. The Opium Suppression Bureau changed names and measures, and tested more or less severe regional formulas, but it continued to draw in revenues.[108]

It was only in 1935 that ideology finally trumped necessity. That year, the government launched a new six-year reduction programme which, this time, it made its best efforts to enforce. It was late in the day, but the regime was in earnest. Its credibility was on the line: the plan, announced on the anniversary day of Lin Zexu's 1839 burning of the foreign opium in Canton, belonged to a policy dubbed the 'New Life Movement', a political creed mixing Confucianism, Christianity and authoritarianism meant to characterize the Kuomintang. The next year, 18,523 drug offenders were arrested and 1,294 sentenced to death. Confiscations swelled, with 370 tons of opiates seized between 1935 and 1939. A fresh eradication drive combined with efforts to push users into yet more treatment centres.[109] User numbers at last began to decline.

The campaign benefited from earlier, positive trends, notwithstanding the cataclysmic conditions affecting China in the interwar period. Even in 1922, after warlords everywhere had recommended poppy farming, the OAC estimated that Chinese opium production stood at no more than 25 per cent of the 1907 level.[110] By then, of course, Hoshi, Voyatzis and their ilk were pouring morphine into the country by multiple illegal means. But the volume of trafficked morphine is calculable, in the period before the 1931 Geneva

Convention, since most supply came from licensed manufacturers whose output was officially collated. Worldwide morphine production reached a 1920s high of around 60 metric tons. It sank to about 25 metric tons, a level regarded by the PCOB as legitimate, in the following decade. The difference was 35 metric tons, the equivalent of about 450 tons of opium. Even if all of this had been diverted into China, it would have represented a tiny proportion of the late Qing total of several thousand tons.[111] As a best estimate, the late Qing opium-smoking population stood at around 15 million, or 3.3 per cent of the population. In 1935, according to a survey, 3.7 million people used opium or its modern equivalents in China, or 0.8 per cent of the population.[112]

Another positive factor was that control was now working with the cultural trend, rather than against it as it had in the nineteenth century. Anti-opium propaganda continued to rely on connecting the drug to downward social mobility. The message was hammered home, in the 1920s and '30s, through texts and pictorials. The pressure was kept up by a powerful National Anti-opium Association, which produced plays, dissertation contests, posters, public speeches, radio programmes and propaganda films shown in cinemas. The association also harassed the warlords and the Kuomintang. It compiled statistics to be provided to the League of Nations, and it urged firmness on Chinese representatives in Geneva. It ensured that there could be no complete return to opium legality, only disbanding in 1937 after the adoption of the six-year reduction plan.[113] The pipe finally ceased to be fashionable. The social elites – civil servants, teachers, professionals – had become less likely to smoke than the average person. The rest of the population followed, setting the direction of the trend downwards.[114]

Yet the Chinese success also belonged to the League of Nations. The first, repressive phase over, the Kuomintang adapted the system to look more like the monopolies prescribed by the League, with a monopoly and tapering supplies. The six-year reduction plan relied on a smoker registration system modelled on those in place in the rest of the region. China may have complained and refused, alongside the Americans, to ratify the League's conventions, but this was what the 1925 Geneva Convention prescribed. The reduction which the Kuomintang belatedly achieved fitted within a regional trend that had commenced earlier, and it made use of the same tools.

China began at last providing statistics to the OAC in the late 1930s. According to the official data, its opium production fell from 5,855 metric tons in 1934 to 890 tons in 1937, the year of the Japanese invasion. To be added to this was Manchurian production, estimated by a U.S. representative on the OAC at 1,271 tons.[115] A substantial share of the Persian and Turkish outputs may also have ended up in China. But this, too, is approximately known since in both countries poppy cultivation was legal and in neither was it subject to quotas. Persia may have produced in the order of 1,000 metric tons in the late 1930s.[116] The picture was more complex in Turkey, but it may have been the source of the equivalent of 300 metric tons in diverted opium.[117] Even if all of this went to China (it did not, since much went to Europe and the United States), this would still have placed Chinese consumption at 8,000 tons in 1935 and something around 3,500 tons in 1937. In 1906, according to this book's estimate, Chinese opium use had stood at 25,000 metric tons.

The opium monopolies had substantially succeeded in their goal of managing drug use downwards. Both total opium use and addict populations fell. Though smuggling persisted, it ostensibly also declined or remained at manageable levels, except as a result of the Japanese invasion of China. Drug control combined with maintenance supply and adequate retail supervision worked. Government monopolies could bring down drug use and could do so without the cycles of repression and violence often associated with prohibition. They were arguably the more effective system, especially when dealing with large user populations.

The practical successes of the Far Eastern monopolies were never recognized; nor was their applicability for containing situations of rampant drug use. By acting as the League's half-in, half-out bad conscience, the Americans obscured the results their exhortations had helped happen. Unrelenting, they insisted that the complete prohibition of drugs other than for medical purposes could only ever be the sole valid goal. That half measures could produce a better outcome was heresy. But the League itself believed in the power of its legal instruments. The lesson that was learned, rather, was that of the supposed triumph of the quota system instituted on manufactured drugs under the 1931 Convention. As experience would show, this only achieved dubious results. Already traffickers were moving geographically, and they had begun to undertake their own manufacturing, inaugurating a business model destined to flourish and grow a thousandfold. For now, the power of policing, especially as bolstered by the 1936 treaty instituting international cooperation, remained dogma.

The Second World War would further contribute to making the prohibitionists look right. It would disrupt international trafficking more effectively than any organized body ever could. Drastically hitting supplies, it would make zero drug use appear within reach. Further bolstering the apologists of supply suppression, it would pave the way for the construction of an even stricter regime under the United Nations. But this was not all. The League had engaged in another experiment pregnant with consequences: the prohibition of marijuana.

6

DRUG PROHIBITION
AT ITS ZENITH

On 20 November 1924, in the middle of the deliberations of the Geneva Opium Conference, the Egyptian delegate Mohamed El Guindy made an off-programme intervention:

> There is, however, another product which is at least as harmful as opium, if not more so, and which my Government would be glad to see included in the same category as the other narcotics already mentioned – I refer to hashish, the product of the cannabis indica or sativa. This substance and its derivatives work such havoc that the Egyptian Government has for a long time past prohibited their introduction into the country (except of course the trifling quantity required for medical purposes). I cannot sufficiently emphasise the importance of including this product in the list of narcotics the use of which is to be regarded by this Conference.[1]

El Guindy's proposal, when submitted, met with 'prolonged applause'. The motion to list hashish was immediately seconded by the Chinese and American delegates, Sze Sao-Ke and Stephen Porter.[2] Malcolm Delevingne was supportive on principle, and so was the French delegate – unsurprisingly, since hashish was already a prohibited drug in France. The only objections came from the representative for India, which had a long tradition of cannabis use, whether as hashish (locally known as *charas*) or as marijuana (*ganja*), including as part of Hindu religious rituals.[3] The India representative was barely able to fend off proposals, by the drafting subcommittee that was appointed, for a comprehensive ban of the 'Indian hemp' resin, medical or not. In the end cannabis was placed on the same restricted list as the other drugs. The full spread of its derivatives, smoked, eaten or drunk, joined opiates and cocaine in the final treaty text.

Domestic interdictions soon followed. In Britain marijuana became forbidden for recreational use under the Indian Hemp Drug Regulations of 1928.[4] In the Netherlands it was made a controlled drug in the same year, and in Germany in 1930.[5] The Hague Opium Convention had paved the way for the adoption, across the world, of laws against the non-medical use of opiates and cocaine: the 1925 Geneva Convention became the basis for spreading anti-marijuana legislation.

Just as the proscription of opium originated in China, not Europe or the United States, marijuana legislation began its career in the Middle East. Like opium, marijuana prohibition came about through the effects of colonialism and the backlash against it, even while it found an alibi in Western scientific discourses. It was telling that the subcommittee against which the India delegate had been forced to battle in Geneva had been composed of an Egyptian, a Turk and a Frenchman. The first modern-era cannabis legislation was passed in Egypt, in 1879, at Ottoman behest.[6] The first modern law criminalizing the use of hashish was the French Loi du 12 juillet 1916.

What were El Guindy's motives? There may have been an element of one-upmanship in his proposal. El Guindy was Egyptian, unlike the representative for India, who was actually British. Having his proposal adopted by the League scored a point for the colonized peoples. They too could be the authors of modern norms. The British authorities in Cairo had recently been embarrassed by an affair in which a Frenchman otherwise known to be engaged in gunrunning and other sulphurous undertakings, Henri de Monfreid, had been routing cannabis from India into Egypt. Lord Allenby, High Commissioner in Egypt, had been sufficiently concerned to compile a report to the Foreign Office.[7] Monfreid, based in colonial Djibouti, offered the potential to make the French look bad. Perhaps El Guindy could imagine what the OAC would make of Monfreid's feats of derring-do after hashish had been listed by the League.

There were nevertheless deeper roots to the Egyptian initiative. Arab texts attest to the consumption of hashish in Egypt, where it was mostly taken with the water-pipe, since at least the twelfth century. Long before Europeans discovered hashish, Egyptians had been debating its vices and virtues. Egyptian poetry described the desirable behavioural changes attributed to it (euphoria, sociability, carefreeness, meditativeness) while adversaries pointed to its undesirable effects (submissiveness, debility, prostitution). Critics focused on the parallel with wine, bringing scripture to bear against established tradition. Though hashish is not mentioned by name in the Koran, it had always had an ambiguous status in observant Muslim societies.[8]

In 1725 the Ottoman Sultan had forbidden hashish, 'which lately is being smoked like tobacco', with punishments including exile, condemnation to the galleys, imprisonment and beatings – though the decree, along with earlier injunctions against opium or coffee, had never been more than proclamatory.[9] In 1875 the grand vizier issued a new circular to the Ottoman provinces prohibiting any further cultivation of cannabis. The order, based on a public investigation into its health effects, concerned a drug 'only consumed by a few amateurs', and it was no more thoroughly applied than earlier measures.[10] The exception was Egypt, where consumption was more widespread. In 1877 Istanbul issued a follow-on order to the effect that all hashish destined for Egypt was to be seized and destroyed. Two years later, the Egyptian khedive himself prohibited the importation and cultivation of cannabis. The 1879 khedival proclamation was followed up with action: a subsequent decree ordered the destruction of cannabis fields, and another prevented keepers of public establishments from selling hashish.[11]

The Egyptian ban mixed traditional motive and modern impulses. The Egyptian elites were proud of their public health and hygiene service: put in place by Muhammad Ali, the country's first hereditary pasha, the service had become a distinguishing feature of the modernizing Egyptian state. In the interpretation of Ali Mubarak, the minister of education and public works and a key supporter, the ban also involved an element of Muslim pride. Mubarak hoped to upstage a ban by Napoleon – supposedly issued during the brief occupation of Egypt in 1798–1801, but not referenced in French sources – writing: 'See how non-Muslim sects ban it! Should not the Islamic sect be the first to do so?'[12]

Yet El Guindy's Geneva proposal, while it built on a background of domestic legislation, also depended on data collected by the colonizer. In support of his intervention, the Egyptian delegate produced a 'Memorandum with reference to haschiche as it concerns Egypt'. This quoted statistics and conclusions that could only have been drawn from the Egyptian Lunacy Department, as it was called, the service in charge of the colony's mental asylums. The service had been run for the better part of the last thirty years by a British medical man: John Warnock. Warnock was convinced that cannabis caused madness, heavily colouring the data from which El Guindy drew.[13]

'I have no doubt that in quite a number of cases there hasheesh is the chief if not the only cause of the mental disease,' opined Warnock.[14] But the British doctor, in turn, owed his conviction to data originally collected in India. In 1872 the Indian government had finalized an inquiry into the dangers of cannabis or, as it was termed, Indian hemp. The review was based on contributions by magistrates, tax collectors, policemen and doctors, though in the end it gave weight only to replies from asylum superintendents. Several of these superintendents had volunteered that large numbers of their inmates had been admitted after using *ganja* (marijuana), with proportions of approximately one-third in Delhi, Bengal, Mysore and so on. 'There can, however, be no doubt that its habitual use does tend to produce insanity,' they opined. 'Of the cases of insanity produced by the excessive use of drugs or spirits, by far the largest number must be attributed to the abuse of hemp.'[15]

These conclusions soon became controversial, and rightly so. As corrective enquiries showed, the data were meaningless. The causes of insanity supposedly observed by asylum superintendents had not been drawn from medical enquiry but only extrapolated from admission papers. These papers were not filled out by the superintendents themselves but by clerks or police based on assertions by third parties or on plain surmise. 'For want of any other reason, it has been necessary to enter under the heading of ganjah several who were merely reported to have indulged in its use,' admitted one of them.[16] Asylum inmates belong to closed and idle populations among which a practice such as the use of *ganja* can swiftly spread. Patients were more likely to have begun smoking the drug after admittance than before.

Another official survey, the 1893–4 Indian Hemp Drugs Commission, managed to debunk the first study. The commission picked apart a total of 1,344 admissions into the British asylums of India. (Example: 'Case No. 1 – (Matabadal Gaola) – In this case the Superintendent is of opinion that the man "was always of weak mind and probably of melancholic habit". There is no evidence that the man began to use the drug before he was insane. The history shows that he began to use the drug at the same time as he showed signs of insanity. This fact, though noted in the history, has been overlooked by the Superintendent."[17]) Out of the 1,344 cases, it concluded that in only 98 could the use of cannabis be reasonably regarded as a factor in having caused insanity. Among them, 38 per cent involved a history of some other cause, such as heredity, syphilis or alcoholism.[18] These conclusions stated that

> There are not a few witnesses who deny this, who say that they have never seen a consumer of the drugs insane, and do not believe that the drugs ever produce insanity. But the much more common impression is that, at all events if used to excess, the hemp drugs may, and often do, produce insanity . . . This popular idea has been greatly strengthened by the attitude taken up by Asylum Superintendents. They have known nothing of the effects of the drugs at all, though the consumption is so extensive, except that cases of insanity have been brought to them attributed with apparent authority to hemp drugs. They have generalized from this limited and one-sided experience.[19]

The cat, unfortunately, was out of the bag. Though, in Britain, what medical commentary came out tended to side with the Hemp Drugs Commission and against the asylum statistics, such was not the impression Warnock retained.[20] In Egypt the data chimed with official suspicion of hashish in the first place. Confirmation bias further helped ensure it became accepted among Warnock's superiors and colleagues. There was, moreover, a third strand to El Guindy's assertions: the Egyptian representative also cited French medical sources in his speech, among whom was Jacques-Joseph Moreau de Tours.[21]

Moreau, it will be remembered, was the 'doctor' who had administered the green jam to Théophile Gautier on his jaunt to the Ile Saint-Louis. A psychiatrist attached to the well-known Charenton asylum, Moreau was the author of a seminal book on hashish dated 1845. Moreau had experimented with the paste while travelling in Egypt and the Levant. His interest was not actually in the drug as such, or in proving or disproving that it caused madness. He hoped, rather, to explore the fundamentals of mental disorder by making use of hashish's effects as an intoxicant: 'Through its effect on the mental faculties, hashish grants those who submit to its uncanny influence the power of studying within himself the moral disorders that characterise insanity, or at least the key intellectual modifications that form the starting point to all categories of mental alienation.'[22] Moreau's view was therefore not that hashish or cannabis, through long-term use, caused madness, but rather that its effects on the subject while intoxicated were a sufficiently good approximation of the state he was interested in researching.

The distinction was quickly lost in his work's recuperation. In the 1850s the psychiatrist Bénédict-Augustin Morel, based on Moreau's account, would list hashish among the substances which according to him led to 'racial degeneracy'.[23] 'The active causes of degeneracy among humans are those which, attacking the brain directly and frequently, produce special deliriums and place those who use them periodically in a state of momentary madness,' wrote Morel.[24] This bridged Moreau's singling out of the drug as a prop to induce temporary madness and the notion that it had permanent effects. There were no clinical studies on hashish such as were being performed at the time on opium or morphine. Morel's inspiration owed more to Rousseau's idealizing of natural man or to tropes about inferior races. ('Among the feelings of the American native . . . there remains no trace of the man who emerged from the creator's hands . . . It is not primitive man, we see in him, but *degenerate man*.'[25]) Hashish nevertheless acquired, in France, a reputation for causing mental enfeeblement. As a pharmacist and writer put it: 'The hashish eater's state is severe: every time he absorbs the drug, he undergoes a hallucinatory state of intoxication, often quite violent, soon leading to dementia, to madness.'[26]

The upshot was that France became the only Western country, in 1916, to list hashish under its first major drug law and the first in the world to criminalize its possession. But Moreau's influence went beyond France. Medical writers quoted him everywhere, occasionally alongside Morel. So did the press, French or foreign, when it reported on hashish: for example the *Pall Mall Gazette* when it passed on the news of the 1875 Ottoman decree. So did, finally, officials such as El Guindy.[27] The marriage of Moreau's notions with popular tropes to form indissoluble truths is all the more striking for occurring not just in France and Egypt but, in parallel, in a third country set to concern cannabis prohibition: Mexico.

In 1860, as part of a short series on intoxicants, the highbrow French daily *Le Journal des débats politiques et littéraires* ran the following extract:

> The excess of hashish can lead to raving madness. There are many examples in Algeria. Last May, an act of savage violence was committed in the grand mosque of the Malekites by a hashish smoker named Hamoud-el-Kahouadji, who runs a café rue Philippe. He smoked no less than a quarter pound a day. 'Suddenly, he was seized with a fit of fury, entered the grand mosque of the rue de la Marine, and jumped on a young Moor, whom he violently bit on the nose. The madman also assaulted the child's father . . . It took considerable trouble to seize him'. The *Akhbar*, which reports the fact, adds: '. . . In the time of the Turks, the manufacturers and even the consumers of this plant were severely punished. It is a wise prohibition which French civilization might usefully borrow from Ottoman barbarousness.'[28]

The irony should not be lost that, while the Egyptians thought they were borrowing their anti-hashish legislation from Napoleon, the French believed with equally dubious justification that their inspiration ought to come from the Ottomans. The piece, however, also makes uncanny comparison with a story published in the Mexican newspaper *El Monitor Republicano* in March 1888:

> We read in *El Pabellón Nacional* that last Saturday around 11 in the morning, there was a great disturbance in San Pablo plaza of this capital city; that the people ran as if they were pursued by an African lion and that the author of such a scandal was a soldier who, under the influence of mariguana, and with knife in hand, frantically attacked the passersby, wounding people left and right.
> The same newspaper notes that a gendarme attempted in vain to detain the man on Molino Bridge, but far from succeeding, he received a wound in the back, and the possessed

soldier could not be captured until, with a club, another gendarme applied a powerful blow to the man's head.[29]

It was the Spanish who had introduced cannabis to South America: in the sixteenth century the Crown had instructed its subjects to sow hemp for fibre. The hemp farms fared only moderately well, but Indian farmhands picked the seed up and, with more success, planted it in their vegetable gardens. They discovered the plant's medical and quasi-medical virtues, and by the eighteenth century it had assumed a place in popular divination rituals under the name *pipiltzinzintlis*. (The Inquisition promptly forbade the practice: the herb, eaten or drunk at this stage in its career, facilitated visions and Devil worship, in its opinion.[30]) That the pagan herb was cannabis had temporarily been obscured, but in the 1770s the polymath scientist José Antonio Alzate proved that *pipiltzinzintlis* and cannabis were one and the same. By 1842 the *Farmacopea Mexicana* listed cannabis as a local herb. Around the same time, it began to be smoked and acquired the name 'mariguana' (later 'marijuana').[31]

Mexican marijuana use long remained anything but widespread. Medical writers knew it best through the European literature on hemp and hashish, in particular O'Shaughnessy, Moreau and the various French authors who quoted Moreau. But marijuana was also sold in *herbarias*, small shops or stands run by local women. Over time, fuelled by the French theories, racial prejudice mingled with discourses on degeneracy to sow suspicion among the intellectual elite. The Mexican prohibition on marijuana, when it passed in 1920, would be called the 'Dispositions on the cultivation and commerce of substances that degenerate the race'.[32] But it was the drug's use around barracks and prisons that ensured it became associated with violent behaviour. Mexican soldiers and prison inmates were the first demographics widely to take up marijuana smoking. As newspapers published stories of soldiers and prisoners committing violent acts while under the drug's influence, the belief spread that marijuana caused not just insanity, but fits of violent rampage.[33]

Modern research has debunked the notion that cannabis use leads to insanity or violence. Something like 190 million people smoke marijuana worldwide, and no surge in random public violence has resulted.[34] Cannabis intoxication may mimic certain aspects of psychoses such as schizophrenia, triggering strange thoughts, auditory hallucinations or socially inapt emotions (for example, smiling instead of feeling sad), but these effects all dissipate. A recent study involving eight hundred subjects performed in New Zealand found no link between cannabis and either anxiety disorders or depression. Large-scale studies show that rates of schizophrenia have not increased, historically, alongside rising marijuana consumption within national populations. The worst that can be said is that marijuana may exacerbate psychotic symptoms in schizophrenics, and that psychotics who use cannabis regularly are more likely to be hospitalized.[35]

How did the belief that marijuana leads to madness become popularly ingrained in settings ranging from India to North Africa and Mexico? The members of the Indian Hemp Commission observed: 'The unscientific or popular mind rushes at conclusions, and naturally seizes on that fact of the case that lies most on the surface . . . An intoxicant would naturally be more readily accepted than other physical causes, because some of its effects as seen in ordinary life are very similar to the symptoms of insanity.'[36] Marijuana intoxication could look outwardly similar to insanity. Morel made the same false generalization from Moreau de Tours. So did newspapers when looking for a cause to the public incidents they wrote up, and so did asylum administrators in India and Egypt.

The developing Mexican discourse on marijuana was in turn relevant to accepted wisdom in an important neighbouring country: the United States. Since the United States was neither a member of the League of Nations nor a signatory to the 1925 Geneva Convention, it did not need to follow their guidance. At the same time, historians struggle to explain the passage of the Marihuana Tax Act of 1937. There had been significant Mexican immigration into the United States between 1915 and 1930, mostly to southwestern states. The immigrants and the hostility to them propagated the lore. 'When they are addicted to the use they become very violent, especially when they become angry and will attack an officer even if a gun is drawn, they seem to have no fear,' testified a Texas police captain. It took several men to handle one who was intoxicated, such was their strength, marijuana producing 'a lust for blood' and 'superhuman strength'.[37] Between 1914 and 1931, 29 states passed laws banning the non-medical sale of marijuana, including California, Colorado and Texas.[38] By one interpretation, the driving force behind these laws was the image of the Mexican immigrant smoking marijuana and committing crimes.

Discussions that preceded the passage of anti-marijuana legislation in the southwestern and western states were prone to make reference to the Mexican origins and/or the violent effects of the drug.[39] The same stories would have prompted the passage of federal legislation.

This 'Mexican hypothesis' is disputed. The historian Jerome Himmelstein writes that 'prior to the 1960s, marihuana was a nonissue in the United States nationally and in most local areas.'[40] It only rarely made the headlines, and theories about a 1930s marijuana panic centred around Mexican immigrants are not supported by the evidence. Himmelstein's thorough investigation of the databases found almost no American press articles on marijuana until 1935 – less than one article per year compared to more than one hundred for alcohol – and only very few thereafter. Marijuana was rarely mentioned in anti-Mexican propaganda. Even in the southwest, both floor debates and newspaper coverage of state marijuana laws were minimal, and their passage was greeted with indifference.[41] A competing explanation, therefore, is that the Marihuana Tax Act was the product of bureaucratic action, especially by FBN commissioner Harry Anslinger (the 'Anslinger hypothesis').

Anslinger was a redoubtable figure who gained the reputation of a hard-boiled anti-narcotics fighter. Physically imposing, square-jawed and in his later years bald, he has been described by some as 'a sort of beefy Mussolini' and 'the ultimate tough cop'. He cultivated this image himself with curt, unforgiving aphorisms. ('Wherever you find severe penalties, addiction disappears.'[42]) Of a modest social background, Anslinger had begun his career as an investigator for the Pennsylvania Railroad, disproving false insurance claims but also pushing back against gang brutality on navvies. He asserted meanwhile that his hatred of drugs harked back to his youth. One day, a woman had begun screaming on the second floor of a neighbour's house. Her husband despatched him to the pharmacy. 'I recall driving those horses, lashing at them, convinced that the woman would die if I did not get back in time ... I never forgot those screams. Nor did I forget that the morphine she had required was sold to a twelve-year-old boy, no questions asked.'[43]

Anslinger was certainly prepared to twist evidence to support legislation on marijuana. During the hearings, he transparently planted gruesome stories in the press. ('The sprawled body of a young girl lay crushed on the sidewalk the other day after a plunge from the fifth story of a Chicago apartment house. Everyone called it suicide, but actually it was murder. The killer was a narcotic known to America as marijuana, and to history as hashish.'[44]) He may have helped sweep under the carpet reports put together by the military in the Panama Canal Zone, dated 1926 to 1933, which portrayed marijuana as neither addictive nor dangerous.[45] During testimonies, he was prepared to trot such stories out as the 'Licata' case, the case of an axe murderer found to have been high on marijuana – without mentioning a prior examination report showing that the culprit had been diagnosed as criminally insane, subject to hallucinations and homicidal impulses.[46]

Yet Anslinger, behind the facade, was a complex man and a deft political operator. Contemporaries described him as humorous, cosmopolitan, musically accomplished, proficient in several languages. His knowledge of German had originally gained him a place in the State Department. As consul in Nassau, the Bahamas, in the 1920s, he had accomplished the feat of convincing the British authorities to cooperate in alcohol prohibition – it had helped earn him his position as an FBN commissioner.[47] In 1956 a senator asked: 'Is it or is it not a fact that the marihuana user has been responsible for many of our most sadistic, terrible crimes in this nation, such as sex slayings, sadistic slayings, and matters of that kind?' The commissioner replied: 'There have been instances of that, Senator. We have had some rather tragic occurrences by users of marihuana. It does not follow that all crime can be traced to marihuana.'[48]

Anslinger at first refrained from throwing his weight behind the Marihuana Tax Act, which remained under consideration for several years before its passage. He instead supported the enactment of more state laws.[49] When pressured, simultaneously, to ensure that powerful sedatives known as barbiturates were listed as narcotics, he resisted having them added to the FBN's load.[50] After the Second World War, he would show the same hesitation with regard to amphetamines. Anslinger was no zealot forever looking to add to the narcotics list. To make such a change, he needed a good reason, preferably one supported by sound political logic.

What, then, accounts for the passage of the Marihuana Tax Act? Without dismissing Mexican influence, explanations fall back on the League and earlier adopters. Could Anslinger resist the prohibition of a drug that had been banned in France in 1916, in Britain in 1928 and in Germany in 1930? If America was seen to fall behind the League, could it remain the champion in the fight, including against opiates? Anslinger attended the 1930s League conferences, communicated regularly with OAC members, and was well attuned to their agendas. He even owed his job, in part, to the international treaties – specifically the 1931 Geneva Convention, which the United States had signed. In 1933, under fiscal strain, the administration had proposed transferring the FBN to the Department of Justice and merging it again with the Prohibition Bureau. The State Department pointed out that a 'reorganization of this nature would be in violation of Article XV of the 1931 Geneva Convention . . . requiring that each signatory maintain a separate, central narcotics office'.[51]

As to El Guindy's own success in 1925, it is easily accounted for. It was a difficult conference already. China and the United States, keen to prove their drug-fighting credentials, endorsed banning marijuana in knee-jerk fashion. None of the intermediary powers – Japan, the Netherlands, Thailand – had any reason to spring to the defence of cannabis, the existence of which they were scarcely even aware. Nor was any industrial or trade interest involved, as they had for a time been on the side of opiates.

In practice this left two powers with a word on the matter: Britain and France. Hashish was already illegal in France. The UK, though its home marijuana consumption was negligible, had a potential problem if cannabis were to be banned in India. There too, however, some regulation of the hemp drug had been trickling through. While concluding that it 'produces no injurious effects on the mind', the 1893–4 Hemp Drugs Commission had highlighted the risk that 'excessive' use might worsen the condition of people already afflicted by, or predisposed to, mental-health problems.[52] Its report recommended the harmonization of hemp taxation, the licensing of cultivation and controlling the number of retail outlets. It also advocated placing limits on the amount an individual could buy. The various Indian presidencies and princely states had been slow to comply, but by the 1920s such controls had been put in place in most of the country.[53] As long as cannabis was not banned outright, especially its medical or quasi-medical use, British India had no reason to oppose its listing by the League.

The Foreign Office, moreover, had other motives to welcome the El Guindy initiative. In Egypt itself, High Commissioner Allenby found the hashish traffic irksome. He described how hashish arrived from Greece and Syria in rubber bags to be thrown off boats and picked up or carried inland on Bedouin camels. 'Hashish has been found in the middle of cotton goods from Manchester, it is put in bundles of newspapers from abroad, it is hidden inside imported goods of all kinds such as tins of petroleum, bricks, millstones, marble columns, hollow bedsteads, barrels of olives, looking glasses etc.'[54] It was proving impossible to put a stop to these practices, and if international action could be taken, that would be welcome.

Finally, there was South Africa. Indian immigrants there had for a long time been smoking cannabis, having brought over the practice from their home country. But Black South Africans also consumed it, and they ostensibly traded hemp with members of the Indian community, in dealings that escaped the purview of white authority. The prospect of two non-white communities finding common ground around a mysterious drug with a reputation for inducing derangement and violence was unlikely to appeal to South Africa's colonial masters.[55] El Guindy's intervention at the Geneva conference was preceded by a letter from the office of the South African prime minister, brought up at the OAC in August 1924. This read: 'I have the honour to inform you that, from the point of view of the Union of South Africa, the most important of all the habit-forming drugs is Indian hemp or "Dagga" and this drug is not included in the International List. It is suggested that the various Governments being parties to the International Opium Convention should be asked to include in their lists of habit forming drugs the following: Indian hemp, including the whole or any portions of the plants cannabis indica or cannabis sativa.'[56]

The prohibition of marijuana would have fateful consequences for the war on drugs decades later, but for now it could be clocked as a victory. The international trade in cannabis was minimal. The plant was barely cultivated at all outside India, the Levant and parts of Africa, where it was locally consumed. International hashish seizures are rarely even mentioned in OAC records; in 1933 and 1934, when they did appear, they occurred only in Egypt, Canada and Romania.[57] Nor did the PCOB, the drug system's main statistical organ, bother to ask member states for production data, only information on international trade, medicinal preparations and confiscations.[58]

As the 1930s drew to a close, the League congratulated itself for major strides accomplished in the fight. It had placed the trade in the main drugs of abuse – opiates, cocaine and now also cannabis – under a stringent system of international certificates. It had inspired member states to set up specialized anti-narcotics units and facilitated their cooperation through shared information and extradition procedures. It had instituted quotas for manufactured drugs, putting an end to diversion from licensed producers. It had helped put a number of traffickers behind bars. That trafficking was merely moving underground was not immediately apparent, and the closing of sea lanes during the Second World War would usefully retard the development of new drug-dealing networks. By 1945 the League's system of control seemed vindicated, awaiting only a few finishing touches. Drug prohibition was inching towards its zenith.

The war put an end to the League of Nations, but its narcotics-control organs were salvaged from ruin. In 1940 Anslinger arranged for the removal of the staff of the DSB and PCOB – the boards supervising quotas and statistics under the Geneva conventions – to Washington. A 1946 protocol transferred the League's drug-control responsibilities to the newly created United Nations. The OAC ceased to sit, but it was reborn under the name Commission on Narcotic Drugs (CND). It now enjoyed American participation, with as representative none other than Anslinger. For a while the world's supervisory organs would all be housed in New York, though the CND relocated to Geneva in 1954.[59]

The war years were bleak for addicts everywhere as supplies collapsed and black-market prices skyrocketed. In the United States, drug-using populations had shifted: the morphine addict who had contracted his or her habit from medical use was giving way to the heroin-using, urban-ghetto white male. Total numbers had fallen: while perhaps numbering 100,000 in the late 1930s, American addicts stood at about half that by 1950.[60] There was a surge in drug use in the occupied countries – Germany, Austria, Japan – in the immediate post-war years as U.S. Army morphine stockpiles seeped into the black market, but this was short-lived.[61] Elsewhere in Europe and North America, drug-user numbers had never been very high. In Britain interwar Dangerous Drugs Act prosecutions had rarely totalled more than one hundred annually.[62] German drug law infractions fell in the 1950s to fewer than 1,000 per year.[63] Canada dutifully compiled estimates of its addict population, medical and non-medical: as of 1949 these numbered 3,500.[64]

As to Asia, during the war the Americans had convinced the British and Dutch to shut down the opium monopolies in their colonies. France promised to follow suit in Indochina in 1945.[65] A major source of illicit supply was, moreover, drying up: China. There, also, the war had disrupted opium availability. Military operations, coming on the heels of the Kuomintang suppression programme, had further hit production. The People's Republic of China turned to opium eradication as soon as it was founded. In language typical of the Communist regime, it issued grand proclamations couched in anti-imperialist terms, opium having been 'forcibly imported into China' in a 'plot to poison' the country, and the cultivator having been forced to grow poppies to support 'the reactionary rule and the decadent lifestyle of the feudal bureaucrats, compradors, and warlords'.[66] A General Order dated February 1950 set out a comprehensive elimination plan, including a propaganda campaign, poppy eradication and addict rehabilitation. By the end of 1952 the government announced it had arrested 82,056 traffickers and sentenced 34,775 to prison or to death, and another 2,138 to labour camps.[67] Within a few years, China was at last rid of opium.

Communist China's elimination of the drug was less brutal than is sometimes supposed. It involved few death penalties: 1 per cent of the sentences dealt.[68] Those who had not been arrested often turned themselves in for lenient treatment. Many people rushed to confess in order to avoid the risk of execution. The People's Republic benefited from earlier efforts by the Nationalist regime, and from opium's long decline in popularity in the decades since the late Qing. Yet there can be no doubt that it was only possible finally to rid the country of the drug by totalitarian means. The broader Communist campaign against 'counter-revolutionaries', which preceded and overlapped that against opium, is officially estimated to have killed 500,000–800,000 people and many more unofficially. After that, fear alone sufficed to dissuade drug offenders. The clampdown was otherwise made effective by the implementation of mass surveillance and denunciation systems typical of totalitarian regimes. Local police stations were staffed with household-register appointees whose role was to report everything that took place in the community under his or her jurisdiction. Organizations such as the Communist Youth League, the Women's Association, the trade unions and residents' associations were asked to keep tabs on their members, leaving no room for anyone to hide.

As to poppy cultivation, the collectivization of agriculture ensured that it could never be resurgent.[69]

This did not prevent Anslinger, in the same period, from accusing China of running narcotics into the free world as part of a subversion effort. At the CND he blamed the People's Republic for running heroin labs and smuggling routes, naming the individuals supposedly involved. In the *New York Times*, he wrote that both to reap profits and to 'demoralize the people of the free world' Communist China was flushing out its surplus drugs to traffickers.[70] (The article recycled a twenty-year-old story on the Ezra family, the masters of the Shanghai–San Francisco route who had been arrested in 1933.) China, not represented at the United Nations at the time, could not rebut his claims, though the Soviets and delegates of other communist countries regularly protested Anslinger's allegations.[71] With a surprising lack of scepticism, the British newspaper *The Times* repeated Anslinger's assertion that China had 'totally reversed' Chiang Kai-shek's opium eradication policies.[72] None of this was more than Cold War fearmongering or obfuscation. Ironically, however, there was a kernel of truth to the story that China's relationship with opium was not dead: the Communists had not revived poppy growing, but the fleeing Nationalists had.

In a zone overlapping northern Burma (now Myanmar), the southern tip of the Chinese province of Yunnan and northwestern Laos lay the territory of a people named the Shan. The Shan, ruled by their own chieftains and numbering around 1 million at the turn of the century, had adopted poppy cultivation from the Chinese. Within British Burma they had been allowed to keep growing opium on the grounds that it was traditional.[73] In 1950 remnants of the fleeing Kuomintang army established themselves in the Shan states. Bordering on Yunnan, the region was a good staging post for raids or even a future invasion into China.

The densely forested, mountainous terrain made it impossible to police for the weak Burmese state. The Kuomintang forces in Burma, numbering several thousand, soon controlled a large swathe of territory going all the way to the sea. They began to buy opium from the Shan tribes, refine it into heroin and take that for sale into Thailand. There, they bought food, clothing and munitions. They also received American supplies in the form of radios and weapons. Shan state opium capacity, at around 60 tons in 1950, would grow to 300–400 tons within a decade.[74] In 1951–2 the Kuomintang forces attempted two attacks into Yunnan, which both failed miserably. Burma protested to the UN, and the threat of embarrassment led to an evacuation to Taiwan. A large clandestine army nevertheless stayed behind with its labs, its networks and its smuggling savvy.[75] Therein lay the origins of the Golden Triangle: the opium-growing and -refining zone overlapping Burma, Laos and Thailand that became one of two major illicit heroin centres in the world from the 1960s onwards.

The second major source of trafficked heroin emerging in this period was the French Connection. Here, too, trafficking cultures exhibited surprising resilience. France, after all, had clamped down on diversion from its morphine factories in the early 1930s. Even after Eliopoulos had moved suppliers to Turkey, his operation had been dismantled. After the Second World War Marseilles mobsters began routing opium from Turkey's Anatolian plateau into Lebanon, where it was churned into morphine base. A Lebanese dealer named Sami El Khoury subverted Beirut airport, customs and police to allow imports in and exports out. From there, the morphine was shipped to Sicily for refining; then, after the Sicilian labs were raided, to southern France. After that it was freight-forwarded to the United States.[76]

Meyer Lansky, one of the few surviving New York Jewish gang leaders, ran the network at the American end. Lansky owned casinos in Havana, and his connections ran through (pre-Castro era) Cuba and Miami, where he had formed an association with the aptly named Trafficante mafia 'family'. The money was laundered through Swiss banks thanks to arrangements by an old gunrunning friend of Lansky named John Pullman.[77] One question concerns the involvement of Charles Lucania, aka 'Lucky' Luciano. According to both Anslinger and the historian Alfred McCoy – whose sources consist mostly of verbal accounts and reports from the FBN – Luciano, a long-time associate of Lansky, was the Connection's mastermind. The gangster, who had once been behind a number of rackets of which narcotics were only one, had been indicted for running a considerable number of brothels in New York in 1936, and he had spent the Second World War behind bars. During the war, however, he may have provided the Office of Navy Intelligence with valuable contacts in Sicily and/or among New York waterfront gangs capable of flushing out subversives. According to this story, Luciano was rewarded with parole in 1946. He and another hundred mafiosi were deported to Italy, from where they went on to establish the long drug-smuggling route that began in Anatolia and ended among his old associates in America.[78]

Yet Luciano has over time become a semi-mythical figure. After 1946 he remained under close surveillance and at risk of extradition. He may have brokered a few contacts, but it is unlikely he enjoyed the freedom, at that stage, necessary for building a large and sophisticated trafficking network. 'Listen,' he told Earl Wilson of the *New York Post Home News*, 'it's not necessary for me to fool around with dope, 'cause I'm not that hard up for money.'[79] It is also unclear whether Luciano actually helped either naval intelligence or the armed forces during the war, and it is just as likely that he bribed his way out of prison.[80] Altogether it seems that Luciano may have played an early role in the establishment of the long-running French Connection, but that the heavy lifting was performed by Lansky and more shadowy French and Italian figures.

Both the Franco-Turkish network and the Golden Triangle remained, in any case, at early stages in their careers. Trafficking at that time was at a low ebb. In 1950 internationally reported drug seizures totalled 59 metric tons of opium, 80 kilograms of heroin and 12 kilograms of cocaine.[81] (See Appendix III for tables.) In 1931, by comparison, seizures had been significantly larger: 56 tons of opium, 943 kilograms of heroin and 70 kilograms of cocaine.[82] By 2015 drug seizures would total 587 tons of opium, 90 tons of heroin and 864 tons of cocaine: a tenfold increase for opium and more than a thousandfold for heroin and cocaine.[83]

Nor was it just that the world's police forces were slow to hunt down dealers. In the United States, the FBN at the ready, drug-related offences were also down. Opium seizures fell from 1,653 kilograms in 1929 to 45 kilograms in 1950, and morphine/heroin seizures from 98 to 22 kilograms.[84] Federal drug Act offences numbered 10,133 in 1929, but only 4,494 in 1950 (plus 1,490 violations of the Marihuana Tax Act).[85] Few people took drugs anywhere, and there were few dealers.

It is in this environment that the American legislature saw fit to pass its most punitive drug laws: the Boggs Act of 1951 and Narcotic Control Act of 1956. The Boggs Act set minimum sentences ranging from two to ten years for drug violations, with longer sentences for repeat offences, including possession.[86] Average prison terms climbed from around forty months before the Act to over seventy months afterwards; almost no offender got under five years, and many got ten, twenty or more.[87]

The 1956 Narcotics Control Act lengthened sentencing again. The minimum for trafficking rose from two to five years for a first-time offence. Possession of marijuana now carried a minimum sentence of two years for the first offence, five for the second and ten for the third. With the exception of a first-time possession offence, the Act forbade judges from suspending sentences or imposing probation. For the first time, a drug offence could carry the death penalty: the sale of heroin by an adult to a youth under eighteen.[88] The sentencing that followed could be frightful. In one instance, an epileptic with an IQ of 69 was given two life sentences for selling heroin to a seventeen-year-old provocateur. In another, a Black veteran with no previous record was sentenced to fifty years without parole for selling marijuana.[89] A prominent doctor complained: 'A man was given ten years for possessing three narcotic tablets. Another man was given ten years for forging three narcotic prescriptions – no sale was involved.'[90]

Such complaints rarely invoked much pity. It was a time of easy triumphs for the prohibitionists. The American Bar Association, finding the Boggs Act excessive, created in 1954 a special committee on narcotics, and in 1955 it formally called for Congress to review and amend federal drug policy. The American Medical Association opened its own investigation into the drug policies in place around the same time.[91] Anslinger shot back with a book entitled *The Traffic in Narcotics*, not all of whose arguments were worthy of his challengers. According to the book, marijuana users found early on that 'the will power is destroyed . . . the moral barricades are broken down and often debauchery and sexuality results.'[92] The FBN commissioner 'proved' that addiction led to crime based on a pre-war Taiwanese report and on FBN files showing that 83 per cent of 'trafficker–addicts' had prior criminal records.[93] In a different era someone might have asked what this actually showed and whether it did not prove, on the contrary, that prohibition was a gift to criminals, but in this case the parliamentarians were impressed. Congressional hearings, running in 1955 and 1956, closed with the passage of the Narcotics Control Act.[94]

Drug users were so few and marginal that the state could afford to treat them like pariahs. It was not that drugs were a terrible menace, but that they had well-nigh ceased to be one. Particularly tough anti-drug legislation was passed in the United States in the 1950s, in response not to a serious drug problem but to the absence of one. The same could be said of the UN drug-control system, which was soon to produce its crowning piece of legislation: the Single Convention of 1961.

With the Chinese supply out, world opium output had by the mid-1950s fallen significantly. Licit world opium production amounted to 820 metric tons in 1955. The lion's share went to three producers: India, Turkey and Iran. Diversion from Indian poppy fields was minimal, as CND assessments confirmed.[95] The situation was different in Iran and Turkey. Though these now both centralized opium purchases through government agencies, helping keep better track of the product, incentives remained high for farmers to sell into the black market. Officially, Iran produced 95 tons of opium and Turkey 222 tons per year. Adjusting the official Iranian and Turkish numbers based on their poppy acreage but keying in Indian yields provides more realistic numbers: 411 tons for Iran and 905 tons for Turkey.[96] To this may be added perhaps 100 tons for Burma. World opium production, even then, would have stood at just under 2,000 tons in 1955. Pharmaceutical industry needs totalled 863 tons, leaving in the order of 1,100 tons to the illegal traffic. This was a fraction of pre-war volumes, which had never been less than 5,000 tons.[97]

For coca the data are hazier, but the world's two main and almost sole producers, Peru and Bolivia, both provided data to the Permanent Central Opium Board in 1954. This placed world output at 13,113 metric tons, of which 700 were needed for medical use. The PCOB, however, estimated that 12,000 tons remained in the Andes to be chewed.[98] If these numbers are to be taken literally, 413 tons would have been left for refining into illicit cocaine, yielding 1.1 tons of the drug – enough to support perhaps 3,500 heavy users worldwide.[99] This is necessarily imprecise, but more accurate cocaine seizures only averaged around 10 kilograms annually.[100] The traffic was minimal and cocaine abuse, in this period, anecdotal. In 1957 the Commission on Narcotic Drugs itself agreed 'that the cocaine traffic was no longer a major problem in most parts of the world'.[101]

None of this dissuaded the commission from pushing for total eradication; on the contrary. The CND, the United Nations' anti-narcotics steering committee, began elaborating plans for direct controls over the opium supply. The idea was to extend to raw materials the quota system that already applied, based on the 1931 Geneva Convention, to manufactured drugs. Raw-material quotas would reflect ultimate medical needs. Member states would submit estimates concerning the amount of opium planted, harvested, consumed domestically, exported and stockpiled. The DSB would be responsible for allocating quotas, and the PCOB would have the power to enquire into discrepancies, conduct inspections and impose embargoes. In exchange for submitting to these conditions, seven named countries were to receive a monopoly on licit sales. The Frenchman Charles Vaille introduced the proposal in the CND in 1951.[102] The project, which soon took the shape of a new UN instrument in drafting named the Opium Protocol, earned Anslinger's vehement support. By 1953 the protocol was ready, in 1954 it was ratified by the Indian government, and by 1959 Iran had acceded to it.[103]

The coca leaf, likewise, was coming under assault in its principal country of production: Peru. The coca leaf was and is still used in the Andes to alleviate hunger, thirst and fatigue, and as a folk remedy to relieve pain. The leaf's cocaine content is small, less than 1 per cent, but coca chewing can provide a physical boost during moments of hard work, especially at the high altitudes where it is typically consumed. It also serves to seal acts of hospitality, marriages or the building of a new house's foundations. In the 1920s and '30s Peru had ignored the League (for reasons independent of cocaine or coca), only agreeing to join the OAC in 1938.[104] But in the 1930s and '40s, a Peruvian 'Indianist' movement, a socially aware political current, began to make its mark nationally. The people composing this movement wanted to pass land and other reforms designed to better the condition of Indigenous Andean people. They were not Indigenous themselves, though, and they took a patronising view of coca chewing. Traditional culture was not something they valued, and their leading experts militated against coca. The leaf's defenders became the conservative elites: coca was a taxable commodity, and it helped finance infrastructure and other budgetary items.[105]

The status quo broke after the Second World War, first under a left-wing government inclined towards social reform, then after a coup installed in power an authoritarian regime closely aligned with the United States. In 1949 the government revoked all existing licences and set up a crude-cocaine monopoly, also charged with regulating cultivation and distribution and with collecting taxes.

With exports placed under control, this theoretically put the lid on smuggling. In the same year, Peru aligned its penal code with international norms – cocaine became criminalized, leading to scores of arrests and seizures.[106] This left open the question of coca chewing: the United Nations stepped into the breach with a special mission to Peru and Bolivia in 1949.

The UN commission visited laboratories, hospitals, schools, missions, prisons, agricultural stations and farms, factories, mines and so on. Its researchers sought evidence of physical characteristics, such as dry skin, missing teeth or low IQ, which it could tie to coca, though it declined to accept notions of 'race degeneration'. It took down statements from the Bolivian and Peruvian military that forbidding coca-chewing among recruits had improved their physical condition.[107] When it came to addiction, it found itself in a quandary. Noting that addiction required compulsive use, a tendency to increase doses and physical dependence, the commission noted: 'In the light of this definition, the observations of the Commission show that coca-leaf chewing is not an addiction (toxicomania) but a habit. It may, however, in some individuals, become an addiction, but generally it can be given up like other habits.'[108] Its conclusions, nevertheless, were foregone: 'The Commission desires, however, to state that the habit of coca-leaf chewing is also dangerous, because the leaves contain a toxic substance – cocaine.'[109] Even if coca chewing did not match the criteria for drug abuse: 'Limitation of the production of coca leaf for chewing should be effected gradually until complete suppression is achieved.'[110]

Ever since 1948, Anslinger had been promoting the idea of a Single Convention to unify, replace and extend the piecemeal controls applicable under the existing treaties. Based on a single legal instrument, all drugs, whether raw or manufactured, would be placed under a set of restrictions applying to cultivation, production, trade, distribution and domestic penal norms. The Single Convention was a far more important piece of legislation than the Opium Protocol, but discussions on both ran in parallel. The CND kept charge of elaborating a draft convention – which was too elaborate a treaty to be left entirely to a conference – while it urged the Opium Protocol upon key opium-producing states.

Anslinger put allies in place to help push them forward: the Canadian Clement Sharman, a colonel and former officer in his country's narcotics service; the American Herbert May, a former pharmaceutical executive and long-time PCOB member; and Charles Vaille, a pharmacist and civil servant who had been a member of the French Resistance and was a staunch prohibitionist. Sharman took the chairmanship of the CND. May became president of the PCOB. Vaille had introduced proposals for the Opium Protocol, and he led much of the preparations for the Single Convention through the 1950s.[111] The commissioner meanwhile maintained friendly relations with the assistant secretary general of the UN, Hoo Chi-tsai, a former Chinese foreign minister who had worked with him on narcotic control in the Far East before the war.[112] Yet Anslinger overshot. He wanted the Opium Protocol to pass as a priority. As a consequence, the elaboration of the Single Convention stalled, holding up both agendas.

Iran's ratification of the Protocol was a significant win. Opium, long cultivated in Iran, had spread down the social ladder in the nineteenth and early twentieth centuries as cultivation took off. Widely taken in pill form or as an additive to infusions, it was sometimes known as the 'hashish of the poor'.[113] Several times, the state had attempted to curtail both cultivation and use. Iran had enacted legislation in 1911 aiming to phase out the non-medical consumption of opium over a period of eight years. It had acceded to the Hague Convention and passed compliant legislation in 1919.[114] In 1926 the League had sent a commission to Iran, and this had recommended a programme of gradual reduction accompanied by infrastructure development and crop substitution.[115] Half heeding this advice, in 1928 Iran had put in place a purchasing monopoly responsible for sweeping the whole of the poppy crop. None of this was effective, however, and both opium cultivation and use had continued to expand. Production rose above 500 tons annually in the 1920s and '30s.[116] Much was smuggled, earning Iran a poor international reputation, but significant quantities were also consumed domestically: in the order of 25 grams (0.9 oz) annually per capita, by one estimate, higher than China at the time.[117] By the early 1950s it was found that output had increased again.[118]

Following a *coup d'état* favourable to American influence, Anslinger approached the Iranians. 'We talked with the Shah of Iran, who agreed to curtail Iranian opium production. We then sent our own Colonel Garland Williams, former head of our New York office, to Iran.' Garland advised complete suppression. 'He organized the Iranian police to deal with the job of suppressing the production in the fields, the opium dens and addiction. Not only Iranian police but also the army and the Iranian customs were enlisted. The clean-up job was efficient and thorough.'[119] The authorities had become alarmed, besides, at spiralling domestic use. A 1955 law banned the cultivation of the poppy, involving heavy sentences – to rise, in 1966, to death for illegal opiate manufacturing or distribution, or possession of over 500 grams (18 oz). The military tore through the poppy fields with mechanical ploughs.[120]

This left Turkey as the principal stumbling block. Unlike Iran, however, Turkey as a country saw very little domestic use; its opium was essentially a cash crop and an economic boon. In a running spat with the Egyptian representative, the Turkish member on the CND remarked: 'The fact that narcotic drugs existed was not sufficient reason to explain illicit consumption; if this were so, all the opium-producing countries would have been seriously affected. Fortunately, this was not the case, and although India and Turkey were major producers, drug addiction in those countries was at an extremely low level.'[121] And later: 'There was little or no addiction in Turkey, which was a producer country . . . The representative of Turkey regretted that the Arab States repeatedly complained of traffic alleged to be coming from neighbouring countries, but did not appear to make any serious efforts to curb the traffic in their own territory.'[122]

Domestically, Turkey regulated opiate distribution and use along international norms. Though it had only acceded to the Hague Convention late, by 1931 it had adopted the international permit system. Cultivation was another matter. In 1933 Turkey put in place an opium purchasing monopoly similar to Iran's.[123] Yet this worked on a declaratory basis, and the state neither issued licences to growers nor controlled possession or quantities in storage, with the result that massive diversion took place.[124] That this went into international trafficking networks was an embarrassment, but neither the UN nor Anslinger were able to pressure the Turkish government into relenting and acceding to the Opium Protocol.

The hold-up was only overcome when the Single Convention, long delayed, was finalized regardless and adopted in conference in 1961. The convention was a comprehensive item of legislation, dealing with the 'cultivation, production, manufacture, extraction, preparation, possession, offering, offering for sale, distribution, purchase, sale, delivery on any terms whatsoever, brokerage, dispatch, dispatch in transit, transport, importation and exportation of drugs'.[125] It contained a tiered schedule of drugs, with opium, morphine, heroin, coca leaf, cocaine and cannabis all listed in schedule 1.[126] It enshrined the systems of import/export certificates and manufactured-drug quotas already in existence. It established production controls on all drugs, not just manufactured drugs. For opium, coca and cannabis, it mandated producer states to establish national agencies for licensing and purchase/collection.[127] The convention specifically included provisions mandating member states to punish drug offences, including possession, with 'adequate punishment particularly by imprisonment or other penalties of deprivation of liberty'.[128] It confirmed as paramount, of course, the principle that drug use should be limited to medical purposes.

With 73 state participants, the Single Convention, and with it the drug prohibition regime, acquired global scope. There remained for a few more years a notable exception: the United States. The Convention's clauses subjecting raw materials to quotas superseded the Opium Protocol. The wording, however, was weaker. In the conference, producer states, Latin American and Asian, had fought the controls the text placed on opium, coca and cannabis, and they had been able to force amendments.[129]

The treaty also admitted exemptions for certain non-medical uses. Peru, though it accepted the principle of prohibition and was prepared to accede to the Single Convention, had led a successful rearguard action on coca chewing. Anthropologists had suddenly discovered coca's place in Peruvian folklore. Local agricultural authorities were sceptical of crop-substitution proposals, and the state, besides, had earmarked taxes on coca for highway construction.[130] As to opium, its quasi-medical use persisted in key countries, such as India and Pakistan. Article 49 of the Single Convention accordingly contained 'reservations' exempting the traditional use of certain listed drugs, namely the coca leaf, smoking and quasi-medical opium, and cannabis, including the resin. Signatories were allowed to 'permit temporarily' the use, production and manufacture of these drugs within their territories, though the quasi-medical use of opium had to be abolished within fifteen years and coca-leaf chewing within 25.[131]

Anslinger, furious, disowned the legislation he had had such a major role in initiating. He tried to derail ratification by friendly member states, and he persuaded the American Senate Foreign Relations Committee to reject the treaty. For a while, he boycotted CND meetings.[32] The situation that had prevailed under the League threatened to repeat itself.

This time, however, the UN Secretariat fought back. In 1962 it announced that 81 nations had approved the Single Convention. The treaty entered into force in spite of Anslinger's opposition in December 1964. The State Department, sensitive to the diplomatic damage if it remained on the sidelines, changed its mind. In May 1967 the United States deposited its ratification, giving its essential imprimatur to this long-withheld and hard-fought instrument.[33]

The Single Convention remains the foundation stone of the world's drug-control order today. Under its aegis, the Committee on Narcotic Drugs acts as the legislative organ of the international drug system. Presently consisting of the representatives of 53 members elected on a rotating basis, it monitors the international drug market and is empowered to make proposals with regard to control and enforcement. It is also responsible for the all-important drug scheduling. An International Narcotics Control Board (INCB) runs the quota system for raw materials and manufactured drugs alike – this replaces the PCOB and DSB originally created by the interwar Geneva Conventions. Finally, a large office for collecting and sharing data and information supports these institutions: having changed names and shapes several times, it is currently called the United Nations Office on Drugs and Crime (UNODC) and is based in Vienna. Two key treaties have since then supplemented the original convention: the 1971 Psychotropic Convention, whose main role has been to extend prohibition to a raft of stimulants and hallucinogenic drugs (amphetamines and LSD, for example), and the 1988 Vienna Convention against the Illicit Traffic in Narcotic Drugs, pledging participants to cooperate against and extradite traffickers, and to clamp down on drug-related money laundering. The system's architecture, nevertheless, remains that established in 1961.[34]

Anslinger may have been sulking, but the United Nations was triumphant. Drug use was down everywhere. Opium smoking, once ubiquitous in the Far East, was in its death throes. China had ceased cultivating the poppy. In India diversion was minimal. Another major source of illegal opium had been hit with a vigorous eradication programme: Iran. Turkey remained a problem, but after it acceded to the

Single Convention it was to be hoped that this last illicit source might also be jugulated. Other trafficking geographies, such as Mexico, remained minor. Peru and Bolivia, finally, had proclaimed themselves open to cooperation with the UN, and cocaine smuggling had well-nigh disappeared.

One country after another reported that their addict populations were vanishing. 'The representative of France mentioned that the addiction problem was not important in his country ... In Denmark, the observer of that country informed the Commission, the number of addicts had not changed substantially. This number, 600, included all persons who, over a period of years, have come to the attention of the narcotics division of the Sanitary Police.'[135] At a 1962 White House conference, President Kennedy celebrated the FBN's accomplishments: 'In recent years we have seen a dramatic reduction in the volume of illegal narcotics ... Under the forceful and purposeful leadership of Commissioner Anslinger the Bureau reduced this misery-producing traffic so effectively, that where 35 years ago addicts could purchase 100 per cent, or pure heroin, the sharply curtailed amount entering the United States today requires traffickers to dilute their product to the point that the addict obtains only 3 to 5 per cent heroin in the packet that he purchases.'[136]

The prohibitionists were victorious. Overcoming the last divisions among themselves, they had defeated their nemesis. Unbeknown to them, they were about to witness the biggest surge in drug use humanity had ever seen.

7

OVERREACH

A t nine in the evening on 12 September 1970, a dark figure crept along the roof of the San Luis Obispo men's prison in California. Over the edge of the roof hung a telephone wire. Low enough to be grabbed, it led to a pole just beyond the perimeter fence. The conditions were right. Earlier, the convict had ticked them off one by one: '*One*: moonless night. *Two*: fog. *Three*: a Saturday night; wait until the patrol car returns from CMC-East with the snack-bar trusties – around 8:30. *Four*: paint white trim on sneakers black. *Five*: write farewell note and leave in locker.'[1]

Still, it had not been easy getting onto that roof. Inside the cell-blocks, even though a football game was playing on TV, a few prisoners remained lurking, not all of them trustworthy. After several attempts, the man had trusted to his luck and slipped into the exercise yard. 'I opened the door, walked onto the prison yard, lit by floodlights. *No one walks the yard in dead of night. Not even the guards.* I stood in front of the tree, directly in front of a window. Inside, facing the window, was Metcalf braying at two cons. Climb the tree two feet in front of the snitch?' Eventually the fugitive snatched at a drooping branch, then another, and vaulted onto the roof.

> I pulled on the handball gloves and lay on the angled roof just under the cable. I hooked my ankles over the wire, reached up my hands, and pulled out head first.
>
> It was hard going. Every ten inches there was a loop that held the telephone cord below the cable. My legs bumped and tangled in the cord. Easy sweeping pulls were impossible. I had

to reach, then wrench ten inches. Hands out. Pulled body. Hauled legs. Ten inches. The cable bounced and swung. A strain to hang on. Weird wrestling motions, my body clinging to the swaying wire. Sweating. Heaving awkwardly. After fifty pulls – a pause. Horrid discovery. Completely exhausted. Lungs gasping. Arms drained. Body limp and weak. Can't go another foot. Only one-third across the wire. Hadn't even reached the road. Exhausted.

My hands couldn't hold the weight of my body. With desperate sexual writhing I embraced the cable with elbows and knees. Rested.

Eventually the climber resumed his crawl, twenty feet above the road. But a patrol car appeared beneath.

A sudden glare of light . . . My denim arms turned lavender in the headlight. The driver leaned over to crush his cigarette in the ashtray. The car passed under me and disappeared.

Now I tumbled into some kind of delirium. Arms crossed, I inched along the wire like a caterpillar. My mind fixed on reaching the fence, so I'd fall to freedom outside the perimeter. Still my hand kept getting tangled in the phone-wire loops. A compulsive wrench to free my hand set the cable bounding wildly. Mouth gasping, face bulging, glasses twisted, sweat dripping . . . From some inner reservoir came LIVE! SURVIVE!, a flow of energy and a curious erotic lightness . . . Hand over hand till fingers hit the pole. Hanging by my legs (I'd practiced it a thousand times in my bunk) I reached and grabbed the spike, dropped my body, wrapped legs around the splintery wood, slid down.

In one bound, he was free. The man staggered up the neighbouring hill, then along a dry creek bed. The cellblock windows shone through the penumbra. On the road ahead, car lights flashed by. Trees appeared. 'Not here. Over there: three trees joined at the roots. A long wait, cars roaring by. Two minutes. Five minutes. Ten minutes. Suppose they didn't come? Had they been busted? Accident? Fuck-up in plans? Could I hitchhike north on Highway I in prison garb? A car. Right blinker flashing. I ran from the shadows. The car door swung open.'

Timothy Leary was fleeing a sentence for marijuana possession, but he was a symbol for much more. A spokesman for drug freedom, the grand apostle of LSD, he was the leading icon of a new, psychedelic movement. As he escaped, a drug craze was likewise in runaway mode from the dead hand of prohibition. The counter-culture of which Leary was a model was not solely responsible for the explosion in recreational drugs that was rippling through the United States, Europe and beyond. At best the hippie movement was associated with the rise of a limited class of drugs. But this was not necessarily how it looked, and soon the movement's antics would be triggering everywhere the repressive reflexes of anti-narcotics authorities.

Leary's trajectory had been erratic even before he found himself in jail. Originally a failed West Point cadet, he had majored in psychology at the University of Alabama, then earned a doctorate at Berkeley. In the 1950s he had married, had two kids and settled in a suburban ranch in the Berkeley hills. He became research director at a psychiatric clinic in Oakland. But Leary was a serial womanizer. On the morning of his 35th birthday, his wife Marianne committed suicide. He resigned from his post and took his children on an extended trip to Europe. When he returned, he was offered a place in psychology research at Harvard. By then, he had already become interested in psychotropic drugs.[2]

Leary was at first attracted to psilocybin, the active compound found in so-called magic mushrooms. His Harvard research tested the substance's uses in experiments on various groups comprising local housewives, writers and fellow psychologists as well as students.[3] In 1961 he was introduced to the more powerful LSD, and became an instant convert. But already the psilocybin programme had been controversial. 'I began to realize that there were only a few subjects and many researchers, which meant that the researchers were taking more of the drug than anybody else,' commented a colleague.[4] In 1962 scandal broke. Leary was accused of having coerced students into taking the drug. The next year, he left Harvard, the more freely to explore LSD's virtues.[5]

LSD was yet another fallen medicine. The Swiss chemist Albert Hofmann first synthesized it in search of a migraine drug for the pharmaceutical company Sandoz in 1943. The substance was one of many he had been experimentally isolating from ergot, a fungus growing on diseased kernels of rye. Ergot is dangerous: it is mainly known as the cause of St Anthony's Fire, an awful disease that causes the fingers and toes to blacken and drop off. Ergotism may also have been responsible for the dancing plague of medieval Europe, a mania by which hundreds inexplicably began to dance until they expired from exhaustion.

Hofmann decided to try his new batch on himself: 'At 4:20 in the afternoon, with his assistants gathered around, he dissolved what he thought was a prudently infinitesimal amount of the drug – 250 millionths of a gram – in a glass of water and drank it down . . . At 4:50 he noted no effect. At 5:00 he recorded a growing dizziness, some visual disturbance, and a marked desire to laugh. Forty-two words later he stopped writing altogether and asked one of his lab assistants to call a doctor before accompanying him home.' Hofmann reached home without accident, but he discovered he had lost the ability to speak. 'When the doctor reached Hofmann's house, he found his patient to be physically sound, but mentally . . . mentally Hofmann was hovering near the ceiling, gazing down on what he thought was his dead body . . . He had been invaded by a demon. When his neighbour arrived with milk, a liquid Hofmann hoped would neutralize the poison, she was no longer gentle Mrs R., but a "malevolent insidious witch", a "lurid mask".'[6] What if his wife and children returned and found him a lunatic?

Hofmann had actually absorbed an enormous dose, five times what is nowadays typically taken for leisure. At low concentrations, Sandoz decided LSD had value in psychiatry and began marketing it under the trade name Delysid. It proposed two possible uses: to elicit the release by patients of repressed psychological material, and to help psychiatrists gain an insight into their world of ideas and sensations. The drug took off in the 1950s among the community of Los Angeles psychological analysts. Prominent subjects included Cary Grant and Anaïs Nin.[7] It was also taken up therapeutically in Britain at various institutions; in a nationwide programme, an estimated 1,500 patients were fed the drug to help them regress their 'inner being' into a child-like state which psychiatrists hoped would release repressed thoughts and feelings.[8]

By 1965 an estimated 30,000 to 40,000 patients around the world were receiving LSD therapeutically.[9] Already, however, therapists were becoming wary of the drug. The replication of early research find-ings was lacking, and many of the results were now said to have been faked. Psychotherapy, which was reaching peak popularity anyway, was finding LSD an unreliable prop. Nor was it entirely safe. For every 1,000 LSD ingestions, one study showed, there were 1.8 psychotic episodes and 1.2 attempted suicides.[10] At the UCLA medical centre, people came in with hallucinations, anxiety attacks and depressed thoughts. Another symptom was a 'psychotic defence reaction'. A doctor testified: 'We talked to one gentlemen who is not in the hospital because the "head culture" supports him. Here is a fellow who took LSD several times and became convinced he was an orange. He withdrew to his room and refused to leave the room for fear that if someone touched him he'd turn into orange juice.'[11]

The hallucinogen had meanwhile been put to even less orthodox uses. In a bizarre episode, the CIA tested LSD, among other substances, as a potential mind-control drug under a long-running project that eventually became known as MK Ultra. Potential means of deployment involved a disorientation bomb alongside more conventional use in interrogation or indoctrination in the style of the film *The Manchurian Candidate*. (In 1964 the British Royal Marines also experimented with LSD with a view to using it on enemy forces.[12]) The CIA began testing LSD in 1953. At first this took place via hospitals and universities, but the agency found these settings too constraining. In parallel, it converted one of its San Francisco safe houses into a field laboratory. Prostitutes would lure customers into the house, where they would be exposed to LSD or psilocybin, usually in a drink or through a spray. Reflecting what the organization thought a brothel should look like, the decor mixed swatches of African fabric with reproductions of Toulouse-Lautrec pictures, tables covered in black velvet and heavy red curtains.[13] Agents observed the punters' behaviour through two-way mirrors. In an even stranger twist, Anslinger himself vetted the programme, seconding two of his star Federal Bureau of Narcotics agents, George White and Charles Siragusa, to supervise the experiments.[14] 'It was fun, fun, fun,' testified White to an official inquiry some years later.[15]

If this went on behind closed doors, Leary's proselytizing could not have been more open. Leary attracted followers into the precincts of a 64-room mansion made available by wealthy well-wishers in the village of Millbrook, upstate New York. It was a 'strange mutation of Thoreau's Walden and a Tantric Buddhist temple', as a *Time* journalist described it. 'In the drafty hall of the main house, part of a grand piano sits on its side, its strings waiting to be plucked. The rooms are furnished with legless tables, bedless mattresses and mandalas on which the eye of the true believer is supposed to "lock" during drug-less exercises.[16] Millbrook, at once model community and pulpit, attracted both urbanites seeking new experiences on weekend retreats and more permanent residents. A visitor listed the activities as fol-lows: 'With some people on a macrobiotic diet, the family around the fireplace smoking pot after dinner . . . palm reading, the reading of Jung, Gurdjieff and Ouspensky, Tantric chants, bells continually ring-ing, wrestling matches, children, popcorn, motorbikes, racoon coats.'[17]

Before leaving Harvard, the psychiatrist had befriended enthusi-asts such as the Beat Generation poet Allen Ginsberg and the novelist Aldous Huxley, author of *Brave New World* as well as *The Island*, his final book, in which the protagonist explores a utopia made possible by a psychedelic drug.[18] Ginsberg had proposed: 'First we would ini-tiate and train influential Americans in consciousness expansion. They would help us generate a wave of public opinion to support massive research programs, licensing procedures, training centers in the intel-ligent use of drugs.'[19] Leary agreed: 'We calculated that the critical figure for blowing the mind of the American society would be four million LSD users and this would happen by 1969.'[20]

Leary aimed to do no less than transform man, to 'change and ele-vate the consciousness of every American within the next few years'.[21] The Millbrook gurus, or the International Foundation for Internal Freedom, as they called it, edited a *Psychedelic Review*. What America needed, this proposed, was a break from 'linear, typographical think-ing' in favour of a 'multilevel Oriental logic'.[22] It all seemed calculated to provoke, as when the 1967 issue explained how to use psychotropic drugs during sex: 'They may feel themselves to be gods, as indeed at that moment they are. Here again we see confirmation through psych-edelics of the ancient Tantric teachings that the lovers have to become gods in order to go beyond the normal spheres of awareness and reach transcendent union.'[23]

Notwithstanding their own dabbling in hallucinogenic drugs, by the mid-1960s the authorities became worried. The medical body was turning against the drug. The *New England Journal of Medicine* had called for an end to LSD research. Sandoz announced that it was terminating supplies. In a first blow, the State of California, the epicentre of the psychedelic revolution, banned the drug in 1966.[24]

Leary, for one, decided to double down. In the same year, with both Millbrook and himself at threat from a first marijuana conviction, he announced he was founding a League for Spiritual Discovery. Half religion and half social movement, this held its first 'public worship service', a play performed in New York's East Village with the title *Death of the Mind*. To the mystified audience, an acolyte of Leary lay on the stage writhing or danced behind a scrim, lost in the depths of an LSD trip. The guru sat front stage, dressed in white, intoning the words: 'Relax, float downstream, trust your divinity, trust your energy processes.'[25] LSD lab courses should become part of college curriculums, Leary explained to a congressional subcommittee. People should be licensed to use it, and training centres established.[26]

The drug had by then been making more adepts. Another proselytizing group was the Merry Pranksters, formed around the meteorically successful author of *One Flew Over the Cuckoo's Nest*, Ken Kesey. Kesey, who had been introduced to LSD as part of Stanford University experiments under CIA sponsorship, gave up literature in favour of tripping. Around him coalesced a loose community including Beat Generation writer Neal Cassady and on occasion Allen Ginsberg. Kesey hosted happenings at his La Honda cabin, where he had repainted the redwoods in Day-glo colours. The Pranksters ran LSD parties called Acid Tests, dressed in the same fluorescent tones. This morphed into a bus tour mixing practical jokes with a travelling show, but the Pranksters more effectively agitated at rock concerts, swinging in their Day-glo finery, pressing Acid Test invitations into the hands of revellers. Kesey eventually hired a band for the Tests, a group of Palo Alto rockers initially called the Warlocks but later renamed the Grateful Dead.[27]

As legal supplies dried up, bootleg manufacturers emerged. Augustus Owsley Stanley, a college dropout and former conman, briefly became America's largest LSD producer. Owsley, like the Pranksters and like Leary, fitted the image of the counter-culture hero. He gifted sound equipment to the Grateful Dead. He bankrolled *The Oracle*, the newspaper of the famous hippie community based in the Haight, San Francisco. He collected orientalia and rare perfumes, and he kept an owl to which he fed live mice. According to his housemates, Owsley received petitioners at his Los Angeles base 'like serfs pleading for a boon from the king . . . enthroned in the nude on a huge fur-covered chair, drying his hair with a hair-dryer'.[28] Owsley had first set up his lab in a bathroom near the Berkeley campus, later to move to Los Angeles, where he began buying chemicals in bulk. Making LSD was dangerous, but he managed to secure the equipment, including a hard-to-procure tableting machine.[29]

Such activities were not small-scale. Because LSD is effective in such small doses, the right tools and chemicals suffice to supply large populations from a single lab. Seeded, in turn, by Owsley was the Brotherhood of Eternal Love, bringing together a group of Laguna Beach surfers and the hippie community of Idyllwild, California.[30] The Brotherhood's primary focus was marijuana, but it saw LSD distribution as a charitable activity, and it sold it at cost. After Owsley exited the market, it became responsible, with distributors in California, Hawaii and Oregon, for up to half of all LSD sales in the United States.[31] The Brotherhood became associated, finally, with a UK-based ring known as the Microdot Gang. The Microdot Gang, improbably, had been put together by a couple of doctors – Richard Kemp and his partner Christine Bott – who had set up shop in a Welsh village named Blaencaron. Kemp, an exceptional chemist, became responsible for a prodigious output. He sold millions of tiny pills ('microdots', available in eight different colours) to a circle of individuals based in London, Birmingham, Lochhead and Swindon, who in turn sold them internationally. His operation briefly grew into the largest in the world.[32]

By then, LSD had begun to be banned everywhere: in the United States in 1970, in the UK in 1971, and under a new UN treaty named the Psychotropic Convention in the same year. In 1966, when California had been the first to clamp down on the drug, Owsley had gone underground. He was caught a few days before the Christmas of 1967 in the town of Orinda, tableting away: found in possession of 217 grams (7.6 oz) of LSD or about 750,000 doses by a group of narcotic agents, he tried to argue that they were for personal consumption.[33] The Brotherhood would last a while longer, but in 1972 forty of its members were arrested – the Drug Enforcement Administration would seize 14 million doses in LSD crystals from four of its underground labs.[34] Kemp's ring, last of all, was busted in a major police action dubbed Operation Julie in 1977.[35]

Leary's existence had long before turned precarious. While returning from a trip to Mexico in 1966, he was detained at the border in Laredo, Texas. The car was searched and a female friend was found to be carrying marijuana, for which Leary foolishly took responsibility. Leary fought the case: he announced that he had become a Hindu and that the drug was really a religious aid, pleading that prohibition was equal to religious discrimination. His argumentation did not go down well with the jury: this being a repeat offence, he was sentenced to thirty years in prison plus a large fine.[36] Leary appealed and got out on bail, gaining time. Three years later he would win a spectacular Supreme Court victory. But he faced continued trouble: the police raided his Millbrook retreat, and his drug infractions were mounting. In 1970 another jury convicted him anew, this time for good. He was remanded to prison for a long term of confinement.[37] It was from this sentence that he would abscond a few months later – the Brotherhood of Eternal Love having paid for and organized his escape.[38] The judge had called Leary 'a menace to this country'.[39]

Such exasperation as the magistrate's was unsurprising, and yet whether the psychedelic or the hippie movement were effectively responsible for the contemporary resurgence in drug use is open to question. No doubt Leary, his followers and his emulators did much to promote and even directly disseminate hallucinogens among a new generation. The hippies openly adopted marijuana, which they considered a gift to mankind and should be legal. It did not follow that all drugs, and the established narcotics in particular, owed them the same debt. There were identifiably two parallel booms: one centred on hallucinogens, closely associated with the new youth culture, and another centred on the more customary drugs of abuse (opiates, cocaine), spreading through a different population and owing its rise to different factors.

Before the rise of 1960s contestation, drugs had featured within the alternative cultural movements that were jazz music and Beat Generation literature. Jazz musicians known to have been on heroin included the trumpeters Fats Navarro and Chet Baker and the saxophonists Wardell Gray and Art Pepper, as well as Stan Getz and, later, Ray Charles. Miles Davis only recovered from addiction in the 1960s. When Billie Holiday lay dying in hospital, New York police raided her room, confiscating heroin among her other possessions and snapping photographs of her *in extremis* to make a scarecrow of her.[40]

The same phenomenon played out on the larger stages that were rock 'n' roll and the pop music of the 1960s and '70s. Heroin addicts who recovered included Keith Richards, Marianne Faithfull and Eric Clapton.[41] Brian Jones of the Rolling Stones died of an overdose in 1969, Jimi Hendrix and Janis Joplin in 1970, and Jim Morrison in 1971.

In 1978 it was the turn of Keith Moon of the Who and in 1979 Sid Vicious of the Sex Pistols. The music itself contained references to drugs. To list only songs from 1966 and 1967, the chorus to Bob Dylan's 'Rainy Day Woman' repeats an instruction to get stoned, The Beatles' 'Lucy in the Sky with Diamonds' formed the acronym LSD, and both 'With a Little Help from My Friends' and the Rolling Stones' 'Mother's Little Helper' were allusions to drugs. So was Frank Zappa's 'Help I'm a Rock', Procol Harum's 'A Whiter Shade of Pale' and, more explicitly, the Velvet Underground's 'Heroin'.[42]

Rebellious youth itself embraced marijuana and hallucinogens because they were forbidden and alternative. Students espoused behaviours that put them at odds with the mainstream, whether that was civil disobedience, growing their hair long or taking drugs.[43] The anthropologist Lewis Yablonsky immersed himself in hippie culture, visiting various 'tribes' or communes. Young men and women, his interviews confirmed, took LSD in search of a new morality: 'I could become an alcoholic. I could ruin my health. I could tear my body down. That's what my father did to himself. If you smoke grass then you're not addicted to it and it is a pleasure to smoke it . . . As for acid, I think that acid is very good for finding out a few things about yourself and the feelings around you.'[44] According to another witness: 'My first trip changed my world. I quit my job and I haven't worked since then. There were a few things that happened to me before my ego buster. I was more selfish and more money-minded and I was more society minded like where I was before. But now, it is kind of a love thing, a humanity thing.'[45] (A sceptic commented: 'Who paves the highway so that daddy's car can bring the hippie to sit there and drop out?'[46])

At the same time, what applied to hallucinogens did not necessarily apply to the other drugs. One intoxicant's rise did not automatically proceed alongside another's. Youthful contestation was a predominantly middle-class phenomenon, while heroin and cocaine use tapped into a different sociological base. Even the flaunting of drugs of all types by rock stars was no more than proof of their entry into mass culture.

The boldest Beat Generation statement on drugs is surely *Junky*, by William S. Burroughs. This takes the reader through a no-holds-barred account of the author's lifelong affair with heroin. But Burroughs's book hardly glamorizes junkies. 'What a crew!' the narrator writes. 'Mooches, fags, flour-flushers, stool pigeons, bums – unwilling to work, unable to steal, always short of money, always whining for credit. In the whole lot there was not one who wouldn't wilt and spill as soon as someone belted him in the mouth and said "Where did you get it?"'[47] (The term *junkie* or *junky* itself originated in 1920s New York, where addicts supported themselves by picking through rubbish dumps.[48]) Nor does Burroughs's work invite the reader to scenes of heroin-induced ecstasy. On the contrary, it is filled with dirt and nausea, and the best things it writes in the drug's favour is that: 'Junk takes everything and gives nothing but insurance against junk sickness.'[49] Of his experience, Burroughs writes: 'In forty-eight hours the backlog of morphine in my body ran out. The solution barely cut the sickness. I drank it all with two Nembutals and slept several hours. When I woke up, my clothes were soaked through with sweat. My eyes were watering and smarting. My whole body felt itchy and irritable. I twisted about on the bed, arching my back and stretching my arms and legs . . . I got up and changed my underwear.'[50]

While middle-class youths experimented with hallucinogens and marijuana, heroin spread among the urban poor. Opiate addiction was associated with 'poverty, urban problems, failure of integration', not the hippie's search for meaning.[51] Contemporaries differentiated between a hippie drug culture, mostly young and middle-class, and a 'negro' drug culture rooted in rebellion against discrimination and lack of opportunity.[52] This contained much racial stereotyping: opiate injecting was equally prevalent among white populations. Yet the point stood that it was disadvantage, not hippie contestation, that fed heroin use.

The same is observed of heroin's spread in other developed countries than the USA. Surveys show that when heroin became more prevalent in Germany it was a working-class phenomenon, with only 23 per cent of users having passed end-of-school exams.[53] In France, when it began to take off, the drug was adopted overwhelmingly by the unemployed.[54] In the UK, likewise, when opiate use began to achieve significant numbers, it was typically men with no or minimal educational achievements who took it, often with a history of delinquency. The vast majority were without jobs.[55]

But that the surge in drugs was not a counter-culture phenomenon is irrefutably confirmed by its chronology. While marijuana and the hallucinogens began to stir in the 1960s, the generalized rise, including heroin and cocaine, began in the 1970s. Illicit drug use as a whole, boosted by the crack epidemic, only reached scale in the 1980s and '90s.

American marijuana statistics are not uniformly available, and the data remain for this period fragmentary, but the drug's uptake can be approached through arrest numbers. Marijuana-related arrests stood at 18,815 in 1965, within their historical ballpark. By 1969 they had multiplied sixfold to number 118,682. A continuous rise was seen thereafter, up to 416,000 in 1975.[56] In the 1950s marijuana had remained an obscure drug few people dared try. By the end of the 1970s the number of Americans smoking it at least once a year had reached the once-unimaginable total of 29.8 million, or 13.3 per cent of the population.[57] The total number declined gently thereafter, to 18.7 million by 1998.[58]

For the other two main illicit drugs, however – heroin and cocaine – the rise clearly took place in the 1970s and '80s. As of 1972, 2.2 per cent of American adults reported having tried cocaine once in their lives: in 1982 this was 26.5 per cent.[59] The peak for cocaine use, including crack, occurred in 1985.[60] Immediately after the Second World War the number of heroin users had been around 50,000. In the late 1960s the total stood at about 100,000.[61] As of 1979 the health services thought there were 427,000 heroin users in the United States. The pre-2000 peak would be reached only in 1997, at 597,000.[62]

The same picture emerges even more markedly elsewhere. In the UK, the Home Office estimated that there were around 3,000 heroin or morphine addicts as of the late 1960s. For cocaine this was a few hundred.[63] By the mid-1980s the country would have an estimated 100,000+ heroin users.[64] Even marijuana use did not pick up in earnest until after 1970. Police seizures of cannabis, at 126 kilograms in 1960, had only risen to 192 kilograms by 1967.[65] By contrast, the median for the 1970s was 6,211 kilograms, and in 1982 UK cannabis seizures totalled 17,440 kilograms.[66] In West Germany, opiate addict numbers held roughly constant at around 4,000 between the mid-1950s and 1970, when they suddenly began to rise. By 1976 the total stood at 40,000.[67] According to one estimate, by the beginning of the 1990s Germany had 100,000 heroin users as well as 30,000–40,000 cocaine users.[68]

Iran offers an example outside the developed world. Though the statistics were imprecise, the mid-1950s eradication campaign caused a steep fall in opium-user numbers, from over a million to the 200,000–300,000 area in 1960. In 1969 the government felt able to relax its hold, and it allowed poppy cultivation to resume. Opiate addicts were asked to register and were steered towards treatment – within two years, 84,000 had done so.[69] When it replaced the shah in 1979, by contrast, the Islamic Republic made a ham-fisted effort to suppress drugs altogether. Police raided areas where addicts congregated and razed entire settlements to the ground. In some years, the regime executed as many as five hundred traffickers, sometimes leaving a body hanging from the gallows for several days to make an example. By the late 1990s, regardless, opiate user numbers had climbed back over 1 million, many of whom now used the far stronger products that are morphine and heroin.[70]

Worldwide, illicit drug trafficking took off in the 1970s and accelerated again in the 1980s and '90s. Globally, seizures of refined opiates (heroin and morphine) stood at a median of 274 kilograms per annum in the 1950s, 953 kilograms in the 1960s, 2,485 kilograms in the 1970s, 10,389 kilograms in the 1980s and 41,434 kilograms in the 1990s. (See Appendix III for tables.) The percentage rate of increase, from the 1960s onward, was approximately constant. But in absolute terms the largest rise actually took place in the 1990s: 31,045 kilograms, itself a multiple of the 1960s and 1970s numbers.

Using seizures as a proxy for trafficking involves certain methodological problems, since increased seizures can also reflect more effective policing. Generally, however, UNODC assumes that approximately 10 per cent of trafficked heroin was seized in the 1980s and 12 per cent in the 1990s. This was twice to three times the probable rate (4 to 5 per cent) for the 1950s. For cocaine, UNODC believes that police effectiveness achieved even higher levels.[71] Yet even allowing for such adjustments, the data point to massive increases in drug trafficking, and show that they occurred in the 1970s, '80s and '90s, with the largest absolute rise in that last decade. Refined opiate seizures increased 150-fold between the 1950s and the 1990s: even if one assumes that anti-narcotic effectiveness tripled, trafficking still increased fiftyfold. For cocaine, the rise was even more staggering: median seizures stood at 10 kilograms in the 1950s, 69 kilograms in the 1960s, 1,933 kilograms in the 1970s, 41,543 kilograms in the 1980s and 320,100 kilograms in the 1990s. Even allowing for considerable improvement in anti-narcotics inception rates, this was a more than thousandfold rise.[72]

What accounts, then, for this flood? If not Leary and his ilk, who or what was at fault for having prompted the tsunami? A hint is given by the arrival on the scene of two more major drug categories: amphetamines and tranquilizers.

Amphetamines, among which are methamphetamines, are chemical stimulants or 'uppers', much like cocaine. Stimulants arouse the brain and nervous system, producing wakefulness, energy and heightened awareness, as well as increased heart rate and blood pressure. They are versatile substances. Amphetamines continue to be used as pharmaceutical products (to treat attention deficit disorder, for example). As drugs of abuse, they are sometimes known as 'speed', while methamphetamine has been known as 'crank' (for its use by motorcycle gangs), 'ice', 'glass', 'crystal meth' and, in Asia, 'yaba' ('crazy drug' in Thai). Meth forms the base for yet another compound: MDMA, or Ecstasy.[73]

The Japanese pharmacologist Nagai Nagayoshi was the first to synthesize methamphetamine, in the late nineteenth century. A Romanian chemist named Lazar Edeleanu, working in Berlin, described the production of amphetamine around the same time.[74] The first commercial application, however, was developed in the United States in 1929 by a chemist named Gordon Alles. Alles, who worked for a Los Angeles laboratory specializing in allergies, was in search of an asthma drug.[75] Much like Albert Hofmann with LSD, he first tried the drug on himself. Early experiments showed that the compound might make a passable decongestant but that it was a poor asthma remedy. It was, however, a potent central nervous system stimulant, triggering a 'feeling of well-being', 'exhilaration' and 'palpitation'.[76]

Alles patented his drug in 1932. Soon thereafter, he and his invention moved to the larger pharmaceutical firm Smith, Kline, & French (SKF). The company sold a spray containing small amounts of the drug for use as a decongestant: the Benzedrine inhaler. From 1937 SKF put Benzedrine on sale in a more concentrated pill form. As such, it was offered as a remedy for narcolepsy, Parkinson's disease and mood elevation in depression. Advertisements came out in the major medical journals. In 1939 Benzedrine brought in sales of $330,000.[77]

A popular myth is that the German army fought the Second World War on an amphetamine high. In 1938 the Temmler pharmaceutical company had introduced a methamphetamine product named Pervitin to the European market. Pervitin was listed for psychiatric use, but the military authorities soon discovered that soldiers were taking it and, based on tests that showed marginal improvements in mental tasks, they authorized it for requisitioning by army doctors. At the height of the French campaign, in April–June 1940, the Wehrmacht issued 35 million pills each month to its soldiers. This sounds like a large number only until it is remembered that the German Army comprised several million men. At six pills per day, this could sustain a high among no more than eight or so army divisions out of a total of 150, without even counting the air force and navy. The military soon became worried, anyway: amphetamines depleted soldiers' energy stores, and it made pilots inattentive. By the end of the year distribution had dropped to 1 million tablets a month. It would fall yet further in 1941 and 1942 as Germany placed methamphetamine, along with amphetamine, under strict regulation.[78]

This did not stop rumours from reaching the British War Office of a drug that made German pilots invulnerable. The British Army and Royal Navy, and the U.S. Army and Marines, possibly distributed more amphetamine pills to their men than the Germans gave theirs. In 1942 Bomber Command decided to supply two half-dose pills to pilots per tour of duty, one to be taken at the beginning and one after the bombing run. The British Army performed its own studies in parallel. Field tests by Field Marshall Montgomery in Egypt, in particular, convinced him of amphetamine's usefulness in raising soldiers' energy levels, and he ordered them distributed to his troops. In total, the British military purchased 72 million Benzedrine tablets from SKF throughout the war. The U.S. Army also adopted the tablet and, from 1943, it was included in combat first-aid kits, with instructions that one half-dose Benzedrine tablet should be taken every six hours for 'extreme' mental fatigue, or two tablets for physical fatigue, up to three times running. The quantities distributed by the American military were never disclosed.[79]

The drug was separately sold in a fourth market: Japan. After the Second World War, this would provide the occasion for a rare, decisive victory in the long war on drugs. Twenty companies manufactured methamphetamine in 1940s Japan, where it was known as Hiropon, the trademark of the Dai-Nippon Seiyaku company. The Japanese authorities, learning of its use by the German military, had distributed Hiropon widely during the war, both to soldiers and to civilian workers. A large number of people became dependent after 1945, whether from having taken the drug in wartime or, more often, because it helped them deal with the harsh conditions of reconstruction. In 1948–9 the Ministry of Health, convinced it faced an epidemic, tightened regulations on distribution. It asked pharmaceutical companies to stop producing the drug. In 1951 the parliament passed legislation criminalizing the unauthorized manufacture, distribution and possession of Hiropon, complete with prison penalties.[80] But makeshift dealers had already learnt how to make it. Law enforcement found methamphetamine labs hidden in factories making paint, tuberculosis remedies, ice cream, window casings, cold perm solution, cosmetics and hair dye. Many labs were mom-and-pop affairs: in May 1953 police searched the Tokyo residence of 46-year-old Tanaka Seiji and his wife. Finding about 10,000 doses plus paraphernalia, they took the couple into custody. The spouses, an investigation revealed, had been making upwards of 1,500 doses of Hiropon per day.[81] A large-scale survey conducted a year later by the Ministry of Welfare found that 550,000 Japanese citizens had become regular methamphetamine users, and that 2 million had tried the drug at least once.[82]

The government responded with a crackdown involving thousands of police in addition to the Narcotics Section. In one all-night investigation, in 1954 in Osaka, 2,000 officers searched nearly eight hundred buildings in various neighbourhoods, netting over three hundred people. The number of suspects taken in that year reached 54,104, or 96 per cent of all drug crime. Almost all convicted offenders received penal sentences, and within the first five years of the law's passage 9,000 violators had served time.[83] Alongside, the government issued anti-Hiropon pamphlets, leaflets and posters, and it backed a press campaign featuring lurid portaits of drug users, printed interviews, cautionary tales by doctors and so on. The authorities, finally, enlisted volunteers to provide counselling to users or help them find employment, and they subsidized medical institutions for treating withdrawal, with mandatory institutionalization. The crackdown worked. By 1956 Hiropon had passed its peak. By 1958 the number of violators had fallen below 1,000. The epidemic was never more than a flash in the pan.[84]

While this was going on, amphetamines were enjoying their pharmaceutical heyday in the USA and Europe. After the Second World War, SKF renewed its Benzedrine marketing push, promoting it as a remedy for psychiatric disorders. An advertisement featured 'a big blue "b" together with photos of an elderly man changing from sad to smiling, illustrating how the drug helps "when persistent depression settles upon the aged patient'".[85] To fight patent expiry, the company released a lookalike: Dexedrine, for use as a weight-loss pill. In 1950 it released Dexamyl, another stimulant and antidepressant. All three pills were heart-shaped: Dexamyl in blue, Dexedrine in yellow, Benzedrine in pink.[86] The three products and their imitators became blockbusters in the USA and the UK. In 1963 American amphetamine sales reached $48 million.[87] In the UK in the same year, amphetamines accounted for 3 per cent of all prescriptions.[88]

From 1940 SKF had begun labelling Benzedrine as prescription-only, and in 1951 the FDA introduced new rules restricting all stimulants to a prescription basis.[89] A grey market developed, whether from recycled Benzedrine inhalers, from enthusiastic prescribing by doctors or, as the 1960s dawned, through diversion from pharmaceutical inventory. A young man explained: 'A typical doctor's appointment would run as follows. I'd fabricate a story, usually to the effect that my girlfriend had moved in with my best male friend on the same day that my brother had committed suicide and/or my mother and/or father either had been admitted to a mental hospital or had died in epilepsy. The doctor would listen, express sympathy, sorrow, etc. (how many of these doctors *could* have believed such nonsense!) . . . Then, in 98 percent of the interviews, he would write a prescription for thirty to one hundred Eskatrols.'[90] Hiropon had not been alone. Amphetamines were on their way to becoming a major black-market drug.

The success of amphetamines in turn points to the fundamental reasons for the groundswell in drug use that began in the 1960s and continues to this day. They had nothing to do with hippies, to whom amphetamines were actually inimical. Allen Ginsberg warned in 1965: 'Speed is anti-social, paranoid making, it's a drag, bad for your body, bad for your mind, generally speaking, in the long run uncreative and it's a plague in the whole dope industry. All the nice gentle dope fiends are getting screwed up by the real horror monster Frankenstein Speedfreaks who are going around stealing and bad mouthing everybody.' Buttons labelled 'speed kills' became common in the San Francisco communes.[91]

Benzedrine may have made progress among jazzmen and the Beat Generation.[92] Amphetamine pills may feature in Burroughs's *Junkie*, but this reflected no more than their general integration into pop culture. The rise of speed was a separate phenomenon from the counter-culture. Perhaps Mick Jagger and the Beatles took amphetamines, but so did the film producer Cecil B. DeMille, the composer Leonard Bernstein, the playwright Tennessee Williams and the movie star Judy Garland. So also, less publicly, did the politicians Anthony Eden and John F. Kennedy.[93]

Amphetamines, far from helping their adherents drop out of conventional society and escape its stifling norms, assisted them in performing better within it and sustaining its competitive pressures. A student who took amphetamines confessed: 'Speed not only made getting [exams] done much easier; it also made subjects that were dry and boring under any other conditions seem very interesting and important.'[94] Likewise, according to another: 'Speed makes the most routine task, function, or conversation take on a different and more tolerable light.'[95] Alternatively, amphetamine use, for example in the variant known as Ecstasy, could be purely hedonistic. Drug users themselves betrayed, in their stated motivations, a simple thirst for fun.[96] Some devotees even reported that they could be 'the most powerful aphrodisiacs known', describing their effect as 'orgasm over your whole body'.[97]

Disposable incomes were rising. Advertising had become ubiquitous. Mass consumption made materialistic pursuits worthy. A sometimes frantic consumerism took hold in the post-war years, social theorists noted, fed at once by the economic boom and fears of a return to the Depression. This new consumerism in turn brought with it what the French sociologist Jean Baudrillard has called a materialistic, new, 'fun morality'.[98] Vladimir Kusevic, a director of the UN's Division of Narcotic Drugs, noted that 'certain psychotropic substances have become "consumer goods" in certain Western countries, resulting in large numbers of dependent persons.'[99] If this sounds too general as an explanation, part of the challenge is to recognize that drugs differed and the motivations varied just as widely for taking them: from the rave-goer popping Ecstasy to the New Age experimenter sampling LSD, from the student preparing for exams with amphetamines to the ghetto-dweller injecting heroin or smoking crack out of enforced idleness. Kusevic elaborated:

> During the last two decades . . . the development of drug abuse has been quite different. In countries where it was unknown, it has appeared; in countries where it touched only the fringe of society, it is now well settled – even in well-to-do

groups and among people to whom it would have been abhorrent earlier. The reasons for this new phenomenon are not the same everywhere because of differences in social economic and cultural structures in different countries. There is no doubt that the condition of life created by the huge development of technology and of the modern 'consumer society' have laid the ground for this new development.[100]

Amphetamines originally owed their success to promotion by the pharmaceutical industry. Because SKF held the patent on amphetamine, or Benzedrine, other firms concentrated at first on the methamphetamine market. Burroughs Wellcome entered the market in 1944 with Methedrine, a product distributed in injectable and pill form. Abbott Laboratories released a methamphetamine product under the trade name Desoxyn shortly thereafter. Other branded products launched in the decades following the Second World War included Clark-O-Tabs Modified, Gerilets Filmtab, Oesoxyn, Meditussin, Methampex, Amerital, Span-RD, Amphaplex, Obetrol . . .[101] An FDA's manufacturer's survey dated 1962 arrived at an annual output of 8 billion standard 10 milligram tablets of amphetamines.[102]

The background was one of emerging medical wonders, including antibiotics, vaccines for diseases such as polio, and the birth control pill. The mental-health market itself was exploding. By the early 1960s some 30 million Americans, or 15 per cent of the population, were on prescription drugs for psychiatric complaints.[103] Pharmaceutical advertising was tapping into a ready seam: a newly born culture of medicating for happiness. There was a solution to everything, and it was commercially available. The notion applied to mental health just as it did in other walks of life.

Nowhere was this more palpable than in the success of yet another category of drugs known as the minor tranquilizers. The first of these sedatives, eventually branded under the name Miltown, was synthesized by a Czech researcher named Frank Berger who had been hired by British Drug House Ltd to research antibiotics. Berger later moved to the American patent medicine firm Carter Products, taking his invention with him. Carter launched Miltown in 1955. Sales immediately leapt. The pill and its emulators promptly achieved a turnover in excess of $100 million.[104] Within a few years, American physicians were prescribing Miltown and its chemically equivalent competitor

Equanil 50 million times annually. Their successor, Valium, would reach an even higher peak in the 1970s, when it became the single most prescribed branded medicine in the world.[105]

These drugs, mild muscle relaxants, were prescribed to ease tension or anxiety. Taken as antidepressants, they helped elevate mood, reduce suicidal impulses and counteract a range of other depressive symptoms. In the 1980s they would be replaced by Prozac, the next wonder drug in the field. Prozac was likewise an overnight marketing success, one of whose principal actors proclaimed that medicine had finally arrived at the stage of 'cosmetic psychopharmacology', a stage in which identities could be 'sculpted' in any desired way.[106] Commercialized medicine had come of age. As Aldous Huxley had once predicted, happiness could be bought in pill form. Perhaps the public could be forgiven for thinking that this applied to substances other than those available from the doctor.

Two clinical trials published in the *Journal of the American Medical Association* in 1955 had initially lauded Miltown as dramatically effective at relieving tension, anxiety and fear states among patients, with no toxicity or risk of addiction.[107] The drug's golden age, though, did not last long. Whether the minor tranquilizers were addictive remained unclear. They induced no quick euphoria. Withdrawal could trigger such symptoms as vomiting, seizures, insomnia and temporary psychosis, but only from much higher doses than typically prescribed. Patients, however, sometimes increased their doses, showing signs of intoxication. When taken off the pills, they complained of feeling nervous and having 'the jitters'.[108] Still more serious, double-blind, placebo-controlled trials coming out in the late 1950s questioned Miltown's very effectiveness. Sales began to fall, and by 1964 Miltown was removed from the pharmacopoeia.[109]

Amphetamines were likewise on borrowed time. By 1960 a number of critical academic appraisals had appeared, including British studies finding strong evidence of a hard core of heavy and constant users. Data from a Newcastle survey of family doctors found that up to a quarter of the mostly middle-aged patients who took amphetamines were 'habituated'.[110] There were dark side effects. Amphetamine users could be asocial, reacting impulsively and violently to perceived insults or threats. The drugs, it was discovered, could trigger paranoid schizophrenia. A 49-year-old lawyer had 'turned up in a Massachusetts mental facility . . . insisting that six cars regularly trailed him, that his son (who was serving in the military) communicated with him from an invisible helicopter overhead, and that the government was spying on him and testing his loyalty for a top-secret mission.' In another case, a 32-year-old man had arrived in a Kansas City hospital 'complaining that his thoughts were being controlled telepathically and that he had been overhearing several of his acquaintances plotting against him'.[111]

Prescriptions began to plateau. The effect, however, was not that amphetamine use fell, but that it increasingly drifted into illicit use. What the doctors became hesitant to prescribe, the customers found a way to appropriate. In 1966 it was found that Abbott Laboratories had sold the equivalent of 2 million doses in powder form to an unlicensed Long Island dealer. In 1969 the owner of a large pharmacy in Kentucky was arrested for having sold large amounts of amphetamine to black-market pushers in neighbouring states. In 1970 a Tennessee jury indicted an employee of the pharmaceutical company Massengill on charges of stealing 380,000 tablets.[112] Eventually, as diversion from licit sources dried up, dealers would learn to make the product on their own. By then, authorities around the world had taken action.

It mattered hugely whether the resurgence in narcotics use was the work of a few agitators and dropouts, or whether it reflected deep-seated societal trends. If the multi-decade explosion in the making was the consequence of fundamental cultural change, itself buttressed by economic shifts, this called for a rethink or at least a considered response. If it was a matter of a few bad eggs, the system could deal with them. The same trap was being laid that had ensnared the Qing. Not completely unjustly, the nineteenth-century Chinese, too, had thought that they merely faced a few supply-side culprits. As the 1960s dawned the anti-narcotics authorities, national and supra-national, were unprepared. Their belief was that they had just slain the dragon and, with the Single Convention, written its epitaph. The spectacle of Timothy Leary preaching the psychedelic revolution was unwelcome.

Nothing spoke louder of the anti-narcotics order and its prevailing concerns than its differing responses to hallucinogens on the one hand and amphetamines on the other. The Commission on Narcotic Drugs dithered on amphetamines for the better part of two decades. It clamped down on LSD almost reflexively. The same may be said, with only a few exceptions, of national authorities. The insidious danger made benign-looking by the pharmaceutical industry was only faced off reluctantly. Preaching by the high priests of the hallucinogenic experience was met promptly and with firmness.

The CND's first significant discussion of amphetamines occurred in the session of 1955. The Greek representative, named Panopoulos, suddenly proposed listing them among the drugs covered by the Single Convention, which was in preparation. Panopoulos 'pointed to the dangers of amphetamines, which contained pervitin, a narcotic substance covered by the 1931 Convention'.[113] (This was of course doubly untrue, and the chairman corrected him.) 'In Greece several deaths had been attributed to the use of cures for obesity and other pharmaceutical preparations with a benzedrine base, sold without restriction in that country as in several others. During the final months before examinations many students were buying preparations with a pervitin base as stimulants, which was very dangerous,' he added with more verisimilitude.

Anslinger objected, opining that controls should be restricted to the national level. 'It was not certain that such products should be considered real narcotic drugs. The commission might ask WHO for its views in the matter.' He was supported by the British delegate: 'While cases of misuse were rare in his country, they were serious and alarming when they did occur. He could therefore readily understand the Greek Government's concern. However, he agreed with the United States representative that the problem should be solved at the national level.' The Canadian delegate likewise concurred.[114] Why rock the boat and upset the pharmaceutical firms? The World Health Organization (WHO) observer who was present did not believe that amphetamines were addictive. They were prescription-only products in a number of countries, and this was enough security against abuse.[115] (Even Panopoulos's game was soon given away: 'Mr Ozkol (Turkey) felt that in view of the fact that ... national controls had failed to eliminate entirely the abuse mentioned by the Greek representative, the Commission should plan on international controls, at least in principle.'[116] The Yugoslav member contributed his support. Greece, Turkey and Yugoslavia were all Opium Protocol holdouts. Amphetamines offered useful diversionary value.)

The subject was not meaningfully raised again until 1965. In that session: 'The representative of Canada drew attention to the growing abuse – particularly among young people – of substances [including amphetamines] which ... had effects that were harmful to the individual and to society itself.'[117] The evidence was that these drugs were being consumed outside medical channels, including by 'young persons' who were 'attracted to certain of these substances on account of their allegedly stimulating and thrilling effects'. Another concern was road safety. Various countries expressed worries, including Switzerland and Sweden, and pharmaceutical companies were criticized for their aggressive marketing. Altogether, nevertheless, the CND remained hesitant and no action was taken.[118]

A WHO expert committee advised that amphetamines be listed under the Single Convention, or placed under measures tantamount to listing, in the same year.[119] Amphetamines were only recommended for scheduling after another four years, in 1969. Even this came at the emergency request of the Swedish delegate, who complained that 'high-dose intravenous abuse of these substances [produced] an intense feeling of euphoria and a form of hyperactivity which was almost maniac. Sexual desire and potency were greatly increased and promiscuous behaviours among addicts were reported. They also become aggressive, took to roaming the streets, driving dangerously and causing accidents, even attacking peaceful pedestrians, and disturbing the peace in general.'[120] The CND put an end to prevarication – but only after time had run out and enough states complained.

By contrast, the moment LSD came under its attention, the commission moved to have it banned. In 1966 the American delegate mentioned the appearance of home-made synthetic drugs, notably certain opiates and LSD.[121] A subcommittee had been formed jointly to study amphetamines, barbiturates (earlier versions of the tranquilizers) and LSD. While deliberations continued on amphetamines and barbiturates, 'The Commission noted the profound concern with which the Committee had viewed the abuse of LSD and substances producing similar effects. Several representatives provided information on the abuse of such drugs in their countries and on legislation which had been enacted to deal with that problem.'[122] This sufficed. No need to consult the WHO or to procrastinate any further. The CND decided: '*Recognizing* the grave danger of this abuse to health and safety in respect to both the individual and to society, [it] *Requests* Governments to take immediate action to control strictly the import, export and production of LSD and substances producing similar ill effects either immediately or readily by conversion, and to place the distribution of these substances under the supervision of competent authorities, [and] *Recommends* that the use of these substances be restricted to scientific research and medical purposes and that their administration be only under very close and continuous medical supervision.'[123] LSD would join the list of the prohibited drugs as a Schedule I drug, alongside heroin, while amphetamines only made it to Schedule II.[124]

Social fears, not health concerns, called the tune. This is confirmed by the medical rationale that was developed to underpin the new ban. The CND/WHO discussions raised two separate yet fundamental issues. The first was whether the new substances, ultimately grouped together under the label 'psychotropic drugs', could simply be added to the Single Convention schedules. The legal experts decided they could not – and as a result a new conference was called, leading to the adoption of a 1971 Convention on Psychotropic Substances. The second question was how to characterize these drugs as addictive substances. Addiction was what singled out prohibited drugs. (A key preamble to the Single Convention reads: '*Recognizing* that addiction to narcotic drugs constitutes a serious evil for the individual and is fraught with social and economic danger to mankind . . .'.[125]) To qualify as a narcotic, a substance had to lure its users into taking ever greater quantities of it and entrap them through painful withdrawal effects. Would this line of argumentation hold with amphetamines, LSD and the other psychotropics?

Opiates functioned as the original model for medically defined addiction. Cocaine, albeit based on questionable data, had been placed alongside them because it approximately conformed to this model. Opiate addiction depends on psychological as well as physical factors, and patterns of opiate consumption often fall short of compulsive use. Yet for heroin, at least, the effects are visible enough, sometimes even spectacular. A doctor provides this classic account of heroin withdrawal:

> Eight to twelve hours after the last dose the addict begins to grow uneasy. A sense of weakness overcomes him, he yawns, shivers and sweats all at the same time while a watery discharge begins to trickle from the eyes and inside the nose which he compares to 'hot water running up in the mouth'. [Later] the yawning may become so violent that it can dislocate the jaw, watery mucus pours from the nose, tears from the eyes. The

pupils are widely dilated, the hair stands up and the skin itself is cold and shows that typical goose flesh which in the parlance of addicts is the original 'cold turkey'.

Now, to add further to the addict's miseries, his bowels begin to act with fantastic violence: great waves of contractions pass over the stomach, causing explosive vomiting, the vomit being frequently blood-stained. So extreme are the intestinal contractions that the surface of the abdomen appears corrugated and knotted, as if a tangle of snakes were fighting beneath the skin . . . As many as sixty large watery stools may be passed in twenty-four hours . . . In a desperate effort to gain comfort from the chills that rack his body he covers himself with every blanket he can find. His whole body is shaken by twitchings and his feet kick involuntarily.

Throughout this period the addict obtains neither sleep nor rest . . . The profuse sweating keeps bedding and mattress soaked. Filthy, unshaven, dishevelled, befouled with his own vomit and faeces, the addict at this stage presents an almost subhuman appearance.[126]

Amphetamines offer parallels with cocaine in that, as stimulants, they induce hyperactivity, which is often followed by sleep disturbance. Heavy long-term users can become exposed to 'amphetamine psychosis'. Amphetamine withdrawal can also include 'visual and tactile hallucinations of worms crawling over [the] body and small animals everywhere'.[127] Amphetamines, however, involve no tolerance mechanism. Any increase is psychological, driven by the desire for more, not bodily adaptation.[128] The drug, besides, rarely induces overdosing. Even methamphetamine seldom kills, except through the deleterious effects of long-term use. Among drug-induced hospital emergencies in the USA in 2010, for example, 30 per cent were cocaine-related whereas less than 7 per cent were for methamphetamine, even though its user population was larger.[129] As to LSD, despite its Schedule 1 classification, it is less dangerous by another degree. The drug involves some measure of tolerance, but this tends to dissipate rapidly. It creates no physical withdrawal effects. Nor do LSD users risk overdosing, though they might believe they can fly and jump out of a window.[130] The World Health Organization faced the problem of reconciling this increasingly diverse set with medical theory.

It also needed, incidentally, to justify marijuana's continuing prohibition. Doing so had been easy while, as in the 1940s and '50s, barely anyone knew anything about this supposedly deadly drug; by the 1960s the folklore around the madness-inducing weed that caused people to kill faced exposure. The WHO was neither prepared nor able to pretend that cannabis was addictive. In an appraisal, it wrote: 'Typically, the abuse of cannabis is periodic but, even during long and continuous administration, no evidence of the development of physical dependence can be detected. There is, in consequence, no characteristic abstinence syndrome when use of the drug is discontinued. Whether administration of the drug is periodic or continuous, tolerance to its subjective and psychomotor effects has not been demonstrated.'[131]

The addiction model, originally built around opiates, did not fit the ramshackle group of substances now being brought under regulation. One solution might have been to question the system that had been established, ask what drugs belonged in it and how, and regulate accordingly. Instead, the WHO decided to reformulate what it meant by addiction.

As of the 1950s both the WHO and the CND had remained happy to use addiction as the key by which to identify narcotics. 'Addiction-producing drugs were detrimental both to the individual and to society, while habit-forming drugs harmed only the individual, and the difference between the two classes had become widely recognized,' explained the CND.[132] From the 1960s, the organization began to retire the term in favour of a new and vaguer yardstick labelled dependence.[133] A WHO expert committee duly reported to the CND: 'In the Expert Committee's opinion, the long-felt need for adapting the present terms "drug addiction" and "drug habituation" to the present state of scientific knowledge and actual practice had now become imperative . . . Dependence, physical or psychic in nature or both, being a feature in common, the Expert Committee recommended that the single term "drug dependence" should be substituted for the terms "drug addiction" and "drug habituation" with the addition of a reference to the type of drug (such as morphine-, barbiturate-, cocaine-, amphetamine-, cannabis-type) on which dependence developed as a consequence of repeated administration.'[134]

Medicine was made to fit the legal framework. Addiction, now relabelled dependence, was and remains a legal, not a scientific, category. Drug prohibition had not been constructed from a scientific consensus, and even less so was it expanded, in the 1960s, based on more precise science. It was the other way around: the scientific consensus was made to fit the mission creep of expanding prohibition.

The WHO itself confessed that its new definition was designed to fit around the enlarged group of the prohibited drugs: 'Frequent misinterpretation of the term "addiction" and its confusion with "habituation", and the increasing variety of substances entering into the considerations of the international narcotics control organs, had led to several attempts to find a general term applicable to abuses of different types of drugs.' It even admitted that the underlying rationale resided in social control, and that it was intoxication and its negative social effects it wished to target. 'The WHO representative recalled, in this connexion, the Expert Committee's view expressed previously, that the primary criterion for the establishment and degree of control was the risk to the community resulting from the drug's liability to be abused.'[135]

'Dependence' was a more pliable term than 'addiction'. It could also mean, as the WHO experts explained, habituation. Scratch the surface, and it was a return to the old label 'habit', with added stigma and the stamp of medical authority. What did it mean with regard to marijuana? According to the WHO: 'Its characteristics are: (a) Moderate to strong psychic dependence on account of the desired subjective effects. (b) Absence of physical dependence, so that there is no characteristic abstinence syndrome when the drug is discontinued. (c) Little tendency to increase the dose and no evidence of tolerance.'[136] What this boiled down to was that the user desired the drug. But do human beings not desire many things? The existing list – opiates, cocaine, cannabis – was disparate enough already. Rather than question it as new challenges arose, the prohibitionists chose to blur the lines yet further. It was a classic case of overreach.

On 14 July 1969, a few months after being elected, President Nixon invited the press to the White House to announce a 'national drive on narcotics use'.[137] As a prominent feature, penalties would be raised on LSD. The famous music festival remained one month away, but Nixon's recollections retrospectively reveal his state of mind: 'To erase the grim legacy of Woodstock, we need[ed] a total war against drugs.'[138] Drugs had become associated with the protest movement against the Vietnam War. In a bitter twist, they had infected American GIs themselves, many of whom were offered opiates by local Saigon dealers. It was more tempting to blame the Woodstock concert-goers and subversion than it was to look for unfathomable social causes. The historian David Musto recalls: 'When I interviewed former Narcotics Commissioner Harry J. Anslinger in 1972, he described his astonishment at the explosion of drug use in the 1960s . . . Anslinger had counted on stiff mandatory sentences, negative drug imagery, and the consensus of national institutions of defense, behind which lay an ignorance of drug users.'[139]

National authorities were just as bewildered elsewhere. In Britain, the government had put together a committee to investigate in 1964 (named the Brain committee, after its chairman, Sir Russell Brain). The report exposed the following concerns:

> We are particularly concerned at the danger to the young. Witnesses have told us that there are numerous clubs, many in the West End of London, enjoying a vogue among young people who can find in them such diversions as modern music or all-night dancing. In such places it is known that some young people have indulged in stimulant drugs of the amphetamine type. Some of our witnesses have further maintained that in an atmosphere where drug taking is socially acceptable, there is a risk that young people may be persuaded to turn to cannabis, probably in the form of 'reefer' cigarettes.
>
> There is a further risk that if they reach this stage they may move on to heroin and cocaine.[140]

Britain placed amphetamines under anti-narcotics control in 1964.[141] Under the Misuse of Drugs Act of 1971, it established LSD as a Class A substance, alongside heroin.[142]

A few years later, another committee reported on cannabis. Cannabis, unlike heroin, did not produce withdrawal effects or physical dependence, this committee found. Nor was it physically dangerous, like barbiturates, amphetamines or tranquilizers, all of which had recently been the causes of hospital admissions and deaths.[143] In light of these observations, the committee's conclusions were somewhat surprising. The most it was prepared to recommend was a reduction in penalties for possession, which under applicable law were the same as for dealing.[144] Even this met a stormy reception in the House of

Commons in 1969 when it was presented – though in practice, the Home Office did reduce maximum sentences for cannabis offences and introduce greater differentiation between possession and sale.[145]

Germany criminalized the possession of drugs for the first time in 1971. Penalties on existing drug-related offences were raised, as they would be again in 1981.[146] The government prepared the passage of the 1971 law with a public relations campaign in which the health minister made most of the idea that Timothy Leary, due to his multiple LSD trips, no longer possessed a normal brain.[147] France updated its own narcotics law in 1970. Possession came under a minimum one-year prison sentence, though judges retained the power to impose rehabilitation as an alternative. Penalties on dealing were increased dramatically, up to forty years for a repeat offence.[148] An expanding core of European governments, including those of both countries, established a 'Groupe Pompidou' to act as a lobby for tough penalties on drugs. Its aim would be to ensure there was no turning back among participant states, thanks to resolutions against the liberalization of cannabis laws or making any distinction between 'soft' and 'hard' drugs.[149]

The Psychotropic Convention, signed in February 1971, ensured the criminalization of non-medical amphetamines, hallucinogens and tranquilizers throughout the rest of the world. There was last-minute resistance: Switzerland, Germany, Belgium and Austria all voted against the convention, though in the Swiss case, at least, this was clearly based on lobbying by the pharmaceutical industry. The new treaty applied the same provisions as the Single Convention to the newly regulated drugs, including a four-part schedule.[150] Its scheduling, however, was not always intuitive. LSD, the weaker mescaline and psilocybin (magic mushrooms) as well as Ecstasy were all placed on Schedule I. Amphetamines, including methamphetamine, were classified as Schedule II. The more conventionally addictive and potentially lethal barbiturates were placed on Schedule III.[151] Admittedly, the differences between schedules were not huge when it came to the regulations imposed by the convention itself.[152] But the treaty had an important normative role: it acted as a model for domestic scheduling by member states, and for the associated penalties. The American authorities, for example, moved amphetamines from Schedule III up to II shortly after its signature.[153]

The Nixon administration promulgated an extensive anti-narcotics programme of its own. In 1970 it passed a Comprehensive Drug Abuse

Act consolidating existing federal drug laws. (This actually introduced scheduling in the USA, with Schedule I containing heroin, LSD and marijuana, Schedule II morphine and cocaine, and Schedule V tranquilizers.[154]) It also reorganized the American anti-narcotics agencies. The Federal Bureau of Narcotics had been replaced, after Anslinger's departure, by a Bureau of Narcotics and Dangerous Drugs (BNDD). An Office of Drug Abuse Law Enforcement (ODALE) was now created, which was to have a parallel role to the BNDD – they were then merged into the Drug Enforcement Administration, or DEA, in 1973. Finally, the government significantly increased the drug-fighting budget. The means allocated to enforcement rose from $43 million in the last Johnson administration budget to $292 million in 1974.[155]

Notably, the Nixon administration's drug programme devoted significant efforts to prevention and rehabilitation alongside enforcement. President Nixon, the callous right-winger, may best be remembered for his declaration of yet another 'war on drugs' in 1971, but he also said, during the passage of the Drug Abuse Act: 'I thought that the answer was simply to enforce the law and that will stop people from the use of drugs. But it is not that. When you are talking about 13-year-olds and 14-year-olds and 15-year-olds, the answer is not more penalties. The answer is information. The answer is understanding.'[156] The Comprehensive Drug Abuse Act reduced most penalties on drug offences, and it did away with almost all federal mandatory minimum sentences.[157] It was followed by a significant boost to treatment programmes: the federal budget for treatment rose above enforcement, reaching $462 million. The administration stimulated the expansion of drug treatment facilities in a number of American cities, also offering synthetic-opiate alternatives to heroin users, with tens of thousands benefiting. It created, finally, a National Institute on Drug Abuse (NIDA), which remains responsible for research and for collecting essential statistics.[158]

Yet no war on drugs was complete without action abroad. The old warhorse of supply suppression had never died; on the contrary. On 14 June 1971, days before he was to make his famous declaration, Nixon summoned the American ambassadors to France, Mexico, Thailand, Turkey, Vietnam and the United Nations to the White House. 'The interdiction of narcotics was to be a first order priority of U.S. foreign policy,' he told them.[159] American military and economic assistance would depend on cooperation in that field. The ambassador to Turkey was given $35 million in loans to offer his host country as an inducement.

Turkey had steadily been reducing the number of provinces where it allowed poppy cultivation as well as its total acreage in the 1960s. It had reorganized, trained and re-equipped its narcotics police, and it had invited in American agents.[160] Before the end of 1971 the government passed a decree ending the cultivation of poppies in the country.[161] After the quarrels of the 1950s, it was quite a coup. The following year, Nixon received the Turkish prime minister Nihat Erim at the White House. Before the cameras, Nixon shook hands with Erim on the same day he was to sign a Drug Abuse Office and Treatment Act.[162]

The Turkish poppy ban would not hold for more than a few years: the proffered financial assistance was too low, and the ban was unpopular in Turkey, where too many farmers depended on the crop.[163] Its legacy would nevertheless endure. America had also dispatched narcotics agents sent to Marseilles. The target was America's principal source of heroin: the French Connection. Leary, the Woodstock-goers and the hippies had convinced the drug crusaders that more than new laws with larger budgets was required. More forceful, visible action had to be taken. War was going to be taken to the drug lords.

PART III
THE SYSTEM
CHALLENGED

8

DRUG LORDS

The period from 1970 onwards saw an explosion in the means devoted to fighting narcotics around the world. As of 1967 the Federal Bureau of Narcotics employed 295 agents: by the year 2000 the DEA would count more than 4,000 field personnel. As of 1967 active staff abroad totalled 23 people. By the early 1990s the DEA possessed 293 agents in 73 foreign offices. The FBN had functioned on an insignificant budget throughout its history. In 1997 the DEA received its first billion-dollar allowance, itself a small slice of the sums allocated to American drug enforcement.[1] There was also a qualitative leap. Ronald Reagan, when president, passed legislative amendments enabling the military to assist in drug enforcement.[2] The change ushered in the deployment of helicopters, gunships, aircraft and special operation units in what had essentially been a detective's field. This is without counting the means allocated to the chase by the countries of the European Union, by UNODC and the UN agencies, or by the states within whose borders it took place, especially in Latin America.

There were victories, even spectacular victories. Another characteristic of the fight is that it featured actions against a handful of drug lords: high-profile figures destined to make it to the front pages of newspapers or as characters in television series. Most of them fell, some in dramatic scenes – epitomized by Pablo Escobar's 1993 killing by multiple gunshots while trying to escape on a house roof. Yet the war was lost. Beefier enforcement did not stem the tide that was the fiftyfold rise in refined opiates and thousandfold surge in cocaine use described in the last chapter. New gang bosses took the place of the old. Trafficking thrived, becoming more diversified both geographically and in its product range. Supply suppression proved once again a costly fool's errand as the sources of drugs, extinguished in one place, merely sprang up in another.

The assault began with the 1970s campaign against the French Connection. President Nixon's strategy was two-pronged, and it was effective. At one end, it leant on the Turkish government to shut down poppy cultivation. At the other, it shamed the French authorities into prosecuting the Marseilles-based heroin refiners and dealers.

These tactics were well adapted to the differing conditions in both countries. In Turkey, opium cultivation, collection and morphine-base refining were all fragmented. There was no gang boss or cartel to be decapitated. From the farmer, the opium gum went to countless small collectors, who were either local notables or the underlings of *caïds* further up the chain. These *caïds* refined the opium gum into morphine base and dealt with the French buyers. Transport was similarly decentralized. There were many routes. A small proportion still passed through Lebanon for shipping out, but by 1970 this outlet was heavily patrolled. Most of the product now moved by road, via Bulgaria, Austria, Yugoslavia and Germany, where the borders were weakly policed.[3] (Inquisitive journalists from *Newsday* crossed the borders into Germany and France multiple times, proudly displaying bags of sugar behind their windshields or on their car seats: they were never stopped.[4]) Extinguishing cultivation was the best way to curtail supply from that side.

At the French end, the bull needed to be taken by the horns. The Marseilles underworld, which handled refining into heroin and smuggling into the USA, remained no more than a loose alliance of gangs. By contrast with Turkey, these nevertheless revolved around a few key bosses and expert chemists. They could be persuaded to quit. The French ganglands were also shot through with rivalries. Cracking down, experience showed, might push the clans to take each other out.

The ground for the French Connection is believed to have been laid in the 1930s, but it is after the Second World War that the networks developed, linking the Anatolian plateau all the way to American street dealers. The Marseilles old-timers had made the mistake of collaborating with the Germans: eliminated or forced to flee, from 1945 they made room for a new generation. The new traffickers, most of them Corsican, coalesced around two main gangs. For a while the

Guerini clan was in the ascendant, led by its chief Antoine Guerini and his three brothers. The second spot was taken by Jo Renucci. (It was Renucci who originally set up the Lebanese route in collaboration with the racketeer and trafficker Samil Khoury, and it is believed he was a friend of Lucky Luciano.) In 1958 Renucci was succeeded by his lieutenants Marcel Francisci and Dominique and Jean Venturi. In the mid-1960s Antoine Guerini fell victim to a gang war. His brothers were soon jailed for a murder that took place on the day of his funeral. The Francisci-Venturi consortium became paramount.[5]

The two clans may have battled it out with guns, but the Francisci–Venturi team enjoyed an edge in that it possessed better political connections. Francisci, like the Guerinis, owed his ascent to his participation in the French Resistance. But while the Guerinis were closest to the socialist mayor Gaston Defferre, the Francisci–Venturi boasted allegiance to the more powerful Gaullist political family. Marcel Francisci, born in 1919, had been made a prisoner of war in 1939 but had escaped and had served with distinction among the Free French. In 1946 he had joined the RPF, the Gaullist political party. Later he would be known to lend financial support to its successor, the UNR/UDR, and to provide protection to its Corsican candidates during campaigns in the unruly French south. Francisci was only ever arrested on minor charges and always quickly released. An American agent seconded to France reported that local police froze every time Francisci was mentioned.[6]

Yet cooperation between the French worlds of trafficking and politics went further. De Gaulle returned to power in 1958 in the midst of a particularly violent war of Algerian independence. An organization of die-hard colonialists named the OAS (Organisation armée secrète) ran a militia performing assassinations and acts of terror in both Algeria and metropolitan France, threatening the state's very integrity. In response, the Gaullist regime resorted to extra-legal means, sponsoring the formation of a freelance SAC (Service d'action civique) to run a dirty war against the OAS. The SAC, numbering around 15,000, recruited heavily among Marseilles mobsters.[7] It also coordinated with the French secret services, the SDECE. There is good reason to believe that the SDECE itself made use of Corsican mob muscle; its agents are known to have crossed the porous line between crime and covert ops.

There is even tentative evidence that some of the SDECE's ops were funded through heroin trafficking into the United States. On 5 April

1971, a New Jersey customs agent discovered 45 kilograms (100 lb) of heroin hidden in a Volkswagen van on board the freighter *Atlantic Cognac*. Its owner, Roger Delouette, was arrested when he came for the car. Under interrogation he claimed to be working for the SDECE. The heroin was an accessory to his mission, he argued. While the French foreign ministry disavowed him, it confirmed that Delouette had been a secret agent. Another five men with SDECE pasts were arrested for heroin trafficking around that time: Ange Simonpieri, Christian David, André Labay, Joe Attia and Michel-Victor Mertz. In 1971 a Paris court convicted Mertz alongside his associate Achilles Cecchini. Cecchini was let go for medical reasons, and it is believed Mertz was quietly released from his five-year sentence.[8] Mertz, a resistance hero, had once saved De Gaulle's life by warning of a bomb plot against him. Though the Algerian war was long over, the SDECE owed a debt to the SAC and its mobster allies, some of whom it continued to employ even as they nurtured the tendrils of the French Connection.

After De Gaulle's departure, this invulnerability began to fray. Georges Pompidou's arrival as president shortly preceded Nixon's declaration of war on narcotics. An embarrassingly high number of French Connection operatives were soon caught in the USA or in third countries. In March 1971 the Paraguayan police arrested Auguste Ricord, who had been running a gang of several men exporting heroin to Miami. The Ricord arrest helped net another French group working from Brazil. Meanwhile American agents seized 82 kilograms (180 lb) of heroin aboard the Italian liner *Rafaello* which they tied to the low-level dealer Richard Berdin. Berdin, grabbed on his way to a New York hotel, informed on a drug ring including several more second-tier French traffickers as well as American mafiosi. This in turn led to the arrest of André Labay, another gangster claiming to be working for the SDECE.[9]

Pompidou had meanwhile installed a new head at the agency, with instructions to carry out a purge. Ties to the SAC were severed, and Alexandre de Marenches, the new SDECE chief, fired 815 people.[10] The French authorities at last moved against the Marseilles gangs and their labs. In March 1972 the police caught Jo Cesari, considered by some 'the best heroin chemist in the world'.[11] Cesari, who had been arrested before, hanged himself during his subsequent incarceration; he told the prison doctor that the heroin seized in the raid was to have been his last batch.[12] Seizures that year rose from 125 to 576 kilograms.[13] The French police caught no fewer than 108 traffickers.[14] The pressure in turn invited infighting among the gangs: gangsters, when released, were suspected of having talked and were often attacked, leading to retaliation. During the first half of 1973 thirty mobsters were murdered in Paris, Marseilles and Lyon. The Paris and Marseilles police forces made yet more arrests, netting another thirty in a single month.[15] Many of the independent dealers and members of the upper rungs fell.

The Guerini clan had already collapsed. This left only the top of the Francisci–Venturi organization in place. Jean Venturi possessed extensive legitimate business interests, including a travel agency, an export firm, a theatre and a painting company. He had briefly worked as a salesman for the spirits company Ricard in Montreal – his superior there was no less than Charles Pasqua, SAC founder, politician and future minister of the interior.[16] Marcel Francisci owned bars and restaurants in Marseilles and Corsica as well as casinos – an ideal front and tool for laundering drug money. He had also made it into Paris society.[17] Both he and Venturi apparently stood too far up the chain to be touched. The likelihood is that they were discreetly persuaded to remove themselves from the trade. Venturi lived until 2011. Marcel Francisci was shot by gunmen in a Paris car park in 1982 in mysterious circumstances.[18] It was not an enviable end, yet both he and Venturi join the list of the drug barons to have enjoyed moneyed and comfortable retirements, alongside William Jardine, Elie Eliopoulos, Hoshi Hajime and Charles 'Lucky' Luciano.

Success at the French end was cemented by Turkish cooperation at the other. Just as seizures rose in France and the trade became more dangerous, the Turkish supply faltered. An army coup had seen the replacement of Prime Minister Sulayman Demirel by Nihat Erim, with whom the American president would shake hands on the White House lawn. Erim announced that the 1971–2 poppy harvest would be the last. The supply collapsed. In the summer of 1972 the anti-narcotics administration reported a heroin shortage on the American East Coast. The drought persisted into 1973, and in September that year Nixon proclaimed: 'We have turned the corner on drug addiction in the United States.'[19]

The Turkish ban was not built to last. In Afyon province – the name itself means 'opium' – about 75,000 farming families grew poppies at the time. The plant was part of the peasants' life: they ate the leaves in salads and flavoured their bread with the seed.[20] The proposed American aid, $35 million, was rightly judged low in Turkey, where no guilt was felt at foreign addiction problems. National elections saw Nihat Erim replaced by Bulent Ecevit at the beginning of 1974. Ecevit had campaigned against the ban. He promptly authorized the resumption of cultivation in seven provinces, to apply to the 1974–5 season, and he instructed the Ministry of Agriculture to replenish seed stocks.[21]

In a final reversal, however, the campaign was saved by technological innovation. Turkey announced that its poppies would now be used for straw conversion into morphine, under a new chemical and mechanical process. This bypassed the collection of opium gum by incision that was so prone to clandestine handling. The new method had the further advantage that it was less labour-intensive than milking poppy sap, leaving the farmers time for other activities or crops even while they continued to draw in revenues. Village leaders became responsible for their farmers' delivery of the poppies, and inspectors were appointed to perform regular checks during harvest. In 1975 the DEA described the controls as 'remarkably effective'. In 1981 the USA gave exclusivity to Turkey and India for opium supplies to its pharmaceutical industry.[22] There would be no more diversion.

The French Connection was dead. Turkish opium had at last been placed under control. It ceased to be diverted in any significant amounts. Its French handlers had died, were behind bars or had quit, and their labs had been shut down. The hydra's head had been cut off. Two more were free to sprout in its place.

The United States Vice Secretary of State Marshall Green made the first known mention of a 'Golden Triangle' where opium production was concentrated, overlapping Burma, Laos and Thailand, at a press conference in 1971.[23] The leader of the Trafficante mafia family, a key French Connection client, had gone on a prospecting tour of Saigon, Hong Kong and Singapore three years before. The Corsicans were already there.[24]

As of 1960 the Golden Triangle's opium output may have stood somewhere around 500 tons. While some of this was refined into morphine base, a large share continued to be consumed as smoking opium or sold raw for refining elsewhere. This output would rise to over 1,000 tons in the 1970s and to 2,000 tons by 1990.[25] Golden Triangle laboratories had by then added the final step to their production processes: refinement into heroin. In terms of potency, this added another multiplier to the fourfold rise in raw volume. Most production, accordingly, was now for export. As the Turkish supply fell, Southeast Asian producers picked up the slack.

The Golden Triangle was born of a triple legacy. First, local opium networks took over from the French and British monopolies once established in Indochina and Burma. Second, trafficking in refined products owed its revival to the relocation of Chinese gangs from the mainland – including that of Du Yuesheng, the gangster who, it will be remembered, had once been master of Shanghai's French Concession. Third, the trade owed its resilience to the infrastructure put in place in the 1950s by the Kuomintang forces in exile.

The French had closed down their Indochinese opium monopoly after the Second World War, but in the colony's dying days they had renewed ties with the drug in order to shore up their crumbling position. The French military, beleaguered and harassed by the Viet Minh, enlisted ethnic and religious factions to safeguard territory, attack enemy supply lines and provide intelligence: hill tribes, Catholic militia from the Tonkin delta, river pirates south of Saigon. These auxiliaries needed to be paid and supplied with weapons. The solution was Operation X, 'a clandestine narcotics traffic so secret that only high-ranking French and Vietnamese officials even knew of its existence'.[26] Led by the SDECE, this entered into full swing between 1951 and 1954. A Mixed Airborne Commando Group (MACG) bought opium in bulk from Hmong and Tai tribal leaders, flew it south and sold it to Binh Xuyen bandits, who served as Saigon's militia and ran its opium traffic. The Binh Xuyen divided their receipts between the MACG and the *deuxième bureau*. Any surplus was sold on to Hong Kong smugglers or Corsican syndicates for shipment to Marseilles.[27]

After independence the South Vietnamese leader Ngo Dinh Diem cleaned up. This included a ferocious battle in and around Saigon in 1955, in which the Binh Xuyen were pushed back into the mangrove forest. Yet when the South Vietnamese regime faced its own insurgency, it resorted to the same means. Its secret police now sourced opium in neighbouring Laos and sold it to a Chinese syndicate in Saigon. The product moved by way of charter airlines operated by Corsicans, the most prominent of which was Air Laos commerciale, run by the 'flamboyant' Bonaventure 'Rock' Francisci (not a relative of Marcel Francisci). Later a Laotian general named Ouane Rattikone decided to take over the trade for himself. He continued to buy from the tribal irregulars who had worked with the French, but he evicted the Corsicans. The Corsicans gone, the intelligence services in Saigon now had the opium brought over on regular commercial flights or on Vietnamese Air Force planes.[28]

A share of this opium was sold for profit in Saigon itself. It continued to be smoked, but some of it was sold as heroin, especially to the increasingly numerous American GIs. The remainder was exported, either refined or as morphine base to be further processed in Hong Kong. The trade there was run by the successors of Du Yuesheng, who during the Second World War had fled to the British colony. After he died, in 1951, Cantonese Triad bosses had taken his operations over, including his chemists. By the early 1970s, ten or so heroin labs were producing the grey no. 3 product sold locally but also pure white no. 4 for export to the USA and Europe. Hong Kong traffickers also sourced some product from Thailand – it was smuggled north on fishing trawlers whose crews transferred their cargo by burying it on desert beaches or dropping it in floating steel drums for picking up.[29]

Opium production in the Golden Triangle was not evenly spread, however. According to a 1968 American Bureau of Narcotics estimate, Thailand's hill tribes harvested approximately 200 tons annually.[30] Laos may have contributed another 100–150 tons.[31] But most of the Golden Triangle opium originated in Burma. It was accordingly in Burma that the first of the late twentieth-century drug lords arose, and against him that the first great hunt began: Khun Sa.

Khun Sa's storied rise was tied to the convoluted Burmese politics. Burma was changed forever when General Ne Win became prime minister in 1958 and installed himself as dictator in 1962. Ne Win imposed a brutal, one-party socialist regime. He also robbed of their autonomy the cultural minorities inhabiting the country's vast and poorly accessible highlands. Both this and his blanket nationalization programme pushed these minorities into revolt. Among the discontented were the Shan, whose settlement overlapped eastern Burma, Laos and Thailand and who speak a language close to Thai. In 1963 Ne Win encouraged the organization of private militias called Ka Kwe Ye (KKY), self-financed through business and trade, whose mission would be to help the government fight the rebels. Many of these defected, though they sometimes returned to the fold when it was convenient to do so. There also remained the Kuomintang generals in exile and their forces to contend with. The ensuing decades saw a disorderly three-way conflict between Rangoon's forces, the Kuomintang remnants and Shan independence fighters, soon to become a four-way conflict through the addition of a Maoist insurgency.[32]

Zhang Qifu, by his original name, was an unlikely champion of the Shan cause. Though his mother was Shan, his father, who had died early, had been culturally Chinese. What education he received was chiefly Chinese. He only assumed the Shan nom-de-guerre 'Khun Sa' past the age of forty, in 1976. Yet he was a talented guerrilla chief and a wily political plotter. He had also been the stepson of one of the main Shan chieftains, helping him raise a following. In 1963 he took the leadership of one of the KKY units nominally loyal to Rangoon: within one year he had defected.[33]

For a while Khun Sa was but one of several commanders and one of several actors on the Burmese opium market, but by 1967 he felt strong enough to challenge the force that remained dominant in the trade: the Kuomintang generals. Khun Sa's guerrilla army had grown to about 2,000 troops. The emerging drug lord put 16 tons of opium gum on a 300-mule caravan and headed for Laos. There the product would be sold to General Ouane, the man who controlled the heroin route to South Vietnam. The sale would enable Khun Sa to enlist yet more men. Sensing danger, the Kuomintang generals waylaid Khun Sa's column just as it reached Ban Khwan, its Laotian destination, where Ouane's morphine-base refinery stood. A firefight ensued, both sides shooting from rifles, heavy machine-guns and mortars. (The press avidly dubbed the fight an 'opium war'.) At that stage, Ouane saw his opportunity and ordered the Air Force to intervene. Both belligerents, bloodied, were forced to retreat. The Laotian general was able to seize the opium for free.[34]

The setback would prove temporary. More trouble brewed as, in an attempt at unification, Khun Sa opened talks with fellow Shan leaders in 1969. The Rangoon authorities got wind of the talks, and Khun Sa was captured and jailed. The silver lining was that the Kuomintang leadership was steadily retreating into the Thai sector of the Golden Triangle, where their welcome was but half-hearted. (One theory is that the Laotian intervention in Ban Khwan was never for real, and that it was contrived between Khun Sa and Ouane to rid themselves of the Chinese.[35]) Another Taiwanese airlift soon drew more of the Kuomintang away from the region.[36] Demand for heroin was about to surge worldwide, and Turkey was ending poppy cultivation. The time was right, if only Khun Sa could get out of jail.

A stroke of luck came when one of Khun Sa's commanders, who had continued fighting, captured a couple of Russian doctors in 1973. They were ransomed for the Shan chieftain, who was released the next year. Khun Sa thereupon united the Shan factions and, proclaiming himself leader of the independence struggle, established new headquarters at a town named Ban Hin Taek, actually in the northwestern hills of Thailand, close to the border. Laos lay in the throes of an insurrection. Khun Sa could now set up his own heroin refineries and smuggling networks. Ban Hin Taek was ideally situated, straddling the main route from Burma's opium-growing regions and through the mountains where the new refineries nested. A dirt road connected to the rest of Thailand what became a boom settlement of two-storey concrete houses, marketplaces, cinemas, brothels and army barracks as well as a Chinese temple and a Shan pagoda.[37]

As business boomed and the Golden Triangle acquired notoriety, the settlement began to attract unwanted attention. It proved an embarrassment to the Thai leadership when Khun Sa began to be called 'King of the Golden Triangle'.[38] The American administration had signed bilateral drug treaties with Thailand and Laos in 1971 and 1972. The DEA's presence was expanding in the region, where by late 1974 it employed 31 agents.[39] The Burmese may have been powerless but Thailand, a long-standing U.S. ally, was another matter. In 1980 the Thai Air Force bombed Khun Sa's base, destroying three chemical storage units. In 1982 Thai rangers stormed Ban Hin Taek. The battle left seventeen soldiers and 130 rebels dead.[40]

Khun Sa's forces were nevertheless able to retreat across the border in good order. They built new headquarters on the other side, where they re-established their refineries.[41] From this new base, they even moved against their last remaining competitor. The last shreds of the Kuomintang presence, including Khun Sa's 1967 nemesis, General Li Wenhuan, had taken refuge in Chiang Mai, Thailand, where they dealt in drugs with corrupt Thai military officers. On 11 March 1984 a truck loaded with 7,000 sticks of dynamite erupted in the driveway of General Li's mansion, destroying the house and leaving a crater 6 metres (20 ft) wide and 2 metres (6 ft) deep. Though Li was away in Bangkok, his heroin apparatus collapsed.[42] In the second half of the 1980s Khun Sa's position was strengthened again by the failure of the Burmese communist insurgency, which allowed him to sweep up even more of the regional opium. In 1987 the DEA estimated that his refineries processed 80 per cent of the Golden Triangle's heroin. By 1989 he commanded more than 15,000 men. In a *Newsweek* interview, the drug lord himself bragged that he drew an annual income of $200 million from his labs.[43]

For several years, Khun Sa remained invulnerable. In 1987, under American pressure, the Thai mounted another assault on his forces. As reported by the government and press, the air force bombed his base, and the army followed in 'hot pursuit'. But in April an American visitor arrived there and saw nothing. When asked about the recent fighting, Khun Sa laughed: 'Oh that. That was a newspaper war.' Thai and Burmese officials had come to explain that they stood to lose millions in drug-suppression funds. So they had worked out a deal: Khun Sa agreed they could come to the border and fire off guns and rockets into the air, helping them claim they were doing their part in fighting this 'monster', and in exchange he was allowed to build a new road leading from his headquarters into Thailand.[44]

It was only as the 1990s dawned that Khun Sa's fortunes took a turn for the worse. In 1990 a New York federal grand jury indicted him for trafficking, the DEA having traced back heroin sold in the United States to his refineries. The American Attorney General called for his extradition.[45] A change in regime made it more likely Burma might oblige.

In 1988 Ne Win had resigned and a new military junta, known as the SLORC, took power in Rangoon. This junta was determined to do away with tribal separatists. In December 1993 the members of the Shan State National Congress assembled in the town of Homong, Khun Sa's base, to proclaim independence and confirm him as leader. This was too much. The next year, a modernized Burmese Army finally began advancing into the region, first cutting off or diverting opium caravans and eliminating the heroin refineries.[46] Khun Sa's lifeblood was being severed. This time, moving away was not an option. Deprived of their main resource, Khun Sa's forces became increasingly brutal, massacring villagers who sold their opium elsewhere.[47] At last, on New Year's Day 1996, the Shan leader surrendered, inviting Burmese troops into Homong and ordering his soldiers to down weapons.

Yet even here, there was more than met the eye. It was a negotiated surrender, and the drug lord and his aides were ceremonially welcomed in Rangoon. Khun Sa retired to a lakeside villa not far from where Ne Win lived. From his new residence, he was allowed to run various investments. He was never extradited.[48] In order to rid themselves of the United Shan Army, moreover, the SLORC had recourse to another long-time drug baron: Lo Hsing-han. Lo was another half-Chinese Shan chief who had originally risen as a KKY commander. He had briefly been paramount in the opium trade when Khun Sa sat in jail in the early 1970s, but he had been caught, in turn, in 1973. In 1980 Lo had been released and empowered to build a new militia. In 1989, with the encouragement of the Rangoon military leaders, he was able to set up a group of heroin refineries at his northern Burmese base and open his own trafficking route into Hong Kong. The quid pro quo was that Lo was to harass Khun Sa's forces. After Khun Sa retired, Lo Hsing-han was left standing. He was never caught again.[49]

Governments and the media enjoy chasing drug lords because they make for high-profile hunts and well-publicized victories when they are captured or killed. The problem is that they are always replaceable. Under Khun Sa as under the Kuomintang generals, Burmese trafficking functioned more like a trading alliance than a centralized organization. Independent merchants owned most of the opium on the convoys, with less than half typically belonging to the overlord protecting them. These merchants paid a percentage tax upfront plus a fixed-price frontier tax for the service. But they were prone to move from one army to the other, from the Kuomintang generals to Khun Sa to Lo Hsing-han, and even the soldiers, who were known to trade on their own account, sometimes melded into former enemy units.[50] A similar system prevailed in refining. Khun Sa's heroin refineries were actually owned by Bangkok-, Hong Kong- and Taiwan-based syndicates who paid him duty in exchange for enjoying the protection of his army.[51] It was easy for these clients to switch allegiance and move their chemists elsewhere. Burmese opiate trafficking, in other words, functioned more like a cartel, or at times overlapping cartels, than like a single fiefdom. When one chief fell, the cartel could always find another.

Drug control did notch up one victory in the Golden Triangle. Between 1970 and 2000 poppy cultivation was significantly brought down in Laos and Thailand. Laos instituted a state monopoly, purchasing opium from farmers for use by the pharmaceutical industry.

It began punishing users harshly, sending them to re-education camps. With help from UNODC, it launched substitute development projects. Over time, China also contributed, providing funds and agricultural experts. From 2002 the programme attracted private agricultural companies which bought tracts of lands and established plantations, employing local farmers. Some villages where crop substitution was not viable were forcibly resettled. This carrot-and-stick approach reduced illicit Laotian poppy acreage close to zero by 2006, when UNODC declared the country poppy-free – though production may have crept up again after 2010.[52]

A comparable approach proved itself effective in Thailand. Initially spurred by a Nixon envoy, successive opium reduction programmes garnered the support of key Thai military and royal figures. Eradication and substitute development initiatives were picked up by the United Nations Fund for Drug Abuse Control (UNFDAC) and by official donors including the USA, Germany and Norway. The programmes at first focused on crop replacement (coffee, tea, silkworms, rice, beans, ornamental flowers and so on), then on the infrastructure to ensure these crops could be brought to market. Alongside, there were education programmes, with the foundation of schools to improve literacy, plus treatment courses and vocational training aimed at reducing local demand. In the last phase, in the 1990s, the government deployed large-scale development schemes, including the establishment of new schools and health facilities in hundreds of communities, the construction of thousands of kilometres of roads, and the electrification of isolated villages. The sequential opium-reduction initiatives took place in the context of a huge rise in GDP per capita.[53] This broad-based approach produced results. At its height, in the mid-1960s, Thai poppy acreage is estimated to have been 18,500 hectares.[54] This declined to less than 7,000 hectares in the 1980s and almost zero in the 2000s.[55]

Both Laos and Thailand proved that local successes could be achieved in the war on drugs. The question, at the same time, is to what extent their poppy acreage simply shifted elsewhere. In the 1980s and '90s Burma picked up the shortfall. The Rangoon government was neither interested in nor capable of enforcing opium eradication, and Burmese substitution programmes all failed.[56] Admittedly, Burmese opium tonnage itself peaked in the early 1990s. By 2000 it had halved, and while Burma has continued to be a significant source of illicit opiates in the twenty-first century, the peak was never recovered.[57]

Yet this was not a problem, from the traffickers' perspective. New opportunities for growing and refining opium beckoned in Mexico, Pakistan and, especially, Afghanistan.

Afghanistan's opium, too, owed a debt to the old East India Company, this time via Pakistan. After Partition, Pakistan had inherited India's opium system. While it had been free of poppy cultivation, it now licensed farmers to grow the crop on small plots. The state collected and sold the opium. In 1955 a processing factory was constructed in Lahore. The next year, cultivation was extended to another four districts including, fatefully, the North-West Frontier province. Pakistan had successfully fought for the 1961 Single Convention to include exemptions for quasi-medical opium use, with a fifteen-year window. In 1967 the government passed a set of Dangerous Drug Rules providing for the gradual restriction of the sector to the medical sphere. The long time window, however, allowed Pakistani poppy cultivation to endure. (Anslinger, who had furiously opposed the exemptions, had been right.) Controls were next to non-existent. The inefficient monitoring of licensed sales allowed traders to bypass the state. In practice there was no reduction.[58]

Around 1975 European buyers, deprived of their long-time Turkish supply, began prospecting in Pakistan. The first heroin labs opened in the same year, on the North-West Frontier and in Baluchistan province. A drought that hit the Golden Triangle in 1978–9 provided a further boost to what would come to be named the Golden Crescent (soon also to encompass Afghanistan). Finally, the Iranian Revolution and the eradication campaign that followed it pushed production into neighbouring Pakistan.[59] By 1979 the country had become the world's leading illicit opium producer with an output of over 800 tons.[60]

Under UN pressure and in the process of implementing strict Islamic moral laws, including on intoxicants, the government passed a 'Hudood Ordinance' in the same year, banning the production, handling and use of opiates.[61] Since Pakistan was not registered with the INCB as a producer for the pharmaceutical market, this amounted to a total ban on poppy cultivation.[62] Opiate manufacturing and distribution were punishable by thirty 'stripes' and five years' imprisonment. Possession of over 1 kilogram of opium was sanctioned with long-term imprisonment and thirty stripes, and in 1997 the possession of 100 grams of heroin would become punishable by death.[63]

None of this had much effect in practice. The Pakistan Narcotics Control Board might try its best to enforce the regulations, but it was woefully ill-equipped. Fifteen years later, it still only possessed Second World War rifles and a total of 29 vehicles, most of them out of order. Seizures rose, and by 1982 between fifteen and twenty heroin labs were being raided every year. But new ones sprouted. The personnel of the Pakistan Narcotics Control Board became notably corrupt and in a few instances actually helped the traffickers. The first lab owner was only prosecuted in 1988.[64]

The problem was that corruption extended higher, to the state's top echelons. Interpol listed General Fazal Haq himself, the governor of the North-West Frontier province, as a drug trafficker.[65] The patron of various anti-narcotics NGOs, Haq was widely alleged to have raided rival heroin factories to bolster his own dominance. A Norwegian investigator connected the traffic all the way to a bank account of General Muhammad Zia-ul-Haq, the president of Pakistan, who was suspected of smuggling heroin in his official plane.[66] A defendant in a drug trial claimed to have financed the 1985 election of Prime Minister Nawaz Sharif. Benazir Bhutto, premier from 1988, announced a war against drugs, but her foreign minister was alleged to have smuggled 400 kilograms (880 lb) of narcotics in bags taken from his rice mills. Suspicions extended to Bhutto's husband, who would have used the ministerial residence itself to engage in trafficking.[67]

Such obfuscation extended to statistics. Official reporting was that, in the 1990s, Pakistani opiate addict population numbered in the millions. Meanwhile a 1980s survey suggested each user injected the considerable dose of 0.9 grams of heroin per day. In combination, the reports led to the conclusion that Pakistan used more opium than was produced worldwide. A historian explains: '*Exaggerating consumption* by officials . . . attract[s] more foreign aid, a good part of which goes into overseas numbered bank accounts.'[68] Pakistan's heroin industry was nevertheless sizeable, in dollar terms. By one more realistic calculation, it had ballooned to $8 billion annually by the late 1980s. This was a substantial share of Pakistan's legal economy and more than its entire foreign trade, helping the country earn the label of 'narco-state'.[69]

Heroin was promised an even brighter future, however, in Afghanistan, into which the trade spilled via army and secret-service involvement. The evidence is that major drug syndicates existed inside the Pakistani Army itself. In June 1986 the police arrested an army major driving from Peshawar to Karachi with 220 kilograms (485 lb) of heroin. Two months later, it stopped an air force lieutenant carrying a package the same size, suggesting it was a standard load. Before the men could be questioned, they escaped under what Pakistan's *Defence Journal* called 'mystifying circumstances'.[70] Yet it was the Pakistani ISI (Inter-Service Intelligence), aided by the CIA, who played the greater role. In 1979, when the Soviet Union invaded Afghanistan, the CIA and its Pakistani allies saw an opportunity to hurt and perhaps inextricably bog down their Cold War foe. They began arming guerrillas. This came just at the point when Pakistan's opiate industry was booming. Heroin offered a simple, inexhaustible means of funding the Afghan resistance.

What role the drug traffic may have played in paying for early weapon deliveries is not known, but they passed through camps set up on the North-West Frontier, where both opium cultivation and heroin refining flourished. Fleeing Afghans began growing opium alongside Pakistani farmers. As the Mujahideen captured land in Afghanistan, they encouraged the peasants to grow the crop there, too. Within a few years, this produced a harvest of several hundred tons. The refined product being more easily portable, guerrilla leaders eventually established heroin labs in Afghanistan itself, adding to what was produced on the North-West Frontier. From 1982 Pakistani army trucks were carrying weapons from Karachi to the border province, where they loaded heroin for the trip back. The funds were moved through the Anglo-Pakistani Bank of Credit and Commerce International (BCCI) – it would go bust, after a lengthy investigation, in 1991.[71]

Afghanistan, too, had its drug lord. Like Khun Sa, he was able to lay claim to a national cause. Gulbuddin Hekmatyar was a fundamentalist Muslim who had protested secularizing reform in the 1960s. News reports claimed he had thrown acid in the faces of unveiled women students. The ISI had nurtured him even before the Soviet invasion. In 1972 he had fled accusations of murder into Pakistan's North-West Frontier. There, the Pakistani agency had set him up as a guerrilla leader for intervening across the border, though initially without scoring any successes. His luck turned in 1979. As the American weapons began flowing in, the ISI insisted that Hekmatyar get the bulk of them. Though he was not alone, he became by the same token the largest dealer in Afghan heroin. He is known to have run six heroin laboratories in Pakistan in addition to what his organization may have been operating in Afghanistan.[72]

As in Burma, it is sometimes difficult to discern to what extent warlord participation in the heroin trade was instrumental and to what extent it became an end in itself. Other guerrilla commanders included Mullah Nasim Akhunzada, the 'heroin king' of the Helmand valley – ostensibly more interested in trafficking than in fighting the Soviets, with whom he was known to agree ceasefires.[73] After Hekmatyar failed to take power in the scramble that took place from 1992, he lost ISI support and eventually departed, abandoning what trafficking infrastructure he may still have controlled.[74] As in Burma, however, his departure did not mean the end of poppy cultivation. The Taliban, who conquered the country in stages between 1995 and 1999, raised taxes on opium, heroin labs and transportation. The Taliban leader, Mullah Omar, occasionally made noises about ending his reliance on heroin income. In 2001, for example, a proclaimed eradication campaign took advantage of a drought having hit production. The idea was to obtain UN recognition and perhaps raise aid money.[75] Actually Afghanistan became entrenched, under the Taliban, as the world's principal supplier of illegal opiates.

Also, as in the Golden Triangle, a system akin to connecting vessels ensured that as output fell in one country, it rose to compensate in the next. During the 1990s Pakistan mounted an attack on its own illicit traffic. Its secular elites were concerned that the heroin industry was becoming the basis for an ISI-supported, fundamentalist stronghold. Benazir Bhutto, who returned as prime minister in 1993, created an Antinarcotics Task Force the next year, and this time there were more arrests. Seizures rose. Pakistan staged a bonfire of 400 kilograms (880 lb) of heroin and opium in Peshawar in February 1999, for example. From its peak of 800 tons, Pakistan's opium output fell to 100–200 tons during the 1990s and even less at the end of the decade.[76]

Afghanistan's rising production more than compensated. The mountainous country enjoyed the advantage that its soil and climate are ideally suited to poppy cultivation. Poppy yields per hectare averaged 40 kilograms in Afghanistan, against 12–14 kilograms in Colombia or Mexico.[77] The country produced approximately as much opium as Burma, in 1995, on a third of the acreage.[78] Afghanistan's output passed the 1,000-ton mark in the late 1980s. This doubled again in the 1990s as Pakistani production fell. By the year 2000, Afghanistan had reached a peak of over 3,000 tons.[79] By then, it was producing more than half the world's illicit opium.[80] It would remain number one in the twenty-first century as its opiate sector continued to expand at a rapid clip.

The finger is sometimes pointed at the secret agencies for this debacle. According to the testimony of a former u.s. ambassador to Pakistan, the ISI remained involved in drug trafficking long after Hekmatyar had departed.[81] The CIA itself played an important role in fostering the Afghan heroin industry at its inception. Nor was this the first time it condoned narcotics trafficking in pursuit of Cold War aims. As the historian of Southeast Asia Alfred McCoy has demonstrated with great persistence and courage, drugs were also made use of in American covert operations during the Vietnam war in the 1960s and '70s and in support of the Nicaraguan Contras in the 1980s.

The CIA originally picked up the use of Hmong guerrillas as auxiliaries in Vietnam, after a five-year hiatus, from the French. Between 1960 and 1974 the CIA maintained a secret army of 30,000 Hmong tribesmen in mountainous northern Laos. These units fought both the Vietcong and Laotian communist insurgents. They guarded radar installations vital to bombing North Vietnam, and they rescued downed American pilots. Conditions were harsh. The Hmong army was collected from a narrow population. It enlisted teenage boys and used food as leverage to keep the villages obedient. Opium, a long-standing Hmong crop, was in this context the only lifeline to hand. The problem was that it needed to be transported: the solution was provided by Air America, a small commercial airline founded by an army major after the Second World War. The CIA acquired indirect control over it, and began using its aircraft to ferry troops and supplies around. Until 1965 Corsican charter airlines were still running the opium south. After the Laotian general Ouane expelled them, that role, too, was taken over by the CIA-owned airline.[82]

Subcommittee and press investigations have revealed that the American government likewise shut its eyes to drug-based fundraising by the Nicaraguan Contras, a guerrilla movement opposing the country's left-wing regime. The Contras, entrenched in neighbouring Honduras, flew cocaine into the USA for the Colombian cartels and allowed traffickers to use their airstrips and fuelling stations to do so. After Congress cut off aid to the Contras in 1984, the principal that was Lieutenant Colonel Oliver North enlisted, at official behest, an American citizen residing in Costa Rica named John Hull, alongside a small team of ex-CIA people. With funds from the sale of American arms to Iran, this group bought aircraft and paid veterans to fly weapons to the Contras. Hull owned a ranch with six airstrips, in particular, that were off limits to local customs or police. But drug pilots en route from Colombia also paid Hull for his services. North's own notebook explicitly referenced the use of CIA airplanes to transport cocaine paste. An FBI investigation into Hull's activities was dropped upon notification that he was working for 'agencies with other operational requirements'.[83] Another Contra-related affair exposed by the *San Jose Mercury News*, which remains controversial, suggests that the CIA may even have shielded cocaine dealers in California itself for several years.[84]

The CIA's preparedness to dabble in or at least shut its eyes to narcotics trafficking has generated considerable excitement among conspiracy theorists. Books continue to come out alleging some grand scheme of oppression, or gleefully pointing at American hypocrisy. It is necessary to point out, however, that the CIA has not been alone in this field. The Pakistani ISI and the French SDECE, at the very least, have demonstrably done like it. At least three factors conspire to make drugs a ready recourse to intelligence agencies. The first is that state failure invites drug dealing just as it invites intervention, including covert intervention, by foreign states. Whether in Burma, Afghanistan or Colombia, the emergence of trafficking networks was made possible by breakdowns in state control spiralling into or bordering on civil war. The second is that trafficking attracts ruthless men for whom hiding and killing are a way of life. As the SDECE's experience attests, these men make obvious recruits for covert missions of a violent kind. Third, drugs offer an ideal means of funding operations for which above-board budgets cannot be found. They are portable and earn high price points per kilo, and their illegality ensures that the trade in them comes with useful payment or money-laundering facilities.

Nor does it follow that the CIA or other intelligence agencies can be made responsible for the millions of drug addicts one finds around the world. No doubt the double standards these agencies practise are reprehensible, but their role in propagating drug use has never been more than marginal. Even in Afghanistan, where arguably the CIA's involvement was the heaviest and where drugs played such an important part, the agency did little more than provide an early impulse to the poppy's progress (though the ISI has arguably been more deeply involved). Afghanistan's heroin production enjoyed its greatest boom after the Soviet war was over, not during it. As UNODC writes: 'Opium production accelerated after the Soviet withdrawal for two reasons: first, it provided a viable source of income for warring factions; and second, it had proven itself to be a viable crop for cultivation and rural livelihood and unlike the destroyed licit agricultural sector, had developed systems and infrastructure which actually functioned.'[85] Afghanistan only overtook Burma as the world's premier poppy grower in 1991.[86] The poppy harvest has continued to grow since then, whether under Afghanistan's warlords, the Taliban or the governments that have succeeded it.

As McCoy himself notes: 'For forty years, the CIA fought a succession of covert wars around these two points at the antipodes of the Asian massif – in Burma in the 1950s, Laos in the 1960s, and Afghanistan in the 1980s . . . The CIA's role in the heroin traffic was an inadvertent consequence of its cold war tactics.'[87] The flourishing of heroin trafficking did not await the intelligence agencies, whose contribution was no more than 'inadvertent'. With the exception of the French Connection, the trafficking networks concerned went on thriving long after the spies were gone. The drug lords of the Golden Triangle and Golden Crescent needed no special agent's supporting hand. Neither, in Latin America, did the cocaine cartels.

The Medellín of the 1960s and '70s was a somnolent place, home to a Colombian version of puritanism and the virtues of frugality, thrift and enterprise, though also beset by a genteel decline reflecting the struggles of its textile factories. Within a decade or so, it had been made famous by a new, far more hip and dangerous industry: cocaine, in which it dealt in tons. It also became home to one of the world's most infamous bandits and perhaps the best-known figure in the entire long war on drugs.

Colombian trafficking first developed around marijuana plantations in the 1970s, when demand was booming in the USA and Europe. In the following decade, the government fumigated most of them.[88] An economic crisis was meanwhile shaking the whole of Latin America as the commodities boom of that era ended and several countries found themselves over-indebted. Fiscal difficulties undermined the state everywhere, favouring corruption and the rise in influence of ruthless men with pocketfuls of hard currency. The same countries were at the same time undergoing demographic explosions. Poor peasants struggling to hold on to their farms were lured into growing coca. For those who drifted, dispossessed, into the towns, the well-paid jobs of refining, transporting or guarding cocaine offered life rafts. For the drug barons, it was easy to hire the more ambitious or desperate among them as gunmen or *sicarios*.

The economic crisis, nevertheless, did not hit Colombia as hard as its neighbours. The country did not default on its debt, and its economy was buoyed by new oil, coal and nickel mining ventures, while even its textile industry adapted and survived.[89] Nor was Colombia even the home of coca: that privilege went to Peru and Bolivia. Two things, rather, favoured it as the future centre of the trade. The first was that it was strategically placed on the road to the all-important United States, where demand for the drug was growing geometrically. The second was that it had a history of violence and lawlessness, ensuring that its drug lords, when they emerged, were the most brutal.

Colombian cocaine was not at first home-grown: it was imported from further south. The product went through four stages. Peruvian or Bolivian peasants grew and harvested the bush. Local dealers processed the leaf into paste. Trafficker organizations refined this paste into the intermediary product that was cocaine base. This, finally, was flown out to the Colombians, who ran the laboratories for transformation into the end product: pure cocaine. The Colombians, of course, also took this cocaine to the United States and Europe and sold it there.

The regional cocaine industry began to take off in the 1970s. Though Peru was equally important, Bolivia provides an example of the boom and the features it assumed, as well as having been the home of one of its first notorious kingpins.[90] The industry was particularly active in the densely forested, central region of Chapare. Small towns swelled in size, turning into centres for buying and selling leaf or paste. Coca farmers sometimes turned to making their own paste. A physically arduous task that took several days, this involved crushing the leaf mixed with corrosive chemicals (sulphuric acid, kerosene and lime) underfoot, then letting the solution dry. By 1985 police estimated that there were 5,000 coca pits in Chapare, one for every eight coca-growing families. Pits pockmarked the forest, criss-crossed by the trails leading to them. Cocaine meanwhile provided employment for people to collect and transport paste, liaise with traffickers to have it taken to market, contract and pay the stompers, provide them with food, transport the materials to the pits, construct them and so on, not including the boon to local restaurants, hotels, tradesmen and jewellers.[91]

Only large *narcos* organizations could churn the paste into cocaine base. The investments were sizeable: at least half a million to a million dollars for one lab. Just the chemicals – sulphuric and hydrochloric acid, potassium permanganate, acetone, ether and ammonia – were expensive. Placed deep into the jungle, the camps where refining took place functioned as self-contained communities complete with laboratories, sleeping quarters, kitchens and latrines. Some even had electric generators, refrigerators, televisions and gymnasiums. Then there were the landing strips, plus the aircraft. Bolivia's cocaine industry was run, accordingly, by around 35 such organizations, most of them family businesses headed by a patriarchal figure.[92]

Much like the Burmese heroin industry, the sector was resilient, apt to recombine if one kingpin fell. Some families shared chemists, pilots, labs, assassins and government contacts. To the casual observer, nonetheless, Bolivian cocaine came to revolve around one egregious figure: Roberto Suárez. Suárez became famous for orchestrating the sensational 'cocaine coup', in which a band of traffickers took over an entire government.

Born in 1932 to one of Bolivia's oldest lineages, a family of diplomats and ranchers, Suárez was a socialite. Well connected and successful, he owned property, and his wife was a former Miss Bolivia. They had four children. It has been rare, historically, for the well-to-do to embrace the illicit drug trade, but Suárez had one advantage: connections. Suárez had made the acquaintance of Klaus Barbie, a former Nazi and the wartime head of the Gestapo in Lyon, who had fled to Latin America. The ex-Nazi, in turn, had introduced Suárez to Luis Arce Gómez, a former chief of intelligence who operated an air taxi business and had been trafficking in cocaine since 1975. Barbie had also served in the Bolivian Interior Ministry and army intelligence, and he had put together a group of bodyguards styling itself the Fiancés of Death. With his backing, Suárez flatly offered General Luis García Meza $1.3 million to launch a coup, the condition being that Arce Gómez be made minister of the interior. A collective of traffickers would fund the military government at will, and they were ready to make a down payment of $70 million to help service Bolivia's foreign debt. On 17 July 1980 the 'cocaine coup' took place.[93]

There followed one of the most unedifying episodes in the long war on drugs. At first, the generals took a percentage cut from cocaine: levying a tax of $2,000 per kilogram provided the government with around $200 million per year. Then they realized they could make more through the 'concentration' of the trade. Arce Gómez established a list of 140 smaller dealers to be 'suppressed' by paramilitary squads, including Barbie's. He, Suárez, their associates and various army officers cashed in. Gómez was reputedly making $200,000 a week personally. He soon owned eleven planes and multiple mansions.[94]

After a while, even Meza began to find the whole display embarrassing. In February 1981 CBS television broadcast a merciless documentary programme accusing Arce Gómez of being Bolivia's number one trafficker. The DEA demanded delivery of the top five cocaine dealers. Meza discreetly moved Gómez to a job at a military academy. He cleaned up the Fiancés of Death, also moving Barbie to a more quiet place. Yet it was only when Meza was ousted in a counter-coup in August 1981 that the whole ring fell. Arce Gómez fled, later to be captured and jailed on a long sentence. Barbie was extradited to France, were he was judged for his wartime crimes against humanity. Astonishingly, Suárez, who had been made to pay a get-out-of-jail $50 million by Meza, lived on to persevere in the trade.[95] In 1983 he was able to meet with the new Bolivian president's narcotics adviser and offer the government the perhaps apocryphal sum of $2 billion in four $500-million instalments.[96] Power, regardless, was passing to the Colombians.

Pablo Escobar was born in 1949, during a particularly disturbing episode of civic strife known in Colombian history as *La Violencia*. His parents were middle-class, his father a middling cattle rancher and his mother a schoolteacher and director, though his grandfather had been a known smuggler. Escobar was no academic success. He dropped out of school just before his seventeenth birthday, three years short of graduation. He started out early as a petty swindler and thief. By the time he was twenty, he and the gang he had assembled had become adept at stealing cars, dismantling them and selling the parts. Later he bribed municipal authorities to be able to resell the vehicles whole, and finally he simply extracted protection money from car owners.[97]

Escobar lacked a towering physical presence: he was short, standing just under five feet and six inches, with a large, round face, black, curly hair which he wore long, and a thin moustache. His authority came from his fearlessness and complete absence of scruples in the face of violence. Escobar the car thief recruited thugs to kidnap people who owed him money or simply for ransom. If the family could not pay, the victim was killed. Sometimes the victim was killed even if the ransom was paid.[98] Around 1974 he started moving cocaine across the Andes, ferrying small doses in 'a rickety stolen Renault' with built-in secret compartments – an activity that earned him a few months in prison.[99] His break came the next year, when he met a young pilot who went by the nickname of Rubin and worked for one of the local cocaine chiefs, named Fabio Restrepo. Escobar met Restrepo and briefly worked with him, then had him killed and took his place. Rubin said of Escobar: 'He was a gangster, pure and simple. Everybody, right from the start, was afraid of him. Even later, when they considered themselves friends, everybody was afraid of him.'[100]

In 1976 the future drug lord was arrested again, on his return from a run in Ecuador. The police found 39 kilograms (86 lb) of cocaine in his car trunk. Escobar tried bribing the judge, but the man turned the money down. But the trafficker hit upon the idea of hiring the judge's estranged brother as his lawyer, prompting the magistrate to recuse himself. The new judge could be bribed, and Escobar was able to shake the charges. It was a close escape, typical of Escobar's uncanny mixture of guile and bravado. Meanwhile the two policemen responsible for the arrest were killed.[101]

The episode that was the rise and fall of Pablo Escobar has come to typify the war on drugs in its post-Nixon phase. It was bloody and breathless, and it enlisted all the stereotypes about drug bosses. Though Escobar's killing was hailed at the time it took place as a victory, with hindsight this victory has come to be recognized as pyrrhic, with scant result to show for the violence unleashed. Beyond the cops-and-robbers story, it serves as a dramatic illustration of the damage wrought by the war on drugs on the countries where it has raged.

Within a few years, Pablo Escobar directly or indirectly controlled the Medellín traffic in cocaine. Business boomed, bringing about a lighting-fast transformation. At first he employed individual drug runners, known in the trade as mules, but soon he was operating a fleet of trucks and planes. His organization absorbed the smaller entrepreneurs, the labs, the distributors. What he could not take over outright, he 'insured': his thugs oversaw the delivery routes, exacting a tax on each kilo shipped and adding the load to his own shipments. Profits were reinvested into more labs and larger aircraft. By 1979

Medellín's drug king was able to construct an estate outside the city on land worth $63 million. There would be an airport, a heliport, six swimming pools and artificial lakes. Escobar had exotic animals flown in – elephants, buffaloes, lions, rhinoceroses, gazelles, zebras, hippos, camels, ostriches – to fill the park.[102]

The gains did not all flow to one man. Medellín itself was transfigured. The price to pay for eating the forbidden fruit having yet to be asked, a city native recalls:

> Medellín jolted alive. Discothèques sprang up in what were once empty overgrown lots along Las Palmas . . . The city's first malls opened and stores selling an unheard-of array of imported items proliferated. Along the main road to the upper-class neighbourhood of El Poblado imported car dealerships mushroomed . . . It became usual to see the small grotto outside the crude little chapel of Sabaneta covered in expensive flowers and the field surrounding it crowded with late model BMWs, Mercedes Benz, and Montero jeeps as drug dealers and their wives and girlfriends paid their respects to the Virgin and expressed their gratitude for being alive.
>
> . . . The adobe farmhouses gave way to concrete bunkers surrounded by security cameras that swivelled menacingly day and night at guarded steel gates painted strident tones of orange and red. Haphazardly planted orchards were transformed into well-manicured lawns dotted with miniature golf courses and huge stadium-like lights that insured against intruders. The road that local property holders had struggled for more than a decade to have paved was suddenly a smooth ribbon of tar and gravel that did not flood in the rainy season . . . And as if this were not enough, a bullring sprang up on land that had once been an empty field owned by a distant relative. Spanish bulls and bullfighters were shipped in and out by jet at huge expense for the pleasure of the local Mafiosi.[103]

Escobar is every so often pictured as a slob who ate only pizza, favoured the company of the soccer teams he bought and hired beauty queens to perform erotic games at his villa.[104] Yet images of gold-chain-wearing drug dealers, even if accurate, also confuse and distract.

Behind this facade surely was hidden a shrewd organizer, capable of masterminding the complex networks essential to handling billion-dollar sums, of whatever origin. Putting together million-dollar labs in remote locations, keeping distributors inside U.S. borders regularly supplied and faithful, maintaining tabs on the myriad payments while ensuring half of them did not go amiss: all this must have demanded detailed, everyday follow-up. Only a skilled businessman could be up to the job. (Another dubious characterization is that the drug lords were all, in spite of their violent nature, devoted family men, from Escobar to Félix Gallardo and El Chapo. Yet they all had multiple mistresses and fathered children out of wedlock.)

Or did it all rely on terror, with obscure but capable lieutenants performing the legwork? How the cartels worked from a business standpoint, their operating model, and their methods of trade remain poorly known. The impression is sometimes that the cartels functioned much like large corporations, and sometimes that they were more akin to markets where the bosses exercised, for a large fee, the judicial arbitration and enforcement normally reserved to the state. Certainly the Medellín cocaine industry was never completely centralized, earning its title as a cartel. Besides federating smaller operators under his protection, Escobar coordinated activities with another three families or gangs, each with their own boss: José Rodriguez Gacha, Carlos Lehder and Jorge Luis Ochoa. From the early 1980s, when the cartel was formed, members shared ties to political interests and oversight of the crucial distribution networks in the United States.[105] Rodriguez Gacha's organization, according to a U.S. Attorney General's report, nevertheless maintained its own more centralized distribution. The report stated: 'He has representatives in South Florida and southern California who are in charge of receiving, inventory control, accounts receivable, and general organizational support. Unlike the representatives of the Pablo Escobar group, who work on commission, Rodriguez's U.S. representatives work on straight salary. They work regular business hours, wear suits and ties, and are instructed to keep a low profile.'[106]

This combination of hierarchy and amorphousness made for equal measures of vulnerability and resistance. Because the cartels involved at least a degree of organizational rigidity, they could be cut down to size if the kingpin was taken down. The Medellín cocaine trade never quite recovered from the falls of Lehder, Gacha and

Escobar – yet neither did it completely die out. Even if one cartel could be destroyed, moreover, the same pattern of competitive collaboration between the regions ensured trafficking in Colombia as a whole would survive. Alongside the Medellín and Cali organizations, there existed a Bogotá and a North Atlantic Coast cartel – this last unit, with a presence in key American cities including Miami, Los Angeles and New York, provided smuggling and money-laundering services to the others.[107] Organizations and methods of trade, finally, are likely to have changed and adjusted to circumstances over time. The Cali cartel, though it, too, possessed a few notorious figureheads, was ostensibly the more adaptable: 'This apparatus utilized taxi cab networks, corrupted officials, and the ability to statistically determine opposing Colombian government activities by means of sophisticated analysis of phone and other records derived from the use of an actual IBM AS/400 super-computer. With shadowy and out of the limelight bosses sporting monikers like "The Chessplayer" and "el Señor", the Cali organization relied far more upon its brains than on the barrel of a gun.'[108] It would pounce when Escobar began to be fatally weakened.

'We're taking down the surrender flag that has flown over so many drug efforts. We're running up the battle flag. We can fight the drug problem, and we can win,' President Reagan announced in 1982.[109] In the USA the cocaine boom was eliciting mounting anguish. Americans had begun taking the drug as crack, a crystalline, concentrated and more dangerous form that is not snorted but smoked. Both import and street prices were falling fast. Cocaine use was hitting record levels.[110]

The United States responded first by putting pressure on governments such as Meza's in Bolivia to perform clean-ups. A similar angle of attack succeeded in the Bahamas, from one of whose islands Carlos Lehder ran his fleet of aircraft, yielding a temporary hit: pressure on the Bahamian government and persistent law enforcement in South Florida caused Lehder to lose his perch in 1983. (Having escaped, he would join Escobar's gang before being captured and extradited in 1987.) As this Caribbean route became less practicable, however, the cartels began to shift their transhipments through Mexico.[111] The American crack epidemic continued unabated.

In 1986 the American president issued a directive declaring drug trafficking a threat to national security for the first time. This allowed the use of military force for fighting drugs overseas.[112] Multiple operations in Latin America based on the deployment of surveillance and military means followed. First came Operation Blast Furnace, a four-month mission during which the u.s. military and DEA worked with Bolivian police to locate and destroy cocaine-processing labs and trafficker airstrips.[113] The next year came Snowcap, designed to cut cocaine output in Bolivia, Peru and Colombia by half within three years. After that would come Safe Haven, Ghost Zone, Support Justice and many more.[114]

Blast Furnace's achievements were not promising. On 14 July 1986 nearly two hundred u.s. troops in full combat gear swooped down on Santa Cruz, a Bolivian trafficking centre, spilling out of c-130 transport planes. Their c-5A aircraft birthed six Black Hawk helicopters. The aim: to take down Roberto Suárez's business, in one of the largest drug busts ever undertaken. The DEA itself sent in twenty agents. But the size of the operation – to the DEA men's own dismay – had blown away any hope of secrecy: 'The first bust was a lab about 50 miles north of their staging base known as El Zorro (The Fox). The site had two airstrips, and 15 large camouflaged tents housing about 75 workers. There was a restaurant, a children's playground and a basketball court. The lab had been manufacturing 700 kilos of cocaine a week. When the Leopards [Bolivian special forces] arrived, however, no-one was at home. The lab had been dismantled and all that remained were a couple of barrels of gasoline and some chemicals.'[115] Two months later, the u.s. forces decided to tackle another major cocaine centre: Santa Ana. On arrival, the eighty Bolivians and thirty Americans who carried out the raid were chased away by a 3,000-strong mob armed with machetes and shouting: 'Kill the Yankees!' They found no drugs and made no arrests.[116]

'Victory over drugs is our cause, a just cause,' proclaimed President George Bush after another three years. Operation Just Cause was about to begin, the 1989 invasion of Panama by 26,000 troops. Panama had been acting as a platform for cocaine-laden aircraft and as a money-laundering centre. Even its president, Manuel Noriega, was wanted in the USA on narcotics charges. The steamroller approach was this time more successful: the coup passed with little resistance, and Panama was forced to clean up its act, at least when it came to drug trafficking.[117] While the canal state was an important waystation, however, it was not a vital centre. As a follow-on, Bush promised the governments of Colombia, Peru and Bolivia record contributions of

$2.2 billion under a programme dubbed the Andean Initiative. The flow of cocaine would fall by 60 per cent over ten years, or so it was hoped.[118] Among the multiple operations belonging to the Andean Initiative was one specifically targeting Colombia: Operation Support Justice. With the Medellín drug barons at the top of its hit list, it would at least achieve media success.

In 1988 *Forbes* estimated the Medellín cartel's income at $8 billion per annum, and it placed Ochoa and Escobar among the world's richest men.[119] Escobar had five more years to live. As for Khun Sa in Burma, however, so for Escobar in Colombia. The seeds of the Medellín king-pin's downfall were planted through his inability to avoid meddling in national politics.

In 1978 Escobar had been elected a substitute city council member in Medellín, and in 1982 he ran for parliament, standing as a substitute for Envigado, a Medellín suburb. Theoretically this granted him par-liamentary immunity, but his election only gave rise to a tumultuous confrontation with Colombia's justice minister, Rodrigo Lara, on the first day he appeared in chamber. Escobar would never forget the humiliation. Six months later, in 1984, the national police raided a large cocaine facility named Tranquilandia, belonging to fellow cartel kingpin Gacha. The police seized 14 tons of cocaine, the largest cocaine seizure in history at the time. The cartel retaliated by eliminating Lara, who was machine-gunned by a passing shooter on a motorbike while sitting in his Mercedes.[120]

The killing of a justice minister was a serious matter, and it could not go unpunished. President Belisario Betancur vowed at Lara's grave to enforce a new extradition treaty with the United States. He placed the country under a state of siege, authorizing the police to confiscate *narcos* assets. The situation looked so bad that Escobar temporarily left the country. The treaty had to be nullified, he decided, and the cartel arranged for a lawsuit to be filed against it. But this strategy only caused him to wade into hotter waters. Escobar bribed the Attorney General for a favourable recommendation. He threatened the judges involved – four recalcitrant judges would be murdered. In November 1985 a guerrilla group named M-19 stormed the Palace of Justice in Bogotá, demanding among other things that the treaty be rescinded. The action caused the death of fifty Palace of Justice employees and eleven of the 24 justices while the guerrillas destroyed 6,000 crimi-nal case files, including the records of proceedings against Escobar.[121]

Shortly thereafter, the Colombian Supreme Court declared the extradition treaty invalid on a technicality. It was but a short-lived victory: days later, a newly elected president, Virgilio Barco, signed it anew. Things threatened to look even more difficult if, as looked likely, the Liberal Party candidate Luis Galán became president in the upcoming elections. On 18 August 1989 a *sicario* with a sub-machine gun shot down Galán as he was making a campaign speech. But the traffickers realized that his appointed successor, César Gaviria, was no better. To get rid of him, the Medellín cartel embarked on the most notorious crime in its career: that November, believing Gaviria was on the flight, the *narcos* planted a bomb on an airliner belonging to the company Avianca, blowing it out of the sky and killing 110 people.[122]

It was a point of no return. Barco again increased the means devoted to fighting the cartel. The Medellín bosses responded with a communiqué declaring 'total and absolute war on the government'.[123] Cartel *sicarios* attacked judges, policemen and informants. They gunned down a former chief of the anti-narcotics police together with several pro-extradition legislators.[124] At some stage, the cocaine barons announced they would kill ten judges for every extradited suspect. (Judges took to wearing hoods in the courtroom so that traffickers could not identify them.[125]) Those who did not want to die were offered bribes. Famously the choice was *plata o plomo* – silver or lead: take a bribe or take a bullet. But while violence had so far been mostly confined to agents of the state, it was now taken to the people of Colombia, with little or no discrimination. Escobar and his allies broadened the fight beyond Medellín and began to deploy car bombs. In Bogotá cars blew up on a daily basis, killing numerous bystanders alongside the intended targets. One bomb hit the headquarters of the DAS, the Colombian anti-narcotics police, killing 64 people.[126] Within two years, 1,500 lay dead.[127]

While the state increasingly responded in kind, the difficulty lay in catching the traffickers on their home ground. Escobar was one of Medellín's biggest but also most generous employers, paying salaries his workers could not hope to make elsewhere. But he also donated funds to build roads, electric lines and floodlit soccer fields. The Medellín drug baron even built a social housing development named after himself, removing people from the slums.[128] 'To many of the poor [Escobar] was not remembered as a man who had led a veritable war against the state, but as a Robin Hood figure who distributed cash and goods and built soccer fields in poor neighbourhoods,' writes a witness.[129] After his death, he would be mourned by thousands. Crowds rioted as his casket was carried through the streets of Medellín, people pushing the bearers aside to open the lid and touch his cold face.[130]

Stalemated, the fight underwent a brief truce. The Colombian forces had cornered and mowed down Gacha at the end of 1989. Escobar was on the run, at the very least prevented from running his business. The Ochoa brothers turned themselves in in exchange for leniency.[131] On 19 June 1991 a new Colombian Constitutional Assembly outlawed extradition. On the same day Escobar surrendered, to be taken to a newly built prison on Mount Catedral, outside Medellín.[132]

La Catedral was no proper prison. It possessed a gymnasium with a sauna, a bar with a lounge and disco, and a soccer field. DEA agents Steve Murphy and Javier Peña toured the place after he had gone: they found a photograph of Che Guevara on the wall and a collection of the *Godfather* movies, but also collected works by Gabriel García Marquez and Stefan Zweig, as well as over the bed 'an ornate, gold-framed portrait of the Virgin Mary painted on inlaid tile'.[133] Escobar was allowed to take in a group of *sicarios* with him and continue running his business from his new base. He was not even obliged to stay inside: police would block off traffic to allow his motorcade to visit the football stadium for a game or for nightclub outings.[134] Yet he was indiscreet enough to ruin his settlement with the government: he hounded two of the cartel families he felt were disrespecting their arrangements, then killed the heads of these families in La Catedral itself. Again, state authority was being openly defied, forcing César Gaviria, now president, to intervene. The army arrived. Escobar was to be moved to another detention point. There was a tense standoff, then the drug boss escaped.[135]

American assistance had by then begun pouring in under the Andean Initiative. A task force of SEALs sailing off the coast had helped take Gacha down. The Americans also contributed surveillance equipment and teams.[136]

Alongside them, Colombia had created a new special police unit named Search Bloc, based in Medellín. Kept separate from the un-trustworthy Medellín police, this was placed under the command of Colonel Hugo Martinez, a low-profile police administrator of 48 who would nevertheless surprise everyone by staying the course until the job was done.[137] Search Bloc took the fight to Escobar's organization on its home ground. The cartel took more casualties. By the end of 1992 twelve of Escobar's top players had been killed in gun battles with the task force, including his best *sicario*, nicknamed Tyson. It was becoming increasingly clear that he was flailing when he offered a $2,000 bounty on every Medellín policeman.[138]

Nor was wanton brutality the solution: the tables began to be turned on Escobar by another group. In January 1993 a hacienda owned by his mother was burned to the ground. Two car bombs exploded in front of apartment buildings where his family members were staying. A third exploded at a property owned by him, injuring his mother and aunt. A people's militia styling itself Los Pepes (for People Persecuted by Pablo Escobar) was bringing his own methods to the cocaine baron. (The group may have been supported by any number of organizations, including Search Bloc itself or the Cali cartel, but most likely it was formed by the Moncada and Galeano families, whom Escobar had attacked while still at La Catedral.) Los Pepes shot Carlos Ossa, Escobar's banker. They gunned down his managers and dealers. They burned the warehouse where he kept his collection of antique cars.[139] Escobar could not fight a war on two fronts.

Besides, there were only so many places where he could safely hide, and at last the Search Bloc started to close in on his position. The fugitive had a close escape when one of his houses was raided, a run-down place where he had been sheltering with two women, a cook and an eighteen-year-old girl he had been 'dating'. In December 1993, by tapping into communications with his son, the Bloc was able to locate him a second time. Hugo Martinez, an officer and the son of the Search Bloc commander, drove over and identified their target by sight in the window of a house, part of a nondescript row of similar two-storey buildings. The Bloc moved in, surrounding the place. As the assault team charged in, Escobar's bodyguard, nicknamed Limón, leapt out of a window and onto the back roof. He began running, but the snipers arrayed in the street behind opened fire and he fell. Escobar followed, having kicked off a pair of flip-flops to jump. As he tried to reach over to a sloping roof of orange tiles on the opposite side, he too was shot multiple times, sprawling forwards. The men scaled the roof and turned the body over, recognizing his bearded face and black curls.[140]

The hunt for Escobar was at an end. It was a victory for justice and, at least cosmetically, for the war on drugs. Five years later, the Commission on Narcotic Drugs would still be boasting: 'Effective law enforcement operations had fragmented the large cartels that once dominated the cocaine trade.'[141] Even then, the massive effort invested in the endeavour had barely proved sufficient, and victory had only been clinched with the help of the extra-judicial means provided by Los Pepes. The Medellín cartel had nevertheless been busted. Cali, or others, could take over.

Twenty-five years on, Escobar's hippopotamuses have thrived and invaded Colombia's rivers, having escaped from the lakes where he kept them. An estimated eighty or more hippos live on, tramping on the native flora, the descendants of the drug lord's original four.[142] The vignette is an apt metaphor for the war on drugs.

Just as the attempt to suppress the opium supply in Turkey and later in the Golden Triangle caused it to move first to Burma and Pakistan and then to Afghanistan, the long string of cocaine-suppression programmes merely moved the drug's sources around. Between 1986 – when the large-scale campaigns began – and the end of the 1990s, coca-leaf output fell in Peru and Bolivia: from 150,000 to 69,000 tons for Peru and from 71,000 to 23,000 tons for Bolivia. Colombia's output rose to compensate, from 18,000 to 261,000 tons.[143] This was even while eradication efforts skyrocketed, from approximately 3,000 hectares uprooted in 1986 to more than 73,000 in 1999.[144]

Colombia, which had seen the most spectacular campaigns – the imprisonment of Lehder, the killing of Escobar, an ensuing clamp-down in Cali – remained at the end of the century responsible for 67 per cent of world cocaine output.[145] Worldwide, the authorities were seizing cocaine to the tune of 360 tons.[146] Anti-narcotics squads were raiding more than 2,000 labs annually.[147] Yet the cocaine that made it to market was more than double what it had been in the mid-1980s.[148] Likewise, according to a u.s. State Department report, the world's illicit supply of opium multiplied five times between 1971, when the axe was taken to the French Connection, and 1999.[149]

A classic argument for anti-narcotics enforcement is that it forces prices up, thereby curtailing demand. But the average street price for cocaine in the usa fell from $400 a gram in 1981 to $170 at the end of the 1990s. Adjusted for inflation, the price decline was even steeper. As to heroin, within ten years from the mid-1980s, average prices fell from $225 to $110 per gram in Western Europe. In the usa heroin prices likewise collapsed by half while purity increased.[150]

Seven years after his predecessor had said effectively the same thing, in 1989 George Bush proclaimed: 'I have some bad news for the bad guys: hunting season is over.'[151] His drug tsar promoted a policy of tough enforcement, promising to reduce drug use by half within a decade. 'This scourge will stop,' he boasted.[152] More cocaine supply-suppression plans followed, with bigger budgets. Operation Support Justice went through four iterations. The u.s. government donated more helicopters to Bolivia and assisted in the launch of more militarized campaigns. For the better part of two decades, it ran a major suppression operation called the Air Bridge Denial Program. This attacked not only air routes into the u.s. but trafficker supply lines between Peru, Bolivia and Colombia. The programme mobilized, beside local police forces, the DEA, the CIA, the FBI and the Coast Guard, plus various institutions operating under the Department of Defense. In 1996 the Department of Defense announced the launch of Operation Laser Strike, with nine countries participating and any number of radars and aircraft. In 2000 President Clinton broke ground on a new 'Plan Colombia' with a $1.3 billion military budget to train anti-drug units, supply helicopters and defoliate coca fields.[153]

None of this can be shown to have had any significant effect. The deck was and remains stacked too heavily against enforcement. To begin with, for all the big budgets, there was a simple inadequacy of means. Between 1980 and 2004 the u.s. government spent $45 billion on drug-supply control in foreign countries.[154] This may sound like an impressive number, but UNODC estimates that the total market for illicit drugs at the end of that period was $320 billion *annually*. Even at the wholesale level (rather than street value), this was $94 billion.[155] In other words, what financial means traffickers were able to deploy outmatched law enforcement by a factor of over fifty.

Even if one chose to count the anti-narcotics budgets of other developed nations (themselves much smaller) and the boots on the ground provided by supplier countries in Latin America and elsewhere, the total would still fall well short. The get-rich-quick potential of illegal drugs ensures that traffickers can always find foot soldiers. The DEA and French anti-narcotics bureau calculated that in the early 1990s the price mark-up for opiates between the Golden Triangle and Europe was 1 to 1,000. For cannabis it was 1 to 300.[156] Opium-to-heroin mark-ups in the time of the French Connection were of a similar order.[157]

Aside from raw financial logic, three factors work to hinder and make ineffective the efforts of anti-narcotics agencies. The first is that traffickers are willing to embrace levels of violence that far exceed what police forces are prepared to deploy, or even what the military may be allowed in a civilian context. The Medellín cartel's bombing of the Avianca flight, with its full load of passengers, just to get at one man whom they were not even certain was on the plane, is sufficient illustration.

Trafficking organizations, moreover, stop at nothing to acquire the best military hardware on the black market. An analyst commented, in the time of the Air Bridge Denial Programme: '[They] have state-of-the-art equipment, including satellite radios, digital decryption devices, and voice privacy mechanisms, that makes it difficult for even the u.s. armed forces to penetrate. General Gorman made this clear when he said, "I have seen equipment used on the aircraft that fly between the United States and Colombia, and I can assure you that it is more sophisticated and more facile [*sic*] than the equipment that I had on my aircraft of the u.s. Air Force in the u.s. Southern Command.""[158] Latin American trafficking organizations have been known to possess equipment including sub-machine guns, rocket launchers, anti-tank rockets, surface-to-air missiles, dynamite, night-vision devices, Kevlar ballistic helmets, helicopters, radio transmitters and 'modern wiretapping equipment', alongside simpler firearms.[159] The same could be said, of course, of the Burmese or the Afghan warlords. Nor is training an issue: the Mexican Zetas, for example, were originally an elite, airborne special forces unit trained for apprehending drug-cartel members. Hired for much higher pay by the Gulf cartel, they decided to go it alone around 2003, becoming a self-standing drug-dealing organization. They have been known to enlist members of the Guatemalan special forces to bolster their ranks.[160]

The second, insuperable hurdle anti-narcotics forces have faced is corruption. The Bolivian 'cocaine coup' provides an illustration at the highest levels of government. It was not alone. Drug dealing became institutionalized in Paraguay under Alfredo Stroessner until his departure in 1989. The Paraguayan leader and his dependents directly managed drug-trafficking enterprises, which became a major source of funds for the armed forces. The same could be said of Panama under both President Omar Torrijos and Manuel Noriega. In the Bahamas various officials including Prime Minister Lynden Pindling and cabinet ministers were exposed during the 1980s for taking bribes from American and Colombian drug traffickers, including Carlos Lehder.[161]

In these high-profile cases, at least, foreign actors and international institutions are able to exert pressure. Part of the American arsenal is an annual certification process by which the president provides Congress with a list of drug-producing and trafficking countries. In order to gain certification, a nation must be confirmed in this process to have 'cooperated fully' with or to have undertaken 'adequate steps' in tandem with u.s. policy. Lack of certification can cost a country military and economic aid, access to multilateral lending institutions and trade preferences.[162]

More insidious and difficult to deal with has been police and judicial corruption, made all the more effective by the stark choice of *plata o plomo* forced on countless humble officers and judges. Most of Mexico's 350,000 police officers made less than $250 per month as of 2010. In 2009, 93 of them were arrested in the central state of Hidalgo for being on the Zeta payroll: some were receiving as much as $225,000 monthly.[163] In the 1980s Bolivian traffickers were known to grant police and town officials between $15,000 and $25,000, more than their annual salary, just to keep quiet for 72 hours and allow a small aircraft to land, pick up a drug load and take off again.[164] An academic study dated 1994 calculated that Mexican drug traffickers spent as much as $500 million in bribes annually, more than double the budget of the Attorney General.[165]

Third, reflective of the huge incentives available to them, drug traffickers have proven infinitely adaptable. Their smuggling techniques have ranged from the most technologically advanced practices to the simplest tricks. In 1997 former Soviet mini-submarines were confiscated in Santa Marta, a Caribbean port, and found to be loaded with cocaine from Colombia.[166] A police officer from Douglas, Arizona, describes a far more basic system: 'Sometimes . . . someone runs to the fence from the Mexican side and lobs a long football-like ball to someone on the other side. There was a report this week from Nogales that people were seen in the surveillance cameras throwing softball-sized aluminium foil balls into the u.s. while others were seen collecting the balls. One of the balls was found to contain an assortment of controlled pills . . . In the days before taller fences, several would jump the fence and scatter in a nice shotgun approach, while only one would be carrying the payload.'[167]

In another tactic, the cartels have been gifted at enlisting local populations in their fight, creating enclaves where the law cannot reach them. Escobar was not alone in showering social works on his community. In the Bolivian town of Santa Ana the *narcos* 'dispensed largesse like village squires', installing street lighting, founding clinics and building a 'house of culture' containing 5,000 books. When in 1989 the police and DEA launched an assault on the town, the population rose in armed resistance, prompting a shootout. The local drug baron was nowhere to be found.[168] The same system prevailed in Burma under Khun Sa and Lo Hsing-han, who were able to pay for infrastructure and social services well in excess of what the central government might provide.

Traffickers have also learnt to keep one step ahead of anti-narcotics forces in their cultivation and manufacturing processes. Fumigation and eradication of coca fields in the Andes merely led cultivation to shift around between countries, from Peru and Bolivia to Colombia and back again. But growers also responded by shifting cultivation within countries. Within Colombia, production moved to more remote regions and agricultural zones, spreading out geographically.[169] A farmer threatened: 'If they fumigate 20 hectares here, we'll cultivate 200 hectares over there. They'll have to get rid of the whole forest.'[170] But growers also adapted through agronomical innovation, such as by increasing plant density, using fertilizers or planting new, faster-growing bush types, boosting yields. As of 1986 the Andean regions produced 240,000 tons of coca leaf on 200,000 hectares. In 1999 it was able to deliver 353,000 tons on 220,000 hectares, a 34 per cent increase in yield. Manufacturing processes also became more efficient, and the pure cocaine yield per ton of leaf increased by an even broader margin.[171]

The same process of adaptation has been at work among illegal amphetamine labs. One of the provisions of the UN's 1988 Convention was to impose restrictions on precursor chemicals, the materials used for making bootleg synthetic drugs. This included ephedrine and pseudo-ephedrine, key amphetamine precursors.[172] However, regulations, while restricting the trade on these products in bulk, left them available without prescription in most countries, in pill or capsule form. Traffickers switched, buying the pills. When, in the

USA, recordkeeping on these was tightened, setting individual limits, dealers sent individuals out in droves each to buy their legal over-the-counter limit. Larger-scale traffickers moved operations to Mexico, and, when that country clamped down, to South Africa, China or India. Some of them switched from ephedrine to phenyl-acetone, a substitute, and when this was barred they began synthesizing phenyl-acetone from other chemicals ('pre-precursors').[173]

The principal result of thirty years of ever tougher supply-suppression efforts, rather, has been deepening and expanding violence. The Colombian violence looked exceptional at the time. It continued after the kingpins fell, and it was nothing compared to what would come to Mexico.

Already in the 1970s Mexican poppy growers and heroin refiners had briefly stepped into the breach created by the dismantling of the French Connection. The authorities, with U.S. assistance, sprayed and destroyed several thousand hectares in the later part of the decade.[174] Mexican output has grown back gradually, and by the year 2016 it counted approximately 26,000 hectares of poppy, yielding 500 tons of opium, or enough to account for 10 per cent or so of world heroin production.[175] Alongside, there existed a profitable business growing marijuana and smuggling it into the USA. Cocaine, however, has been the making of the Mexican drug cartels.

The petty Sinaloan gangster Felix Gallardo – soon to be known as the godfather or 'El Padrino' – took control of the trade towards the beginning of the cocaine boom, assisted by Ernesto 'Don Neto' Fonseca and Rafael Caro Quintero, both of whom were marijuana smugglers. Gallardo began dealing in cocaine in 1977 or 1978, and he appears to have first struck a deal with Gacha of the Medellín cartel.[176] The Mexicans picked up Colombian product and moved it north and over the border, though for now they played second fiddle to the Colombians, who retained control of the vital American distribution.

El Padrino imposed a peace of sorts, but this collapsed in the 1980s. The DEA agent Enrique 'Kiki' Camarena had infiltrated Gallardo's network. In 1984, based on information provided by him, a squad of Mexican soldiers raided and destroyed a 1,000-hectare marijuana plantation known as 'Rancho Bufalo'. In February 1985 Camarena was abducted. He was tortured for at least two days and killed. But the DEA responded with another investigation leading to the arrests of Don Neto and Rafael Quintero. Although El Padrino escaped, he was on America's wanted list, undermining his position as kingpin. Gallardo divided the cartel into regional fiefdoms: the Tijuana route, on the Californian border, went to one family, the Arellano Felix, while Ciudad Juarez, on the Texan border, went to the trafficker Amado Carrillo Fuentes, soon to be known as the 'lord of the skies' for his possession of a large fleet of cocaine-smuggling aircraft. The Sinaloan, Pacific coast operations, through which the drugs moved north from Colombia, fell into the hands of three men: Ismael 'El Mayo' Zambada, Hecto Palma 'El Güero' and Joaquín Guzmán, also known as El Chapo.[77] Gallardo was arrested in 1989. The Sinaloans, supported by Carrillo Fuentes, soon entered into a long-running conflict with the Arellano Felix. Involving several shootouts in Tijuana and Guadalajara, the fight notably included the inadvertent killing of Cardinal Juan Jesus Posadas Ocampo, Archbishop of Guadalajara.[78] He was but one of the thousands and even tens of thousands of victims to come.

The second step towards never-ending drug wars was that the Mexicans acquired control of u.s. distribution, creating far higher stakes. The long fight against the Medellín and then the Cali cartel had taken its toll, but it was the Mexican traffickers, not anti-narcotics enforcement, that benefited. The Sinaloa–Tijuana clash was the first of many vendettas, some of them nationwide. The twenty-first century would see gruesome killings, beheadings and the routine shooting of bystanders. As Sinaloa and Ciudad Suarez went on to battle it out with the Gulf, then the splinter group that was Los Zetas, far more blood would be spilled.[79] Difficult as it was to believe after the closure of Escobar's saga, at the time, drug-related violence in Latin America was only in its first innings.

As the twentieth century came to a close, the rise of El Chapo to worldwide fame and the headlong rush of the Mexican drug cartels into blood-soaked anarchy lay in the future. That two decades of muscular supply suppression in Latin America and in South and Southeast Asia had achieved nothing was not yet clear, or at least not clear to all. The surrender of Khun Sa, the killing of Escobar: the headlines had been good, no matter what story the data told. The Commission on Narcotic Drugs congratulated itself: 'Improved cooperation between law enforcement authorities had contributed to some of the largest drug seizures, forcing traffickers to constantly shift transportation routes in moving illicit drugs to markets. Improved judicial systems had made it more difficult for drug traffickers to buy their freedom, while tougher extradition laws denied them the national havens that they once could count upon.[180]

In 1998, faithful to its mandate, the UN called a conference for one more push against drugs. What it envisaged was a fight to the finish, a last, victorious battle. Attendance was correspondingly high-level, involving multiple heads of state. '"Yes" to the challenge of working towards a drug-free world,' proclaimed Kofi Annan, the secretary general, to the assembled dignitaries.[181] The UN would commit to reducing worldwide drug use 'substantially' by the year 2008. An attending political declaration promised new strategies for 'overcoming the world drug problem [and] to reduce both the illicit supply of and the demand for drugs'.[182] Belying its supposed novelty, it would involve tighter transnational cooperation, more crop eradication and tougher enforcement. That neither coca nor poppy acreage were falling did not matter: there would be more efforts 'with a view to eliminating or reducing significantly the illicit cultivation of the coca bush, the cannabis plant and the opium poppy'.[183]

Others, however, wished to draw the lessons. For them, the paltry results of the latest iteration of the war on drugs were proof enough that it could not be won. Nor was the level of violence it produced something they could continue to contemplate. Ever more strongly enforced prohibition was not the answer. It was time for other solutions, or at least for an earnest debate.

9

THE CONSENSUS
CRUMBLES

A few days before the special UN session of 1998, an open letter landed on Kofi Annan's desk. A long list of academics, journalists, diplomats, legislators and cabinet ministers from countries belonging to the six continents had had enough. 'We believe that the global war on drugs is now causing more harm than drug abuse itself.'[1]

Prohibition, they wrote, had only empowered organized crime, helped corrupt governments, stimulated violence and distorted both commercial markets and moral compasses. The UN had an essential role to play in combating the harm from drugs, but only if it was willing to face tough questions about past efforts. A fresh response was required, focused on health, education and development rather than on yet more interdiction efforts. 'Realistic proposals to reduce drug-related crime, disease and death are abandoned in favour of rhetorical proposals to create drug-free societies,' the letter complained. 'Mr. Secretary-general, we appeal to you to initiate a truly open and honest dialogue regarding the future of global drug control policies – one in which fear, prejudice and punitive prohibitions yield to common sense, science, public health and human rights.'[2]

For ten years or so already, public challenges to the drug-control order had been gathering. Drug prohibition had always had its critics: politicians who found its characterizations excessive, doctors who resented the misappropriation of addiction theory, artists who complained of the constraints on their creativity. The failures of the war on drugs in its post-Nixon phase, from the 1980s onwards, now encouraged a large number of people to speak out for the first time.

The first protests emerged in the USA, the country most actively and visibly committed to the fight. As the 1998 address confirmed, however, challengers to the consensus were by then arising everywhere.

Historically, there was no lack of alternative models to drug prohibition. The alternative best known to contemporaries was the free-for-all that had prevailed in the United States and Britain in the nineteenth century and into the early twentieth. But even the nineteenth century offered other precedents: the regulatory regime reliant on pharmacy laws long prevalent in France, Germany and a number of other European countries, for example. What one might call the Franco-German or the Continental model neither punished nor explicitly outlawed recreational use, permitting drugs to be sold only in pharmacies and on prescription. (This model had witnessed far lower rates of opiate use than in the USA or UK.) The apparatus of prohibition consists of an overlay of punitive legislation – national and international – over a set of pharmacy laws. Remove the punitive superstructure and there remains a system by which drugs are legally limited to the medical sphere, albeit one that shows far fewer teeth in punishing contraband and infringement. It might be called prohibition lite. Under it, drugs revert to what they were originally – medicines – and are treated as such at every step.

A third paradigm available for historical comparison is offered by the Southeast Asian opium monopolies of the interwar period. This consisted of government monopolies of varying geometry, sometimes encompassing cultivation and/or production, sometimes the retail trade, and always imports and exports. Under the regime that became most typical of the end of that period, consumers were registered, with the effect that the supply of drugs was limited to established users and closed to new applicants. The idea was that user numbers would trend down, but the same mechanisms could be deployed to manage the pains of a stable or growing population. The principle was that of another model for dealing with drugs of addiction: the British system as it emerged in the wake of the 1926 Rolleston Report.

The post-Rolleston drug regime was the product of a classically British compromise. It existed in practice more than in the law, and it may even be described as encompassing two conflicting systems, one run by doctors and the other by the Home Office, coexisting in a state of mutual respect. When this balance was lost, in the late 1960s, the system shrivelled without the intervention of any fundamental legal change. Yet the so-called British system was important because, even as it entered the end of its life, it became a point of reference for those seeking alternatives to the war on drugs, especially in the USA. Its central feature was also destined to become a key weapon in the armoury of drug-control challengers elsewhere: drug maintenance.

At the initiative of Sir Malcolm Delevingne, under-secretary at the Home Office responsible for drugs, Britain had during the First World War passed the anti-narcotics directive known as DORA Regulation 40b. This was formalized and extended in the first major piece of British anti-narcotics legislation: the Dangerous Drugs Acts of 1920. Delevingne, who also became the chief drug-fighter on the League of Nations' Opium Advisory Committee, was for 'stamping out addiction' as the Americans were doing.[3] The law, however, specified that listed drugs were allowed for legitimate medical purposes. Delevingne felt compelled to turn to the Ministry of Health in order to establish what exactly this meant. At stake was whether prescribing to addicts on the grounds that they could not do without their drug – a practice known as maintenance – constituted a legitimate medical purpose.

The task of investigating the matter was given to a Departmental Committee on Morphine and Heroin Addiction, chaired by Sir Humphrey Rolleston. All the Rolleston committee members were medical men, though one was also an analyst at the Home Office. While the committee did not quite speak with one voice, its key members, including Rolleston himself, were convinced of the need to protect the addict from the ravages of penal law. The result was an official statement that the long-term prescription of drugs to patients to treat their addiction was legitimate medical practice. Addiction was a private matter that belonged nowhere else but in the relationship between patient and medical practitioner. The Home Office need not be notified, let alone allowed to punish either doctor or patient.[4]

The report, published in 1926, did not have the force of law, but its recommendations were written up in a memorandum distributed among the medical- and dental-care professions. The medical world would decide who deserved to receive morphine, heroin or cocaine. Anyone who dealt in or took drugs outside it remained at the mercy of law enforcement. (That there were few addicts and that they were predominantly middle-class people viewed as respectable helped cement the compromise.) Tribunals were established to decide, in borderline cases, whether there were 'sufficient medical grounds for the administration of the drugs by the doctor concerned', leaving the Home Office the last word under this delicate balancing act.[5]

In the USA maintenance had briefly survived the passage of the first great piece of anti-narcotics legislation, the 1914 Harrison Act. A number of outpatient clinics dispensing heroin and cocaine pre-existed the Act, and many more were set up after its passage.[6] The new law permitted a doctor or druggist to dispense drugs 'in the course of his professional practice only'. Whether this included main-tenance was no clearer than under Britain's Dangerous Drugs Act. The difference was that the question was resolved, in the USA, in the courts. The issue was probed by the Supreme Court in the 1920 case of a Pittsburgh physician, Jin Fuey Moy, who had been selling mor-phine prescriptions to addicts for the purpose of maintaining their habit. Moy was condemned for providing or selling prescriptions to persons who were not his usual patients and 'for the mere purpose ... of enabling such persons to continue the use of the drug'. The defend-ant was a known 'dope doctor', and the precedent was therefore not entirely clear-cut. *United States vs. Behrman*, dated 1922, laid all remain-ing doubts to rest: Behrman, a doctor, had given prescriptions for grains of heroin, morphine and cocaine to a patient named Willie King, yet 'King did not require the administration of either morphine, heroin, or cocaine by reason of any disease other than such addiction.'[7] The court condemned Behrman. Maintenance, the jurisprudence now said, was illegal.

The American maintenance clinics swiftly closed. Anslinger would liken them to 'stations to spread leprosy and smallpox'.[8] Maintenance was rejected in favour of the search for a cure. In order to keep addicts out of prison, the Public Health Service opened two institutions known as narcotic farms, located in Lexington, Kentucky, and Fort Worth, Texas. The farms, which opened in the 1930s, pro-vided a three-phase treatment: a thirty-day profiling phase that began with ten days of detoxification, a phase of several months employed in farm work or crafts, and a final phase of preparation for the return to the outside world.[9] The Lexington facility also ran an addiction research centre. Where exactly the farms fitted within the penalization of drug use was ambiguous. Their original reason for existence was to separate those convicted on possession charges from traffickers. But attendance was usually compulsory, and a secondary aim was to keep addicts under confinement while they were being rehabilitated. For this reason and for their forbidding aspect, they were sometimes called 'prison farms'.[10] The author of *Junky*, William S. Burroughs, provides his own unique take on them: 'There was nothing wrong with the accommodations, but the inmates were a sorry-looking lot. In my section, there were a bunch of old bums with the spit running out of their mouths. You are allowed seven days to rest in population after medication stops. Then you have to choose a job and go to work. Lexington has a complete farm and dairy.' After these seven days, Burroughs, sick from withdrawal, absconded in search of drugs with a group of inmates.[11]

Apart from this option of dubious worth, the American drug user, if caught by law enforcement, faced the harsh penalties of incarceration. As sentencing toughened in the 1950s, prominent organizations such as the American Bar Association and the American Medical Association became alarmed. Having failed to derail the legislation which, in that decade, enshrined the ever harder penalization of drug users, they turned to the British system for a potential way out.[12] If the addict could discreetly be maintained on his or her drugs by a doctor, perhaps he or she could be kept out of Anslinger's clutches in the first place. Maintenance, though not quite an alternative form of legalization, can if generalized become tantamount to user decriminalization, albeit under medical supervision. Prominent writers on drugs of addiction came to vaunt the British system, notably Alfred Lindesmith, a long-time critic of the nexus between addiction theory and punitive drug laws, and Lawrence Kolb, an addiction researcher and the Lexington farm's first director.[13] Into the 1970s two major research institutions, one private (the Drug Abuse Council) and one public (the National Institute on Drug Abuse) would be conducting major studies of the history of British drug policy.[14]

The paradox was that just as it was being rediscovered across the Atlantic, the British system came under attack at home. In the next twenty years, it was Britain who ended up adopting America's harsher model, not vice versa.

Ostensibly the Rolleston compromise collapsed because a handful of gullible doctors were discovered to be prescribing heroin pills to addicts who were obviously reselling them on the black market. In the background stood official distress at the seeming glorification of drugs in 1960s youth culture and rises in drug use. The Home Office checked on the proper functioning of the Rolleston norms through an interdepartmental committee: this reported in 1961 that all was well. Such was not the conclusion of the second report of the Brain committee, named after its chairman Sir Russell Brain, published in 1964. A few doctors were making large prescriptions to patients who could only be reselling the pills. Indeed, the case narrowed down to that of one London doctor, Lady Isabella Frankau, whose philosophy was that addicts should never be denied what they asked for: 'In 1962 one doctor alone prescribed almost 600,000 tablets of heroin (i.e. 6 kilogrammes) for addicts. The same doctor, on one occasion, prescribed 900 tablets of heroin (9 grammes) to one addict and, three days later, prescribed for the same patient another 600 tablets (6 grammes) "to replace pills lost in an accident".'[15]

The committee's solution was, first, to raise supervision one notch by asking doctors to notify addicts to a central authority and, second, to restrict the right to prescribe dangerous drugs to authorized treatment centres.[16] Nothing changed in the law. On paper, the Rolleston system was modified even less fundamentally than the Brain committee recommended: theoretically individual doctors continued to be allowed to prescribe heroin or cocaine, provided they obtained a licence to do so. From 1968, nevertheless, practices changed, causing the old system to wilt. The Home Office had taken control, breaking the balance that had prevailed for forty years. It issued more than five hundred licences, but almost all of them went to psychiatrists, all hospital-based.[17]

The psychiatrists decided that addicts could and should be cured through abstinence. Clinics or 'drug-dependency units' could theoretically still dispense drugs for addict maintenance but, endowed with fresh ambition and matching support staff (doctors, nurses, social workers, psychologists), they adopted the loftier goal of full rehabilitation. The drug-dependency units moved away from prescribing heroin except as a bridging measure: between 1971 and 1978, just as British opiate use began to boom, the amount of heroin they prescribed fell by 40 per cent. Most clinics had by the mid-1970s adopted a strict withdrawal programme in lieu of long-term prescribing.[18]

Just as it was attracting increasing interest abroad, then, the long-prevalent British practice of drug maintenance was coming into disuse. More than the rectification of a prescribing particularity, this was a shift away from drug liberalism: if addicts are able to obtain drugs at will, at least for private consumption, from doctors rather than street dealers, their habit is effectively decriminalized and the black market sidelined. At the same time, since the shift in the British system did not rely on legal change, it could be reversed again. This is what happened in the 1990s when, partly as a result of pressure from the mounting AIDS epidemic, some of the drug-dependency units picked up heroin maintenance anew. By then, however, a lively debate over the merits of drug prohibition in general had taken hold both at home and beyond British shores.

The United States and other developed countries were pouring significant means into supply suppression in Latin America and Southeast Asia. So far they had little to show for it. The war on drugs was not leading to falls in user numbers. This was the first trigger for contestation. The second was the AIDS epidemic. People who injected drugs were dying from AIDS and they were passing the disease around. Illegality was helping neither tracking nor prevention. Both factors, emerging in the second half of the 1980s, gave vent to the first systematic challenge to prohibition in at least half a century.

The signatories to the 1998 letter included a number of political figures nationally known in their home countries alongside jurists, diplomats and personalities from journalism and the arts. Prominent American figures involved in the fight included the mayor of Baltimore Kurt Schmoke and ex-Secretary of State George Shultz. Ten years earlier, Schmoke had been one of the very first to call for a national drug-policy overhaul. His proposal – to legalize all drugs, whether marijuana, heroin or crack cocaine – had attracted significant media attention at the time and acted as a catalyst for the nascent drug debate.[19] George Shultz had been Secretary of State under Reagan and was as such one of the architects of the conflict's late militarization. His support for a change of tack spoke loudly as to suppression's supposed successes in Latin America.

Equally important were the academics – sociologists, historians and, in particular, criminologists – who fed the debate with data and questioned its assumptions. Key contributors included the criminologist Arnold Trebach and the political scientist Ethan Nadelmann. Nadelmann's Lindesmith Center, founded in 1994, coordinated the open letter to Kofi Annan. It would merge in 2000 with Trebach's Drug Policy Foundation, founded in 1987, to form the Drug Policy

Alliance (DPA). In the twenty-first century the DPA would go on to play a key role in the legalization of marijuana in multiple American states. Significant debate participants otherwise included the historian David Courtwright, the sociologist James Inciardi and, in Europe, the French sociologist Anne Coppel and the Dutch criminologist Tim Boekhout van Solinge, to name but a few.

The star of liberal economics Milton Friedman was another 1998 signatory. Though Friedman was not a regular drug commentator, his involvement was important because it stood for the philosophical argument for liberalization. The University of Chicago economist had made the case against drug prohibition as early as 1972. In a *Newsweek* opinion piece, just as Nixon was beginning to take down the French Connection, Friedman had warned: 'We cannot end the drug traffic. We may be able to cut off opium from Turkey – but there are innumerable other places where the opium poppy grows. With French cooperation, we may be able to make Marseilles an unhealthy place to manufacture heroin – but there are innumerable other places where the simple manufacturing operations involved can be carried out. So long as large sums of money are involved – and they are bound to be if drugs are illegal – it is literally hopeless to expect to end the traffic or even to reduce seriously its scope.'[20]

Friedman's argument was a return to Mill's ideas on liberty and the sanctity of individual choice: 'On ethical grounds, do we have the right to use the machinery of government to prevent an individual from becoming an alcoholic or a drug addict? For children, almost everyone would answer at least a qualified yes. But for responsible adults, I, for one, would answer no. Reason with the potential addict, yes. Tell him the consequences, yes. Pray for and with him, yes. But I believe that we have no right to use force, directly or indirectly, to prevent a fellow man from committing suicide, let alone from drinking alcohol or taking drugs.'[21] For his follower Thomas Szasz, a professor of psychiatry, the right to use drugs was 'more basic than the right to vote', a matter of sovereignty over one's own body.[22] Szasz rejected equally the notion that habitual drug use constituted either a crime or a disease, denying any validity to the theory that the drug addict was by nature unfree.[23] Prohibition, in the libertarian view, violated the individual's right to freedom from coercion. The state had no authority to impose treatment, let alone a prison term, on the user: 'An ill person generally has the right to refuse medical treatment even when such treatment is necessary to preserve that person's life. Individuals have the right to refuse treatment because the value of controlling one's own destiny outweighs the economic, social and emotional costs of a premature death.'[24]

The libertarian argument was important because it tended to be made by right-wing commentators who might otherwise have sided with hard-line prohibition. As such, it would play a key role in the twenty-first-century legalization of marijuana. Libertarian legalizers, nevertheless, were few. Even the war on drugs' vocal critics tended to be wary of grand legalization proposals. The debate principally ran along utilitarian, not ideological, lines. Even after legalization, it was pointed out, sales to minors would presumably still attract penalties, so drug-related incarceration would not entirely end. If drugs, like alcohol, were taxed, they would likely continue to generate smuggling.[25] Proposals to change the system, then, ranged widely. Some wished to legalize certain drugs only, typically marijuana but in some cases also psychotropics such as LSD. Others merely sought to remove the criminal penalties on drugs, especially on possession – an alternative to decriminalization being depenalization, a policy by which offenders were not prosecuted or at any rate not jailed, but continued to carry a criminal record. Continued prohibition, finally, could be tempered with 'medicalization', in various permutations akin to the British system in its post-Rolleston days.[26]

Liberalizing criticism of prohibition likewise came to rely on three main practical arguments. First, prohibition threatened public health by forcing users to resort to unsafe practices. Second, the war on drugs enriched gangs and fostered violence. Third, the means deployed in policing and incarceration were wasted and better used in treatment. To this was added, in the USA specifically, a fourth point: that the war on drugs fell predominantly on African Americans and was inherently racist.

'The unintended victims of drug prohibition policies', argued Nadelmann, 'are the 30 million Americans who use illegal drugs, thereby risking loss of their jobs, imprisonment, and the damage done to health by ingesting illegally produced drugs; viewed broadly, they are all Americans, who pay the substantial costs of our present ill-considered policies, both as taxpayers and as the potential victims of crime.'[27] Consumers of injected drugs bought from the street pumped adulterated substances into their bodies, sometimes comprising materials more dangerous than the drugs themselves. Bootleg pills sold as LSD or Ecstasy might well be deadly alternatives, and the youth who bought them undercover on a night out had little way of knowing. Black-market purchases, the fear of asking for treatment because it might attract criminal sanction: such were the results of prohibition, and they put lives at risk. The AIDS epidemic made the danger yet more imminent. 'AIDS is a greater threat to our survival than all of the drugs combined,' warned Trebach. 'Properly designed drug maintenance (even those providing for medical heroin and other feared drugs) and needle-exchange programmes should be advocated as essential elements in all AIDS-control strategies and bills.'[28] AIDS was not even the only danger. In 2017 UNODC estimated that 585,000 people died worldwide as a consequence of drug use; among these deaths, 50 per cent were from hepatitis C and another 10 per cent from AIDS, both of which can be contracted through unsafe injecting practices.[29]

Anti-narcotics enforcers had long argued that drugs fostered crime. The trope had been a favourite of Anslinger, who used it to scare legislators into toughening drug laws. The Swedish minister of health, Margot Wallström, speaking at the UN, complained of girls 'falling in love with an older boy with drug problems, then dropping out of school, and then turning to crime'.[30] Crime, the liberalizers countered, was the product of prohibition, not of the drugs themselves. Perhaps the worry should not be imaginary marijuana-fuelled axe murderers, but the thousands of victims of a Pablo Escobar empowered by smuggling riches. Kurt Schmoke, in his initial call for a debate, had argued that legalization would cut the grass from under the dealers' feet and drastically reduce violent crime.[31] Prohibition itself boosted criminal statistics by making drug dealing or using an offence. 'Producing, selling, buying, and consuming strictly controlled and banned substances is itself a crime that occurs billions of times each year in the United States alone. In the absence of drug prohibition laws, these activities would obviously cease to be crimes,' began Nadelmann.[32] Perhaps users also committed crimes such as robberies or muggings to feed their habit; but illegality, by making drugs more expensive, only made such infractions more common. Legalization, on the contrary, would reduce drug-related violence, especially by criminal gangs: 'Legalization of the drug market would drive the drug-dealing business off the streets and out of the apartment buildings, and into legal, government-regulated, tax-paying stores. It would also force many of the gun-toting dealers out of business.'[33]

Related to crime was the question of law enforcement, incarceration, the associated budgets and whether they were well spent. During the Californian campaign for marijuana legalization, the former San José police chief Joseph McNamara would be quoted as saying: 'I know from thirty-five years in law enforcement. Today, it's easier for a teenager to buy pot than beer. Proposition 19 will tax and control marijuana just like alcohol. It will generate billions of dollars for local communities, allow police to focus on violent crimes, and put drug cartels out of business.'[34] It was not just the billions spent overseas in eradication programmes or the hunt for elusive drug lords. Pursuing addicts and street dealers cost police time and money, reformers argued. Incarceration itself was expensive. A German study dated 1981 estimated the costs of drug repression, including that of keeping 5,000 people in jail, at a minimum of DM 2.5 billion (€1.25 billon) annually.[35] Would this not be better spent on anti-overdosing pills or job creation in poor areas? The funds freed from incarceration could be used to subsidize social programmes, treatment and prevention.[36]

Added to this bill was the racial bias which drug prohibition evinced and perpetuated, reformers believed. The American statistics were stark. As of the mid-1990s 78 per cent of American marijuana users were white, as well as 71 per cent of cocaine users and 41 per cent of heroin users, yet 74 per cent of federal prisoners on drug offenses were Black and 16 per cent Hispanic.[37] This could not be explained by the higher penalties on drug dealing, had relatively more dealers been Black. Actually, a survey from the same period found that Blacks represented no more than 16 per cent of dealers and whites 82 per cent.[38] Penalties fell more heavily on minority populations, especially those who were Black, feeding a cycle of ghetto lawlessness and repression. This bias had been fed by the passage of tough laws against crack cocaine, whose use was more prevalent among deprived African American communities. In 1986 Congress had introduced mandatory sentences of five to ten years on offences involving as little as 5 grams of crack – by comparison to a threshold of 500 grams for powder cocaine. Though tough laws on crack played well to Republican electoral agendas, they were, moreover, a bipartisan effort, betraying institutional bias. President Bill Clinton failed to overturn the blatant discrepancy between sentencing on crack and powder cocaine when he got the chance.[39] Racial disparity was growing with incarceration rates, regardless of the party in power: between 1976 and 1996 white drug arrests climbed by 86 per cent, while Black drug arrests increased 400 per cent.[40] That the war on drugs perpetuated racism was a key libertarian argument; it would feature in the legalization of marijuana and in its preparatory campaigns in the 2010s.[41]

The argument in favour of prohibition was rarely articulated. It benefited, rather, from simple inertia and the public's belief that if something was illegal, there had to be good reasons. The case was nevertheless advanced formally by James Wilson, who had been Nixon's chairman of the National Advisory Council for Drug Abuse Prevention, in the review *Commentary* in 1990. Wilson ridiculed Friedman and the liberalizers. He rightly praised the Nixon administration's success in the fight against the French Connection. His statistics, and his chronology, were more questionable. In the ensuing two decades, rates of heroin use had remained approximately flat, Wilson contended, whereas they would have risen had the drug been legalized. The point would have been statistically more valid on marijuana, and it rather ignored exponential rises in amphetamines and cocaine, including crack cocaine use. Wilson also criticized the British system, which in his opinion had led to skyrocketing opiate use; he seemed unaware that the heroin wave he was describing had actually coincided with the system's relinquishment. But Nixon's former council chairman only really made one main point. The war on drugs was being neither won nor lost: the problem was contained. Prohibition kept user numbers down. Were it relaxed, they would skyrocket.[42]

Ultimately, the entire debate hinged on that question. It did not matter that prohibition placed the lives of injecting users at risk or that incarceration cost money if one accepted that it kept drug use down drastically. The prospect of creating tens of millions of new addicts dwarfed the disappointments of floundering supply suppression overseas. Nor were reformers able to offer a firm rebuttal. Researchers consulted the decriminalization of marijuana in certain Australian states in the 1980s and '90s and the 'coffee-shop' policy of cannabis toleration practised in the Netherlands. Neither data set was conclusive. Cannabis use had increased in the Australian states concerned, but the rise was not significant. Dutch marijuana consumption had remained broadly stable for years, then doubled between

1984 and 1996 – but similar trends could be observed in countries that had not liberalized, such as Canada, Norway or the UK.[43] A weakness of the reforming camp was that it tended to concede implicitly that legal availability would lead to higher rates of use by at least some margin.[44] From historical example, this is far from clear. Past surges in drug use have obeyed sociocultural trends often irrespective of availability. It suffices to compare nineteenth-century India to China, or twentieth-century Turkey to Iran. There remained the unknowable question: would a relaxation of the rules cause drug use to shoot upwards?

Pointing at the injustice of the war on drugs was not enough. Perhaps it was costly and ineffective: to convince a sceptical or an apathetic public, reformers needed to prove that legalization was safe. Because it involved assessing a leap into the unknown, this was, in turn, an impossible task. The emergence of an active, multi-sided debate was an important development to the course of the long war on drugs, but for now it was insufficient to force a reversal. Would attitudes about drugs and the risks they involved themselves change? There was the possibility that they might with yet another shift in the forever fraught concept that was addiction.

The popular meaning of the term 'addiction' has changed in the past couple of decades. The word is proudly displayed in Dior perfume advertisements. Video games are vaunted as addictive in their own marketing material. Routinely, everything and anything is described as addictive, from coffee to shopping or from jogging to social media. Negative connotations have disappeared, or they have been downgraded so much that the concept has lost its teeth. Yet somehow drug addiction remains in its own category. Ask someone why drugs should remain illegal and the knee-jerk response is: they are addictive.

In the aftermath of the WHO's abandonment of the word 'addiction' in favour of 'dependence', medical organizations were deserting the concept – the American Psychiatric Association, for example, dropped it in favour of 'substance use disorder'.[45] Yet while the terms changed, at heart remained the age-old question: did drugs make the user sufficiently unfree to justify his or her punishment or forcible confinement by the state?[46] Historically, addiction theory had been born of medical observation. The problem was that such observation centred on patients, failing to take into account casual or healthy users. A more complete picture started to emerge after the Second World War and especially from the 1960s as sociologists became involved – Alfred Lindesmith was a forerunner – as psychiatrists took a second look, and as governmental and other healthcare institutions began to produce more systematic data.

The first thing this research confirmed was that many people took drugs, even opiates, without becoming addicted. Contracting a habit, it showed, did not automatically follow from experimenting with drugs. One piece of evidence concerned returning veterans from the Vietnam war, who were systematically subjected to drug tests. GI urinalysis tests showed that 5.5 per cent used heroin. The actual proportion was likely higher, as soldiers faked the test because they needed to pass it to be discharged: the rate has been estimated at between 11 and 19 per cent. One study found that 95 per cent of them were clean of opiates a year after their return; within three years, only 2 per cent of returning GIs had continued to use the drug with any regularity.[47] Context was everything: once removed from the horrors of war, the need for the drug disappeared, however hooked many of these GIs had become.

More robust data are produced by the American Substance Abuse and Mental Health Services Administration (SAMHSA). SAMHSA has been estimating, based on surveys, the nationwide number of users for an array of intoxicants. The data are compiled both in past-year and past-month format: that is, SAMHSA estimates how many people have been using each drug at least once a month and, separately, once or more in the last year. In 1995 there were 428,000 past-year but only 196,000 past-month heroin users. The difference, 232,000 people, had taken the drug that year yet were not sufficiently addicted to have used it at least once a month. For cocaine, including crack, the past-year total was 4,682,000 and past-month 1,873,000.[48] For both drugs, this suggested, the majority of users were casual, prepared to take the drug occasionally but not dependent enough to use it once a month, let alone every day.

The psychiatrist Norman Zinberg, a National Institute on Drug Abuse researcher, found concrete examples of such casual or controlled use. One of his interviewees was a forty-year-old carpenter, a man who had been married for sixteen years and had three children. The man had been using heroin for ten years at weekends only. Exceptionally he had used heroin midweek, but not in the last five years.[49]

When asked how he avoided becoming an addict, another interviewee replied: 'Well, I have responsibilities, you know, and I keep my use down. If I wasn't married and I didn't have my son or my business, then I think my chances of becoming an addict would be very strong.'[50] Zinberg's research focused on opiates. Over a long period, 23 per cent had used less than once per month on average, 36 per cent monthly and 41 per cent weekly.[51] Zinberg remarked: 'The argument [for prohibition] implies a straight-line arithmetical relationship between use and misuse, which does not exist . . . It is likely that current social policy is discouraging primarily those who use drugs only moderately, while heavy users, to whom the substance is more vital, are flouting the law in order to make their "buys".'[52]

Alongside compulsive users whose existence was undeniable, there existed others for whom a subculture of controlled consumption kept addiction at bay. Several subjects reported engaging in daily activities while high, such as taking their children to a sporting event, washing the floor, talking with people, working or playing the piano.[53] These users developed their own rules, often enforced through peer pressure: special sanctions such as 'do not use every day' or limiting use to weekends, confining it to safe physical or social settings, or rituals to prevent it from invading their personal life.[54] Controlled users tended to shun addicts. One might chastise another for manifesting junkie-like behaviour: being dirty or disorderly, being unable to master the drug's effects, spending too much on drugs, cheating others and so on.[55] Nineteenth-century China, too, had developed social codes differentiating respectable and excessive opium smoking, reserving it to specific classes, settings or occasions.

More recently, researchers have sought to rate addiction mathematically, or at least to place the various intoxicants on a single scale. One study asked experts to rank eighteen substances on how easily they 'hooked' people and how difficult they were to quit. Marijuana ranked fourteenth in its addictiveness, behind nicotine (first), alcohol (eighth) and caffeine (twelfth). Hallucinogens (Ecstasy, LSD and psilocybin), ranked yet further down the list.[56] Sliding away from addiction, another attempt at ranking intoxicants looked at the risk of overdose, defined as the ratio between a lethal dose and the most commonly taken, regular dose. The lower the ratio, the more dangerous the drug. Heroin had a tenuous safety ratio of 5, alcohol was at 10, cocaine at 15 and marijuana over 1,000.[57]

Such comparisons have not always helped probe the addiction–prohibition paradigm. On the contrary, they can easily drift into a vaguer labelling whereby intoxicants are generally seen as harmful, implicitly or explicitly making the case for control. One such approach sought to develop a 'rational' scale for assessing the overall harm from intoxicants. Harm was defined as including physical and social harm (defined as cost to society and family, to healthcare systems, social care and law enforcement), and the risk of dependence. Dependence itself was made to include three parameters: intensity of pleasure, psychological dependence and physical dependence. The scoring, performed by the members of a panel, was equally arbitrary.[58] (Heroin came first and alcohol fifth, with marijuana and the psychotropics once again towards the bottom.) Another, EU-sponsored study renounced addiction in favour of what might be termed the social-democratic definition of dependence: 'heavy use over time'. The concept, the authors found, 'fits better with models of public health, bringing in health and social consequences over and above the criteria currently derived from medical classifications'.[59] The need to regard the addict as unfree was circumvented altogether, individual freedom being in any case 'subsidiary' to the 'common good'. Drugs were bad according to how much they burdened the social-security system – though here, too, alcohol struggled to look good.[60]

Still more problematic was that addiction simultaneously enjoyed a fresh lease of life with the development of brain science. In 1973–4 a group of Stanford University and Johns Hopkins academics had discovered that the brain contains receptors capable of bonding with morphine molecules. It was later shown that these receptors interacted with a multiplicity of endogenous chemicals whose function it was to relieve the stresses of danger or pain. The discovery paved the way for a revival of addiction as a measurable, relapsing brain disease.[61]

How the interaction of morphine or other intoxicants with neuronal receptors constituted or caused addiction was not explained, but another invention came to the researcher's rescue: the brain scan. Scans allow researchers to show what parts of the brain react to drug intake, lighting them up. They show that some of these areas change in volume over time, including the right amygdala, a section believed to be active in processing emotions and memory.[62] A key finding has been that this impact is particularly strong during adolescence and until the age of 21, when the brain remains more plastic, potentially causing long-term alterations.[63]

Brain imaging does not explain how these potentially durable alterations create a habit mechanism. It is purely descriptive. Scans also show that the brain returns to normal after periods of abstinence of varying length – fourteen months, for example, for a meth user.[64] Research based on scans has, moreover, been drug-specific, again primarily centred on opiates. If anything, differences highlighted by brain imaging have proved that lumping illicit drugs together as addictive is questionable from a scientific point of view.[65] The problem was fixed with yet another discovery: dopamine. The release of dopamine, an organic chemical involved in the brain's pleasure and reward mechanisms, is common to a multiplicity of intoxicants and to all drugs of abuse. As researchers explain: 'At the receptor level, these increases elicit a reward signal that triggers associative learning or conditioning. In this type of Pavlovian learning, repeated experiences of reward become associated with the environmental stimuli that precede them.'[66] The attenuated release of dopamine over time from the repeated use of drugs could even explain tolerance, smaller increases in dopamine being observable among tolerant subjects.[67]

Dopamine's involvement in withdrawal mechanisms is more difficult to pinpoint.[68] Dopamine, moreover, can be shown to be involved in the mental rewards from much more than just drugs. Alcohol, too, triggers dopamine rushes, in addition to acting on its own identifiable receptors. That these rewards abate with repetition is nothing new: the law of diminishing returns applies to all pleasurable activities, whether jumping into cool water on a hot day or eating chocolate.[69]

Brain science has nevertheless helped drug addiction make a comeback as something grounded in biological fact verifiable by science. Healthcare and drug-control organizations highlight brain theory in their pamphlets, even while their documents concede that genetic, psychological and environmental factors ('lack of parental supervision', 'community poverty') remain important in circumscribing addiction.[70] The American National Institute on Drug Abuse explains: 'Our brains are wired to increase the odds that we will repeat pleasurable activities. The neurotransmitter dopamine is central to this. Whenever the reward circuit is activated by a healthy, pleasurable experience, a burst of dopamine signals that something important is happening that needs to be remembered. This dopamine signal causes changes in neural connectivity that make it easier to repeat the activity again and again without thinking about it, leading to the formation of habits.'[71]

In lay parlance, the idea of the 'hijacked brain' has taken the place of the nineteenth-century 'disease of the will'.[72] Just as sociological and psychiatric data were becoming available to nuance received wisdom, inventions such as the brain scan intervened. For all the graphic precision, brain mapping does not interact with knowledge about the neurochemistry of drug use to produce a theory of addiction. It is very unlikely that cellular analysis can ever explain the complex social behaviours involved in the habitual recourse to any of the illicit drugs, let alone to all of them as a group. The illusion that it does, however, reinforced the drug-debate stalemate, cementing the inertia protecting the drug-control system from its challengers.

At a CND session on the drug treaties, the American representative rebuffed calls for reform on the grounds that 'addiction is a disease of the brain.'[73] Opinions on drugs and drug control were too hard to budge. Neither public views on drug control nor views on addiction and on the drugs themselves were liable to shift materially. The reformers simultaneously understood that they needed to change tack. Rather than seek to dismantle the system, they would turn to altering it from the inside. The result was a credo known as harm reduction.

Harm reduction is a broad church, and it has enjoyed some overlap with the legalization movement. Harm reductionists have included the historian David Courtwright, who rejected liberalization for its over-ambition and lack of detail, but also on occasion the Drug Policy Alliance, the creation of the key liberalizing critics of the war on drugs Arnold Trebach and Ethan Nadelmann. The DPA's website writes: 'Our mission is to advance those policies and attitudes that best reduce the harms of both drug use and drug prohibition, and to promote the sovereignty of individuals over their minds and bodies.'[74] Europe-based harm-reductionist lobby groups have included the Beckley Foundation, the Transnational Institute and the British association Release, to name but a few. The Beckley Foundation, the creation of the British heiress Amanda Feilding, informally succeeded Timothy Leary, without the theatrics, in the defence of LSD and other psychotropics. The Transnational Institute, left-leaning and less bold on drug reform, has taken up harm reduction as one of several social causes. Release is distinguished by its consultative status with the powerful Economic and Social Council of the UN, a body ranking above UNODC.[75]

Harm reduction focuses on practical reforms to health and legal systems, a number of which were tested in various countries in the 1980s and '90s. Outside the devotion of greater means for treatment, it has involved three chief policies. The first and most basic has consisted of needle and syringe exchange programmes, occasionally extending to safe injection rooms. The second has included opiate maintenance provision, generally on substitute opiates but sometimes on heroin itself. The third has involved the removal of penalties on possession, whether on marijuana only or on all drugs.

The first needle exchange programme opened in Amsterdam in 1984, with the aim of preventing the spread of hepatitis B. The idea was that if multiple users avoided sharing the same needle, they would not spread intravenously transmittable diseases. The policy soon received a significant impulse as health services everywhere woke up to the existence and implications of AIDS. Programmes opened in one European country after another, and they had spread throughout the EU by 1993. Syringe exchange programmes also opened, more haltingly, in a variety of American states, having met significant opposition at the federal level and been denied funding.[76]

Going one step further were supervised injection rooms, also known as drug consumption rooms. Here the user is provided with not just a clean syringe but an environment where he or she can be free from the depredations of street consumption. Crucially, the rooms are overseen by personnel equipped to intervene in case of an overdose, especially by administering the inhibitor Naloxone. Injection rooms first opened in the 1990s in Switzerland, followed by Germany, the Netherlands and Australia. Later adopters have included Canada, Luxembourg, Norway, Spain and France, and such rooms are under consideration in a few more jurisdictions.[77] In the context of prohibition, supervised injection rooms have been more controversial than syringe exchange programmes. They more explicitly condone drug injecting and require the police to turn a blind eye. Still more controversial, nevertheless, has been drug maintenance.

In the 1930s a group of German scientists developed a synthetic opiate named methadone, destined to serve during the Second World

War to relieve Germany's morphine shortage. One among many such derivates, it initially attracted little attention, though the Lexington farm took it up as a tool to palliate withdrawal symptoms during the inmates' initial weaning phase. Then, in 1962, the New York City Health Research Council asked the Rockefeller University academic Vincent Dole to assemble a team to research heroin addiction. While reading up, Dole came across a book by a young Harlem psychiatrist, Marie Nyswander, entitled *The Drug Addict as Patient*. He convinced her to join. Dole and Nyswander experimented on various substitutes, including codeine and morphine. They eventually picked methadone, which Nyswander knew from work in Lexington.[78]

Methadone produces, in tolerant users, longer-lasting effects than other opiates without triggering a euphoric high. It has the power both to block the high produced by heroin (an effect labelled the 'narcotic blockade') and to eliminate withdrawal pains. It can also be administered orally. Dole and Nyswander introduced it to maintenance, and the results were spectacular: more than 90 per cent retention in treatment and the virtual cessation of heroin use. The two researchers were rewarded with the prestigious Lasker Prize. A few years later, Nixon seized on their results to create a Special Action Office for Drug Abuse Prevention, with the maintenance convert Jerome Jaffe in charge. By 1975 the United States possessed over four hundred methadone programmes, serving more than 75,000 patients.[79]

Ironically, methadone maintenance soon petered out in the USA while it bloomed in other countries, where it had initially been greeted with scepticism. Methadone, after all, even if it is not heroin, is also a scheduled drug. Drug warriors consider methadone maintenance a form of surrender. Quitting it can be also difficult – clinical studies have shown relapse rates of 50 to 70 per cent after it was discontinued.[80] Though methadone has continued to be available throughout most of the USA, its accessibility became patchier, often limited to clinics, with more use for detoxification and less under maintenance programmes.[81] By contrast, in the 1980s, methadone use began expanding in other developed countries. Australia, for example, produced national methadone guidelines in 1985. These make the drug available from general practitioners, and users pick up their prescriptions in pharmacies.[82] Methadone maintenance has likewise become established in a number of European countries, though in some, such as Sweden and France, the synthetic opiate buprenorphine has become the alternative of choice.[83]

Heroin maintenance made its own return around the same time. The British drug-dependency units that had been created to substitute for the old, post-Rolleston system were struggling to cope as opiate use spread. The arrival of AIDS threatened to take a heavy toll. A clinic in Merseyside, in the neighbourhood of Liverpool, initiated one of the first syringe exchange programmes. Local police agreed they 'wouldn't hang around outside and target clients'.[84] Emboldened, the Merseyside staff decided to expand the service to include heroin maintenance, for which it was already licensed. The programme was rounded out with counselling, plus employment and housing assistance. The Merseyside project, though it at first made waves, brought about a revival of British heroin maintenance, including among licensed general practitioners.[85]

Switzerland, which was afflicted with one of the highest rates of opiate use in Europe, took a similarly bold step shortly thereafter. The programme enlisted 1,000 volunteer heroin addicts, launching at first experimentally in 1994. Later expanded and having been vetted by referendum in 1997, it is still running. The Netherlands launched a heroin maintenance trial next, in 1996, and Denmark in 2009. Canada initiated a similar programme in 2005 named the North American Opiate Medication Initiative (NAOMI).[86] Heroin is provided to patients at one clinic: the Providence Crosstown clinic in Vancouver. The total number of patients treated has remained small, in the low hundreds. None has died under the clinic's supervision, however, which also relies on a safe injection room. A reporter describes the results as follows:

> John Pinkney can trace his drug use back to the age of 6, when he was first prescribed Ritalin. By his 20s, he was using heroin and other street drugs. Now in his late 50s, he says his life is in a much better place. He has a part-time job. He brags about owning a television and furniture – the kinds of things others might take for granted, but were hard-fought for someone struggling with drug addiction. 'I have a two-bedroom apartment,' Pinkney said. 'I have things. I got my TV and my pet and living room furniture and bedroom furniture. You know, it's like I got my life back.'[87]

Yet the most radical harm-reduction initiative was its third and final tier: user decriminalization. The best-known exercise in the field has probably been the Dutch cannabis 'coffee-shop' regime. A 1960s public debate on marijuana had led to the formation of another commission of inquiry: the Baan commission, named after its chairman Pieter Baan, chief inspector of mental health. The Baan report, published in 1972, was noncommittal: it was divided on the health effects of marijuana, and it raised the problem of the Dutch commitments under the international treaties. But Dutch heroin use was rising, and the government wished to prioritize law enforcement against hard drugs. In 1976 a new Opium Act (as the Dutch drug laws continued to be called) drew a distinction between cannabis products and drugs believed to present greater risks, including heroin, cocaine, amphetamines and LSD. Penalties for dealing in hard drugs were raised. The possession of marijuana and hashish in amounts up to 30 grams (1 oz) was conversely downgraded to a misdemeanour.[88]

The government shrank from full legalization out of respect for its treaty obligations. Decriminalization, as a result, was a compromise measure. The Dutch regime was left with the contradiction that the sale or possession of small quantities was tolerated, including in coffee shops, but cultivation and wholesale handling remained fully criminalized.[89] In the early 1990s the government again considered legalization, or at least extending toleration to local cultivation and wholesale activities. This met with direct opposition from the French president Jacques Chirac, who attacked the proposal in the name of cooperation against crime and the 'harmonization' of EU drug policy. The Dutch authorities backtracked, lowering the permitted amount of coffee-shop sales to boot.[90] The number of coffee shops has declined since then, falling below 1,000 after the turn of the century.[91]

Yet bolder and higher-profile has been the decriminalization experiment that took place in Portugal from 2001. There, it was not just the possession of cannabis that was decriminalized, but all illicit drugs.

Portugal stood in the midst of a heroin epidemic, with accompanying infectious diseases and AIDS. Its per capita heroin use was the highest in Europe. The government, wishing to make changes, appointed an expert commission whose key figure was João Goulão, a doctor and founder of the country's network of drug-abuse treatment centres. Goulão knew the pitfalls of criminalization at first hand:

the justice system further isolated users, worsening their prospects. He believed that treating or ending addiction was best done *in situ* within communities, not in jails or compulsory centres. For this to be made possible, drug possession first needed to be decriminalized.[92]

The reform he recommended was enacted in July 2001. (Goulão would go on to become Portugal's 'drug tsar' through multiple administrations, and he would become an international ambassador for harm reduction.) The possession of drugs below certain thresholds ceased to be a criminal offence in Portugal. Users were now referred to a district-level commission for the dissuasion of drug addiction made up of three people: a lawyer, a social worker and a medical professional. The commissions were empowered to impose a fine, psychological counselling and/or other minor sanctions or, if the user was (or is) judged addicted, referral to an education programme. Trafficking has remained punishable in Portugal, quite severely.[93]

Several European countries have since then decriminalized the possession of some or all drugs. Though Portugal has tended to overshadow them in terms of public attention, actually Italy and Spain decriminalized drug possession before it. Spain reformed its drug laws in 1983. A new provision distinguished soft from hard drugs, with two different ranges of penalties for trafficking and none for possession. Though there have been borderline cases and ambiguities, such as relating to gratuitous transfer, drug possession has remained exempt from punishment (other than through a fine if practised in a public place) since then.[94] Italy passed a new drug law in 1975 that redefined chronic drug use as an illness. Personal use and the possession of small quantities were downgraded to administrative offences. The system underwent a brief hiatus between 1990 and 1993, when the possibility of prison for possession was reintroduced – although only with short sentences and in repeat cases – and when the offence was reinstated as criminal. Since then, though drug users may be subject to penalties such as the temporary suspension of their drivers' licence, drug possession has ceased to be a crime in Italy.[95] Estonia, in 2002, was the next country to decriminalize after Portugal. Other European countries to have decriminalized the possession of all drugs in later years include Bulgaria, Croatia, the Czech Republic, Latvia and Slovenia.[96]

None of this, unsurprisingly, went unnoticed. Harm reduction pushed ever more insistently at prohibition's boundaries. Criticism of the war on drugs, willy-nilly, was translating into practice. In an increasing number of countries, the authorities were becoming less willing to stick to the script. Their policies were beginning, from the turn of the century, to make a nasty dent in the shiny coachwork of drug control. It would have been surprising if the anti-narcotics system had not fought back. As the 1990s closed and as harm reduction began to make visible progress in various jurisdictions, it began to attract pushback.

Harm reduction works, its partisans protested. The epidemiological evidence has been that needle or syringe exchange programmes save lives. Supervised injection rooms help distribute information about safe injecting and put users in touch with social and medical services. They prevent overdoses from becoming lethal, and do not appear to encourage a greater number of people to inject drugs.[97]

The Portuguese decriminalization, though sometimes contested, is generally considered to have produced good results. Total drug use continued to increase in the years following the reform, but the data are distorted by the large share taken by cannabis. Both drug use by youths and drug injecting fell.[98] A few years later, Portugal's rates of opiate, cocaine and amphetamine use stood no higher than in a typical European country, and far lower than in the United States.[99] By 2015 its incidence of injected drug use, principally heroin, had dropped significantly compared with 2000.[100] Critics have complained that the number of people imprisoned for drug possession was already low before the reform, and that the total of arrests plus administrative citations remained high afterwards.[101] The effects on crime and incarceration were nevertheless notable. The proportion and number of offenders sitting in Portuguese prisons for drug-related offences – including offences committed under the influence or to pay for drug purchases – both fell sharply. Prison overcrowding ended.[102] More generally, the main decriminalizing countries have not stood out for increased levels of drug use. The data are patchy, but whether for opiates, cocaine or amphetamines, country rates merely vary, with no discernibly higher rates for the countries that have decriminalized possession compared to those that have not.[103]

None of this prevented harm reduction from coming under strenuous criticism as it began to make headway. In 1998 the American drug tsar Barry McCaffrey labelled harm reduction 'a hijacked concept that has become a euphemism for drug legalization'.[104] The hijacked concept met a stubborn resistance both institutionally and diplomatically. Prohibitionist stalwarts included Japan and Russia. In Europe France was long a hold-out, later replaced by Sweden.[105] Hard-fought discussions took place at the CND over needle exchange programmes, with EU countries leading the charge against opposition from the USA, Brazil, Japan and Russia, among others.[106] In 2000, for example, at the CND: 'Concern was expressed about the policy of some Governments that permitted the establishment of drug-injection rooms for drug abusers or the provision of heroin to them. Some felt that such a practice ignored the extent of the problem. One considered that it amounted to abandoning drug abusers.'[107] The clash continued into 2008, with the 1998 action plan for achieving a 'drug-free world' coming up for review, when a group of 26 countries publicly expressed their frustration at the failure to agree on a harm-reduction mandate.[108]

The competing concept the UN institutions and anti-narcotics forces promoted was demand reduction. But while this may sound similar to harm reduction, the two philosophies overlap only in a limited way, in the general sense that they both approve of treatment measures. Demand reduction focuses on the hope that information and propaganda will dissuade potential users from experimenting with drugs. On the contrary, harm reductionists begin from the assumption that such efforts have long been proven to be futile, and it is best to focus on damage limitation. While demand and harm reduction both involve treatment, moreover, they differ radically in the type of care they offer. Demand reduction essentially envisages treatment as an exhortation to abstinence. Its central feature is rehabilitation, with at best a short-term role for substitutes such as methadone. Maintenance is anathema because it is perceived to perpetuate drug use. As to user criminalization, at least implicit in demand reduction is the notion that the higher the penalty, the more strongly will anyone be dissuaded from using drugs. This is in straight contradiction to harm reduction.

The 1980 CND report, as an illustration, listed a number of demand-reduction initiatives. These included the opening of rehabilitation centres in Mexico, American education programmes on the risks of marijuana, an Italian ministerial decree curtailing methadone distribution, and precursor-chemical controls in the German Democratic Republic.[109] Such was not the style of measures likely to appeal to harm reductionists. The best compromise that could be found, in 1998, was to declare that to the existing goal of preventing the use of drugs should be added that of 'reducing the adverse consequences of drug abuse'. This, though, was little more than papering over the cracks: 'While China, Japan, the Russian Federation, the United States and several other countries are in favour of traditional demand reduction efforts (prevention) in order to reduce demand, most European countries, as well as Australia and Canada, tend to support policies that also contain elements of harm reduction (such as needle-exchange programmes) so as to reduce drug use-related HIV/AIDS rates and/or keep them low.' Meanwhile: 'Harm reduction programmes should not be carried out at the expense of, or be considered substitutes for, activities designed to reduce the demand for illicit drugs.'[110]

International bodies are first and foremost diplomatic forums. Their position is only as good as that of their member states, or what consensus their member states are able to muster. The CND's views only reflected such politics. Yet the INCB, part of whose role it is to oversee the due implementation of the conventions, also stepped in. In 1999 it wrote that any state that permitted supervised injection rooms 'could be considered in contravention of the international drug control treaties'. Subsequent reports followed a similar line, singling out Australia, Canada, Germany, the Netherlands, Norway, Spain and Switzerland.[111] In parallel, the board suddenly challenged the Dutch coffee-shop system, calling it an incitement in its annual reports. (The Dutch replied that their Opium Act remained in compliance with the treaties, which impose the demand that each participant criminalize possession only 'subject to its constitutional limitations'. The objection is less valid, however, when it comes to penalizing the traffic itself: Dutch tolerance also turns a blind eye to cannabis sales, which may have been what attracted the INCB's ire.[112])

If harm reduction made progress around the world it was surreptitiously, country by country. China was long a key opponent of reform. After several decades of having been rid or almost rid of drugs, its government had discovered at the end of the 1980s that narcotics use was making a comeback. It used the 150th anniversary of the First Opium War in 1990 to conduct a patriotic education campaign. The message was that, starting from that war, China had experienced a series of defeats and humiliations at the hands of Western imperialists, a situation that had only been rectified after the Communists took power. Being soft on drugs was unthinkable.[113] On the contrary, a new get-tough strategy became the order of the day. A 1990 law introduced fresh jail sentences up to life imprisonment or, in severe cases, the death penalty for those convicted of smuggling, trafficking or manufacturing.[114] From 2000, nevertheless, China began to embrace measures for reducing the vulnerability of injecting drug users to AIDS. It established its own methadone programmes: soon, it would have more than five hundred methadone clinics. By 2009 thirteen Asian states were prescribing methadone or buprenorphine, including Cambodia, Bangladesh and Thailand, though the practice has remained illegal in Russia.[115]

Separately, a 2002 report by the legal affairs section of UNODC ruled that substitution and maintenance treatments as well as drug-injection rooms were compatible with the drug treaties.[116] UNODC may be junior to the CND and INCB, but it is also filled with experts inclined more towards practical solutions than to member-state politics. It was an important change when it began supporting alternatives to incarceration, a euphemism for the decriminalization of possession: 'Where appropriate, governments should consider providing treatment and rehabilitation to drug abusing offenders, either as an alternative or in addition to conviction or punishment.'[117] The INCB, finally, had been critical of the Portuguese decriminalization before the fact. Perhaps mindful of the disastrous political fallout if it came out with a formal condemnation, following a mission to the country in 2004 it concluded that Portugal remained in compliance with the treaties.[118]

Harm reduction, with each inroad, was chipping at the drug-control consensus. Its policies, by the turn of the twenty-first century, were enjoying piecemeal adoption around the world. Institutional sniping notwithstanding, their proponents were often able to squeeze under the UN agencies' radar. If such initiatives as user decriminalization and maintenance came to make headway, moreover, they stood to make a fundamental, practical difference to the drug-control order.

Such achievements nevertheless remained local and fragile. For all the subterranean change, as the twenty-first century dawned, prohibition remained paramount. The apparatus of narcotics suppression survived, and even thrived. The treaties retained, in their strictest expression, the support of powerful states, and the UN institutions were not standing idly by. In a sense, furthermore, harm reduction represented a step back from the legalizing challenge that had arisen alongside it. Harm reduction sought to mitigate rather than end prohibition. With it, legalization, the idea that the war on drugs was failing and required a redesign, had given way to a more modest compromise approach. The debate that had sprung up in the 1980s, however, was not over. Three developments would impart a new dynamic to calls for reform: the opioid epidemic that was beginning to spread throughout the United States, sudden progress in the legalization of marijuana, and continued violence in Latin America.

10

OPIATE OVERDOSE

From 1995 a group of pharmaceutical companies began flooding the American market with prescription opioids – drugs synthetically derived from and/or similar to opiates. A large dependent population quickly arose. The regulators were powerless, or rather their efforts were stifled by the pharmaceutical origins of the drugs and the efforts of their big-capital manufacturers and distributors. Deaths by overdose ensued on a large scale. At the height of the epidemic, the American overdose toll rose to the equivalent of one Vietnam War per year. By the end of 2020 the crisis had killed at a minimum 300,000 people and as a best estimate 500,000.[1]

From a historical perspective, two observations jump out. First, the parallel with the late nineteenth-century spread of opiate addiction from iatrogenic causes is stunning. The opioid epidemic that has hit the United States was born of irresponsible prescribing married with regulatory capture by pharmaceutical companies, like its predecessor. The only difference was that it took place on a far grander scale. It is hard to escape the thought that, one hundred years later, they ought to have known better. A second salient feature has been the powerlessness of law enforcement. If one administration has distinguished itself in the whole affair, it has been the DEA. Yet faced as it was with a malfunctioning regulatory model and surging user demand, it could achieve little more than damage limitation. When the information on drugs is faulty and deep-seated factors favour increasing uptake, supply suppression is powerless. This has been a recurrent theme of this book.

The opioid epidemic has, more basically, made a mockery of the war on drugs. It is not just that historical precedents that ought to have been institutionalized were forgotten. The American government allowed its death toll from opioids to rise far above that of illicit drugs for years on end. While it did next to nothing at home, it continued to run anti-narcotics campaigns in Asia and Latin America and pretend that its drug problem was the work of a few traffickers, especially foreign ones. Astonishingly, even now the epidemic has yet to run its course. While it has morphed into an illegal opiate crisis, its pharmaceutical origins remain clear for all to see. Twenty years on, the official response to this entirely preventable tragedy has remained business as usual.

The crisis has helped make the argument for harm reduction. In 2017 the FDA commissioned an expert report to draw lessons from what had taken place and make proposals for the future. This contained no silver bullet, but several of its recommendations – such as initiatives to forestall overdose deaths – were harm-reduction staples.[2] The same ideas have been catching on in the mainstream press and among state governments, some of which have been boosting their methadone or buprenorphine programmes.[3] Separately, from 2014, the Department of Justice at last came out with measures to reduce drug-related incarceration, especially for low-level offenders.[4]

Of more direct impact on the drug-control order, the opioid epidemic has done subterranean damage to the position of its American protector. The United States' incontinence at home has torpedoed its credibility abroad as the defender of a sacrosanct anti-narcotics system. The grand champion of supply suppression has feet of clay. This has made it all the more patent that opioids themselves have made the war on drugs impossible to win – if that were not already the case. Though the catastrophe, mostly confined to the USA, has been only one factor behind the inexorable rise in drug use in the first two decades of the twenty-first century, it has certainly ruled out any fall. The demand for drugs has skyrocketed, making the goal of a drug-free world recede into an ever more mythical future.

The villains of the piece have undoubtedly been the large pharmaceutical manufacturers and distributors, or a small set of them. At the heart of this set, notoriously, was one of them: Purdue Pharma. In 1962 Arthur Sackler, a psychiatrist who had once run a medical advertising company, joined with his brothers Mortimer and Raymond to acquire the minor pharmaceutical firm Purdue Frederick. The company, once known for selling tonics, at first added laxatives, an earwax remover and an antiseptic to its range. Then, in 1972, its British subsidiary developed a formula, known as Continus, for the slow release of a pill's contents into the patient's system. This extended-release technology was used for the improvement of several drugs: first an asthma drug, later morphine. MS Contin, as this last product was branded, was used in terminal care. It was a major commercial and medical success in its own right. The Sackler family rose to such social heights as to lend their name to galleries at the Smithsonian Institute, the New York Metropolitan Museum of Art and London's Royal Academy, and to projects at the universities of Princeton, Harvard and Beijing. By the 1990s, though, the MS Contin patent was running out. The Sacklers – Arthur's nephew Richard having now taken a leading role – subdivided Purdue Frederick, creating Purdue Pharma to focus on new pain treatments. In 1995 Purdue Pharma launched OxyContin, a delayed-release pill for oxycodone, a synthetic opiate with a potency between that of morphine and heroin.[5]

Purdue led the pack through its aggressive sales tactics. Other firms selling opioids on extended-release systems included Pfizer (morphine), Janssen (tapentadol), Endo (oxymorphone), Mallinckrodt (hydromorphone), Teva (oxycodone) and Insys (fentanyl). With the possible exception of Insys, Purdue was the most egregious in its marketing practices, and the others largely rode on the back of its promotional efforts.[6] OxyContin's unique selling proposition was that it was a powerful yet non-addictive analgesic. How anyone could still believe, at the turn of the twenty-first century, that an opiate with a strength superior to morphine's was not addictive seems incredible. Yet Purdue took two lines of attack to support this claim.

The first relied on the extended-release mechanism. The OxyContin sales pitch was that other painkillers needed to be taken every three or four hours, whereas it acted continuously over twelve hours, without highs and lows. This reduced the drug's abuse potential, Purdue reassured concerned doctors, helping avoid the risk of addiction. (The company's own submissions to the FDA did not quite support this claim, showing a high after three hours and a rapid decline in narcotic concentration in the blood thereafter.[7])

Purdue's second tactic was to brandish academic statements purportedly proving that opiates were not addictive when administered medically. The first of these was a 1980 letter to the *New England Journal of Medicine*, in which two doctors stated that, among thousands of hospital patients treated with opioids, almost none had become addicted. The piece was not a research article, and it provided no data – such as whether the drugs had been administered for an operation, for example, or for how long after it. Purdue now promoted its drugs for the treatment of chronic pain. Its sales efforts ensured that the pills were used for long-term administration, not post-operative or terminal care relief. Long-term prescribing maximized the likelihood of addiction. The second supposed academic proof which Purdue deployed was an article published by another pair of medical researchers, Russell Portenoy and Kathleen Foley, in 1986 in the journal *Pain*. This examined the history of cancer patients who had been given opioid painkillers over several years. Only a few had become addicted and, from this result, the authors concluded that opioid therapy was safe. The sample size was small, however: a mere 38 patients. The journal had initially refused the article.[8]

What was lacking in terms of substance was made up for in high-volume sales efforts. Purdue spent several times the advertising budgets of its rivals. It employed hundreds of sales reps. When they ceased to suffice, it licensed the product to Abbott Laboratories, which was able to deploy a sales force of another three hundred people. Soon, nearly 1,000 reps were pushing OxyContin across the country. In 1995 the USA had possessed 35,000 pharmaceutical sales reps. A decade later, it counted 110,000, many of them selling opioids.[9] Purdue targeted its message at the least knowledgeable: primary care doctors, whose sole pain-management training was at medical conferences, and dentists. A Purdue sales manager testified: 'They told us to say things like it is "virtually" non-addicting. That's what we were instructed to do . . . You'd tell the doctor there is a study, but you wouldn't show it to him.'[10] Doctors received OxyContin advertising paraphernalia including hats, mugs and CDs. Purdue held pain-management seminars and ran education programmes, flying doctors to resorts where they were invited to dinners, golf outings and spa treatments. At one stage it gave out OxyContin coupons, which patients could redeem for a one-time free prescription at a participating pharmacy.[11]

As to Insys, still more dangerous than OxyContin was its pharmaceutical product Subsys, containing fentanyl – a substance multiple times more potent than heroin and highly likely to prove fatal in high doses.[12] Subsys was approved for cancer patients experiencing adverse reactions to other opioids. Yet the vast majority of doctors Insys targeted were not oncologists. Insys sales representatives meanwhile pushed medical practitioners to increase the doses they prescribed, a practice known as titration. In an internal motivational video, a salesperson performed a rap about the drug while a man dressed as a giant Subsys bottle danced around. 'I love titration, yeah, it's not a problem,' they sang. 'I got new patients and I got a lot of them.' As the company's head of sales admitted at a trial years later, he had 'no morals, ethics [or] values'.[13]

Demand took off vertically. Sales of OxyContin rose from $48 million in 1996, the year after it received FDA approval, to over $1 billion in 2000.[14] Problems emerged as early as the year 2000, with reports of widespread diversion, tampering and misuse. The FDA responded by asking Purdue to change the label and remove the claim that extended release reduced the risk of abuse.[15] But it was easy for patients to get around extended release anyway. The label read: 'Tablets are to be swallowed whole, and are not to be broken, chewed or crushed. Taking broken, chewed or crushed OxyContin tablets could lead to the rapid release and absorption of a potentially toxic dose of oxycodone.'[16] For many, this was more a recipe than a warning. Doctors were routinely giving a full run of thirty pills to their patients: if the patient did not complete the run, others were often prepared to raid his or her toiletries cabinet.[17] By 2003 OxyContin sales had almost doubled again. In 2009 they reached $3 billion, and opioid sales of all brands three times that level.[18] Within a few more years, drugs containing hydrocodone would become the most prescribed medicine in the United States, and opioid painkillers, with more than 200 million scripts, the most prescribed class of drugs.[19] Overdose fatalities climbed alongside revenues. From 5,000 in 1999, the death toll passed the 10,000 annual mark in 2003, then the 15,000 mark in 2007.[20]

Beyond their aggressive sales methods, the opioid manufacturers were savvy at recuperating a nascent medical trend. Their marketing was egregious, but demand was not created from nowhere. Purdue, Insys and the others also benefited from and built on changes in attitudes to pain and its medication. Prescription opioids had originally been intended for postoperative or terminal cancer patients, as morphine continued to be used. The novelty was that they began to be made available for managing chronic pain. Though Purdue's lever into the market was its extended-release invention, there had to be a perceived need for a market to exist in the first place.

In the 1980s the WHO had adopted the principle of a rising scale of painkillers in palliative care, in a guideline that became known as the WHO ladder. For a while this remained confined to postoperative or terminal care, but such ideas eventually drifted into an altogether different field. By the 1990s professional and patients' organizations such the American Pain Society, the Veterans Association and the American Society for Pain Management Nursing had begun to argue that relieving pain was not just a duty for doctors treating patients in postoperative or terminal situations, but in general. Chronic pain was an illness begging for treatment, they asserted. Its symptoms could even be measured: pain became the 'fifth vital sign' (after the more mathematically calculable temperature, blood pressure, pulse and breathing rate). Sufferers from bad knees, back pain, arthritis, severe headaches, the aftermath of sporting accidents: they too must have access to the potent painkillers that had hitherto been reserved to extreme or exceptional situations. If pain could be measured, finally, so could the doctors' performance in treating it – and with this rose the pressure to prescribe.[21]

The pharmaceutical companies had found a furrow and ploughed it deeper. They found advocates eager to speak at their conferences: people like Russell Portenoy, the author of the *Pain* article recuperated by Purdue, but also the editor of the *Journal of Pain and Symptom Management* and the author of textbooks on the topic. They subsidized pain societies and websites, such as Partners Against Pain and the American Pain Foundation, both founded in 1997. (The American Pain Foundation was disbanded in 2012 after it came under a Senate committee investigation.[22]) They funded front groups such as the American Academy of Pain Medicine to educate doctors on chronic-pain treatment and to run academic journals for publishing favourable reviews. They lobbied key practitioners and medical boards to endorse the concept of the fifth vital sign. They advertised directly to consumers – the United States being one of two countries, alongside New Zealand, where consumer advertising of prescription drugs is allowed – so that they and their associations might in turn pester doctors for the opioids to which they were told they had a right.[23]

Not all doctors and pharmacists were innocent. Predictably, a few became aware of the unique financial opportunity that was offered them, and a few sufficed to turn over large volumes: they were the so-called dope doctors and pill mills. One Kentucky doctor prescribed more than 2 million pills to 4,000 patients over 101 days, seeing 133 patients per day in an office without electricity. Another was caught writing eight hundred prescriptions a month, the equivalent of one every ten minutes.[24] Distributors were sometimes no better. In one West Virginian town whose population was 2,924, a pharmacy recorded ordering 258,000 pills in a single month.[25] Another town, with a population of 406, was showered with an average of 900,000 pills per year between 2005 and 2011.[26] Pain clinics opened everywhere to partake in the bonanza. In Florida their number grew from a few dozen to more than seven hundred by 2009.[27]

Suggestions that Purdue, the other manufacturers or the distributors might be responsible for such excesses were met with ferocious denials, helped by their capture of the highest regulatory instances. Purdue consistently blamed its patients. In 2001 Michael Friedman, its executive vice president, testified before a congressional hearing convened to look into the alarming increase in opioid abuse. The marketing of OxyContin had been 'conservative by any standard', he maintained. 'Virtually all of these reports involve people who are abusing the medication, not patients with legitimate medical needs.'[28]

That Purdue had been able to convince the FDA to approve Oxy-Contin for chronic pain treatment on the thin evidence it provided was in itself surprising. That all the regulator demanded in 2001 was a change in labelling is instructive. The year after OxyContin's release, the examiner who had approved the original application left the FDA. After a stint at another pharmaceutical company, he began working for Purdue.[29] By 2003 dire warnings were coming out of academic journals. That year Endo Pharmaceuticals sought FDA approval for Opana, an oxymorphone drug with a strength superior to that of OxyContin. The FDA rejected the application after several patients in the clinical trial had overdosed. Endo performed new trials, however, enrolling more people and weeding out those who showed signs of addiction or misuse early on. In 2006 it was able to present the data it wanted to the FDA, which approved the narcotic pill.[30] (The FDA would force Endo to withdraw Opana in 2017.[31])

Opioid manufacturers went so far as to craft and impose their own prescribing norms. They lobbied such bodies as the Joint Commission for the Accreditation of Healthcare Organizations, responsible for certifying hospitals and clinics, to promote their solutions for the treatment of chronic pain. They pressed the Federation of State Medical

Boards to develop guidelines for pain treatment along the same lines, proposing to pay for their distribution. Consistently, the industry either subverted its regulatory instances or bogged them down into paralysis. Over the decade to 2015, a Pain Care Forum drawing together the industry, patient-advocate organizations and medical interests spent close to three-quarters of a billion dollars pushing policies, writing legislation and funding elected officials to promote opioids and/or oppose curbs on prescribing. Within a few years, the norms Big Pharma had helped write were adopted in 35 states. Some states went further, with laws effectively giving doctors immunity from prosecution for prescribing opioids except in blatant criminal cases.[32] In 2009 the FDA was planning a programme known as REMS, including mandatory opioid training for doctors and pharmacists and the enrolment of patients on higher-strength opioids on a national registry. The Pain Care Forum and the American Pain Foundation struck back, gathering petitions against the programme from what it described as 'people with pain'. The measures were withdrawn, including compulsory training, and the programme was eviscerated.[33]

The DEA struck back, as, increasingly, did prosecutors in the hardest-hit states. In 2005 the DEA appointed a new head to its Office of Diversion Control, a pharmacist and lawyer by training named Joe Rannazzisi. Rannazzisi began with a 'distributor initiative' to remind wholesalers of their obligations. When these warnings were ignored, he took legal action, beginning with the largest firms – the first time the DEA attacked a Fortune 500 company. In 2008 three companies were condemned – AmerisourceBergen, McKesson and Cardinal Health – though the fines were low.[34] Separately, in 2007, a West Virginian prosecutor indicted Purdue and got it to admit guilt to the felony charge of misbranding its products. Purdue agreed to pay a penalty of $600 million. Three of its executives pleaded guilty to misdemeanours: its president, its general counsel and its chief medical officer. The executives were fined a total of $34.5 million, placed on probation for three years and assigned four hundred hours of community service. There was, however, a hitch: as the result of a last-minute compromise, the conviction applied to Purdue Frederick, not Purdue Pharma. The manufacturer of OxyContin remained free to step up its sales efforts.[35]

The distributors likewise managed to thwart the DEA's increasingly intrusive interventions. Rannazzisi returned to the charge in 2011, successfully going after the Florida distribution centre of Cardinal

Health. In total, the DEA would bring at least seventeen cases against thirteen distributors and one manufacturer, helping the government levy nearly $425 million in fines.[36] But the industry was not lying supine. Lobbyists convinced Congress to adopt a bill named the Ensuring Patient Access and Effective Drug Enforcement Act. This required the DEA to warn pharmacies and distributors before moving to withdraw their licences, and it made it more difficult to freeze suspicious shipments. The DEA fought the bill, supported by the Attorney General. It passed, however, in spite of this opposition in 2015. Rannazzisi was pushed aside from his post, soon to retire from the organization after a thirty-year career. Immediate suspension orders on opioid shipments plummeted.[37]

DEA and court actions did have an intimidating effect. In 2010 Purdue released a new version of the drug with an 'abuse-deterrent formula', harder to crush for obtaining an instant high. (The FDA would continue to approve new opioid formulations, not all of them containing 'abuse-deterrent' safeguards.[38]) Deaths from prescription opioid overdoses, though they did not start falling, reached a plateau after 2011. The problem, however, was that by then a large population had become opiate-dependent. When prescription products became harder to obtain, users turned to heroin. A large share of the opioid-consuming population transitioned to illicit opiates. In one study 80 per cent of heroin users surveyed reported having begun with prescription opioids.[39]

The Mexican cartels were more than ready to meet this new customer base halfway. Dealers drove into rural states where pain prescriptions had spiked. They moved in as the pill mills moved out. Heroin was cheaper than opioids anyway.[40] The death toll rose again. But an even more dire development awaited: the cartels learnt to make fentanyl, which is cheaper and safer to produce because it does not require growing poppy in fields, only procuring precursor chemicals. It is also easier to smuggle because it is far more concentrated.[41] They began lacing heroin with fentanyl, in concentrations unknown to their customers. Fatalities from their illicit brethren overtook those from prescription opioids, climbing to 20,000 in 2015.[42] In 1999, by comparison, opiates had been responsible for fewer than 2,000 fatalities by overdose.[43]

Only massive, American-style class-action lawsuits have been able to bring the big corporations to heel. With some estimates placing the bill at $500 billion, the consequences promise to be epic.[44] More settlements have recently been agreed involving manufacturers and distributors.[45] But nemesis has been approaching in the form of a consolidated lawsuit being judged in Ohio, which is bringing over 2,500 plaintiffs, including numerous counties, cities and individuals, against everyone involved: the manufacturers, the distributors, the insurers, their shareholders, their directors, people such as the Sacklers and those, like Portenoy, who evangelized for them.[46]

The founders of the fentanyl maker Insys have been convicted of racketeering conspiracy, and face twenty years in prison.[47] Purdue Pharma declared bankruptcy in September 2019, reaching at the same time a settlement deal with 24 states and more than 2,000 cities, counties and other plaintiffs. The company agreed to pay what it claims is worth $12 billion, including cash and the assignment of future profits. The Sacklers also remain exposed to the consolidated lawsuit. They nevertheless appear to have been transferring billion-dollar sums offshore. Alongside Purdue, they also own another company named Rhodes Pharma, for making generic opioids.[48]

That it is the courts that have finally been bringing the companies and individuals responsible for this debacle to account will only make it more difficult for the lessons to be learned. Congress has not been mooting new legislation, the DEA has not been given new powers to clamp down, and the FDA has not been asked to de-list prescription opioids. The Centers for Disease Control and Prevention issued new, stricter prescribing guidelines in 2016.[49] Yet opioid prescribing for chronic pain has not ceased. New opioids are coming onto the market. Nor have the patient organizations nurtured by Big Pharma disappeared. On the contrary, they have been complaining that their supply is being curtailed.[50] The death count, meanwhile, has not been falling: as of 2019, it had merely flatlined at the very high level of several tens of thousands per year.[51]

In a last twist, the Sacklers have been seeking an international career for OxyContin through yet another one of their companies: Mundipharma. Active throughout the world, Mundipharma has been organizing seminars in Brazil, China and elsewhere to help doctors overcome 'opiophobia'. It has hired 'pain ambassadors' to preach to doctors in Colombia, Brazil, South Korea, the Philippines and Singapore. In Spain Mundipharma has been using 'naked celebrities' for publicity, hiring 'a string of topless actors, musicians and models [to tell] fellow Spaniards to stop dismissing aches and pains as a normal part of life'.[52]

It remains to be seen whether the chronic prescription of opioids will catch on in other parts of the world, though the crisis has affected Canada almost as badly as the United States.[53] The opioid epidemic has essentially been the result of regulatory failure. Countries with different and less commercialized medical systems therefore ought to be shielded from it.[54] Annual drug-related deaths in the EU remained, as of 2018, within the same ballpark as in the 1990s, at 8,300.[55] The American problem has nevertheless been making healthcare providers and regulators elsewhere nervous, particularly in Europe. The epidemic was partly the product of cultural change, namely the rising idea that all pain must be medicated away to the fullest extent, and cultural trends often cross the Atlantic eastward. As a social commentator has noted, the United States and Europe have both become 'psycho-pharmacological societies', creating fertile ground for the abuse of pain medications.[56]

Popular wisdom nicknaming OxyContin 'hillbilly heroin' proved greater than the FDA's.[57] Why green-light opioids if opiates are illicit? Anslinger, who had fought so hard to keep quasi-medical drug use out of the Single Convention, must have been turning in his grave. Conversely, it seems hard to believe that, if heroin itself had been legalized, it would not have come with better safeguards, beginning with restrictions on promotion and advertising. Fatalities from the opioid epidemic have exceeded the total number of deaths by overdose from heroin and cocaine combined between the passage of the Harrison Act and the FDA's approval of OxyContin.[58] There is no better testament to the paradoxes of the war on drugs as it has been waged in the United States. A century of drug prohibition had been for nothing.

The opioid epidemic's effects, like OxyContin itself, have worked on extended release. Alongside, another development has had a more immediate impact on drug control. A second body blow was dealt to the system, this one more benign in human terms. In the 2010s marijuana was legalized in eleven American states plus the District of Columbia – though it has remained prohibited at the federal level – and in two countries: Canada and Uruguay.

Marijuana legalization has followed different routes in these different jurisdictions. In Canada it began with medical cannabis – a step contravening at least in spirit the international conventions, which schedule cannabis among the drugs that have no medical utility – but full legalization came suddenly and at the initiative of the government. In the American states it was also preceded by the authorization of medical use, but full legalization was the result of popular ballots. Uruguay had long tolerated drug possession. Its legalization of cannabis nevertheless came suddenly, and it was government-led. In both the United States and Canada, meanwhile, reform has followed from shifts in public perception. Even in Canada, public opinion, according to polls, had long been ready for legalization. In Uruguay, however, opinion only shifted in marijuana's favour after the passage of the new law: opinions on intoxicants, unsurprisingly, are also shaped by their legal status.

The late 1960s and the 1970s had seen an early movement in favour of legalizing marijuana in a multiplicity of geographies. The governments of Australia, the UK, Canada, the Netherlands and the United States all convened public committees within ten years of each other. Their reports tended to dispel received wisdom on the terrible dangers of cannabis, though they felt compelled to warn about the need for more research.[59] 'We suspect that illegality may play an important role in problem definition where drugs are concerned,' the American report drily noted.[60] In Canada, the Le Dain Commission found the prohibitionist regime 'grossly excessive'. It recommended a number of reforms including the decriminalization of marijuana possession, though nothing came of it.[61]

The American commission had also opined: 'The Commission feels that the criminalization of possession of marihuana for personal use is socially self-defeating.'[62] President Nixon, who had just declared war on drugs, was not prepared to oblige, yet things began to change after his departure.[63] Such organizations as the American Bar Association, the American Medical Association and the American Academy of Pediatrics all endorsed decriminalization. Spearheading liberalization efforts was the National Organization for the Reform of Marijuana Laws (NORML), founded in 1970 by a young lawyer named Keith Stroup. 'We do not advocate the use of marijuana,' Stroup told a reporter, 'but we know of no medical, legal, or moral justification for sending those to jail who do use it.'[64] Destined to return as a powerful force in the twenty-first century, NORML enjoyed its first moment in the sun under Jimmy Carter. Stroup became friendly with

Peter Bourne, Carter's drug-policy expert, and the association gained access on intimate terms to the White House.[65] In 1977 Carter himself publicly expressed support for federal measures.[66] By 1978 eleven states had decriminalized marijuana possession.[67]

Reform was stopped in its tracks by a scandal involving Bourne, who was forced to resign after it was discovered he had written an illegal prescription for Quaaludes, a regulated sedative, for his attractive young secretary.[68] More basically, the public was not ready for liberalization. Surveys from the period suggested that a majority might be persuaded to decriminalize possession, but three-quarters of Americans disagreed that 'you can use marijuana without ever becoming addicted to it' and almost as many believed that smoking it would make people want to try heroin.[69] A countervailing force to NORML soon emerged in the form of concerned parents' associations. The backlash began with a collective founded in Atlanta in 1976 by Marsha Schuchard, aka Manatt, a mother of three living in the aptly named suburb of Druid Hills. Schuchard agitated and lobbied against liberalization and for toughening the rules such as by banning the sale of smoking paraphernalia. Perhaps her greatest coup was to enlist the backing of Robert DuPont, the head of the NIDA and a methadone maintenance pioneer. In 1979 she founded PRIDE (Parents Resource Institute for Drug Education), which had its own newsletter.[70] More parental associations formed – by 1980 there were three hundred of them nationwide – to raise the battle cries of 'D.A.R.E.' (Drug Abuse Resistance Education), 'Drug-Free' and, after Ronald Reagan's election, 'Just Say No.'[71] Meanwhile several of the state decriminalization laws had been reversed – South Dakota's, for example, as early as 1977.[72]

Liberalization would only come slowly, beginning with the legalization of marijuana for medical purposes, which itself has involved two distinct steps: the approval of cannabis extracts, such as THC, for medical use, and the authorization of marijuana itself, the leaf, for use in treatment. In 1980, for example, the FDA approved oral THC for prescription to patients undergoing chemotherapy.[73] The authorization of plant-based preparations would take longer. Likewise, in Europe today, most countries have approved some or all of the existing, cannabis-based pharmaceutical products, but only fourteen allow the medical use of marijuana preparations themselves, several on the basis of exceptional or compassionate motives only and under special access schemes.[74]

Sensing a weak link, the legalizers of the 1990s decided to press for the passage of laws authorizing medical marijuana in selected American states, beginning with California. The leaf had been identified for use in five main therapeutic areas: appetite stimulation. analgesia, controlling nausea, mastering neurologic disorders and treating glaucoma. A particular application was pain or nausea relief among cancer sufferers, including patients undergoing chemotherapy.[75] Individuals who had run out of other options were demanding access.

In 1995 a group of long-time local activists placed on California's citizens' ballot a law authorizing patients to cultivate or have a caregiver cultivate cannabis for their medical use, an initiative known as 'Proposition 215'. Their cause gained a fighting chance when they accepted the support of Ethan Nadelmann. Nadelmann brought in both Bill Zimmerman, a canny political consultant with a ballot track record, and donors for a campaign, beginning with the hedge-fund billionaire George Soros. Proposition 215 passed in 1996 with 56 per cent of the vote.[76] The Drug Policy Alliance (DPA, the Trebach–Nadelmann foundation) and an organization started by former NORML employees known as the Marijuana Policy Project (MPP) then decided to build on this success to push for citizens' ballots in more states. Polls showing a minimum of 55 per cent support made a state eligible for targeting. The donors forked out more money for campaigns. Within four years, they won another six states: Alaska, Oregon and Washington in 1998, Maine in 1999, and Nevada and Colorado in 2000. By 2013 medical-cannabis laws had passed in twelve more states, a few by votes in the legislature but most by popular ballot.[77]

Medical marijuana likewise acted as a Trojan horse in Canada, but through a different route. Hopes for decriminalization had emerged in 1992 under the Conservatives and in 1993 under the Liberals. A new law came into effect in 1996 allowing possession under 30 grams (1 oz) of marijuana or 1 gram of hashish to be dealt with by summary proceedings. The government claimed this amounted to depenalization, even if possession remained on the books as a criminal offence. Meanwhile a 1995 survey showed that 69 per cent were in favour of either a non-criminal fine or no legal restraints on marijuana possession at all.[78]

It was through the courts, however, that tangible change arrived. In several cases running from the year 2000, Canadian judges began ruling that denial of access to medical cannabis was a violation of rights. This set a precedent not just for marijuana possession for medical use, but in general. The government reacted by allowing medical marijuana, in 2002, under a regime run by Health Canada, the country's department of health. (The authority itself grew the cannabis, though it privatized production after 2012.) This, however, only consolidated the drug's progress. The production and sale of marijuana and its derivates for medical purposes would form the bedrock of a future Canadian industry that has expanded into recreational cannabis and become a major international actor. The courts, meanwhile, continued to throw out possession charges.[79]

For a decade, prospects fluctuated with electoral politics. The Liberals introduced a liberalization bill in 2003 under Jean Chrétien, but it was delayed several times and never passed. A return to power by the Conservatives left the ambiguous status quo in place and even threatened a return to stricter terms, as the government promised a new anti-drug strategy based on tougher criminal penalties. Yet conditions turned favourable again as Justin Trudeau, prime minister from 2015, appointed a panel known as the Task Force on Cannabis Legalization and Regulation. Headed by Anne McLellan, a former Liberal cabinet member who had held both the health and justice portfolios, this comprised representatives from various stakeholder groups, including health research, law, policing and social work. Trudeau had made an electoral promise anyway, and opinion polls showed that Canadians strongly favoured legalization. The panel confirmed that it recommended the reform, and cannabis, medical and recreational, became legal in Canada on 17 October 2018.[80]

In the United States, opinion was likewise primed by the twenty-first century's second decade. In 2016 lifetime marijuana use among the American adult population reached 47 per cent: the number of people who had tried the drug at least once in their lives approached the majority mark.[81] According to a 2013 poll 77 per cent of Americans believed that cannabis could legitimately be used as a medicine, and a majority, 52 per cent, supported legalization for recreational use.[82] The reform campaigners pounced, though their first attempt would draw a blank.

In 2010 Richard Lee, a long-time activist who owned a cannabis dispensary in Oakland and ran an 'Oaksterdam University', launched a proposal known as 'Proposition 19' to legalize recreational marijuana in California. Lee invested $1.5 million of his own earnings to draft the proposition and gather the required 400,000+ signatures to put it on the ballot. He garnered support from libertarian public speakers and from California's American Civil Rights Union (ACLU). The more politically savvy organizations that were NORML, the MPP and the DPA, however, withheld their active support, mistrusting the electoral dynamics – though some of their financial backers decided to contribute at the last minute. It may not have helped that one month before the vote, Governor Arnold Schwarzenegger reduced the punishment for the possession of an ounce or less to an infraction with a $100 fine. The initiative failed.[83]

Grassroots campaigners were luckier in Washington and Colorado, where the fight moved next. In Washington state, the lawyer and ACLU director Alison Holcomb led the campaign. In Colorado, Mason Tvert took the lead, a long-time activist with a folksy style who would go on to join the MPP. Holcomb pursued the middle-of-the-road voter, addressing upfront issues such as restrictions on youth and home cultivation. Tvert, who faced a well-funded opposition in the shape of the Save Our Society from Drugs lobby group, ran a combative billboard campaign.[84] When Governor John Hickenlooper added his opposition, Tvert attacked him for having made a fortune on alcohol – in this case the brewing business. The DPA and MPP meanwhile supported the campaigns, making essential financial contributions. In Colorado, Republican and libertarian sympathizers also weighed in, helping sway conservative voters. The vote was won with 56 per cent in Washington and 55 per cent in Colorado. Both initiatives became law in December 2012.[85]

The floodgates had opened. In the aftermath, nine states introduced decriminalization bills and another nine full legalization bills.[86] In November 2014 Oregon and Alaska became the third and fourth states to legalize marijuana completely. They were followed by California, Maine, Massachusetts and Nevada in 2016.[87] Illinois, Michigan and Vermont would soon join them.[88] In 2016 a poll found that 60 per cent of Americans supported marijuana legalization.[89] Prohibition, of course, remains in full force at the federal level. Yet in 2017 another poll found that 71 per cent of Americans opposed federal intervention in legalizing states.[90] Marijuana has, moreover, become legal in the capital itself: Washington, DC, legalized the drug in 2014, allowing home cultivation of up to six plants and possession of up to 2 ounces (60 grams). The law, actively supported by Keith Stroup, who was still serving as legal counsel for NORML, passed by the largest majority in the country: 65 per cent.[91]

As to Uruguay, it had decriminalized the possession of all the main drugs in 1974 – although what qualified as possession was left to the judge's discretion, so that some incarcerations for use continued. As in the United States, a popular movement eventually coalesced in the early twenty-first century in favour of the full legalization of cannabis. Formed in 2006, the Movement for Cannabis Legalization was joined by young, left-wing politicians and more discreetly by clandestine cannabis growers and users. The Federation of University Students, LGBT organizations and the National Union of Workers as well as various academics, lawyers, doctors and artists became fellow travellers. This informal coalition gained political attention when it obtained an audience with the president in 2007, and again during the campaign of 2009. Support remained too narrow, however, to force a change in legislation.[92]

In 2011 a 63-year-old woman was imprisoned after cannabis plants had been found in her house: her case gathered media attention and convinced a cross-party group of deputies to get together and draft legislation. The disastrous violence hitting Latin America as a result of the war on drugs, though it remained less stark in Uruguay itself, acted as a backdrop. At that stage, polls showed that 66 per cent opposed marijuana legalization, with only 24 per cent in favour. The parliamentarians forged ahead regardless, motivated by public-health goals and the desire to put an end to black-market activity and the associated violence. In December 2013 the law made it onto the statute books. Cannabis had become legal in Uruguay. Remarkably, public opinion turned around as the reform cleared the chamber of deputies: 78 per cent declared it was preferable, after all, to the old status quo.[93]

Legalization means the full regularization of cultivation, retail and use, medical and recreational, not just decriminalization. Differing sets of regulations have nevertheless been instituted in these three geographies. All keep track of production, potency and distribution, but in different ways.

Uruguay set up an Institute for the Regulation and Control of Cannabis to authorize and monitor crops, harvesting and distribution. Private growers remit the marijuana, which can only be sold in pharmacies. The institute keeps close tabs on potency, namely THC and CBD concentrations. Buyers must be eighteen or older, and they must register. The law also allows sales through regulated private clubs, and home cultivation of up to six plants and an annual limit of 480 grams (160 oz). As of February 2018, there were sixteen pharmacies dispensing cannabis for non-medical use in the country, with 34,696 people registered to buy from them. By February 2019, 115 cannabis clubs had been registered with 3,406 members, and 6,959 people had obtained a licence for domestic cultivation.[94]

Canada has a more complex, two-tier system reflecting its federal constitution. The federal government is responsible for setting norms for growers, including the types of cannabis products to be made available for sale. It also sets rules on promotional activity, packaging and labelling, notably to ensure that products are not targeted at underage users. Distribution and sale are governed by provincial or territorial authorities. Systems vary. In some provinces, the entire retail chain is state-controlled; in others, the province controls wholesale distribution but not retail; and in two provinces the system is fully private. Some provinces have placed caps on the number of licensed stores. Some, but not all, also allow home cultivation, generally up to a limit of four plants, and some have set the minimum age higher than the federal level of eighteen years old. Each province has its own excise stamps. Health Canada, finally, provides added oversight: it is responsible for regulating the medical-cannabis industry, but because the large growers are active in both the medical and recreational segments, in practice it also has power over what is sold to the non-medical user.[95]

The system is yet more varied in the United States, where reforming states have each legalized separately and marijuana remains banned federally. Oversight has sometimes been awarded to liquor boards, sometimes to newly established cannabis regulatory bodies, and in one state to the department of agriculture. Regulations typically match those in place for alcohol, with marijuana forbidden to people under 21. Some states allow counties and municipalities to continue banning retail sales locally. Enterprises must be licensed to produce, market or sell cannabis products. With the exception of Washington, DC, possession remains everywhere limited to 1 ounce (30 grams). The legalizing states likewise permit home cultivation, typically up to a six-plant limit, and raise varying rates of excise.[96] Some states, finally, have expunged the criminal records of former cannabis offenders – a measure also seen as a matter of racial justice – notably California and Massachusetts.[97] Both producers and retailers meanwhile continue to labour under federal restrictions. Cannabis cannot cross state lines, for example, even between legalizing states. The greatest restriction concerns banking and payment facilities: because banking is federally regulated, cannabis-sector participants have no access. Dispensaries have had to hoard cash or find other activities to front for their marijuana sales.[98]

While legalization in the American states remains at threat from federal intervention, a countervailing factor may bolster it for the long term: the arrival of big capital. A number of cannabis companies, originally set up for the medical market but most of them having branched out into the recreational segment, have become large enough to obtain stock-exchange quotations: Canopy Growth, Aurora Cannabis, Aphria, Tilray, Cronos Group, Curaleaf, Trulieve ... All are Canadian and primarily listed in Toronto, but some are also traded on NYSE or Nasdaq. Many have been hotly tipped stocks by *Forbes* and the ticker-tape boffins.[99] Canopy had, at the time of writing, a multi-billion-dollar value, and Aurora and Aphria had market capitalizations above U.S.$1 billion.

The CEO of Aurora Cannabis writes: 'We're in the early days of what we know is going to be a massive global industry. In fiscal 2019, our Sky Class facilities are now established as the industry standard for efficiency and scale: we are leaders in cultivation ... We've now grown into 25 markets, through targeted acquisitions and strategic partnerships, and we will continue to expand globally.'[100] Pictures of the company's 'state-of-the-art' production facility show huge greenhouses with automated pulleys lifting bushes and workers in laboratory gowns examining the leaves.[101] Alongside its medical products, Aurora owns a number of 'consumer' brands: Aurora, San Rafael, Whistler, AltaVie and Woodstock. Its medical and consumer turnover remain about equally split.[102] Aurora describes its AltaVie brand as follows: 'Superior cannabis products designed for the premium customer segment. AltaVie users are curious and discerning about life and searching for physical, mental and emotional enrichment.'[103] Fifty years on, perhaps Timothy Leary's preaching has not fallen on deaf ears after all.

The decriminalization of marijuana possession has meanwhile been catching on around the world. In 2015 Jamaica passed legislation reducing the possession of small quantities to a petty offence.[104] In 2018 the South African Constitutional Court ruled that the consumption of marijuana in private homes was not a punishable act – an all the more significant development given that South Africa has been, historically, a major consumer nation.[105] Though a New Zealand referendum legalizing cannabis was narrowly defeated in October 2020, decriminalization remains on the agenda.[106]

Medical marijuana has been making its own progress in Europe. A number of THC or CBD pharmaceutical products have gained approval by various national authorities: the most widely validated has been Sativex, a spray for treating muscle spasticity in multiple sclerosis. A few countries have also allowed the prescription of herbal cannabis for alleviating the symptoms of medical conditions ranging from multiple sclerosis, HIV and cancer to Tourette's syndrome. The Netherlands took the lead in 2003, but it has been followed by a large group of countries, including the UK, Denmark, Germany, Italy, Portugal and Switzerland.[107] Denmark, Germany and Portugal have even allowed domestic cultivation for supplying the medical market – Aurora Cannabis runs production facilities in all three of these countries, and Aphria is preparing to do so in Germany.[108]

The authorization of medical cannabis having been the first step to full legalization in Canada and the American states, one might expect recreational marijuana eventually to make it on the agenda in some European countries at least. This is where harm reduction may act as a brake on legalization, however. In many European countries, marijuana possession has been decriminalized in practice, potentially robbing any campaigns for legalization of their momentum.

European policies on recreational marijuana have been sitting on a broad spectrum, from the *de jure* decriminalization of possession in Portugal, Spain and the Czech Republic to full prohibition in Sweden or France, as well as intermediate *de facto* decriminalization in countries such as the Netherlands, Belgium, Luxembourg, Switzerland and Germany.[109] In 1994 the German Federal Constitutional Court, in a key ruling, cleared the way for the decriminalization of cannabis use. The possession of cannabis was thereafter depenalized with different thresholds in various *Länder*.[110] Several German cities have proposed to allow cannabis dispensaries within their precincts, though this has gone no further than a pilot project in Frankfurt. In the Netherlands, where cannabis use has long been tolerated, multiple municipalities have asked for a relaxation of measures against cultivation; while the government has denied their requests, judges have been known to refuse to condemn growers.[111] Finally, in Spain, followed by Belgium, the UK, France and Slovenia, grassroots associations labelled 'cannabis social clubs' have emerged and started to engage in collective cultivation for private use. As of 2014, for example, there were seventy such clubs in Britain. In Spain, where possession is legal, the clubs only break the law by growing the plant. Elsewhere, they operate completely illegally (though their members may not always be aware of it), but they have rarely been raided.[112]

A second factor militating against further legalizations has been pushback from the UN-led drug-control institutions. The INCB already considers that medical marijuana violates the drug treaties. The principle is at best ambiguous: the conventions allow cannabis to be used for medical research, but not treatment. But in any case, medical cannabis laws have violated articles 23 and 28 of the Single Convention, which stipulate that, if a government allows the cultivation of cannabis, it must establish an exclusive, national purchasing agency.[113] This is not how medical cannabis markets have been established in most jurisdictions. Concerning the decriminalization of possession, the conventions leave the loophole that enforcing criminal penalties remains subject to each signatory's constitutional principles.[114] Legalizing entities such as the American states, however, can hardly claim recourse to that exception while marijuana remains prohibited at the federal level. Even policies of practical toleration have been viewed dimly by the UN organs. In 2006 UNODC reiterated that, under the conventions, cannabis must be controlled with the same severity as heroin and cocaine, complaining that the toleration of cannabis led to 'confusion' in the global community.[115] As to Canada and Uruguay, of course, they are simply in open breach of the treaties.

On 12 February 2019 a New York jury convicted Joaquín Guzmán Loera, aka El Chapo, on multiple charges of drug trafficking and money laundering.[116] The cartel leader, once Mexico's most powerful, faced life in prison. He might have twice escaped from Mexican jails, but there was no prospect of freedom this time. El Chapo boasted a longer career and had trafficked more narcotics than the once legendary Pablo Escobar. He was responsible for cartel wars, assassinations, rapes, mutilations and the wholesale corruption of his country's law enforcement and political classes. His victims, direct and indirect, numbered in the thousands. His conviction was a red-letter day for justice.

Anyone who thought it would make any difference to the volume of drugs trafficked into the United States or elsewhere had not been paying attention. El Chapo's Sinaloa cartel, after having defeated its Tijuana enemies, had briefly established a claim to dominance over Mexico's drug traffic. After that, it had gone to war with the Gulf cartel, and then with Los Zetas. At the same time as it was diversifying into methamphetamine and fentanyl, it had spread its tentacles deep into South America but also into Europe, where it sold drugs, and into Asia, where it purchased precursor chemicals. While El Chapo sat in court, the business had continued to boom, for Sinaloa as for the others. Worldwide, as confirmed by seizure data, cocaine, fentanyl and meth trafficking had all been expanding. Behind one kingpin, besides, stood another: Ismael 'El Mayo' Zambada, the man who had held the fort while Guzmán had been imprisoned the first time, and possibly the real brains behind the operation.[117]

As a corollary, violence had likewise spiralled upwards. Mexico had degenerated, in the opening decades of the twenty-first century, into dark and disturbing practices as Los Zetas broke up into yet another splinter group, La Familia, and as new cartels arose to defy Sinaloa, such as Tijuana's Jalisco. Instances of cartel torture have included starvation, beatings, sexual abuse, knee-capping and wounding with knives or industrial tools in various parts of the body prior to murder, as well as the use of acid, fire, electricity, water, excrement and animals. Cartel violence has produced dismembered bodies and bodies partially dissolved in vats of acid. Beheadings have become common. In 2009 the retired general Mauro Enrique Tello Quiñonez was kidnapped along with his aide and driver, then killed. He had just been hired to set up a hundred-man anti-drug unit. His body had burns on his skin, and his hands and wrists were broken. An autopsy revealed he had suffered broken knees and been shot eleven times.[118]

Felipe Calderón, president of Mexico between 2006 and 2012, attempted to bring down the cartels through military means. The offensive and the associated violence, whether on officials, between cartels or on bystanders, left an estimated 60,000 dead and 20,000 missing.[119] Nor has the escalating brutality been confined to Mexico or even Latin America. In 2001, for example, when he took office, the Thai prime minister Thaksin Shinawatra vowed to eradicate drug trafficking. In 2003 he proclaimed a nationwide 'war on drugs'. Human Rights Watch has calculated: 'The government crackdown has resulted in the unexplained killing of more than 2,000 persons, the arbitrary arrest or blacklisting of several thousand more, and the endorsement of extreme violence by government officials at the highest levels.'[120]

Neither of these so-called wars produced any effect on the drug supply. Nor were they ever likely to. In 2016 UNODC estimated that the world's total area under poppy cultivation was 305,000 hectares. This is half the size of the state of Delaware, or about the size of Luxembourg. Global coca acreage was even smaller.[121] Poppy and coca fields have always been able to find somewhere to hide. Traffickers, likewise, have never lacked a supply of poor or desperate youths to recruit. Even safeguards against money laundering are being circumvented: traffickers have become adept at using Bitcoin and the 'darknet'.[122]

Even if poppy and coca plants could somehow all be fumigated or uprooted, besides, the cartels have already discovered other avenues for expansion. Fentanyl, heroin's deadlier cousin, has been one of them. Another has been methamphetamine, commonly known as yaba in Southeast Asia. In 2015 methamphetamine became the most widely used drug in China, Japan, the Philippines and Singapore, and the region turned into the main recipient of methamphetamine worldwide.[123] But Southeast Asia has also become an important centre for meth production in its own right.

In 2018 the Australian police led an operation combining twenty agencies from Asia, North America and Europe against a man named Tse Chi Lop. Tse, a Canadian national born in China, has like many of the drug lords of the past spent a stint in prison: in 1998 he was sent to jail for a few years by a New York court. Tse was a member of a heroin-smuggling ring from the Golden Triangle, and this is where he disappeared again thereafter. He soon became the kingpin or one of the barons of an organization, nicknamed Sam Gor by police forces, spanning East Asia, Australia and New Zealand and specializing in crystal meth.

UNODC has estimated Sam Gor's meth revenues at $8 billion per year. It is believed to be handling the drug in tons, exporting it to at least a dozen countries. Anti-narcotics officials have described the Sam Gor syndicate as 'enormously wealthy, disciplined and sophisticated – in many ways more sophisticated than any Latin American cartel'.[124] (Like Latin American kingpins, too, Tse is rumoured to fly family on private jets to extravagant parties, bet big on horses and maintain a team of bodyguards, this time consisting of Thai kickboxers.) Perhaps the most notable, though, is the location of Sam Gor's production facilities. In late 2016 a young Taiwanese man was caught at Rangoon airport carrying bags of white powder. His captured phone pointed towards a local address where police found over a ton of crystal meth. Further investigations led into the Shan state, Khun Sa's old home base. A reporter has described the scene:

> Along the road to the village of Loikan in Shan State . . . high-end suvs thunder past trucks carrying building materials and workers.
> The Kaung Kha militia's immaculate and expansive new headquarters sits on a plateau nestled between the steep green hills of the jagged Loi Sam Sip range. About six kilometers away, near Loikan village, was a sprawling drug facility carved out of thick forest. Police and locals say the complex churned out vast quantities of crystal meth, heroin, ketamine and yaba tablets – a cheaper form of meth that is mixed with caffeine. When it was raided in early 2018, security forces seized more than 200,000 liters of precursor chemicals, as well as 10,000 kg of caffeine and 73,550 kg of sodium hydroxide – all substances used in drug production.[125]

The Sam Gor syndicate has a lineage that can be traced back to the Opium Wars, via Chinese opium networks, the British colonial regime in Burma, the flight of the Kuomintang generals into the region and Khun Sa's Shan insurgency. Drug trafficking cultures and networks possess a resilience that can span multiple generations. Their durability and their adaptability, as the switch from opiates to meth manufacturing shows, defy the imagination. Perhaps Tse will be caught, but will it have any impact?

The mounting violence, its futility, the inexhaustible permanence of trafficking networks: all this increasingly made the case for policy relaxation. In practice, in spite of the continuing rise in trafficking, incarceration flattened out, in the first two decades of the twenty-first century, in a number of national systems. In the United States, drug-offender prison populations stopped climbing. America had been incarcerating a dramatically growing number of people for drug offences in the three previous decades: from 38,680 in 1972 to 480,519 in 2002. In 1997, the last year for which such data were available, 172,797 people were sitting in prison on possession offenses alone.[126] Based on federal and state prison data, these numbers plateaued thereafter and even began to decline: from 337,872 offenders on drug charges in 2003 to 268,900 in 2017.[127]

Drug-related incarceration rates were likewise stable in most European countries: the EU total was 57,048 in 2002 and 62,601 in 2019.[128] Incarcerations have fallen in Germany, the Netherlands, Spain and Sweden, though not in the UK, France or Italy. How many prison inmates were purging possession charges has not been tallied, but sentencing in selected countries provides a glimpse. At the period's approximate midpoint, the Netherlands boasted the highest likelihood of incarceration for a possession arrest: 20 per cent. (The absence of marijuana possession charges artificially drives this rate up, compared to other countries.) France stood at 12 per cent, Germany at 7 per cent and Britain around 4 per cent. Scandinavian countries exhibited rates in the low single digits, with Finland at zero.[129]

Many countries in Asia have kept a zero-tolerance approach to drugs, for example Indonesia, the Philippines and Singapore. Indonesian drug laws prescribe the death penalty for narcotics trafficking. In the Philippines, the possession of 5 grams of marijuana is an offence punishable with twelve years in jail.[130] In China, nevertheless, though drug use remains unlawful, possession was downgraded in 2008 from a criminal offence to a contravention punishable by administrative sanction. Though the new rehabilitation centres to which offenders have been assigned often resemble custodial environments, the law also envisages community-based rehabilitation.[131]

The UN's decade for achieving a drug-free world was coming to a close in 2008. As the deadline approached, UNODC wrote: '*Drugs are everywhere*, say alarmed parents. *The drug problem is out of control*, cries the media. *Legalize drugs to reduce crime*, say some commentators. Such exasperation is understandable in the many communities where illicit drugs cause crime, illness, violence and death. Yet, worldwide statistical evidence points to a different reality: drug control is working and the world drug problem is being contained.'[132] The claim for containment was twofold, based first on a supposed flattening in trafficking trends in the last quarter-century, and second on lower rates of opiate addiction compared to a century before. In reality, any recent flattening was hard to see, based on UNODC's own statistics: it relied entirely on marijuana, while the evidence was that trafficking in heroin and cocaine had increased twenty- to fiftyfold in that time span.[133] The trend would continue upwards in the years to come. As to century-long comparisons of opiate-abuse rates – themselves based on the dubious assumption that smoking opium is the same as injecting heroin – they would soon be vitiated by the opioid epidemic.

In a small concession, the CND became empowered, after 2008, to endorse some harm-reduction measures. The commission, for example, asked member states to scale up 'evidence-based interventions to prevent HIV infection among people who use drugs'. It recommended to their attention a WHO, UNODC, UNAIDS *Technical Guide for Countries to Set Targets for Universal Access to HIV Prevention, Treatment and Care for Injecting Drug Users*, which endorsed needle exchange programmes.[134] For the first time, in 2012, it considered recommending alternatives to incarceration. In a resolution, the CND encouraged member states 'to consider allowing the full implementation of drug-dependence treatment and care options for offenders, in particular, when appropriate, providing treatment as an alternative to incarceration'.[135]

The question was whether this was not, from the perspective of the drug-control consensus, a case of too little, too late. The last decade has seen an increasingly direct challenge to the international drug-control system. The violence had not stopped by 2008, and the UN's 1998 call for one last push against drugs had visibly failed. The critique of prohibition that had first emerged in the 1990s resurfaced. The novelty, however, was that it now came from state actors themselves. It also burst the banks of the developed world. In the last ten years, two powerful calls for reforming the drug-control system have emerged, both originating in Latin America.

In 2009 three former presidents – Fernando Henrique Cardoso of Brazil, César Gaviria of Colombia (the same man Escobar had tried to kill by blowing up the Avianca plane) and Ernesto Zedillo of Mexico – joined with a wider group of Latin American personalities to demand fundamental change. Two years later, the Global Commission on Drug Policy was born, a caucus encompassing South American luminaries – the ex-president of Chile Ricardo Lagos and the writer Mario Vargas Llosa, for example, in addition to the original three – but also American and European business and political figures such as Richard Branson, George Shultz, Javier Solana and Paul Volcker. Most spectacularly, its roster included Kofi Annan, former Secretary-General of the United Nations, the very man who had issued the 1998 call for a 'drug-free world'.[136]

The Global Commission on Drugs has called for a paradigm shift in the war on drugs. In its own words it 'broke the taboo' on drug control's supposed successes and actual consequences, drawing from data on health, trafficking, legal trends and economics. It has called the war on drugs a war on people: farmers losing their crops or lands, citizens denied health and sometimes life, individuals sentenced to long prison terms. It has also rebutted two of supply suppression's central tenets: that it raises drug prices, thereby reducing demand, and that pursuing trafficking kingpins has been a useful strategy – though at the same time it has called for concentrating policing efforts on 'the most dangerous . . . actors of the illegal market'.[137] Finally, it has made ambitious proposals ranging from harm reduction to extensive legalization measures. In 2018 the Global Commission made the case for unrestricted legalization:

> A fundamental question regarding illegal drugs is still rarely asked. Who should assume the control of these substances that bear serious risks for health – the state or organized crime? We are convinced that the only responsible answer is to regulate the market, to establish regulations adapted to the dangerousness of each drug, and to monitor and enforce these regulations. This is already the case for food, for legal psychoactive substances, for chemicals, for medications, for isotopes and many other products or behaviors that comprise a risk of harm . . . The regulation of currently illegal drugs is not only possible, it is necessary.[138]

The formation of the Global Commission on Drugs echoed the address to Kofi Annan of 1998, with a larger, more geographically diverse and yet more high-profile backing – as well as the difference that the former UN Secretary-General had now switched sides. Yet to translate into change, it needed political action. The second attack on the drug-control order has taken place in the diplomatic arena itself, and it has demonstrated the potential for mustering a coalition for reform beyond what had long looked conceivable.

In 2013 a meeting of the presidents of Mexico, Colombia and Guatemala called, independently of the first initiative, for a re-evaluation of UN drug policies. In the same year, this was picked up by the Organization of American States. Though the OAS's message was eventually toned down at the behest of the United States, the UN agreed to move its next ten-year review session up to 2016 to accommodate the need for a debate.[139] The session itself was the occasion for preparations at the CND in 2014, including a set of subsidiary meetings known as a high-level segment. Both sets of debates were characterized by open tension between the partisans of the entrenched order and a reforming coalition ranging from Latin America (Mexico, Uruguay and Guatemala having been the most vocal nations) to Europe (the Czech Republic, Norway, Portugal, Switzerland, the EU as a block) as well as Asia and the Pacific (India and New Zealand).[140] While some demanded more flexibility in drug control, the Japanese delegate belittled 'so-called harm reduction'.[141] When Uruguay proposed to amend the treaties, the Algerian representative responded: 'We must cover our ears.'[142]

The 2016 UN session itself contained no radical resolutions. Though the debates were less triumphant than they had been in 1998, the policy menu remained heavy on traditional supply-suppression and demand-reduction recipes.[143] The speeches, most of them lacking in originality, were nevertheless leavened by defiant declarations by Enrique Peña Nieto, the Mexican president; Milton Romani Gerner, the representative of Uruguay; and the Colombian president Juan Manuel Santos Calderón. 'The approach essentially based on prohibition – the so-called war on drugs that began in the 1970s – has not succeeded in diminishing the worldwide production, trafficking or consumption of drugs,' said Peña Nieto. 'A consensus is beginning to emerge in favour of meaningful reform of the international drug regime.'[144] Romani extolled harm reduction and his own country's marijuana legalization. 'The war on drugs has ended. It was a senseless war with a fundamentalist approach characterized by rigid exhibitionism and one-track thinking, which has also been brought to an end,' he declared.[145] As to Santos Calderón, he asked: 'After so many lives cut short, so much corruption and violence and so many young lives wasting away in prisons, can we say that we have won the war? Can we say, at least, that we are winning it? Unfortunately, the answer is a resounding no.'[146]

Such talk, in the context of the staid, diplomatic lingo that is deployed at these conferences, was revolutionary. It remains to be seen how much effect it will have. The obituary of drug prohibition has been written before, no doubt. The global drug-control order is governed by treaties which, in the absence of a broad momentum to do so, cannot be changed. Its institutions – the CND, INCB and UNODC – respond ultimately to impulses from their member states. So long as a majority, or even just a few powerful countries, remain opposed to alterations to the prevailing order, none will take place. That Russia remains a prohibitionist champion and that China has so much vested, ideologically, in looking tough on drugs does not bode well for reform. At the same time, the position of another prohibitionist heavyweight, the United States, has been weakened, first by its high-profile failure to contain the home-made opioid epidemic and second by its state-led legalization of marijuana. Canada's open defiance of the conventions will be difficult to overlook. Adding to dissention, a number of countries, no longer confined to Europe, have begun pushing the envelope ever further on harm reduction.

The Latin American states, in addition to their inherent diplomatic weight, moreover hold the card that they are the home of coca cultivation and much else. That Bolivia has been able to thumb its nose at both the United States and the CND on the matter of coca chewing is instructive. It will be remembered that the 1961 Single Convention gave it 25 years to phase out the practice. Not only has Bolivia done nothing of the kind, but in 2006 it elected as president Evo Morales, a former coca grower who took an enthusiastic view of traditional chewing. At a session in 2009 the CND gave Bolivia another ten years to comply.[147] Morales at first tried to have the treaty amended, but when this failed Bolivia simply denounced (that is, withdrew from) the convention. Yet within a year, in 2013, it was able to accede anew, the number of states opposing its re-accession falling below the required quorum. Even better: it was permitted to do so with a 'reservation' on coca-leaf chewing.[148] When, in 2015, the United States attempted to punish the country by decertifying it, the Bolivian government shrugged its shoulders and signed off the associated aid.[149]

In one of its reports, the Global Commission on Drug Policy foresaw the possibility that selected states might withdraw from the conventions, taking Bolivia for a model, or enter into 'respectful non-compliance', like Canada.[150] Even if no change is ever made to the conventions, the risk to the drug-control order is that, in the absence of reform, it sinks into irrelevance. Piecemeal non-compliance, alongside harm reduction, raises the threat of systemic destruction from the inside.

UNODC has been sounding increasingly concerned over the last few years. The agency has evidently been aware that its member states are divided. Harm reduction has appeared with rising frequency in its recommendations. 'The flexibility inherent in the international drug control conventions should, to the maximum extent possible, be used to offer individuals (men, women and children) with drug use disorders the possibility to choose treatment as an alternative to conviction or punishment,' it noted in the aftermath of the 2016 UN session.[151] Following the stormy CND meetings of 2014, UNODC remarked that there were no 'simple answers' to the drug problem.[152] In its language, demand reduction has become increasingly leavened with references to human rights and to development. This draws the lessons from the ceaseless failures of supply suppression, though also from its occasional successes – the rare instances when suppression efforts have prevailed, as in Thailand, having been accompanied by important strides in economic development and the large-scale deployment of physical and social infrastructure.[153]

Chiefly, however, the realization has crept in that far from having been defeated or even contained, drug trafficking has been constantly spreading. Drug dealing has been conquering new geographies: in Africa, for example. Benin, Tanzania and Kenya were serving as platforms for distribution into Europe from South America or Pakistan and increasingly into African countries themselves.[154] In 2019 UNODC drastically revised its worldwide numbers upwards, in part to reflect a new estimate for opiate and other drug users in Nigeria.[155] Even more ominous than geographical expansion has been the traffic's ever wider product diversification. Amphetamines have been overtaking opiates and cocaine in user terms. New psychoactive substances (NPS), new synthetic or plant-based intoxicants, have appeared in an ever more bewildering array. 'The problem of NPS is a hydra-headed one in that manufacturers produce new variants to escape the new legal frameworks that are constantly being developed to control known substances. These substances include synthetic and plant-based psychoactive substances, and have rapidly spread in widely dispersed markets,' the agency has noted.[156] Scheduling cannot keep up. There have been too many NPS – 251 of them by 2012 – and their composition is changing constantly. Some countries have been independently introducing 'emergency scheduling', such as the UK, the Netherlands and Germany (Britain passed a contested, blanket Psychoactive Substances Act in 2016), but others have given up and now track them through their weaker pharmacy laws.[157]

Finally, there is the sheer size of the traffic. The 2019 UNODC report made for grim reading. More people used illicit drugs than ever, and 30 per cent more than a decade before. Opiates, cocaine, amphetamines and other stimulants, hallucinogens such as LSD or Ecstasy: all were at record highs. The number of NPS had doubled compared to a few years before, reaching a total of five hundred. Poppy acreage in Afghanistan, after twenty years of reduction efforts, was at its second largest ever and up 60 per cent compared to a decade earlier.[158] All this while trafficking, ever plastic and malleable, was yet again running rings around law enforcement:

> The monitoring of the modi operandi of drug traffickers and their trafficking routes needs to capture the dynamics and incentive systems inherent to drug trafficking. There is a need to understand, in particular, the complexity and variability of the spectrum of drug trafficking modalities. The dynamics of the recent opioid crisis in North America, which are now coming to light, highlight the need to address both sophisticated trafficking of large shipments in containers and the smuggling of small packages containing NPS and synthetic opioids (fentanyl analogues) via the postal system. Some end users buy their products directly online or via the darknet, posing additional challenges. This changing landscape is a far cry from the situation of just two decades ago, with mostly organic psychoactive substances being trafficked across borders.[159]

The Latin American statesmen's appeal for change in 2013 had given rise to a report by the Organization of American States. This was less a discussion of prohibition's successes and failures or even a policy document than an effort to peer into the future. The idea was to alert policymakers to what could happen. Though designed for the Americas, it could equally have applied to the world drug-control order.

The document envisaged four scenarios: *together*, *pathways*, *resilience* and *disruption*. The first scenario, 'together', was the closest to business as usual, with the difference that confronting trafficking would be met by stronger public-safety institutions. 'Pathways' included trying out 'alternative legal and regulatory regimes', beginning with cannabis. 'Resilience' supposed that states enhance their education and healthcare-based response to drugs and drug violence, foreseeing the triumph of harm reduction. 'Disruption', finally, supposed that states go their separate ways, with key producer and transit countries deciding that the fight, too costly and unbalanced, was best abandoned.[160] Continuing prohibition, legalization, harm reduction or a disorderly breakdown: two hundred years into the war on drugs, it remains impossible to predict which of these potential realities will come to pass.

CLOSING OBSERVATIONS

I n the course of writing this book, I have been asked several times what alternative or alterations I would propose to drug prohibition. My conception of the historian's role is epistemological, not prescriptive: to describe the past as best I can, not translate it into blueprints for the future. Historians labour to show by what processes, accidents and misunderstandings we got where we are. This is quite different from showing the way forward. Asked how we might do so, the best response might be the celebrated words of the London cabbie: 'I wouldn't start from here.'

If the war on drugs is not being won – and clearly, anyone who is prepared to write that it has been going on for two hundred years does not believe it is – is legalization the answer? Is there at least a blank-slate response, if blank slates ever existed in human affairs? There can be no single reply. What to do with drugs depends on a society's given tolerance for risk balanced against its regard for individual freedom, its ability to enforce norms and the associated costs. Drugs are dangerous, some more than others. Certain activities are also dangerous, though we tolerate and even celebrate them. Mountaineering, for example. Mountain climbing in selected American locations causes six hundred deaths per million people.[1] Fatalities from cocaine, including crack, oscillate between 350 and 700 per million in the USA and Europe.[2] Paragliding in Germany has been measured at 460 deaths per million, and climbing Mount Everest at 15,600. Where should the limit be set? Should paragliding be banned? Certainly it would be a shame, as it must be fun – but then, so probably is playing with cocaine. Rather than set artificial red lines, I will therefore keep my closing observations to the past, and limit them to three.

The first is that supply suppression has not worked. Of course, there have been successes. The dismantlement of the French Connection is one. The effective elimination of diversion in India and Turkey are two more. Thailand has managed to get rid of its poppy fields. China under the CCP was able to solve its opium problem. The historian James Windle has rightly highlighted a few more such successes, all incidentally confined to opiates. Both India and Turkey, however, were helped in that they were vetted as official suppliers of opium to the pharmaceutical market. Thailand only triumphed as the country was economically transformed, and even then its illicit drug industry simply moved next door. China eliminated opium through totalitarian measures that might not be practicable in the country itself today, let alone elsewhere.

But the key obstacle has been that, as drug production is pushed down in one place, it resurfaces in another. The outsized economic incentives created by prohibition ensure it does so, as Friedman warned in his 1972 *Newsweek* piece. In this context, moreover, it is worth noting that harm reduction offers no solution. Only liberalization can remove the incentives to trafficking – and the associated violence. Maintenance policies, by establishing legal sources alongside the black market, can undercut illicit dealers and take their customer base, or part of it, away from them. This, though, is but a half measure, especially as maintenance applies only to opiates: addiction provides the medical rationale for making maintenance distributions, and there is no such thing as marijuana or Ecstasy maintenance. One question this leaves hanging is whether some supply-suppression efforts offer better returns than others. My hunch is that crop eradication and similar actions are especially useless. Probably law enforcement works best when it is deployed closest to home. I leave the point to criminologists, who are better equipped to make it.

The second observation I wish to volunteer is that the criminalization of the drug user has been a monumental historical blunder. There is a philosophical question at stake: should someone go to jail, or even be given a criminal record, for having done something harmful only to him- or herself? But condemning users, the evidence shows, is also wasteful. Compare incarceration rates on drug offences in the USA and in the EU, then look at their respective drug-use incidences. The USA incarcerates something like five times more people, yet its population uses more drugs across almost every category. Portugal is right. Imprisoning drug users keeps them away from healthcare, and it only makes the problem worse. The criminalization of the drug user, never intuitive, was the fruit of particular historical circumstances. It made its grand entry in The Hague, where it was informed by colonial paternalism on the one hand and Qing desperation on the other. It also owed something to prevailing medical views. But addiction and the theories behind it have served the user shockingly poorly. As a medical category, addiction was theorized with the aim of healing. It became the excuse for punishing. Had vice notions of addiction prevailed, I cannot help thinking, they would have produced less punitive governance models, perhaps in the style of those that apply to prostitution or gambling.

Third, and finally, it is time to recognize that the illicit drugs as a group are a historical category, and not a scientific one. They are all fallen medicines, but their original applications as medicines varied widely. From a blank-slate perspective, each would warrant being regulated completely differently. It is not just that they are addictive in different ways, and some not at all. The risks associated with them bear no comparison one to another. Based on recent data produced by the American agency NIDA, for example, annual fatalities per thousand heroin users stand at a rate of 7.3. For cocaine this is 0.7.[3] For amphetamines the rate is yet lower, and for hallucinogens or marijuana it is basically nil. Such divergent levels of risk ought to justify different regulatory regimes. The legalization of cannabis in a handful of countries and American states recognizes this fundamental difference with respect to one widely consumed drug. Lumping together illicit drugs also impedes research into their medical uses. This book has discussed the late resurgence of medical marijuana, but other drugs are potentially concerned. Research shows that some psychotropics (psilocybin, LSD, MDMA) may be of value in treating otherwise intractable mental illnesses. The UK's Advisory Council on the Misuse of Drugs, for one, has recommended that they be rescheduled accordingly. This has been denied, ostensibly because it would clash with the treaties.

The Opium Wars were the original sin of drug prohibition. The drug-control system grew from an attempt to remedy their evils. Other drugs were later grafted into this system from administrative or political convenience: in chronological order, cocaine, marijuana, hallucinogens and amphetamines. Commonly labelled narcotics, they were placed together on the neat ladder that were the drug-control schedules. They had in common with opium that they had once been medicines, but they were otherwise fundamentally different. Regulation, had history followed a different course, might have reflected these differences in nature. Such has not been the case: these fascinating yet fraught substances became and have remained opium's orphans.

APPENDIX I

OPIUM SMOKER NUMBERS IN NINETEENTH-CENTURY CHINA

A number of contemporary statisticians – and, after them, historians – have attempted to calculate how many people were opium smokers in turn-of-the-century China.[1] Typically, observers have taken the total quantity of opium consumed in the country and divided this number by the likely average consumption for a median user. This is also what this book does. The total Chinese opium output was only known approximately. Median consumption per user could only be estimated based on surveys, adding a second layer of imprecision. Dividing by an average also introduces a statistical skew if a distribution is spread between two extremes: a small number of very heavy users and a large number of light users. Using the median consumer's level of use will lead to overstating the total number of users, because heavy users, even if few in number, will take up a large share of total output. This method, nevertheless, is the only one to provide a degree of precision. Total output could be estimated with some confidence because it was the object of significant scrutiny by tax assessors. Typical use can be cross-checked against other geographies, and even other opiates.

The best estimate of peak Chinese opium output is to be found in the Chinese delegation's report to the Shanghai commission. This contained three possible estimates: a low point by the Board of Revenue for 1906, a midpoint for 1905 by Hosea Ballou Morse, a British commissioner of customs and statistical secretary, and a higher point based on 1906 customs reports. The Board of Revenue total, at 148,100 piculs (1 picul = 60.3 kg, almost the same as a chest), narrowly based on fiscal returns, appears to have been an underestimate. Morse's calculation, which was based on a combination of fiscal data and surveys based on personal investigation, stood at 376,000 piculs. Morse himself hints that the actual total may have been a little higher. The Board of Revenue total, the highest, was 584,800 piculs. Yet the Board of Revenue had good reason to overstate this number. The Chinese government and its delegation needed to show that the 1907 ban was working. Making the 1906 total as high as possible helped show a fall thereafter. The Board of Revenue 1906 estimate was based on the 1907 numbers upped by a significant but artificial percentage to account for success in eradication. The best guess probably therefore sits between Morse and the Board of Revenue, the average of the two coming out at 480,000 piculs or chests. To this must be added the more precisely known but much smaller net import total of 29,000 chests.

Two further adjustments must be made. First, the raw opium was boiled before it could be smoked, leading to a reduction in volume of 37.5 per cent – this statistic being based on the Shanghai commission report. Second, opium ashes, or dross, were recuperated by den operators to be smoked again. This increased the opium available for smoking again by about 30 per cent, according to the same report. (Newman makes much higher dross adjustments, but the more opium remained to be used from ashes, the less would enter the initial smoker's system in the first place.)

As to the number of smokers, average opium use per smoker is provided in an earlier report produced by the imperial custom service, itself based on a collection of surveys performed in the various Chinese provinces. While both the methods and the data ranged widely from one province to the next, the averages have a certain statistical robustness. These surveys contained estimates for 'beginner', 'average' and 'heavy' smokers, with medians of 4.2 grams, 11.1 grams and 32.8 grams per day respectively. The average of 11.1 grams is almost certainly high. A French survey dated 1907 for the Cochin-China region of Indochina showed a rate of 1.5 grams per day, though 4.1 grams among Chinese users. In Taiwan, in 1900, 169,064 registered opium smokers consumed 125 tons, or 2 grams per day, though this ignored smuggling. Meanwhile, even if no more than 10 per cent of China's opium users qualified as 'heavy' smokers, this on its own would account for 3.3 grams. A reasonable average might weight equally the 'beginner', the 'average' and the much lower Cochin-China result, for a result of 5.6 grams per day. This may be compared to the heroin equivalent consumed by the average modern user. The 2009 UNODC *World Drug Report* estimated that 13 million users consumed 375 tons of heroin, or 79 milligrams per day. Very roughly, heroin can be assumed to be one hundred times more potent than smoked opium, so this would tally with a daily opium dose of 7.9 grams.

The data are summarized in the table below. The Chinese population at the time is assumed to have totalled 450 million.

	Low	High
Chinese output (piculs)	480,000	584,800
Net imports (chests)	29,000	29,000
Raw consumed (metric tons)	30,690	37,012
Net after boiling (metric tons)	19,182	23,133
Dross recuperation (metric tons)	5,755	6,940
Total consumed (metric tons)	24,937	30,073
Median daily use (grams)	11.1	5.6
Median annual use (kg)	4	2
Number of users	6.2 million	15.0 million
Percentage of the population	1.4%	3.3%

APPENDIX II
LEAGUE-ERA OPIUM
REGIME STATISTICS

The League of Nations collated statistics on both licit and illicit drug output, trade and consumption, based on data provided by governments.[1] Data quality was variable, especially in the early years, but it was better on the Asian opium franchises and monopolies, which were well equipped to collect them. Gaps in the series have been filled with piecemeal information brought up at OAC sessions but somehow not included in the annual reports, and, for Indochina, with a quasi-official French source.

SMOKING OPIUM (KG)

	Burma	Straits Settlements	Malay States	Taiwan	Hong Kong	Indonesia	Indochina	Thailand
1922	30,778	51,492	56,900	54,166	13,999	64,450	68,254	50,160
1925	18,180	46,323	82,791	41,991	8,826	51,014	60,200	54,634
1926	16,928	53,549	92,755	40,236	7,379	n.a.	59,689	55,462
1927	14,570	52,692	95,707	37,323	11,068	59,103	n.a.	60,483
1928	14,451	50,814	79,831	34,970	9,350	61,797	68,267	61,486
1929	13,756	43,553	78,378	31,967	6,803	58,806	70,493	58,170
1930	12,171	33,346	59,571	36,359	7,264	49,278	n.a.	49,436
1931	10,361	24,855	36,873	33,218	6,562	35,788	55,487	37,336
1932	11,270	24,897	29,882	27,418	4,878	24,427	41,315	30,077
1933	12,081	23,146	30,131	22,878	2,243	18,355	30,532	27,314
1934	13,325	26,378	42,006	19,879	1,207	16,650	28,458	26,882
1935	13,612	25,462	42,652	19,236	655	14,512	32,514	27,307
1936	14,107	19,066	37,311	17,910	587	15,577	34,506	27,416
1937	18,988	21,019	38,233	16,920	840	20,550	51,491	30,355

REGISTERED SMOKERS

	Burma	Straits Settlements	Malay States	Taiwan	Indonesia
1922	n.a.	n.a.	n.a.	42,923	n.a.
1923	n.a.	n.a.	n.a.	n.a.	142,730
1925	19,219	n.a.	n.a.	34,359	129,289
1926	15,879	n.a.	n.a.	31,982	126,186
1927	14,003	n.a.	n.a.	29,536	97,317
1928	13,364	n.a.	n.a.	27,378	101,048
1929	12,151	40,956	76,898	25,022	100,730
1930	11,269	42,751	107,906	38,480	92,830
1931	10,297	43,106	70,953	31,236	74,916
1932	19,955	n.a.	64,988	25,008	62,977
1933	20,678	23,290	37,526	18,844	48,969
1934	20,936	54,217	57,353	16,643	41,066
1935	19,025	25,625	62,016	15,048	39,365
1936	18,503	27,016	39,080	13,574	34,985
1937	18,165	27,150	52,097	12,063	41,360

NET OPIUM REVENUES/FISCAL RECEIPTS

	Burma	Straits Settlements	Malay States	Taiwan	Hong Kong	Indonesia	Indochina	Thailand
1923	4.4%	43.6%	16.9%	3.8%	23.3%	7.1%	13.8%	20.0%
1924	3.5%	38.9%	15.0%	4.8%	20.0%	6.3%	11.3%	17.9%
1925	2.9%	23.3%	13.4%	1.1%	11.3%	5.8%	9.2%	18.2%
1926	3.4%	30.5%	14.6%	3.4%	10.2%	5.4%	6.3%	16.7%
1927	2.9%	34.0%	13.4%	3.5%	11.6%	4.8%	6.7%	15.5%
1928	3.1%	32.3%	12.3%	2.7%	11.0%	4.9%	5.2%	15.3%
1929	2.5%	15.1%	14.0%	2.0%	8.3%	5.3%	4.7%	15.4%
1930	3.0%	23.0%	13.0%	3.0%	7.2%	6.1%	9.5%	14.1%
1931	2.0%	18.6%	10.7%	2.9%	6.6%	4.2%	n.a.	11.6%
1932	2.7%	13.2%	8.2%	2.3%	5.0%	4.4%	4.7%	11.0%
1933	2.8%	19.0%	7.4%	1.8%	0.8%	2.8%	0.0%	6.9%
1934	2.8%	22.4%	8.2%	1.5%	0.5%	1.7%	0.0%	8.5%
1935	2.4%	21.7%	7.5%	1.3%	0.0%	1.4%	4.7%	8.9%
1936	2.6%	20.7%	6.1%	1.3%	0.0%	1.1%	4.7%	7.5%
1937	4.5%	20.6%	5.2%	1.0%	0.0%	1.4%	12.9%	7.8%

APPENDIX III
POST-WAR DRUG SEIZURES

The table below shows worldwide seizures for the main controlled-drug categories, in kilograms.[1] This is based on UN data series, as found in the reports of various agencies (the CND, INCB and UNODC). The series are only as good as the information provided by member states; the data, therefore, can only be incomplete, though collection improved over time. Because the data have been erratic, the totals are presented here as three-year averages (for example, the number for 1950 is an average for 1949–51). Stimulants chiefly comprise amphetamines, not including Ecstasy. For the last few years, the source data group heroin and morphine together.

	Opium	Morphine	Heroin	Cocaine	Cannabis	Stimulants
1950	46,194	39	93	18	136,580	n.a.
1955	42,074	128	118	11	180,050	n.a.
1960	42,684	232	245	20	328,477	n.a.
1965	43,004	583	302	131	326,302	n.a.
1970	37,207	997	856	391	3,216,444	450
1975	43,920	562	1,802	2,095	2,272,303	416
1980	58,854	1,335	3,398	9.909	5,935,192	1,160
1985	38,013	447	8,365	37,508	4,950,000	4,250
1990	40,000	5,033	23,400	291,567	3,351,267	4,302
1995	188,133	12,733	29,300	310,267	3,791,933	7,546
2000	186,529	31,113	47,193	354,249	5,165,624	32,315
2005	312,133	51,257	58,778	680,312	6,620,379	33,876
2010	535,679	126,526		668,687	7,297,305	94,940
2015	591,667	118,000		899,667	7,114,000	199,333

REFERENCES

PROLOGUE

1 Quoted in David Anthony Bello, *Opium and the Limits of Empire* (Cambridge, MA, 2005), p. 155, full text pp. 313–15.

2 Ibid., p. 121; Jonathan Spence, 'Opium Smoking in Ch'ing China', in *Conflict and Control in Late Imperial China*, ed. Frederic Wakeman and Carolyn Grant (Berkeley, CA, 1975), p. 158; Wang Hongbin, *Jindu shijan* (Beijing, 1997), p. 43.

3 Bello, *Opium*, p. 117. The timing of certain anti-opium provisions on trafficking and, by extension, imports, is disputed. Wang attributes key measures to the late 1790s, while Bello believes the Qing court only launched its campaign in 1813. What is not disputed is that possession became criminalized in 1813. See Wang, *Jindu shijan*, pp. 34–6; and Bello, *Opium*, pp. 307–8.

4 Based on Wang's imports for 1812–14 divided by average use based on Imperial Customs data. Wang, *Jindu shijan*, pp. 53–4; *China Imperial Maritime Customs Reports on Opium* (Shanghai, 1864–1909), vol. IV, pp. 60–63. For the method, which for reasons of comparability excludes dross, see Appendix 1.

5 The earliest available English estimates are for 1827–30. For these numbers, see Virginia Berridge, *Opium and the People*, 2nd edn (London, 1999), p. 274.

6 'President Launches Drive on Narcotics', *New York Times*, 28 November 1954, quoted in *Drugs and Drug Policy in America: A Documentary History*, ed. Steven Belenko (Westport, CT, 2000), p. 197. For a critique of American-centric views, see James Windle, 'How the East Influenced Drug Prohibition', *International History Review*, 35 (2013), pp. 1185–99.

7 UNODC, *World Drug Report* (Vienna, 1997–), 2019, vol. I, p. 29.

8 Ibid., p. 7.

9 Including Ecstasy: ibid., pp. 29–30.

10 Ibid. (2017), vol. IV, p. 16.

11 Ronald Renard, 'The Making of a Problem: Narcotics in Mainland Southeast Asia', in *Development or Domestication? Indigenous Peoples of Southeast Asia*, ed. Don McCaskill and Ken Kampe (Chiang Mai, 1997), p. 310; Windle, 'How the East Influenced Drug Prohibition', p. 1189.

12 Renard, 'Narcotics in Mainland Southeast Asia', pp. 309–10.
13 Patrick Jory, 'The Vesantara Jataka, Barami, and the Bodhisatta-Kings: The Origin and Spread of a Thai Concept of Power', *Crossroads*, 16 (2002), pp. 36–78.
14 Windle, 'How the East Influenced Drug Prohibition', p. 1190.
15 The source, perhaps not altogether reliable, is a Dutch East India Company report dated 1671: Hans Derks, *History of the Opium Problem: The Assault on the East, ca. 1600–1950* (Leiden, 2012), p. 214.
16 James Rush, *Opium to Java: Revenue Farming and Chinese Enterprise in Colonial Indonesia, 1860–1910* (London, 1990), pp. 4–5.
17 Rudolph Matthee, *The Pursuit of Pleasure: Drugs and Stimulants in Iranian History, 1500–1900* (Princeton, NJ, 2005), pp. 114–16 and 207.
18 Joseph Gagliano, *Coca Prohibition in Peru* (Tucson, AZ, 1994), pp. 25–8 and 37–45.
19 Ibid., pp. 48–75.
20 Stephen Platt, *Imperial Twilight: The Opium War and the End of China's Last Golden Age* (London, 2018), pp. 210–11.
21 Bello, *Opium*, pp. 116–18.
22 Fu Lo-shu, *A Documentary Chronicle of Sino-Western Relations (1644–1820)*, 2 vols (Tucson, AZ, 1966), vol. 1, pp. 162–3.
23 Bello, *Opium*, p. 120.
24 Fu, *A Documentary Chronicle*, p. 380; Platt, *Imperial Twilight*, p. 211.

1 FORBIDDEN CITIES

1 Rudolph Matthee, *The Pursuit of Pleasure: Drugs and Stimulants in Iranian History, 1500–1900* (Princeton, NJ, 2005), p. 97.
2 David Anthony Bello, *Opium and the Limits of Empire* (Cambridge, MA, 2005), p. 142; Zheng Yangwen, *The Social Life of Opium in China* (Cambridge, 2005), pp. 11–12.
3 Zheng, *Social Life of Opium*, p. 26; Frank Dikötter, Lars Laamann and Zhou Xun, *Narcotic Culture: A History of Drugs in China* (London, 2004), pp. 25–6.
4 Dikötter et al., *Narcotic Culture*, pp. 32–3.
5 Ibid., pp. 58–9.
6 Ibid., pp. 60–61.
7 Zheng, *Social Life of Opium*, pp. 72–7.
8 Ibid., pp. 49–52.
9 Dikötter et al., *Narcotic Culture*, pp. 58–60.
10 Ibid., p. 36.
11 Wang Hongbin, *Jindu shijan* (Beijing, 1997), pp. 53–4.
12 Bello, *Opium*, pp. 124–5 and 177–80.
13 The existence of a Mughal monopoly seems to have been disproved: Emdad-ul Haq, *Drugs in South Asia: From the Opium Trade to the Present Day* (Basingstoke, 2000), pp. 15–19.
14 David Edward Owen, *British Opium Policy in China and India* (London, 1934), pp. 22–7 and 44–5.
15 Haq, *Drugs in South Asia*, p. 22; Peter Ward Fay, *The Opium War, 1840–1842* (Chapel Hill, NC, 1975), pp. 12–13.

16 Fay, *The Opium War*, pp. 13–14; Carl Trocki, *Opium, Empire, and the Global Political Economy* (London, 1999), p. 70; Brian Inglis, *The Opium War*, 2nd edn (London, 1979), p. 92.

17 Owen, *British Opium Policy*, pp. 61–2; Inglis, *The Opium War*, p. 71; Fay, *The Opium War*, p. 47; Stephen Platt, *Imperial Twilight: The Opium War and the End of China's Last Golden Age* (London, 2018), pp. xvii–xxi.

18 Fay, *The Opium War*, pp. 49–54.

19 Owen, *British Opium Policy*, p. 74.

20 Inglis, *The Opium War*, pp. 68–70.

21 Chang Hsin-pao, *Commissioner Lin and the Opium War* (Cambridge, MA, 1964), p. 21.

22 Fay, *The Opium War*, p. 49; Platt, *Imperial Twilight*, pp. 216–17.

23 Jonathan Spence, 'Opium Smoking in Ch'ing China', in *Conflict and Control in Late Imperial China*, ed. Frederic Wakeman and Carolyn Grant (Berkeley, CA, 1975), p. 166.

24 Platt, *Imperial Twilight*, pp. 201–2.

25 Melissa Macauley, 'Small Time Crooks: Opium, Migrants, and the War on Drugs in China, 1819–1860', *Late Imperial China*, 30 (2009), pp. 1–47, at p. 32.

26 Chang, *Commissioner Lin*, p. 33.

27 Macauley, 'Small Time Crooks', p. 21.

28 Ibid., p. 20.

29 Ibid., p. 36.

30 Ibid., pp. 1–2.

31 Wang, *Jindu shijan*, pp. 53–4; Michael Greenberg, *British Trade and the Opening of China, 1800–42* (Cambridge, 1951), p. 221.

32 Greenberg, *British Trade*, p. 221.

33 Calculated as follows: 40,000 chests = 5.28 million lb, less 37.5 per cent for boiling, divided by 400 million people. Population reference in John Fairbank, *The Cambridge History of China: Late Ch'ing, 1800–1911*, 2 vols (Cambridge, 1978), vol. 1, pp. 108–9.

34 Virginia Berridge, *Opium and the People*, 2nd edn (London, 1999), p. 274.

35 Bello, *Opium*, pp. 122–3.

36 For dollar values at the time, from which prices are derived, see Chang, *Commissioner Lin*, p. 223. Prices presented here are an average between Bengal and Malwa. They are expressed in Spanish silver dollars, about equal to a U.S. dollar at the time. One *tael* was worth approximately 1.3 silver dollars.

37 Macauley, 'Small Time Crooks', p. 19.

38 Zheng, *Social Life of Opium*, pp. 67–70.

39 Fairbank, *Cambridge History of China*, vol. 1, pp. 108–9.

40 Ibid., p. 12; Julia Lovell, *The Opium War* (London, 2011), p. 42.

41 Philippe Le Failler, *Monopole et prohibition de l'opium en Indochine: le pilori des chimères* (Paris, 2000), p. 13; Chantal Descours-Gatin, *Quand l'opium finançait la colonisation en Indochine* (Paris, 1992), pp. 31–3.

42 Richard Newman, 'Early British Encounters with the Indian Opium Eater', in *Drugs and Empires: Essays in Modern Imperialism and Intoxication, 1500–1930*, ed. Patricia Barton and James Mills (Basingstoke, 2007), pp. 67–9.

43 Data derived from Chang, *Commissioner Lin*, p. 223.

44 Platt, *Imperial Twilight*, p. 211, whose source is *Da Qing Renzong Rui (Jiaqing) huangdi shilu*, juan 270, p. 12a. I am indebted to Professor Wang Li of Jilin University for the translation of this preamble.

45 Zheng, *Social Life of Opium*, pp. 56–7; Jiang Qiuming and Zhu Qingbao, *Zhongguo jidu licheng* (Tianjin, 1996), p. 20.

46 Charles Gutzlaff, *Journal of Three Voyages along the Coast of China in 1831, 1832, and 1833* (London, 1834), p. 113.

47 Bello, *Opium*, p. 159.

48 Dikötter, *Narcotic Culture*, pp. 105–6.

49 Gutzlaff, *Journal of Three Voyages*, pp. 127–9; Platt, *Imperial Twilight*, p. 334.

50 Platt, *Imperial Twilight*, p. 211.

51 Fairbank, *Cambridge History of China*, vol. 1, pp. 13–21; R. Bin Wong, 'Opium and Modern Chinese State-Making', in *Opium Regimes: China, Britain, and Japan, 1839–1952*, ed. Timothy Brook and Bob Tadashi Wakabayashi (Berkeley, CA, 2000), p. 191.

52 Macauley, 'Small Time Crooks', pp. 10–16.

53 Platt, *Imperial Twilight*, pp. 205–8.

54 Fairbank, *Cambridge History of China*, vol. 1, p. 21.

55 Macauley, 'Small Time Crooks', pp. 12–14.

56 Platt, *Imperial Twilight*, pp. 215–16.

57 Ibid.; Bello, *Opium*, pp. 124–5.

58 Bello, *Opium*, pp. 125–7.

59 Platt, *Imperial Twilight*, pp. 293–4.

60 James Polachek, *The Inner Opium War* (Cambridge, MA, 1992), pp. 103–5.

61 'Memorial on Legalizing Opium, June 10, 1836', in *The Search for Modern China: A Documentary Collection*, ed. Jonathan Spence (New York, 1999), pp. 111–14.

62 'Memorial on Banning Opium, October 1836', ibid., pp. 114–19.

63 Platt, *Imperial Twilight*, pp. 311 and 334.

64 Bello, *Opium*, pp. 135–6; 'Annexed Laws on Banning Opium, July 1839', in *Documentary Collection*, ed. Spence, pp. 120–21.

65 Wang, *Jindu shijan*, pp. 101–6; Bello, *Opium*, p. 137.

66 Inglis, *The Opium War*, pp. 75–80; Owen, *British Opium Policy*, pp. 83–9.

67 Greenberg, *British Trade*, pp. 220–21.

68 Ibid.

69 Chang, *Commissioner Lin*, pp. 22–3; Inglis, *The Opium War*, pp. 66–82.

70 Owen, *British Opium Policy*, pp. 114–15; Jesse Palsetia, *Jamsetjee Jejeebhoy of Bombay* (New Delhi, 2015), pp. 32–6; Anonymous, *The Rupture with China and Its Causes* (London, 1840), p. 8.

71 Fay, *The Opium War*, pp. 131–2.

72 Ibid., p. 62.

73 Ibid., pp. 32–7.

74 Ibid., pp. 132–5.

75 Greenberg, *British Trade*, p. 30.

76 Fay, *The Opium War*, p. 120.

77 Platt, *Imperial Twilight*, pp. 258–63.

78 Fay, *The Opium War*, p. 61; Janin Hunt, *The India–China Opium Trade in the Nineteenth Century* (London, 1999), pp. 92–4.

79 Fay, *The Opium War*, pp. 44–5.
80 Alain Le Pichon, *China Trade and Empire: Jardine, Matheson & Co. and the Origins of British Rule in Hong Kong, 1827–1843* (Oxford, 2006), p. 35.
81 H.C.G. Matthew, ed., *Oxford Dictionary of National Biography*, 60 vols (Oxford, 2004), vol. xv, p. 841.
82 Palsetia, *Jamsetjee Jejeebhoy*, pp. 12–22.
83 Fay, *The Opium War*, p. 138.
84 Anonymous, *The Rupture with China*, p. 59.
85 Ibid., pp. 20–31.
86 Ibid., pp. 34–5.
87 James Matheson, *The Present Position and Prospects of the British Trade with China* (London, 1836), p. 1.
88 Ibid., pp. 3 and 33–8.
89 Palsetia, *Jamsetjee Jejeebhoy*, p. 41.
90 Platt, *Imperial Twilight*, p. 238.
91 Ibid., pp. 297–304.
92 H. Hamilton Lindsay, *Letter to the Right Honourable Viscount Palmerston on British Relations with China* (London, 1836), pp. 12–13.
93 Platt, *Imperial Twilight*, p. 318.
94 Ibid., p. 421.
95 Chang, *Commissioner Lin*, pp. 121–6.
96 Platt, *Imperial Twilight*, pp. 336–8.
97 Chang, *Commissioner Lin*, p. 104.
98 Fay, *The Opium War*, pp. 118–20.
99 Platt, *Imperial Twilight*, pp. 323–4.
100 Fay, *The Opium War*, pp. 124–5.
101 Bello, *Opium*, pp. 177–80 and 211–12.
102 Fay, *The Opium War*, pp. 129–31.
103 Ibid., pp. 135–6.
104 Ibid., pp. 140–41.
105 Ibid., p. 172; Lovell, *Opium War*, p. 59.
106 Fay, *The Opium War*, p. 144; Lovell, *Opium War*, pp. 59–60. Lin's order may be found in Jehu Lewis Shuck, *Portfolio Chinensis* (Macao, 1840), pp. 84–99.
107 Fay, *The Opium War*, p. 145.
108 Platt, *Imperial Twilight*, p. 351.
109 James Matheson to William Jardine, 1 May 1839, in Le Pichon, *Jardine, Matheson*, pp. 358–68.
110 Data drawn from Fay, *The Opium War*, p. 375; and *Parliamentary Papers: Papers Relative to the Opium Trade in China, 1842–1856* (London, 1857), p. 50.
111 'Chinese Letter to the Queen of England', *The Times*, 19 November 1839, p. 6.
112 *Canton Press*, 16 November 1839, p. 2.
113 Matthew, ed., *National Biography*, vol. xv, p. 841.
114 Platt, *Imperial Twilight*, pp. 7 and 351–2.
115 Fay, *The Opium War*, pp. 146–7.
116 Ibid., pp. 147–50.
117 Platt, *Imperial Twilight*, p. 355.
118 Ibid., pp. 355–6.
119 Fay, *The Opium War*, pp. 153–66.

120 Ibid., pp. 158–76.
121 Ibid., p. 161.
122 Lovell, *Opium War*, pp. 69–70.

2 OPIUM WARS

1 Peter Ward Fay, *The Opium War, 1840–1842* (Chapel Hill, NC, 1975), pp. 207–8 and 261–4.

2 Ibid., p. 345; Julia Lovell, *The Opium War* (London, 2011), pp. 111–15.

3 Lovell, *Opium War*, pp. 130–33.

4 As Lovell points out, the notion originated in the 1836 legalization debate: ibid., pp. 51–2.

5 Fay, *The Opium War*, pp. 194–5; or Stephen Platt, *Imperial Twilight: The Opium War and the End of China's Last Golden Age* (London, 2018), p. 371.

6 Quoted in Platt, *Imperial Twilight*, p. 411.

7 Roundell Palmer, *Statement of Claims of the British Subjects Interested in Opium* (London, 1840), p. 3.

8 See www.ukpublicspending.co.uk/uk_year1840_0.html, last accessed on 1 November 2018.

9 In the 1830s: *Parliamentary Papers, Papers Relative to the Opium Trade in China, 1842–1856* (London, 1857), p. 50.

10 Brian Inglis, *The Opium War*, 2nd edn (London, 1979), p. 223.

11 Lovell, *Opium War*, pp. 109–11. The account that follows is chiefly derived from Lovell's book.

12 Fay, *The Opium War*, p. 341.

13 Granville Loch, *Closing Events of the Campaign in China* (London, 1843), p. 113.

14 Ibid., p. 107.

15 Ibid., pp. 108–10.

16 Fay, *The Opium War*, p. 362.

17 Loch, *Closing Events*, pp. 170–71.

18 Ibid., pp. 173–4.

19 David Anthony Bello, *Opium and the Limits of Empire* (Cambridge, MA, 2005), pp. 138–40.

20 Melissa Macauley, 'Small Time Crooks: Opium, Migrants, and the War on Drugs in China, 1819–1860', *Late Imperial China*, 30 (2009), pp. 37–9.

21 Bello, *Opium*, p. 163.

22 Fay, *The Opium War*, p. 368.

23 Ibid., p. 370; Platt, *Imperial Twilight*, pp. 412–13; Jesse Palsetia, *Jamsetjee Jejeebhoy of Bombay* (New Delhi, 2015), pp. 107–34.

24 *The Record*, 30 July 1840, p. 4.

25 *Morning Herald*, 1 January 1840, p. 4, and 7 April 1840, p. 4; 'The Opium War', *Northern Star*, 15 February 1840, p. 4.

26 Quoted for example in T. H. Bullock, *The Chinese Vindicated* (London, 1840), pp. 94–5; for the war's reception, see more broadly P. E. Caquet, 'Notions of Addiction in the Time of the First Opium War', *Historical Journal*, 58 (2015), pp. 1009–29.

27 *Hansard's Parliamentary Debates* (London, 1803–), Third Series, vol. LIII, House of Commons, 9 April 1840, c. 950.

28 Ibid., vol. LIV, House of Lords, 12 May 1840, cc. 34–43.

29 James Matheson to William Jardine, 1 May 1839, in Alain Le Pichon, *China Trade and Empire: Jardine, Matheson & Co. and the Origins of British Rule in Hong Kong, 1827–1843* (Oxford, 2006), p. 369.

30 H. Hamilton Lindsay, *Is the War with China a Just One?* (London, 1840); *Hansard's Parliamentary Debates*, Third Series, vol. LXVIII, House of Commons, 4 April 1843, cc. 453–7.

31 *The Rupture with China and Its Causes* (London, 1840), pp. 3–4; a key tract written to order was Samuel Warren, *The Opium Question* (London, 1840).

32 A. S. Thelwall, *The Iniquities of the Opium Trade with China* (London, 1839), pp. 9–10.

33 *The Record*, 2 March 1840, p. 4.

34 'Iniquities of the Opium Trade with China', *The Times*, 15 August 1839, p. 6.

35 *Morning Chronicle*, 27 March 1840, p. 4.

36 Hosea Ballou Morse, *The International Relations of the Chinese Empire*, 3 vols (London, 1910–18), vol. I, p. 556.

37 David Edward Owen, *British Opium Policy in China and India* (London, 1934), p. 211.

38 J. Y. Wong, *Deadly Dreams: Opium, Imperialism and the Arrow War* (Cambridge, 1998), pp. 262–7.

39 For the incident: ibid., pp. 43–79; and Jack Beeching, *The Chinese Opium Wars* (London, 1975), pp. 213–18.

40 Wong, *Deadly Dreams*, pp. 157–73 and 223–40; Lovell, *Opium War*, pp. 253–5.

41 Account taken from Beeching, *Chinese Opium Wars*, pp. 248–93; and Lovell, *Opium War*, pp. 258–62.

42 Beeching, *Chinese Opium Wars*, pp. 296–327.

43 Ibid., pp. 263–4; Wong, *Deadly Dreams*, pp. 413–15.

44 Beeching, *Chinese Opium Wars*, pp. 181–93; Morse, *International Relations of the Chinese Empire*, vol. II, p. III.

45 Owen, *British Opium Policy*, pp. 221–2.

46 Ibid., pp. 222–3.

47 John Fairbank, *The Cambridge History of China: Late Ch'ing, 1800–1911*, 2 vols (Cambridge, 1978), vol. I, pp. 285–309.

48 Owen, *British Opium Policy*, pp. 242–73.

49 'Memorandum on Opium from China', International Opium Commission, *Report of the International Opium Commission, Shanghai China, February 1 to February 26 1909* (Shanghai, 1909), p. 53.

50 Bello, *Opium*, p. 294.

51 Jiang Qiuming and Zhu Qingbao, *Zhongguo jidu licheng* (Tianjin, 1996), p. 84.

52 Jonathan Spence, 'Opium Smoking in Ch'ing China', in *Conflict and Control in Late Imperial China*, ed. Frederic Wakeman and Carolyn Grant (Berkeley, CA, 1975), p. 161.

53 Wang Hongbin, *Jindu shijian* (Beijing, 1997), pp. 225–6.

54 Bello, *Opium*, pp. 222–3.

55 The customs inspector general estimated them to be about equal in 1881: *China Imperial Maritime Customs Reports on Opium* (Shanghai, 1864–1909), vol. IV, pp. 1–4.

56 'Memorandum on Opium from China', International Opium
 Commission, *Report*, pp. 48–57.
57 Zheng Yangwen, *The Social Life of Opium in China* (Cambridge, 2005),
 pp. 114–17.
58 Ibid., p. 148.
59 Ibid., pp. 156–7.
60 Frank Dikötter, Lars Laamann and Zhou Xun, *Narcotic Culture:
 A History of Drugs in China* (London, 2004), pp. 64–5.
61 Ibid., pp. 62–3.
62 R. K. Newman, 'Opium Smoking in Late Imperial China:
 A Reconsideration', *Modern Asian Studies*, 29 (1995), pp. 765–94, at pp. 777–8.
63 Zheng, *Social Life of Opium*, p. 125.
64 Justus Doolittle, *Social Life of the Chinese*, 2 vols, 2nd edn (New York,
 1876), vol. II, p. 355.
65 *Final Report of the Royal Commission on Opium*, 6 vols (London, 1893–5),
 vol. I, p. 42.
66 See for example Elizabeth Chang, *British Travel Writing from China,
 1798–1901*, 4 vols (London, 2010), vols III and IV.
67 Newman, 'Opium Smoking in Late Imperial China', p. 777; Dikötter,
 Narcotic Culture, pp. 61–2.
68 William Hector Park, ed., *Opinions of over 100 Physicians on the Use
 of Opium in China* (Shanghai, 1899), pp. 30–31.
69 Doolittle, *Social Life of the Chinese*, pp. 351–2.
70 Zheng, *Social Life of Opium*, p. 193.
71 Dikötter, *Narcotic Culture*, p. 120.
72 Kathleen Lodwick, *Crusaders against Opium: Protestant Missionaries
 in China, 1874–1917* (Lexington, KY, 1996), p. 135.
73 Ibid., p. 136.
74 Macauley, 'Small Time Crooks', p. 17.
75 Newman, 'Opium Smoking in Late Imperial China', p. 781.
76 Park, *Opinions of over 100 Physicians*, pp. 30–31.
77 Alexander Des Forges, 'Opium/Leisure/Shanghai', in *Opium Regimes:
 China, Britain, and Japan, 1839–1952*, ed. Timothy Brook and Bob Tadashi
 Wakabayashi (Berkeley, CA, 2000), pp. 176–9.
78 An early example of this approach, also followed by Newman, is
 Frederick Storrs Turner, *British Opium Policy and Its Results to India
 and China* (London, 1876), pp. 248–53.
79 'Memorandum on Opium from China', International Opium
 Commission, *Report*, p. 57.
80 *China Imperial Maritime Customs*, pp. 60–63.
81 UNODC, *World Drug Report* (Vienna, 1997–), 2017, vol. II, p. 32.
82 Ibid., vol. I, p. 9.
83 Lovell makes this very point in her book: Lovell, *Opium War*, pp. 333–60.
 For a balanced assessment of perhaps overenthusiastic attempts at
 rehabilitation, see Macauley, 'Small Time Crooks', p. 17.
84 National Institute on Drug Abuse Online Database, *Number of National
 Drug Overdose Deaths Involving Select Prescription and Illicit Drugs,
 1999–2018*, www.drugabuse.gov, accessed on 22 May 2020.
85 *Final Report of the Royal Commission*, vol. I, pp. 109–10.

86 Ibid.

87 Lodwick, *Crusaders against Opium*, pp. 130–32.

88 *Final Report of the Royal Commission*, vol. I, p. 41, italics in original.

89 Hans Derks, *History of the Opium Problem: The Assault on the East, ca. 1600–1950* (Leiden, 2012), pp. 164–70 and 213–37; George Bryan Souza, 'Opium and Tobacco in the Indonesian Archipelago, 1619–1794', in *Drugs and Empires: Essays in Modern Imperialism and Intoxication, 1500–1930*, ed. Patricia Barton and James Mills (Basingstoke, 2007), pp. 42–6.

90 James Rush, *Opium to Java: Revenue Farming and Chinese Enterprise in Colonial Indonesia, 1860–1910* (London, 1990), pp. 30–31.

91 Ibid., pp. 24–5.

92 Ibid., p. 58.

93 Richard Newman, 'Early British Encounters with the Indian Opium Eater', in *Drugs and Empires*, ed. Barton and Mills, pp. 62–7.

94 Ibid., p. 66; *Final Report of the Royal Commission*, vol. VI, pp. 7–8; John Richards, 'The Moral Economy of Opium in Colonial India', in *Drugs and Empires*, ed. Barton and Mills, p. 78.

95 *Use of Opium and Traffic Therein: Message from the President of the United States* (Washington, DC, 1906), pp. 35–7; Cheng U. Wen, 'Opium in the Straits Settlements, 1867–1910', *Journal of Southeast Asian History*, 2 (1961), pp. 52–75, at p. 52.

96 Ashley Wright, *Opium and Empire in Southeast Asia: Regulating Consumption in British Burma* (Basingstoke, 2014), pp. 23–33 and 45–9.

97 Chantal Descours-Gatin, *Quand l'opium finançait la colonisation en Indochine* (Paris, 1992), pp. 20–21.

98 'Statement by the Siamese delegates to the International Opium Commission', International Opium Commission, *Report*, pp. 329–30.

99 Rush, *Opium to Java*, pp. 83–5.

100 Alexander Barton Woodside, *Vietnam and the Chinese Model* (Cambridge, MA, 1971), pp. 269–70.

101 Descours-Gatin, *Quand l'opium finançait la colonisation*, pp. 42–52.

102 Ibid., p. 23.

103 Philippe Le Failler, *Monopole et prohibition de l'opium en Indochine: le pilori des chimères* (Paris, 2000), p. 66.

104 Descours-Gatin, *Quand l'opium finançait la colonisation*, pp. 91–7.

105 Ibid., pp. 145–8 and 197.

106 Rush, *Opium to Java*, pp. 213–22.

107 Wright, *Opium and Empire*, pp. 97–8.

108 'Statement by the Siamese Delegates', International Opium Commission, *Report*, pp. 329–30.

109 'Regulations and Restrictions Regarding Opium in Great Britain and Its Possession', ibid., pp. 162–7.

110 Cheng, 'Opium in the Straits Settlements', p. 74; *Proceedings of the Committee to Inquire into Matters Relating to the Use of Opium in British Malaya* (Singapore, 1924), pp. 22–3.

111 Calculations based on International Opium Commission, *Report*, pp. 162–7, 193, 300 and 330; Wright, *Opium and Empire*, p. 98; and Descours-Gatin, *Quand l'opium finançait la colonisation*, pp. 210–11.

112 *Final Report of the Royal Commission*, vol. II, pp. 87.

113 Descours-Gatin, *Quand l'opium finançait la colonisation*, pp. 38–9.

114 Rush, *Opium to Java*, pp. 140–43.

115 Ibid., pp. 166–7.

116 Ibid., pp. 199–208.

117 Wright, *Opium and Empire*, pp. 37–9.

118 Ibid., pp. 49 and 59–60.

119 Cheng, 'Opium in the Straits Settlements', pp. 61–74.

120 Wright, *Opium and Empire*, pp. 110–11; Emdad-ul Haq, *Drugs in South Asia: From the Opium Trade to the Present Day* (Basingstoke, 2000), p. 56.

121 'Statement by the Siamese Delegates', International Opium Commission, *Report*, p. 330.

122 Bob Tadashi Wakabayashi, 'From Peril to Profit: Opium in Late-Edo to Meiji Eyes', in *Opium Regimes*, ed. Brook and Wakabayashi, pp. 58–64.

123 Ibid., pp. 66–7; 'Control of Opium in Japan', International Opium Commission, *Report*, p. 250.

124 'Control of Opium in Japan', International Opium Commission, *Report*, pp. 250–52; Miriam Kingsberg, *Moral Nation: Modern Japan and Narcotics in Global History* (Berkeley, CA, 2014), p. 11; *Use of Opium and Traffic Therein*, p. 220.

125 *Use of Opium and Traffic Therein*, pp. 24–5; Kingsberg, *Moral Nation*, pp. 20–21.

126 Kingsberg, *Moral Nation*, pp. 21–2.

127 Ibid., pp, 22–3.

128 Ibid., pp. 23–4.

129 'Control of Opium in Japan', International Opium Commission, *Report*, p. 278.

130 Ibid., p. 275.

131 Kingsberg, *Moral Nation*, pp. 26–7.

132 'Control of Opium in Japan', International Opium Commission, *Report*, p. 280.

133 Alma Bamero, 'Opium: The Evolution of Policies, the Tolerance of the Vice, and the Proliferation of Contraband Trade in the Philippines, 1843–1908', *Social Science Dilman*, 3 (2006), pp. 49–83, at p. 59.

134 Kingsberg, *Moral Nation*, p. 27.

3 PARADISE LOST?

1 Théophile Gautier, 'Club des hachichins', *La Revue des deux mondes*, 1 February 1846, pp. 520–35. What follows is taken from this fictionalized account.

2 Arnould de Liedekerke, ed., *La Belle époque de l'opium*, 2nd edn (Paris, 2001), pp. 62–5.

3 James Mills, *Cannabis Britannica: Empire, Trade, and Prohibition, 1800–1928* (Oxford, 2003), p. 19.

4 Ibid., pp. x–xi and 52–5.

5 Ibid., pp. 25–30.

6 Howard Wayne Morgan, *Drugs in America: A Social History, 1800–1980* (Syracuse, NY, 1981), p. 20.

7 Mills, *Cannabis Britannica*, p. 33.

8 Ibid., pp. 43–6.

9 *Description de l'Egypte*, 23 vols (Paris, 1809–28), vol. v, p. 220.

10 Ibid., p. 226.

11 Ibid., p. 220.

12 Gautier, 'Club des hachichins', pp. 523–4; Alethea Hayter, *Opium and the Romantic Imagination* (London, 1968), p. 21.

13 Jean-Jacques Yvorel, *Les Poisons de l'esprit* (Paris, 1992), p. 10.

14 Morgan, *Drugs in America*, pp. 3–4; Virginia Berridge, *Opium and the People*, 2nd edn (London, 1999), p. 66.

15 Virginia Berridge, *Demons: Our Changing Attitudes to Alcohol, Tobacco, and Drugs* (Oxford, 2013), pp. 15–16.

16 Berridge, *Opium and the People*, pp. 38–48.

17 William Howitt, 'Nooks of the World – a Visit to the Whitworth Doctors', *Tait's Edinburgh Magazine* (April 1839), p. 239.

18 Berridge, *Opium and the People*, pp. 4 and 11–17; Steven Belenko, ed., *Drugs and Drug Policy in America: A Documentary History* (Westport, CT, 2000), p. 4.

19 Quoted in Samuel Crumpe, *An Inquiry into the Nature and Properties of Opium* (London, 1793), pp. 52–3.

20 Thomas De Quincey, *Confessions of an English Opium-Eater*, 2nd edn (London, 1856), pp. 267–8.

21 'Confessions of an English Opium-Eater', *Lady's Monthly Museum* (April 1823), p. 96.

22 'Confessions of an English Opium-Eater', *British Review and London Critical Journal* (December 1822), p. 475.

23 'Confessions of an English Opium Eater', *Eclectic Review* (April 1823), p. 371.

24 Liedekerke, *La Belle époque de l'opium*, p. 55.

25 Fitz Hugh Ludlow, *The Hasheesh Eater* (New York, 1857).

26 Barry Milligan, *Pleasures and Pains: Opium and the Orient in Nineteenth-Century British Culture* (Charlottesville, VA, 1995), pp. 10–11.

27 Charles Baudelaire, *Les Paradis artificiels, opium et haschisch* (Paris, 1860), p. 74.

28 Ibid., p. 26.

29 Heinrich Laehr, 'Ueber Missbrauch mit Morphium-Injektionen', *Allgemeine Zeitschrift für Psychiatrie* (1872), pp. 349–53.

30 Ibid., pp. 351–2.

31 Berridge, *Opium and the People*, pp. 136–7; David Musto, *Drugs in America: A Documentary History* (New York, 2002), pp. 200–201.

32 Belenko, *Drugs and Drug Policy in America*, p. 4.

33 Berridge, *Demons*, p. 111; Berridge, *Opium and the People*, pp. 139–40.

34 John Chardin, *Travels in Persia, 1673–1677* (New York, 1988), p. 245.

35 A. S. Thelwall, *The Iniquities of the Opium Trade with China* (London, 1839), pp. 4–5; 'British Opium Trade with China', *Leeds Mercury*, 7 September 1839, p. 3.

36 'On the Preparation of Opium for the Chinese market', *Foreign Quarterly Review* (October 1839), pp. 120 and 138.

37 John Jones, *The Mysteries of Opium Reveal'd* (London, 1700), p. 32.

38 Crumpe, *An Inquiry into the Nature and Properties of Opium*, p. 217.

39 Terry Parssinen, *Secret Passions, Secret Remedies: Narcotic Drugs in British Society, 1820–1930* (Manchester, 1983), p. 85.
40 See Berridge, *Opium and the People*, pp. 150–69; and Louise Foxcroft, *The Making of Addiction: The 'Use and Abuse' of Opium in Nineteenth-Century Britain* (Aldershot, 2007).
41 Belenko, *Drugs and Drug Policy in America*, pp. 26–7; David Courtwright, *Dark Paradise: A History of Opiate Addiction in America* (Cambridge, MA, 2001), pp. 87–9.
42 Johan Edman and Börje Olsson, 'The Swedish Drug Problem: Conceptual Understanding and Problem Handling, 1839–2011', *Nordic Studies on Alcohol and Drugs*, 31 (2014), pp. 503–26.
43 Virginia Berridge et al., 'Addiction in Europe, 1860s–1960s: Concepts and Responses in Italy, Poland, Austria, and the United Kingdom', *Contemporary Drug Problems*, 41 (2014), pp. 551–66.
44 Albrecht Erlenmeyer, *Die Morphiumsucht und ihre Behandlung*, 2nd edn (Leipzig, 1883), p. 7.
45 Ibid., pp. 12–13.
46 See for example 'A Remarkable Case of Morphia Addiction', *British Medical Journal*, 11 May 1889, pp. 1051–2; Robert Jones, 'Notes on Some Cases of Morphinomania', *Journal of Mental Science* (July 1902), pp. 478–95; 'Morphine Habit Treated by Gradual Withdrawal', *Medical and Surgical Reporter*, 18 April 1891, p. 446.
47 Eduard Levinstein, *Morbid Craving for Morphia* (London, 1878), pp. 6–7.
48 R. Burkart, *Die chronische Morphiumvergiftung und deren Behandlung* (Bonn, 1880), p. 23.
49 Benjamin Ball, *La Morphinomanie*, 2nd edn (Paris, 1888), pp. 10 and 18; Henri Guimbail, *Les Morphinomanes* (Paris, 1891), pp. 11–12.
50 Ernest Chambard, *Les Morphinomanes, étude clinique, médico-légale et thérapeutique* (Paris, 1890), pp. ix–xi; Daniel Jouet, *Etude sur le morphinisme chronique* (Paris, 1883); Maurice Notta, 'La Morphine et la morphinomanie', *Archives générales de médecine* (November 1884), pp. 561–83.
51 Erlenmeyer, *Die Morphiumsucht*, p. 8.
52 Eduard Levinstein, *Die Morphiumsucht* (Berlin, 1877), p. 4.
53 Norman Shanks Kerr, *Inebriety or Narcomania*, 3rd edn (London, 1894), pp. 5–8. See also Berridge, *Opium and the People*, pp. 151–60.
54 Ibid., p. 12.
55 Ibid., pp. 41 and 117.
56 T. D. Crothers, 'The Disease of Inebriety and Its Treatment', *The Lancet*, 19 November 1887, p. 1011.
57 'Section on Nervous and Mental Diseases', *Medical News*, 29 July 1905, p. 236.
58 'Morphine Addiction', *Journal of the American Medical Association*, 16 November 1907, p. 1708.
59 Paul Rodet, *Morphinomanie et morphinisme* (Paris, 1897).
60 'Aus der Gesellschaften', *Zentralblatt für die gesamte Neurologie und Psychiatrie*, 1 September 1884, p. 403; Schröder, 'Über Behandlung der Morphinisten', *Allgemeine Zeitschrift für Psychiatrie*, 68 (1911), pp. 276–7.
61 Rodet, *Morphinomanie et morphinisme*, pp. 35–43.

62 Ibid., pp. 201–3; Paul Garnier, 'De l'état mental et de la responsabilité pénale dans le morphinisme chronique', *Annales médico-psychologiques* (January 1886), pp. 351–78; Otto Remertz, 'Morphinismus und Entmündigung', *Archiv für Psychiatrie und Nervenkrankenheiten*, 53 (1914); 'Schmidbauer, Einfluss des Morphinismus auf die civil- und strafrechtliche Zurechnungsfähigkeit', *Allgemeine Zeitschrift für Psychiatrie* (1887), pp. 160–61.

63 *The Times*, 'The Alleged Poisoning Case at Wimbledon', 9 December 1881, p. 8; 'George Henry Lamson Was Yesterday Convicted', 15 March 1882, p. 9; 'The Case of Dr. Lamson', 15 April 1882, p. 13; 'The Lamson Case', 17 April 1882, p. 6; 'The Plea of Insanity in the Lamson Case', 21 April 1882, p. 4; 'The Convict Lamson', 28 April 1882, p. 7; and Benjamin Ball, 'L'Empoisonneur Lamson', *L'Encéphale* (1882), pp. 209–13.

64 Quoted in 'The Plea of Insanity in the Lamson Case', *The Times*, 21 April 1882, p. 4.

65 Ball, 'L'Empoisonneur Lamson', p. 213.

66 Richard Davenport-Hines, *The Pursuit of Oblivion: A Global History of Narcotics, 1500–2000* (London, 2001), p. 95; H. Richard Friman, 'Germany and the Transformations of Cocaine, 1860–1920', in *Cocaine: Global Histories*, ed. Paul Gootenberg (London, 1999), p. 84.

67 Joseph Spillane, *Cocaine: from Medical Marvel to Modern Menace in the United States, 1884–1920* (Baltimore, MD, 2000), pp. 7–15.

68 Ibid., p. 22.

69 Davenport-Hines, *The Pursuit of Oblivion*, pp. 113–17.

70 Albrecht Erlenmeyer, 'Über Cocainsucht', *Deutsche Medizinal-Zeitung*, 7 (1886), p. 483.

71 Michael Gossop, *Living with Drugs*, 6th edn (Aldershot, 2007), pp. 147–9.

72 J. B. Mattison, 'Cocaine Dosage and Cocaine Addiction', *The Lancet*, 21 May 1887, p. 1026.

73 'The Cocaine Habit', *Medical and Surgical Reporter*, 31 October 1891, p. 710. See also Spillane, *Cocaine*, pp. 33–6.

74 Spillane, *Cocaine*, pp. 41–2.

75 Ibid., pp. 82–7.

76 Ibid., pp. 71–3.

77 Samuel Hopkins Adams, *The Great American Fraud* (Chicago, IL, 1906), p. 43.

78 Paul Gootenberg, *Andean Cocaine: The Making of a Global Drug* (Chapel Hill, NC, 2008), p. 21.

79 William H. Hefland, 'Mariani et le vin de coca', *Revue d'histoire de la pharmacie*, 68 (1980), pp. 227–34.

80 Gootenberg, *Andean Cocaine*, p. 28.

81 Joseph Spillane, 'The Manufacture, Sale and Control of Cocaine in the United States, 1880–1920', in *Cocaine: Global Histories*, ed. Gootenberg, pp. 23–7.

82 Friman, 'Germany and the Transformations of Cocaine', pp. 84–6.

83 Gootenberg, *Andean Cocaine*, pp. 31–44 and 63–4.

84 Ibid., pp. 125–8.

85 Marcel de Kort, 'Conflicting Interests in the Netherlands and Dutch East Indies, 1860–1950', in *Cocaine: Global Histories*, ed. Gootenberg, p. 132.

86 Davenport-Hines, *The Pursuit of Oblivion*, pp. 112–13; Mark Pendergrast, *For God, Country and Coca-Cola: The Definitive History of the World's Most Popular Soft Drink* (London, 2000), pp. 21–5.

87 Pendergrast, *For God, Country and Coca-Cola*, pp. 41–4.

88 Ibid., p. 87.

89 Ibid., p. 88.

90 Ibid., pp. 63–4 and 88.

91 P. E. Caquet, 'France, Germany, and the Origins of Drug Prohibition', *International History Review*, 43 (2021), pp. 207–25, at p. 211.

92 Obersteiner, 'Der chronische Morphinismus', *Deutsche Medizinal-Zeitung* (1883), pp. 288–9.

93 Emil Bihler, 'Ein Fall von tödlicher Opiumvergiftung', *Deutsches Archiv für klinische Medizin* (1899), pp. 483–91.

94 As suggested, for example, in Davenport-Hines, *The Pursuit of Oblivion*, p. 84.

95 Morgan, *Drugs in America*, pp. 29–30.

96 Courtwright, *Dark Paradise*, pp. 9–28.

97 Ibid. Using the same method and data, but with an 0.67 gram per day morphine use, or 5.6 grams opium, and a one-third discount for medical use, yields 120,000 users.

98 Spillane, *Cocaine*, pp. 59–64 and 115.

99 Ibid., pp. 91–2.

100 Parssinen, *Secret Passions*, pp. 71–3.

101 David Musto, *The American Disease: Origins of Narcotic Control*, 2nd edn (Oxford, 1987), pp. 21–2 and 91.

102 Spillane, *Cocaine*, pp. 144–5.

103 James Broh, ed., *Gesetze und Verordnungen betreffend den Drogen-, Gift- und Farbenhandel* (Berlin, 1899), pp. 9–10; 'No 2676 – Loi contenant Organisation des Ecoles de pharmacie', *Bulletin des Lois de la République*, IIIe Série, vol. VIII (October 1803), pp. 121–9; Friedrich Ludwig Augustin, *Die königlich Preußische Medicinalverfassung* (Potsdam, 1818), pp. 494–6; 'No 12,115 – Loi sur la vente des substances vénéneuses', *Bulletin des Lois du Royaume de France*, IXe Série, vol. XXXI (February 1846), p. 302.

104 Broh, *Gesetze und Verordnungen*, pp. 39–53; Levinstein, *Die Morphiumsucht*, pp. 154–5.

105 Alfred Adlung, *Grundriss der Geschichte der deutschen Pharmazie* (Berlin, 1935), p. 86.

106 'France et Indochine', International Opium Commission, *Report of the International Opium Commission, Shanghai China, February 1 to February 26 1909* (Shanghai, 1909), p. 122.

107 It is always difficult to prove a negative, but neither the academic literature nor keyword searches in databases covering the main newspapers yield more than a tiny number of drug-related articles for the period.

108 Roger Dupouy, *Les Opiomanes, mangeurs, buveurs, et fumeurs d'opium* (Paris, 1912), pp. 287–92; Liedekerke, *La Belle époque de l'opium*, pp. 126–31 and 266–310.

109 Docteur Ox, 'Si vous aimez la vie, craignez la morphine', *Le Matin*, 9 July 1912, p. 1.

110 'Après le drame de la morphine, un drame de la cocaïne', *Le Petit Parisien*, 25 December 1912, pp. 1–2.

111 Yvorel, *Les Poisons de l'esprit*, pp. 217–20.

112 Paul Bonnetain, *L'Opium* (Paris, 1886).

113 Dupouy, *Les Opiomanes*, pp. ii–iii.

114 'Negro Cocaine Evil', *New York Times*, 20 March 1905, p. 14.

115 Spillane, *Cocaine*, pp. 94–5; Musto, *Drugs in America*, pp. 360–61.

116 Musto, *American Disease*, p. 8.

117 '6,000 Opium Users Here', *New York Times*, 1 August 1908, p. 6.

118 Belenko, *Drugs and Drug Policy in America*, pp. 14–15.

119 'The Opium Habit in San Francisco', *Medical and Surgical Reporter*, 10 December 1887, p. 684.

120 *New York Times*, in Belenko, *Drugs and Drug Policy in America*, p. 24.

121 'The Female Drug Drunkard: Health in the Household', *Current Literature* (December 1889), p. 480.

122 'Women Using Narcotics', *New York Times*, 10 January 1897, p. 13.

123 Yvorel, *Les Poisons de l'esprit*, pp. 107–8.

124 William Rosser Cobbe, *Doctor Judas* (Chicago, IL, 1895), pp. 12–13.

125 Ibid., p. 27.

126 Marcel Mallat de Bassilan, *La Comtesse morphine* (Paris, 1885), pp. 278–9.

4 SHANGHAI AND THE HAGUE

1 Hosea Ballou Morse, *The International Relations of the Chinese Empire*, 3 vols (London, 1910–18), vol. III, pp. 347–59.

2 Frank Dikötter, Lars Laamann and Zhou Xun, *Narcotic Culture: A History of Drugs in China* (London, 2004), p. 109.

3 Zhou Yongming, *Anti-Drug Crusades in Twentieth-Century China: Nationalism, History, and State Building* (Lanham, MD, 1999), pp. 20–21.

4 Dikötter et al., *Narcotic Culture*, p. 108.

5 John Fairbank, *The Cambridge History of China: Late Ch'ing, 1800–1911*, 2 vols (Cambridge, 1978), vol. II, pp. 375–411.

6 Carnegie to Grey, 21 July 1906, The National Archives [TNA], FO 371/37/30586, ff. 345–6.

7 J. B. Brown, 'The Politics of the Poppy: The Society for the Suppression of the Opium Trade, 1874–1916', *Journal of Contemporary History*, 8 (1973), pp. 97–111; Virginia Berridge, *Opium and the People*, 2nd edn (London, 1999), pp. 176–82.

8 *Hansard's Parliamentary Debates* (London, 1803–), Third Series, vol. ccxxv, House of Commons, 25 June 1875, c. 571.

9 Dated 1876, 1886, 1889, 1891, 1893, 1895 and 1906. The SSOT also intervened on questions over the opium tariff at various dates.

10 *Hansard's Parliamentary Debates*, Third Series, vol. cccxxxv, House of Commons, 3 May 1889, cc. 1143–92.

11 Ibid., vol. ccclii, 10 April 1891, cc. 285–304.

12 Ibid., cc. 309–15.

13 Ibid., c. 344; Kathleen Lodwick, *Crusaders against Opium: Protestant Missionaries in China, 1874–1917* (Lexington, MD, 1996), p. 57.

14 *Hansard's Parliamentary Debates*, Fourth Series, vol. XIV, House of Commons, 30 June 1893, cc. 591–601.

15 Ibid., cc. 615–20.

16 Berridge, *Opium and the People*, pp. 183–4.

17 Wu Wen-Tsao, *The Chinese Opium Question and British Opinion and Action* (New York, 1928), pp. 101–2.

18 *Final Report of the Royal Commission on Opium*, 6 vols (London, 1893–5), vol. VI, pp. 93–7. For a balanced critique of the commission's work, see Richard Davenport-Hines, *The Pursuit of Oblivion: A Global History of Narcotics, 1500–2000* (London, 2001), pp. 136–9.

19 Joshua Rowntree, *The Opium Habit in the East: A Study of the Evidence Given to the Royal Commission on Opium, 1893–4* (London, 1895); *Hansard's Parliamentary Debates*, Fourth Series, vol. XXXIV, House of Commons, 24 May 1895, cc. 278 and 324.

20 Brown, 'The Politics of the Poppy', p. 109; Lodwick, *Crusaders against Opium*, pp. 122–3; R. K. Newman, 'India and the Anglo-Chinese Opium Agreements, 1907–14', *Modern Asian Studies*, 23 (1989), pp. 525–60, at pp. 533–4.

21 *Hansard's Parliamentary Debates*, Fourth Series, vol. CLVIII, House of Commons, 30 May 1906, cc. 494–500.

22 Ibid., cc. 500–505.

23 Ibid., cc. 505–15.

24 Wang Hongbin, *Jindu shijan* (Beijing, 1997), pp. 269–77.

25 Joseph Gundry Alexander, *Interviews with Chinese Statesmen with Regard to the Opium Traffic* (London, 1894), pp. 5–20.

26 Wang, *Jindu shijan*, pp. 269–77.

27 Lodwick, *Crusaders against Opium*, pp. 52–3.

28 Ibid., pp. 30–32.

29 Alan Baumler, ed., *Modern China and Opium* (Ann Arbor, MI, 2001), pp. 66–71; Jiang Qiuming and Zhu Qingbao, *Zhongguo jidu licheng* (Tianjin, 1996), pp. 185–7; Newman, 'India and the Anglo-Chinese Opium Agreements', p. 531.

30 Newman, 'India and the Anglo-Chinese Opium Agreements', p. 535; 'Sir J. Jordan to Sir Edward Grey', 30 November 1906, TNA, FO 371/37/40331, ff. 379–81.

31 Newman, 'India and the Anglo-Chinese Opium Agreements', pp. 547–56.

32 Hamilton Wright, 'The International Opium Commission', *American Journal of International Law*, 3 (1909), pp. 828–68, at pp. 842–3.

33 'Sir Edward Grey to Sir M. Durand', 17 October 1906, TNA, FO 371/22/35165, f. 110.

34 Elizabeth Kelly-Gray, 'The Trade-Off: Chinese Opium Traders and Antebellum Reform in the United States, 1815–1860', in *Drugs and Empires: Essays in Modern Imperialism and Intoxication, 1500–1930*, ed. Patricia Barton and James Mills (Basingstoke, 2007), pp. 220–28.

35 Ibid., p. 228.

36 Ibid., p. 229.

37 Stephen Platt, *Imperial Twilight: The Opium War and the End of China's Last Golden Age* (London, 2018), p. 416.

38 Ibid., pp. 417–20; Arnold Taylor, *American Diplomacy and the Narcotics Traffic, 1900–1939* (Durham, NC, 1969), p. 16.

39 Michael Hunt, *The Making of a Special Relationship: The United States and China to 1914* (New York, 1983), pp. 171–97.

40 Ibid., pp. 88–94 and 232–41.

41 Alma Bamero, 'Opium: The Evolution of Policies, the Tolerance of the Vice, and the Proliferation of Contraband Trade in the Philippines, 1843–1908', *Social Science Dilman*, 3 (2006), pp. 49–83, p. 68; David Courtwright, *Dark Paradise: A History of Opiate Addiction in America* (Cambridge, MA, 2001), pp. 80–81; Ian Tyrrell, *Reforming the World: The Creation of America's Moral Empire* (Princeton, NJ, 2010), p. 147.

42 Wilbur Crafts, *Protection of Native Races against Intoxicants and Opium* (New York, 1900).

43 Taylor, *American Diplomacy*, pp. 34–40; Tyrrell, *Reforming the World*, pp. 150–51.

44 Tyrrell, *Reforming the World*, pp. 152–3.

45 Alexander Zabriskie, *Bishop Brent* (Philadelphia, PA, 1948), pp. 67–70.

46 David Musto, *The American Disease: Origins of Narcotic Control*, 2nd edn (Oxford, 1987), p. 25.

47 Zabriskie, *Bishop Brent*, pp. 98–9.

48 *Use of Opium and Traffic Therein: Message from the President of the United States* (Washington, DC, 1906), pp. 11–18.

49 Ibid., p. 31.

50 Ibid., pp. 51–2.

51 Bamero, 'Opium: The Evolution of Policies', p. 69; Tyrrell, *Reforming the World*, p. 154.

52 Tyrrell, *Reforming the World*, pp. 156–7.

53 'Opium Traffic between India and China', 8 January 1906, TNA, FO 371/22/1026, ff. 1–3.

54 Zhou, *Anti-Drug Crusades*, p. 24.

55 *Hansard's Parliamentary Debates*, Fourth Series, vol. CLVIII, House of Commons, 30 May 1906, cc. 494–515.

56 'Question Asked in the House of Commons', 18 June 1906, TNA, FO 371/37/31748, f. 302; 'Importation of Opium into China', 11 April 1906, TNA, FO 371/22/12455, ff. 16–20; 'The Archbishop of Canterbury to Sir Edward Grey', 25 September 1906, TNA, FO 371/22/32438, ff. 90–91.

57 Tyrrell, *Reforming the World*, p. 159.

58 'India Office to Foreign Office', 2 November 1906, TNA, FO 371/22/36924, f. 152.

59 The United States, Austria–Hungary, China, France, Germany, Britain, Italy, Japan, the Netherlands, Persia, Portugal, Russia and Siam; William McAllister, *Drug Diplomacy in the Twentieth Century* (London, 2000), p. 28.

60 International Opium Commission, *Report of the International Opium Commission, Shanghai China, February 1 to February 26 1909* (Shanghai, 1909), p. 9.

61 Ibid., pp. 27–30.

62 Ibid., p. 10.

63 Taylor, *American Diplomacy*, pp. 53–4.

64 International Opium Commission, *Report*, p. 46.

65 Ibid., pp. 46–7.

66 Ibid., p. 48.

67 Ibid., pp. 49–50.

68 Ibid., pp. 51–2.

69 Ibid., p. 84.

70 Ibid., pp. 61–2.

71 Ibid., p. 51.

72 Jacques Dumarest, *Les Monopoles de l'opium et du sel en Indochine* (Lyon, 1938), pp. 79–81.

73 International Opium Commission, *Report*, pp. 62–5.

74 Marcel de Kort, 'Conflicting Interests in the Netherlands and Dutch East Indies, 1860–1950', in *Cocaine: Global Histories*, ed. Paul Gootenberg (London, 1999), pp. 141–2.

75 International Opium Commission, *Report*, pp. 51–2.

76 Ibid., p. 84.

77 William J. Collins, 'An Address on the Ethics and Law of Drug and Alcohol Addiction', *The Lancet*, 16 October 1915, pp. 847–50.

78 Paul Jennings, 'Policing Drunkenness in England and Wales from the Late Eighteenth Century to the First World War', *Social History of Alcohol and Drugs*, 26 (2012), pp. 69–92.

79 Virginia Berridge, *Demons: Our Changing Attitudes to Alcohol, Tobacco, and Drugs* (Oxford, 2013), p. 63.

80 Berridge, *Opium and the People*, pp. 165–9.

81 Samuel Hopkins Adams, *The Great American Fraud* (Chicago, IL, 1906), p. 3.

82 Norman Clark, *Deliver Us from Evil: An Interpretation of American Prohibition* (New York, 1976), pp. 50–118.

83 Steven Belenko, ed., *Drugs and Drug Policy in America: A Documentary History* (Westport, CT, 2000), pp. 30–31.

84 Musto, *American Disease*, pp. 38–9.

85 'Memorandum by Mr. Brunyate', 21 July 1910, TNA, FO 371/22/29029, ff. 67–79.

86 Taylor, *American Diplomacy*, pp. 86–9.

87 *International Opium Conference, The Hague, December 1, 1911–January 23, 1912: Summary of the Minutes (Unofficial)* (The Hague, 1912), pp. 1–17.

88 *The International Opium Convention, 1912, and Subsequent Relative Papers* (London, 1921), pp. 236–7.

89 Ibid., p. 237.

90 Ibid., p. 238.

91 *International Opium Conference, Summary of the Minutes*, pp. 44–6.

92 H.C.G. Matthew, ed., *Oxford Dictionary of National Biography*, 60 vols (Oxford, 2004), vol. XII, pp. 23–4.

93 *International Opium Convention*, p. 240.

94 Taylor, *American Diplomacy*, pp. 107–13; *Deuxième conférence internationale de l'opium, La Haye, 1–9 juillet 1913* (The Hague, 1913), pp. 1–51.

95 *Troisième conférence internationale de l'opium, La Haye, 15–25 juin 1914* (The Hague, 1914), pp. 18–19.

96 Ibid., pp. 42–3.

97 David Bewley-Taylor, *The United States and International Drug Control, 1909–1997* (London, 1999), p. 165.

98 Joseph Spillane, *Cocaine: From Medical Marvel to Modern Menace in the United States, 1884–1920* (Baltimore, MD, 2000), pp. 112–13.

99 Ibid., pp. 135–8.

100 Musto, *American Disease*, pp. 32–5.

101 Belenko, *Drugs and Drug Policy in America*, pp. 35–7.

102 'Say Drug Habit Grips the Nation', *New York Times*, 5 December 1913, p. 8.

103 David Musto, *Drugs in America: A Documentary History* (New York, 2002), pp. 375–8.

104 Howard Wayne Morgan, *Drugs in America: A Social History, 1800–1980* (Syracuse, NY, 1981), p. 106.

105 Musto, *American Disease*, p. 46.

106 Ibid., pp. 47–8.

107 Ibid., pp. 17–21 and 54–7.

108 Courtwright, *Dark Paradise*, pp. 103–6.

109 Belenko, *Drugs and Drug Policy in America*, pp. 49–53.

110 Zhou, *Anti-Drug Crusades*, pp. 34–5.

111 Xavier Paulès, 'Anti-Opium Visual Propaganda and the Deglamorisation of Opium in China, 1895–1937', *European Journal of East Asian Studies*, 7 (2008), pp. 229–62.

112 James Windle, *Suppressing Illicit Opium Production: Successful Intervention in Asia and the Middle East* (London, 2016), pp. 18–19.

113 Alexander Hosie, *On the Trail of the Opium Poppy*, 2 vols (London, 1914), vol. II, pp. 266–7.

114 Ibid., pp. 287–8.

115 Paul Brouardel, *Cours de médecine légale de la Faculté de médecine de Paris*, 14 vols (Paris, 1895–1909), vol. XII, p. 58.

116 'La Vente de l'opium', *Journal de pharmacie et de chimie* (1908), p. xlvi.

117 Howard Padwa, *Social Poison* (Baltimore, MD, 2012), p. 116.

118 Jean-Jacques Yvorel, *Les Poisons de l'esprit* (Paris, 1992), pp. 237–8; 'Projet de décret, Conseil d'état', Archives Nationales [AN]/BB/18/2488/2.

119 Virginia Berridge, 'War Conditions and Narcotics Control: The Passing of Defence of the Realm Act Regulation 40B', *Journal of Social Policy*, 7 (1978), pp. 285–304, at pp. 287–91.

120 Yvorel, *Les Poisons de l'esprit*, pp. 238–40; 'Opium – Dossier de principe', AN/BB/18/2488/2.

121 Berridge, 'War Conditions and Narcotics Control', pp. 291–2.

122 *Journal Officiel*, Débats parlementaires, Sénat, 27 January 1916, p. 25. See also Yvorel, *Les Poisons de l'esprit*, pp. 255–7.

123 *Journal Officiel*, Documents parlementaires, Sénat, 22 July 1915, doc. 250, p. 141.

124 Berridge, 'War Conditions and Narcotics Control', pp. 296–8.

125 Ibid., p. 299.

126 Terry Parssinen, *Secret Passions, Secret Remedies: Narcotic Drugs in British Society, 1820–1930* (Manchester, 1983), p. 137.

127 Hugh N. Linstead, *Poisons Law* (London, 1936), pp. 149–50.

128 Ibid., p. 134.

129 Taylor, *American Diplomacy*, p. 119.

130 McAllister, *Drug Diplomacy*, pp. 36–7; Taylor, *American Diplomacy*, pp. 143–4.

131 De Kort, 'Conflicting Interests in the Netherlands', p. 124.

132 'Résumé des réponses au questionnaire sur l'opium', League of Nations, Advisory Committee on Traffic in Opium and Other Dangerous Drugs, *Procès Verbal of Sessions* (Geneva, 1921–40), Second Session, 1922, pp. 26–7.

133 Ibid., p. 24; League of Nations, Advisory Committee on Traffic in Opium and Other Dangerous Drugs, *Summary of Annual Reports of Governments* (Geneva, 1926–40), 1931, pp. 17–18.

5 GANGSTERS

1 The affair is detailed in 'Illicit Drug Traffic, Report of the Trial at the Basle Court of Justice', TNA/FO 7403/965/87, reproduced in *The Opium Trade, 1910–1941*, 6 vols (Wilmington, DE, 1974), vol. VI, pp. 42–6.

2 William McAllister, *Drug Diplomacy in the Twentieth Century* (London, 2000), pp. 44–5; Arnold Taylor, *American Diplomacy and the Narcotics Traffic, 1900–1939* (Durham, NC, 1969), pp. 148–9.

3 League of Nations, Advisory Committee on Traffic in Opium and Other Dangerous Drugs, *Procès Verbal of Sessions* (Geneva, 1921–40), First session (1921), p. 17.

4 Ibid., pp. 44–8.

5 Alan A. Block, 'European Drug Traffic and Traffickers between the Wars: The Policy of Suppression and Its Consequences', *Journal of Social History*, 23 (1989), pp. 315–37, at p. 319.

6 Ibid., pp. 319–20.

7 Kathryn Meyer and Terry Parssinen, *Webs of Smoke: Smugglers, Warlords, Spies, and the History of the International Drug Trade* (Lanham, MD, 1998), pp. 24–5.

8 Advisory Committee on Traffic in Opium, *Procès Verbal of Sessions*, Ninth session (1927), pp. 105–6.

9 Ibid., Twelfth session (1929), pp. 16–19.

10 Ibid., Fifth session (1923), p. 215.

11 Thomas Pietschmann, 'A Century of International Drug Control', *Bulletin on Narcotics*, LIX (2007), pp. 70–71.

12 James Mills, *Cannabis Nation: Control and Consumption in Britain, 1928–2008* (Oxford, 2013), pp. 24–5.

13 Tilmann Holzer, *Die Geburt der Drogenpolitik aus dem Geist der Rassenhygiene: Deutsche Drogenpolitik von 1933 bis 1972* (Norderstedt, 2007), pp. 163–4; Jonathan Lewy, *Drugs in Germany and the United States, 1819–1945* (Baden-Baden, 2017), pp. 142–3.

14 Mills, *Cannabis Nation*, pp. 36–8.

15 Harry Jacob Anslinger, *The Murderers: The Story of the Narcotic Gangs* (London, 1962), pp. 141–2.

16 David Musto, *The American Disease: Origins of Narcotic Control*, 2nd edn (Oxford, 1987), pp. 146–7.

17 Steven Belenko, ed., *Drugs and Drug Policy in America: A Documentary History* (Westport, CT, 2000), pp. 173–5; John McWilliams, *The Protectors: Harry J. Anslinger and the Federal Bureau of Narcotics, 1930–1962* (Newark, NJ, 1990), pp. 46–7.

18 Advisory Committee on Traffic in Opium, *Procès Verbal of Sessions*, Twelfth session (1929), p. 6.

19 Taylor, *American Diplomacy*, pp. 288–91; *Conference on the Limitation of the Manufacture of Narcotic Drugs, Geneva 27 May–13 July 1931* (Lake Success, NY, 1947), p. 16.

20 Taylor, *American Diplomacy*, pp. 294–8.

21 *Conference for the Suppression of the Illicit Traffic in Dangerous Drugs (Geneva, June 8th–26th, 1936)* (Geneva, 1936), pp. 2–3.

22 Anslinger, *The Murderers*, p. 60.

23 Ibid., pp. 62–3.

24 Ibid., pp. 60–62; Harry D'Erlanger, *The Last Plague of Egypt* (London, 1936), pp. 265–6.

25 Meyer and Parssinen, *Webs of Smoke*, pp. 118–19.

26 Anslinger, *The Murderers*, pp. 62–3.

27 Meyer and Parssinen, *Webs of Smoke*, p. 119; Block, 'European Drug Traffic', p. 327.

28 Anslinger, *The Murderers*, p. 64.

29 D'Erlanger, *The Last Plague of Egypt*, pp. 253–4.

30 Thomas Russell, *Egyptian Service, 1902–1946* (London, 1949), pp. 241–2 and 246–7.

31 Ibid., pp. 243–4; Anslinger, *The Murderers*, pp. 66–9.

32 D'Erlanger, *The Last Plague of Egypt*, pp. 255–61; Russell, *Egyptian Service*, p. 245.

33 Advisory Committee on Traffic in Opium, *Procès Verbal of Sessions*, Ninth session (1927), pp. 2–6.

34 Ibid., Tenth session (1927), pp. 109–17, and Eleventh session (1928), pp. 275–339.

35 Ibid., Twelfth session (1929), pp. 149–60, and Thirteenth session (1930), pp. 143–8; Taylor, *American Diplomacy*, pp. 231–2.

36 Taylor, *American Diplomacy*, p. 235; *Conference on the Limitation of the Manufacture of Narcotic Drugs*, pp. 7–16. Imports and exports also became subject to quotas, in addition to the certificates.

37 'Rapport au Conseil', Advisory Committee on Traffic in Opium, *Procès Verbal of Sessions*, Sixteenth session (1933), pp. 8–9.

38 Ibid., pp. 9–10.

39 League of Nations, Advisory Committee on Traffic in Opium and Other Dangerous Drugs, *Summary of Annual Reports of Governments* (Geneva, 1926–40), 1931, p. 26.

40 Statistics collated ibid., 1926–36.

41 Pietschmann, 'A Century of Drug Control', p. 77.

42 Anslinger, *The Murderers*, p. 64.

43 Meyer and Parssinen, *Webs of Smoke*, pp. 132–5.

44 Ibid., p. 117.

45 Ibid., pp. 235–7.

46 McWilliams, *The Protectors*, p. 132.

47 Meyer and Parssinen, *Webs of Smoke*, pp. 254–8.

48 McWilliams, *The Protectors*, pp. 133–4.

49 Ibid., p. 135; Alfred McCoy, *The Politics of Heroin: CIA Complicity in the Global Drug Trade* (New York, 1991), pp. 26–8.

50 Russell, *Egyptian Service*, pp. 245–9; D'Erlanger, *The Last Plague of Egypt*, pp. 266–8.
51 Anslinger, *The Murderers*, p. 74.
52 Ibid., pp. 74–6; McWilliams, *The Protectors*, pp. 132–3.
53 Advisory Committee on Traffic in Opium, *Procès Verbal of Sessions*, First session (1921), pp. 22–3.
54 McAllister, *Drug Diplomacy*, pp. 47–53.
55 An added twist was that the United States did not ratify the treaty on which the PCOB was reliant, but New Zealand helpfully agreed to nominate an American to that committee.
56 Taylor, *American Diplomacy*, pp. 158–60.
57 Advisory Committee on Traffic in Opium, *Procès Verbal of Sessions*, Fifth session (1923), pp. 17–18.
58 Ibid., pp. 10–17.
59 McAllister, *Drug Diplomacy*, pp. 65–6.
60 Ibid., pp. 58–9.
61 *Première conférence de l'opium, Procès-verbaux et annexes* (Geneva, 1924–5), pp. 7–9.
62 Ibid., pp. 19–22.
63 Ibid., pp. 50–55 and 61–8.
64 Ibid., pp. 115–16.
65 *Actes de la deuxième conférence de l'opium, Séances plénières, compte-rendu des débats*, 2 vols (Geneva, 1924–5), vol. I, pp. 35–6 and 425–45.
66 Ibid., pp. 74–7.
67 Ibid., pp. 77–83.
68 Ibid., pp. 132–3; McAllister, *Drug Diplomacy*, pp. 69–70.
69 McAllister, *Drug Diplomacy*, p. 75.
70 Ibid., p. 76; 'Compte-rendu des séances de la délégation des seize', *Actes de la deuxième conférence de l'opium*, vol. II; *Première conférence de l'opium, Procès-verbaux et annexes*, p. 117.
71 *Première conférence de l'opium, Procès-verbaux et annexes*, pp. 120–21.
72 McAllister, *Drug Diplomacy*, pp. 80–81; Emdad-ul Haq, *Drugs in South Asia: From the Opium Trade to the Present Day* (Basingstoke, 2000), p. 95.
73 Advisory Committee on Traffic in Opium, *Procès Verbal of Sessions*, Eighth session (1926), p. 36; Advisory Committee on Traffic in Opium, *Summary of Annual Reports of Governments* (1928), pp. 18–21.
74 Advisory Committee on Traffic in Opium, *Procès Verbal of Sessions*, Fifteenth session (1932), p. 4.
75 Advisory Committee on Traffic in Opium, *Summary of Annual Reports of Governments* series, 1926–35.
76 Ibid.; *Commission d'enquête sur le contrôle de l'opium à fumer en Extrême Orient* (Geneva, 1930–31), pp. 22–3 and 173; *Proceedings of the Committee to Inquire into Matters Relating to the Use of Opium in British Malaya* (Singapore, 1924), pp. 16–18.
77 John Jennings, *The Opium Empire: Japanese Imperialism and Drug Trafficking in Asia, 1895–1945* (Westport, CT, 1997), pp. 23–5.
78 *Proceedings of the Committee to Inquire into the Use of Opium in British Malaya*, pp. 45–6.

79 Ibid., pp. 47–65.

80 Advisory Committee on Traffic in Opium, *Summary of Annual Reports of Governments* (1929–30), pp. 62–3.

81 Haq, *Drugs in South Asia*, pp. 100–102.

82 *Commission d'enquête sur le contrôle de l'opium à fumer en Extrême Orient*, pp. 62–111.

83 Data drawn from the Advisory Committee on Traffic in Opium, *Procès Verbal of Sessions* and *Summary of Annual Reports of Governments* series, 1926–37.

84 Advisory Committee on Traffic in Opium, *Procès Verbal of Sessions*, Twenty-second session (1937), pp. 26–7.

85 Advisory Committee on Traffic in Opium, *Summary of Annual Reports of Governments* (1935), pp. 24–5.

86 Ibid., 1926–37; Advisory Committee on Traffic in Opium, *Procès Verbal of Sessions*, Twenty-second session (1937), p. 30.

87 Jacques Dumarest, *Les Monopoles de l'opium et du sel en Indochine* (Lyon, 1938), p. 154; Philippe Le Failler, *Monopole et prohibition de l'opium en Indochine: le pilori des chimères* (Paris, 2000), p. 317.

88 Dumarest, *Les Monopoles de l'opium et du sel*, p. 122; Advisory Committee on Traffic in Opium, *Summary of Annual Reports of Governments*, 1932–7.

89 Advisory Committee on Traffic in Opium, *Summary of Annual Reports of Governments*, 1926–37.

90 Edward Slack, *Opium, State, and Society: China's Narco-economy and the Guomindang, 1924–1937* (Honolulu, HI, 2001), pp. 63–9.

91 Jennings, *The Opium Empire*, pp. 47–9.

92 Ibid., pp. 32–7.

93 Ibid., pp. 54–6.

94 Ibid., pp. 56–9.

95 Ibid., p. 107.

96 McAllister, *Drug Diplomacy*, p. 105.

97 Jennings, *The Opium Empire*, pp. 77–89 and 101–2.

98 Ibid., pp. 92–8; McAllister, *Drug Diplomacy*, pp. 114–15; Timothy Brook, 'Opium and Collaboration in Central China, 1938–1940', in *Opium Regimes: China, Britain, and Japan, 1839–1952*, ed. Timothy Brook and Bob Tadashi Wakabayashi (Berkeley, CA, 2000), pp. 329–37.

99 Zheng Yangwen, *The Social Life of Opium in China* (Cambridge, 2005), pp. 188–9.

100 Brian Martin, *The Shanghai Green Gang: Politics and Organized Crime, 1919–1937* (New York, 1996), pp. 67–77.

101 Ibid., pp. 114–31.

102 Ibid., pp. 178–80.

103 Ibid., pp. 145–6; Meyer and Parssinen, *Webs of Smoke*, p. 157.

104 Slack, *Opium, State, and Society*, pp. 71–2.

105 Alan Baumler, ed., *Modern China and Opium* (Ann Arbor, MI, 2001), p. 135; Jiang Qiuming and Zhu Qingbao, *Zhongguo jidu licheng* (Tianjin, 1996), p. 255.

106 Frank Dikötter, Lars Laamann and Zhou Xun, *Narcotic Culture: A History of Drugs in China* (London, 2004), pp. 126–7.

107 Ibid., pp. 130–32.

108 Alan Baumler, 'Opium Control versus Opium Suppression', in *Opium Regimes*, ed. Brook and Wakabayashi, pp. 273–81; Zhou Yongming, *Anti-Drug Crusades in Twentieth-Century China: Nationalism, History, and State Building* (Lanham, MD, 1999), pp. 78–80.

109 Zhou, *Anti-Drug Crusades*, pp. 80–84; Slack, *Opium, State, and Society*, pp. 106–9.

110 Advisory Committee on Traffic in Opium, *Procès Verbal of Sessions*, Second session (1922), p. 7.

111 Assuming a 7–8 per cent morphine content. The Qing-era data are provided in Appendix 1. Morphine data based on the *Summary of Annual Reports of Governments* series.

112 Zheng, *Social Life of Opium*, p. 186.

113 Xavier Paulès, 'Anti-Opium Visual Propaganda and the Deglamorisation of Opium in China, 1895–1937', *European Journal of East Asian Studies*, VII (2008), pp. 229–62, at p. 236; Edward Slack, 'The National Anti-Opium Association and the Guomindang State, 1924–1937', in *Opium Regimes*, ed. Brook and Wakabayashi, pp. 249–58.

114 Paulès, 'The Deglamorisation of Opium in China', pp. 261–2.

115 Advisory Committee on Traffic in Opium, *Procès Verbal of Sessions*, Twenty-third session (1938), p. 15.

116 *Commission of Enquiry into the Production of Opium in Persia, Report to the Council* (Geneva, 1926), p. 42; Advisory Committee on Traffic in Opium, *Summary of Annual Reports of Governments*, 1936–7.

117 This takes the difference between estimated production in 1924, when Turkey had yet to ratify any of the opium treaties, and legitimate production calculated as of the late 1930s, with data drawn from the *Summary of Annual Reports of Governments* series.

6 DRUG PROHIBITION AT ITS ZENITH

1 James Mills, *Cannabis Britannica: Empire, Trade, and Prohibition, 1800–1928* (Oxford, 2003), p. 167; *Records of the Second Opium Conference, Plenary Meetings, Text of the Debates*, 2 vols (Geneva, 1924–5), vol. 1, pp. 39–40.

2 *Actes de la deuxième conférence de l'opium, Séances plénières, compte-rendu des débats*, 2 vols (Geneva, 1924–5), vol. 1, p. 140.

3 Ibid., pp. 140–42; Mills, *Cannabis Britannica*, pp. 49–50.

4 James Mills, *Cannabis Nation: Control and Consumption in Britain, 1928–2008* (Oxford, 2013), p. 10.

5 Sebastian Scheerer, *Die Genese der Betäubungsmittelgesetze in der Bundesrepublik Deutschland und in den Niederlanden* (Göttingen, 1982), pp. 75–6; Andreas Siebel, *Drogenstrafrecht in Deutschland und Frankreich* (Frankfurt am Main, 1996), pp. 31–2.

6 Liat Kozma, 'Cannabis Prohibition in Egypt, 1880–1939: From Local Ban to League of Nations Diplomacy', *Middle Eastern Studies*, XLVII (2011), pp. 443–60, at p. 445.

7 Mills, *Cannabis Britannica*, pp. 180–81; James Mills, 'Colonial Africa and the International Politics of Cannabis: Egypt, South Africa and the Origins of Global Control', in *Drugs and Empires: Essays in Modern*

Imperialism and Intoxication, 1500–1930, ed. Patricia Barton and James
Mills (Basingstoke, 2007), p. 178.

8 Ahmad M. Khalifa, 'Traditional Patterns of Hashish Use in Egypt', in
Cannabis and Culture, ed. Vera Rubin (The Hague, 1975), pp. 198–203.

9 Marinos Sariyannis, 'Law and Morality in Ottoman Society: The Case of
Narcotic Substances', in *The Ottoman Empire, the Balkans, the Greek Lands:
Towards a Social and Economic History*, ed. Elias Kolovos (Istanbul, 2007),
pp. 315–17. I am indebted to Dr Haggai Ram for these references and for
his considerations on the subject.

10 *Pall Mall Gazette*, 19 May 1876, p. 4; *House of Commons Parliamentary
Papers, Reports from Her Majesty's Representatives in Egypt, Greece, and
Turkey on Regulations Affecting the Importation and Sale of Haschisch*
(London, 1893), pp. 19–22.

11 *Reports from Her Majesty's Representatives in Egypt, Greece, and Turkey*,
pp. 2–3; Kozma, 'Cannabis Prohibition in Egypt', p. 445. I am indebted
to Dr Liat Kozma for her help and considerations on the subject.

12 Kozma, 'Cannabis Prohibition in Egypt', pp. 455–7.

13 Mills, *Cannabis Britannica*, pp. 183–4.

14 Ibid., p. 184.

15 Ibid., pp. 82–4.

16 Ibid., pp. 85–90.

17 *Report of the Indian Hemp Drugs Commission, 1893–94*, 7 vols (Simla, 1894),
vol. II, p. 1.

18 Ibid., vol. I, p. 239.

19 Ibid., vol. I, pp. 225–6.

20 Mills, *Cannabis Britannica*, pp. 140–44.

21 *Records of the Second Opium Conference*, vol. I, p. 133.

22 Jacques-Joseph Moreau de Tours, *Du Hachisch et de l'aliénation mentale,
études psychologiques* (Paris, 1845), p. 34.

23 Bénédict-Augustin Morel, *Traité des dégénérescences physiques, intellectuelles
et morales* (Paris, 1857), pp. 148–53.

24 Ibid., p. 154.

25 Ibid., p. 38.

26 Ernest Bosc, *Traité théorique et pratique du haschich et autres substances
psychiques: cannabis, herbes magiques, opium, morphine, éther, cocaïne*
(Paris, 1895), pp. 75–6.

27 *Pall Mall Gazette*, 19 May 1876, p. 4.

28 Emile Deschanel, 'Des excitans', *Le Journal des débats politiques et
littéraires*, 12 July 1860, p. 1.

29 Quoted in Isaac Campos, *Home Grown: Marijuana and the Origins
of Mexico's War on Drugs* (Chapel Hill, NC, 2012), p. 81.

30 Ibid., pp. 52–4.

31 Ibid., pp. 58–73 and 82.

32 Ibid., pp. 119–25.

33 Ibid., pp. 90–98.

34 UNODC, *World Drug Report* (Vienna, 1997–), 2019, vol. I, p. 29.

35 Mitch Earleywine, *Understanding Marijuana: A New Look at the Scientific
Evidence* (Oxford, 2002), pp. 144–8.

36 *Report of the Indian Hemp Drugs Commission*, vol. I, p. 225.

37 Steven Belenko, ed., *Drugs and Drug Policy in America: A Documentary History* (Westport, CT, 2000), pp. 137–8.

38 Ibid., p. 133.

39 Ibid., p. 143.

40 Jerome Himmelstein, *The Strange Career of Marihuana* (Westport, CT, 1983), p. 38.

41 Ibid., pp. 38–43.

42 David Courtwright, ed., *Addicts Who Survived: An Oral History of Narcotic Use in America before 1965* (Knoxville, TN, 1989), pp. 11–12.

43 Harry Jacob Anslinger, *The Murderers: The Story of the Narcotic Gangs* (London, 1962), pp. 17–18.

44 'Marijuana: Assassin of Youth', *American Magazine*, July 1937, quoted in Belenko, *Drugs and Drug Policy in America*, p. 145.

45 Ibid., pp. 148–50.

46 John McWilliams, 'Through the Past Darkly: The Politics and Policies of America's Drug War', *Journal of Policy History*, III (1999), pp. 5–41, at p. 16.

47 John McWilliams, *The Protectors: Harry J. Anslinger and the Federal Bureau of Narcotics, 1930–1962* (Newark, NJ, 1990), pp. 31–2; David Musto, *The American Disease: Origins of Narcotic Control*, 2nd edn (Oxford, 1987), pp. 210–11.

48 Belenko, *Drugs and Drug Policy in America*, p. 147.

49 Himmelstein, *The Strange Career of Marihuana*, pp. 56–8.

50 Ibid., p. 89.

51 McWilliams, *The Protectors*, pp. 88–9.

52 Mills, *Cannabis Britannica*, pp. 118–21.

53 Ibid., p. 133.

54 Ibid., pp. 180–81.

55 James Mills, 'Colonial Africa and the International Politics of Cannabis', pp. 168–72.

56 Ibid., pp. 166–7.

57 League of Nations, Advisory Committee on Traffic in Opium and Other Dangerous Drugs, *Procès Verbal of Sessions* (Geneva, 1921–40), Eighteenth session (1934), p. 16.

58 Permanent Central Opium Board, *Report of the Permanent Central Opium Board* (Geneva, 1946–65), 1955, pp. 11–12.

59 William McAllister, *Drug Diplomacy in the Twentieth Century* (London, 2000), pp. 138–41 and 154–5; David Bewley-Taylor, *The United States and International Drug Control, 1909–1997* (London, 1999), pp. 115–17.

60 David Courtwright, *Dark Paradise: A History of Opiate Addiction in America* (Cambridge, MA, 2001), pp. 119–22.

61 Henry Richard Friman, *Narco-Diplomacy: Exporting the U.S. War on Drugs* (Ithaca, NY, 1996), pp. 67–71.

62 Terry Parssinen, *Secret Passions, Secret Remedies: Narcotic Drugs in British Society 1820–1930* (Manchester, 1983), pp. 164–6.

63 Scheerer, *Die Genese der Betäubungsmittelgesetze*, p. 72.

64 Commission on Narcotic Drugs, *Summary of Annual Reports of Governments* (Lake Success, NY, 1944–86), 1949, pp. 16–19.

65 McAllister, *Drug Diplomacy*, pp. 150–52.

66 Zhou Yongming, *Anti-Drug Crusades in Twentieth-Century China: Nationalism, History, and State Building* (Lanham, MD, 1999), pp. 95–6.

67 Ibid., p. 100.

68 Ibid., p. 107.

69 Ibid., pp. 105–9.

70 Issue dated 5 May 1954, quoted in Belenko, *Drugs and Drug Policy in America*, pp. 186–7.

71 Bewley-Taylor, *The United States and International Drug Control*, pp. 109–10.

72 'Illicit Traffic in Opium', *The Times*, 6 May 1952, p. 5.

73 Alfred McCoy, *The Politics of Heroin: CIA Complicity in the Global Drug Trade* (New York, 1991), pp. 108–9; Ashley Wright, *Opium and Empire in Southeast Asia: Regulating Consumption in British Burma* (Basingstoke, 2014), pp. 7–8.

74 McCoy, *The Politics of Heroin*, pp. 162–73; Commission on Narcotic Drugs, *Reports on Sessions* (New York, 1946–), Fifth session (1950), p. 77.

75 McCoy, *The Politics of Heroin*, pp. 174–5.

76 Ibid., pp. 38–9.

77 Ibid., pp. 40–45.

78 Ibid., pp. 30–38; McWilliams, *The Protectors*, pp. 135–6.

79 Kathleen Frydl, *The Drug Wars in America, 1940–1973* (New York, 2013), p. 101.

80 McWilliams, *The Protectors*, pp. 136–8; Kathryn Meyer and Terry Parssinen, *Webs of Smoke: Smugglers, Warlords, Spies, and the History of the International Drug Trade* (Lanham, MD, 1998), pp. 283–6.

81 Commission on Narcotic Drugs, *Reports on Sessions*, Nineteenth session (1964), p. 11.

82 Ibid.

83 UNODC, *World Drug Report* (2017), vol. I, p. 15.

84 Bureau of Narcotics, *Traffic in Opium and Other Dangerous Drugs* (Washington, DC, 1928–67), 1929, p. 27, and 1950, pp. 16–18.

85 Ibid., 1929, p. 25, and 1950, p. 33.

86 Belenko, *Drugs and Drug Policy in America*, pp. 195–6.

87 Bureau of Narcotics, *Traffic in Dangerous Drugs*, 1958, pp. 20–31 and 39.

88 Belenko, *Drugs and Drug Policy in America*, pp. 203–6; Himmelstein, *The Strange Career of Marihuana*, pp. 90–91.

89 Courtwright, *Addicts Who Survived*, p. 19.

90 Belenko, *Drugs and Drug Policy in America*, pp. 207–8.

91 Ibid., pp. 199–201.

92 Harry Jacob Anslinger, *The Traffic in Narcotics* (New York, 1953), p. 21.

93 Ibid., pp. 267–8.

94 Belenko, *Drugs and Drug Policy in America*, pp. 202–3; McWilliams, *The Protectors*, pp. 111–16.

95 Commission on Narcotic Drugs, *Summary of Annual Reports of Governments* (1955), p. 39, and 1955 ADD, pp. 15–17; Permanent Central Opium Board, *Report of the Permanent Central Opium Board* (1955), pp. 26–7; Commission on Narcotic Drugs, *Reports on Sessions*, Seventh session (1952), pp. 4–5, and Twelfth session (1957), p. 13.

96 Contemporary estimates were that Iran may have actually produced in excess of 700 tons of opium annually: Permanent Central Opium Board,

Report of the Permanent Central Opium Board (1955), pp. 9–10. Conversely, however, the figure of 905 tons for Turkey may be overstated, judging from pre-war data: Advisory Committee on Traffic in Opium, *Summary of Annual Reports of Governments* (1926), pp. 13–24, has an estimate of 565 tons for 1924, a date at which no reason existed to under-report.

97 Permanent Central Opium Board, *Report of the Permanent Central Opium Board* (1956), p. 31.

98 Ibid., 1955, p. 11.

99 Calculations based on historical UNODC leaf/cocaine conversion rates and on Joseph Spillane, *Cocaine: From Medical Marvel to Modern Menace in the United States, 1884–1920* (Baltimore, MD, 2000), p. 115, for average use.

100 Commission on Narcotic Drugs, *Summary of Annual Reports of Governments* (1950–59).

101 Commission on Narcotic Drugs, *Reports on Sessions*, Twelfth session (1957), p. 18.

102 McAllister, *Drug Diplomacy*, pp. 176–82.

103 Ibid., p. 196.

104 Paul Gootenberg, *Andean Cocaine: The Making of a Global Drug* (Chapel Hill, NC, 2008), pp. 213–16.

105 Joseph Gagliano, *Coca Prohibition in Peru* (Tucson, AZ, 1994), pp. 126–31.

106 Ibid., pp. 152–4; Gootenberg, *Andean Cocaine*, pp. 232–3.

107 United Nations, *Report of the Commission of Enquiry on the Coca Leaf* (Lake Success, NY, 1950), pp. 7–8 and 23–30.

108 Ibid., p. 31.

109 Ibid., p. 32.

110 Ibid., p. 96.

111 McAllister, *Drug Diplomacy*, pp. 157–8 and 167–8.

112 Bewley-Taylor, *The United States and International Drug Control*, p. 75.

113 Rudolph Matthee, *The Pursuit of Pleasure: Drugs and Stimulants in Iranian History, 1500–1900* (Princeton, NJ, 2005), pp. 106–7.

114 Ibid., p. 222.

115 *Commission of Enquiry into the Production of Opium in Persia, Report to the Council* (Geneva, 1926), pp. 54–6.

116 League of Nations, Advisory Committee on Traffic in Opium and Other Dangerous Drugs, *Summary of Annual Reports of Governments* (Geneva, 1926–40).

117 Anthony Neligan, *The Opium Question with Special Reference to Persia* (London, 1927), p. 28.

118 Commission on Narcotic Drugs, *Reports on Sessions*, Fifth session (1950), p. 79.

119 Anslinger, *The Murderers*, pp. 203–4.

120 James Windle, *Suppressing Illicit Opium Production: Successful Intervention in Asia and the Middle East* (London, 2016), pp. 40–41.

121 Commission on Narcotic Drugs, *Reports on Sessions*, Twelfth session (1957), p. 12.

122 Ibid., Fifteenth session (1960), p. 17.

123 Advisory Committee on Traffic in Opium, *Summary of Annual Reports of Governments* (1929–30), p. 54, 1932, p. 33, and 1933, pp. 29–30.

124 Windle, *Suppressing Illicit Opium Production*, pp. 50–51.

125 United Nations, *Single Convention on Narcotic Drugs, 1961* (New York, 1972), p. 39.
126 Ibid., pp. 50–54.
127 Ibid., pp. 20–37. National agencies had a supervisory role only over the collection of coca or cannabis.
128 Ibid., p. 39.
129 McAllister, *Drug Diplomacy*, pp. 205–7.
130 Gagliano, *Coca Prohibition in Peru*, pp. 157–8.
131 United Nations, *Single Convention on Narcotic Drugs*, pp. 46–7.
132 Bewley-Taylor, *The United States and International Drug Control*, pp. 148–9; McAllister, *Drug Diplomacy*, pp. 216–17.
133 Bewley-Taylor, *The United States and International Drug Control*, p. 155; McAllister, *Drug Diplomacy*, pp. 217–18.
134 Bewley-Taylor, *The United States and International Drug Control*, pp. 136–7 and 166–8.
135 Commission on Narcotic Drugs, *Reports on Sessions*, Sixteenth session (1961), p. 21.
136 Bureau of Narcotics, *Traffic in Dangerous Drugs* (1962), p. 21.

7 OVERREACH

1 Story told in Timothy Leary, *Flashbacks: An Autobiography* (London, 1983), pp. 291–6.
2 Jay Stevens, *Storming Heaven: LSD and the American Dream* (London, 1987), pp. 126–9.
3 Ibid., p. 138.
4 Ibid., p. 160.
5 Ibid., p. 162; David Black, *Acid: The Secret History of LSD* (London, 1998), pp. 59–61.
6 Stevens, *Storming Heaven*, pp. 4–5.
7 Ibid., pp. 11–12 and 64–6.
8 Black, *Acid*, p. 65.
9 Steven Belenko, ed., *Drugs and Drug Policy in America: A Documentary History* (Westport, CT, 2000), pp. 270–71.
10 Ibid., p. 271; Stevens, *Storming Heaven*, p. 173.
11 Lewis Yablonsky, *The Hippie Trip* (New York, 1968), p. 252.
12 Dessa K. Bergen-Cico, *War and Drugs: The Role of Military Conflict in the Development of Substance Abuse* (Boulder, CO, 2012), pp. 67–8.
13 Stevens, *Storming Heaven*, pp. 82–3; Black, *Acid*, pp. 37–8.
14 John McWilliams, *The Protectors: Harry J. Anslinger and the Federal Bureau of Narcotics, 1930–1962* (Newark, NJ, 1990), pp. 165–73.
15 Richard Davenport-Hines, *The Pursuit of Oblivion: A Global History of Narcotics, 1500–2000* (London, 2001), p. 262.
16 Stevens, *Storming Heaven*, pp. 208–9.
17 Ibid., pp. 216–19.
18 Belenko, *Drugs and Drug Policy in America*, pp. 271–2.
19 Stevens, *Storming Heaven*, p. 146.
20 Ibid., p. 192.
21 Stevens, *Storming Heaven*, p. xvii.

22 Timothy Leary and Ralph Metzner, 'Editorial', *Psychedelic Review* (1967), p. 3.

23 'On Programming Psychedelic Experiences', ibid., p. 16.

24 Stevens, *Storming Heaven*, pp. 280–81 and 291.

25 Ibid., pp. 326–7.

26 Ibid., pp. 284–5.

27 Ibid., pp. 240–48.

28 Ibid., p. 313.

29 Ibid., pp. 309–18.

30 Ibid., pp. 351–2; Black, *Acid*, p. 112.

31 Black, *Acid*, p. 131.

32 Ibid., pp. 136–47; Lyn Ebenezer, *Operation Julie: The World's Greatest* LSD *Bust* (Talybont, 2010), pp. 14–16, 38–9 and 122–4.

33 Stevens, *Storming Heaven*, pp. 345–51.

34 Black, *Acid*, pp. 132–4.

35 In 1977: Ebenezer, *Operation Julie*, pp. 112–14.

36 Stevens, *Storming Heaven*, pp. 267–8.

37 Ibid., pp. 352–5.

38 Ibid., p. 356; Black, *Acid*, pp. 112–13.

39 Belenko, *Drugs and Drug Policy in America*, pp. 291–2.

40 Humberto Fernandez and Therissa Libby, *Heroin: Its History, Pharmacology, and Treatment* (Center City, MN, 2011), pp. 236–7; Davenport-Hines, *The Pursuit of Oblivion*, p. 282.

41 Fernandez and Libby, *Heroin*, p. 238.

42 Davenport-Hines, *The Pursuit of Oblivion*, p. 331.

43 Kathleen Frydl, *The Drug Wars in America, 1940–1973* (New York, 2013), p. 345.

44 Yablonsky, *Hippie Trip*, pp. 119–21.

45 Ibid., p. 141.

46 Ibid., p. 281.

47 William S. Burroughs, *Junky* (London, 2008), p. 39.

48 David Courtwright, *Dark Paradise: A History of Opiate Addiction in America* (Cambridge, MA, 2001), p. 113.

49 Burroughs, *Junky*, p. 104.

50 Ibid., p. 106.

51 Thomas Bewley, 'Drug Dependence in the USA', *Bulletin on Narcotics* (1969), pp. 13–30.

52 Jock Young, *The Drugtakers: The Social Meaning of Drug Use* (London, 1971), pp. 148–68.

53 As of 1985: Andreas Siebel, *Drogenstrafrecht in Deutschland und Frankreich* (Frankfurt am Main, 1996), p. 162.

54 Ibid., p. 167.

55 John Strang and Michael Gossop, eds, *Heroin Addiction and the British System*, 2 vols (Milton Park, 2005), vol. I, pp. 81–7; John Giggs, 'Epidemiology of Contemporary Drug Abuse', in *Policing and Prescribing: The British System of Drug Control*, ed. David Whynes and Philip Bean (Basingstoke, 1991), pp. 167–8.

56 State-level arrests: Drug Abuse Council, *The Facts about 'Drug Abuse'* (New York, 1980), p. 159.

57 Past-year data: Substance Abuse and Mental Health Services Administration, *National Household Survey on Drug Abuse: Detailed Tables* (Rockville, MD, 1998–), 1998, Table 104A.

58 Ibid.

59 Blended rate based on two population categories: National Institute on Drug Abuse, *Cocaine Use in America: Epidemiologic and Clinical Perspectives* (Rockville, MD, 1985), p. 40.

60 SAMHSA, *National Household Survey*, 1998, Table 104A.

61 Bewley, 'Drug Dependence in the USA', pp. 13–30; David Musto, *The Quest for Drug Control: Politics and Federal Policy in a Period of Increasing Substance Abuse, 1963–1981* (New Haven, CT, 2002), pp. 38–9.

62 SAMHSA, *National Household Survey*, 1998, Table 104A.

63 Bruce Johnson, 'Understanding British Addiction Statistics', *Bulletin on Narcotics* (1975), pp. 49–66.

64 Strang and Gossop, *Heroin Addiction and the British System*, p. 80.

65 Advisory Committee on Drug Dependence, *Cannabis* (London, 1968), p. 8.

66 Based on CND and INCB series: see Appendix III for sources.

67 Tilmann Holzer, *Die Geburt der Drogenpolitik aus dem Geist der Rassenhygiene: Deutsche Drogenpolitik von 1933 bis 1972* (Norderstedt, 2007), p. 355; Henry Richard Friman, *Narco-Diplomacy: Exporting the U.S. War on Drugs* (Ithaca, NY, 1996), p. 95.

68 Detlef Briesen, *Drogenkonsum und Drogenpolitik in Deutschland und den USA: Ein historischer Vergleich* (Frankfurt am Main, 2005), p. 306.

69 Commission on Narcotic Drugs, *Reports on Sessions* (New York, 1946–), Twenty-fourth session (1971), pp. 64–9; Alfred McCoy, *The Politics of Heroin: CIA Complicity in the Global Drug Trade* (New York, 1991), pp. 468–9.

70 Fariborz Raisdana, 'The Drug Market in Iran', *American Academy of Political and Social Science*, DLXXXII (2002), pp. 149–66, at pp. 153–60.

71 UNODC, *Global Illicit Drug Trends* (New York, 1999–2003), 1999, pp. 14–15, 40 and 51.

72 For data and sources, see Appendix III.

73 Nicholas Parsons, *Meth Mania: A History of Methamphetamine* (Boulder, CO, 2014), pp. 1–4.

74 Ibid., pp. 46–7; Nicolas Rasmussen, *On Speed: The Many Lives of Amphetamine* (New York, 2008), p. 22.

75 Rasmussen, *On Speed*, p. 6.

76 Ibid., pp. 16–17.

77 Ibid., pp. 21–3 and 40–41.

78 Ibid., pp. 54–5.

79 Ibid., pp. 65–84.

80 Bert Edström, 'The Forgotten Success Story: Japan and the Methamphetamine Problem', *Japan Forum*, XXVII (2015), pp. 519–34, at pp. 522–6.

81 Miriam Kingsberg, *Moral Nation: Modern Japan and Narcotics in Global History* (Berkeley, CA, 2014), pp. 183–4.

82 Edström, 'Japan and the Methamphetamine Problem', p. 526.

83 Kingsberg, *Moral Nation*, pp. 190–91.

84 Ibid., pp. 191–8; Edström, 'Japan and the Methamphetamine Problem', pp. 527–8.

85 Rasmussen, *On Speed*, pp. 114–15.

86 Ibid., pp. 116–19 and 130–31.

87 Ibid., p. 163.

88 Ibid., p. 172.

89 Ibid., p. 101; David Herzberg, *Happy Pills in America: From Miltown to Prozac* (Baltimore, MD, 2009), p. 91.

90 Lester Grinspoon, *The Speed Culture: Amphetamine Use and Abuse in America* (Cambridge, MA, 1975), pp. 4–5.

91 Rasmussen, *On Speed*, pp. 183–8.

92 Ibid., pp. 91–2.

93 Parsons, *Meth Mania*, pp. 52–3.

94 Grinspoon, *Speed Culture*, pp. 34–5.

95 Ibid., p. 35.

96 Max Glatt, *The Drug Scene in Great Britain* (London, 1967), pp. 45–52.

97 Grinspoon, *Speed Culture*, pp. 97–9.

98 Quoted in Rasmussen, *On Speed*, p. 180.

99 Vladimir Kusevic, 'Drug Abuse Control and International Treaties', *Journal of Drug Issues*, 1 (1977), pp. 35–53, at p. 37.

100 Ibid., p. 35.

101 Parsons, *Meth Mania*, pp. 49–50.

102 Rasmussen, *On Speed*, p. 178.

103 Ibid., p. 163.

104 Herzberg, *Happy Pills*, pp. 25–6.

105 Ibid., p. 29.

106 Ibid., pp. 175–6.

107 Ibid., p. 31.

108 Ibid., pp. 83 and 107–9.

109 Ibid., p. 39.

110 Rasmussen, *On Speed*, pp. 137–8.

111 Ibid., p. 139.

112 Grinspoon, *Speed Culture*, pp. 23–4.

113 Commission on Narcotic Drugs, *Summary Record of Sessions* (New York, 1946–), Tenth session (5 May 1955), p. 9.

114 Ibid., pp. 9–10.

115 Ibid., p. 11.

116 Ibid., pp. 11–12.

117 Commission on Narcotic Drugs, *Reports on Sessions*, Twentieth session (1965), p. 16.

118 Ibid., pp. 40–44.

119 Ibid.

120 Ibid., Twenty-third session (1969), pp. 62–9; William McAllister, *Drug Diplomacy in the Twentieth Century* (London, 2000), pp. 227–8.

121 Commission on Narcotic Drugs, *Reports on Sessions*, Twenty-first session (1966), p. 35.

122 Ibid., p. 38.

123 Ibid., p. 46.

124 United Nations, *Convention on Psychotropic Substances, 1971* (New York, 1971), pp. 17–18.

125 United Nations, *Single Convention on Narcotic Drugs, 1961* (New York, 1972), p. 13.

126 Thomas Dormandy, *Opium: Reality's Dark Dream* (New Haven, CT, 2012), pp. 198–9.

127 Grinspoon, *Speed Culture*, p. 156.

128 Michael Gossop, *Living with Drugs*, 6th edn (Aldershot, 2007), p. 152.

129 Parsons, *Meth Mania*, p. 9; UNODC, *World Drug Report* (Vienna, 1997–), 2012, p. 25.

130 Stevens, *Storming Heaven*, pp. 84–5; Gossop, *Living with Drugs*, pp. 117–30.

131 Advisory Committee on Drug Dependence, *Cannabis*, p. 75.

132 Commission on Narcotic Drugs, *Reports on Sessions*, Sixth session (1951), p. 22.

133 Virginia Berridge et al., eds, *Concepts of Addictive Substances and Behaviours across Time and Place* (Oxford, 2016), pp. 67–9.

134 Commission on Narcotic Drugs, *Reports on Sessions*, Nineteenth session (1964), pp. 7–8.

135 Ibid., p. 8.

136 Advisory Committee on Drug Dependence, *Cannabis*, p. 76.

137 Roy Reed, 'President Urges a National Drive on Narcotics Use', *New York Times*, 15 July 1969, pp. 1 and 18.

138 Davenport-Hines, *The Pursuit of Oblivion*, p. 339.

139 David Musto, *The American Disease: Origins of Narcotic Control*, 2nd edn (Oxford, 1987), p. 252.

140 Brain Committee Report, *Drug Addiction: Second Report of the Interdepartmental Committee* (London, 1965), p. 6.

141 Davenport-Hines, *The Pursuit of Oblivion*, p. 254.

142 Ibid., p. 269.

143 Advisory Committee on Drug Dependence, *Cannabis*, p. 14.

144 Ibid., pp. 17–21; James Mills, *Cannabis Nation: Control and Consumption in Britain, 1928–2008* (Oxford, 2013), pp. 141–50.

145 Mills, *Cannabis Nation*, pp. 150–56.

146 Siebel, *Drogenstrafrecht*, pp. 33–5.

147 Ibid., pp. 182–3.

148 Ibid., pp. 40–41.

149 Ibid., pp. 44–5.

150 Kusevic, 'Drug Abuse Control', pp. 39–41.

151 United Nations, *Convention on Psychotropic Substances*, pp. 17–20; Gossop, *Living with Drugs*, p. 157.

152 United Nations, *Convention on Psychotropic Substances*, pp. 3–9.

153 Rasmussen, *On Speed*, pp. 219–20.

154 Belenko, *Drugs and Drug Policy in America*, pp. 278–83.

155 Musto, *Quest for Drug Control*, pp. 90–98 and 107–13; Musto, *American Disease*, p. 257.

156 Musto, *Quest for Drug Control*, p. 73.

157 Frydl, *The Drug Wars in America*, p. 361.

158 Musto, *Quest for Drug Control*, pp. 97–8; Musto, *American Disease*, pp. 258–9.

159 Nasuh Uslu, *The Turkish–American Relationship between 1947 and 2003* (New York, 2003), p. 236.

160 Ibid., pp. 231–2.

161 Ibid., pp. 236–7.

162 McCoy, *The Politics of Heroin*, p. 390.

163 Uslu, *The Turkish–American Relationship*, pp. 233–4 and 244–5.

8 DRUG LORDS

1 Bureau of Narcotics, *Traffic in Opium and Other Dangerous Drugs* (Washington, DC, 1928–67), 1967, pp. 2–8; Richard Davenport-Hines, *The Pursuit of Oblivion: A Global History of Narcotics, 1500–2000* (London, 2001), pp. 342–6.
2 Pierre-Arnaud Chouvy, *Opium: Uncovering the Politics of the Poppy* (Cambridge, MA, 2010), p. 107.
3 Newsday, ed., *The Heroin Trail* (London, 1975), pp. 11–26 and 44–9.
4 Ibid., pp. 58–61.
5 Ibid., pp. 74, 92–6 and 136–7; Henrik Krüger, *The Great Heroin Coup* (Walterville, OR, 1980), pp. 37–9; Alfred McCoy, *The Politics of Heroin: CIA Complicity in the Global Drug Trade* (New York, 1991), pp. 61–6.
6 Newsday, *The Heroin Trail*, pp. 78–84 and 135–40.
7 Ibid., pp. 85–6 and 130–31.
8 Ibid., pp. 119–20; Krüger, *The Great Heroin Coup*, pp. 92–6.
9 Krüger, *The Great Heroin Coup*, pp. 97–9.
10 Ibid., p. 41.
11 Ibid., p. 100.
12 Newsday, *The Heroin Trail*, pp. 75–7.
13 Ibid., p. 88.
14 Krüger, *The Great Heroin Coup*, p. 114.
15 Ibid., pp. 110–12.
16 Newsday, *The Heroin Trail*, pp. 143–7.
17 Ibid., pp. 135–6.
18 'Marcel Francisci Shot Dead; Tied to "French Connection"', *New York Times*, 16 January 1982, p. 23.
19 Cornelius Friesendorf, *U.S. Foreign Policy and the War on Drugs: Displacing the Cocaine and Heroin Industry* (London, 2007), pp. 46–7 and 53–4.
20 James Spain, 'The United States, Turkey and the Poppy', *Middle East Journal*, 29 (1975), pp. 295–309, at p. 304.
21 Ibid., pp. 299–302.
22 Ibid., p. 308; James Windle, *Suppressing Illicit Opium Production: Successful Intervention in Asia and the Middle East* (London, 2016), pp. 58–9.
23 Chouvy, *Politics of the Poppy*, p. 23.
24 McCoy, *The Politics of Heroin*, pp. 74–6.
25 For estimates in various periods: UNODC, *Global Illicit Drug Trends* (New York, 1999–2003), 2001, p. 49; Ronald Renard, *The Burmese Connection: Illegal Drugs and the Making of the Golden Triangle* (Boulder, CO, 1996), p. 105; McCoy, *The Politics of Heroin*, pp. 222–3. For a warning on output estimates: Yawnghwe Chao Tzang, *The Shan of Burma: Memoirs of a Shan Exile* (Singapore, 2010), pp. 56–7.
26 McCoy, *The Politics of Heroin*, pp. 132–3.
27 Ibid., pp. 134–8.
28 Ibid., pp. 154–5, 203–15 and 299–304.
29 Ibid., pp. 268–79; Chouvy, *Politics of the Poppy*, pp. 66–7.
30 McCoy, *The Politics of Heroin*, p. 287.
31 Ibid., p. 299.

32 Chouvy, *Politics of the Poppy*, p. 25; Yawnghwe, *The Shan of Burma*, pp. 18–24; Renard, *Burmese Connection*, p. 59.

33 Yawnghwe, *The Shan of Burma*, p. 176.

34 Ibid., pp. 176–7; McCoy, *The Politics of Heroin*, pp. 355–63; Renard, *Burmese Connection*, pp. 59–60.

35 Renard, *Burmese Connection*, p. 60; Bertil Lintner, *Burma in Revolt: Opium and Insurgency since 1948* (Boulder, CO, 1994), p. 245.

36 Friesendorf, U.S. *Foreign Policy*, p. 49.

37 Lintner, *Burma in Revolt*, p. 244.

38 Chouvy, *Politics of the Poppy*, p. III.

39 Friesendorf, U.S. *Foreign Policy*, p. 55.

40 McCoy, *The Politics of Heroin*, pp. 418–19; Lintner, *Burma in Revolt*, pp. 261–3.

41 Lintner, *Burma in Revolt*, pp. 264–5.

42 Ibid., pp. 246–51; McCoy, *The Politics of Heroin*, p. 430.

43 UNODC, *Global Illicit Drug Trends*, 2001, p. 47; McCoy, *The Politics of Heroin*, p. 431.

44 Lintner, *Burma in Revolt*, p. 306.

45 Ibid., p. 305; McCoy, *The Politics of Heroin*, p. 434.

46 McCoy, *The Politics of Heroin*, pp. 435–6.

47 Lintner, *Burma in Revolt*, pp. 326–7.

48 McCoy, *The Politics of Heroin*, pp. 438–9.

49 Chouvy, *Politics of the Poppy*, pp. 25–7; Renard, *Burmese Connection*, pp. 61–2 and 69–70; Lintner, *Burma in Revolt*, p. 307.

50 Martin Jelsma et al., ed., *Trouble in the Triangle: Opium and Conflict in Burma* (Chiang Mai, 2005), pp. 9–12.

51 Lintner, *Burma in Revolt*, p. 254.

52 Windle, *Suppressing Illicit Opium Production*, pp. 102–19.

53 Ronald Renard, *Opium Reduction in Thailand, 1970–2000: A Thirty-Year Journey* (Bangkok, 2001), pp. 69–III.

54 Ibid., p. 7.

55 Ibid., pp. 36–7; Windle, *Suppressing Illicit Opium Production*, p. 64.

56 Lintner, *Burma in Revolt*, p. 317.

57 Renard, *Burmese Connection*, p. 105; UNODC, *Global Illicit Drug Trends*, 2001, p. 49.

58 Windle, *Suppressing Illicit Opium Production*, pp. 81–2; James Windle, 'Insights for Contemporary Drug Policy: A Historical Account of Opium Control in India and Pakistan', *Asian Journal of Criminology*, VII (2012), pp. 55–74, at p. 65.

59 Windle, 'Insights for Contemporary Drug Policy', pp. 65–6; Amir Zada Asad, *The Politics and Economics of Drug Production on the Pakistan–Afghanistan Border* (Aldershot, 2003), p. 37; Commission on Narcotic Drugs, *Reports on Sessions* (New York, 1946–), Sixth special session, 1980, pp. 30–31.

60 Chouvy, *Politics of the Poppy*, p. 29.

61 Asad, *Drug Production*, p. 31.

62 International Narcotics Control Board, *Report of the International Narcotics Control Board* (Geneva, 1969–), 1979, pp. 21–2.

63 Windle, *Suppressing Illicit Opium Production*, pp. 87–8.

64 Windle, 'Insights for Contemporary Drug Policy', p. 85; Asad, *Drug Production*, pp. 37–8.

65 Dessa K. Bergen-Cico, *War and Drugs: The Role of Military Conflict in the Development of Substance Abuse* (Boulder, CO, 2012), p. 109.
66 McCoy, *The Politics of Heroin*, pp. 481–2.
67 Asad, *Drug Production*, pp. 48–9.
68 Ibid., pp. 46–7, emphasis in original.
69 McCoy, *The Politics of Heroin*, p. 23.
70 Asad, *Drug Production*, p. 50.
71 McCoy, *The Politics of Heroin*, pp. 477–80; UNODC, *Global Illicit Drug Trends*, 2001, p. 33; Bergen-Cico, *War and Drugs*, pp. 108–9.
72 McCoy, *The Politics of Heroin*, pp. 475–6; Asad, *Drug Production*, pp. 52–3.
73 Chouvy, *Politics of the Poppy*, p. 33.
74 McCoy, *The Politics of Heroin*, p. 505.
75 Ibid., pp. 508–20; UNODC, *Global Illicit Drug Trends*, 2001, p. 35, and 2002, pp. 5–6.
76 McCoy, *The Politics of Heroin*, pp. 502–4.
77 UNODC, *Global Illicit Drug Trends*, 1999, p. 21.
78 Commission on Narcotic Drugs, *Reports on Sessions*, Fortieth session, 1997, p. 3.
79 Windle, *Suppressing Illicit Opium Production*, p. 140; UNODC, *Global Illicit Drug Trends*, 2001, pp. 32–3.
80 UNODC, *Global Illicit Drug Trends*, 2002, p. 16.
81 Jelsma, *Trouble in the Triangle*, p. 178.
82 McCoy, *The Politics of Heroin*, pp. 287–304.
83 Ibid., pp. 489–91.
84 Ibid., pp. 493–6; Bergen-Cico, *War and Drugs*, pp. 54–9.
85 UNODC, *Global Illicit Drug Trends*, 2001, pp. 32–3.
86 Chouvy, *Politics of the Poppy*, p. xiii.
87 McCoy, *The Politics of Heroin*, p. 15.
88 Jean-Pierre Minaudier, *Histoire de la Colombie de la conquête à nos jours* (Paris, 1997), pp. 298–9.
89 Ibid., pp. 295–8.
90 On Peru, see Paul Gootenberg, *Andean Cocaine: The Making of a Global Drug* (Chapel Hill, NC, 2008), pp. 292–300.
91 Clare Hargreaves, *Snowfields: The War on Cocaine in the Andes* (London, 1992), pp. 28–39.
92 Ibid., pp. 60–65.
93 Ibid., pp. 71–3 and 107–8.
94 Ibid., pp. 108–10.
95 Ibid., pp. 112–18.
96 Ibid., p. 67.
97 Gootenberg, *Andean Cocaine*, p. 305; Mark Bowden, *Killing Pablo*, 2nd edn (London, 2016), pp. 19–26.
98 Bowden, *Killing Pablo*, pp. 26–7.
99 Gootenberg, *Andean Cocaine*, pp. 305–6.
100 Bowden, *Killing Pablo*, pp. 30–32.
101 Ibid., pp. 32–3.
102 Ibid., p. 36.
103 Mary Roldán, 'Cocaine and the "Miracle" of Modernity in Medellín', in *Cocaine: Global Histories*, ed. Paul Gootenberg (London, 1999), pp. 168–70.

104 Bowden, *Killing Pablo*, pp. 36–40.
105 Ibid., p. 33; United States Attorney General, *Drug Trafficking: A Report to the President of the United States, 3 August 1989* (Washington, DC, 1989), p. 18.
106 United States Attorney General, *Drug Trafficking*, pp. 18–19.
107 Ibid., p. 19.
108 Robert Bunker, ed., *Narcos over the Border: Gangs, Cartels, Mercenaries, and the Invasion of America* (London, 2010), p. 40.
109 Friesendorf, *U.S. Foreign Policy*, p. 80.
110 Ibid., pp. 81–2.
111 United States Attorney General, *Drug Trafficking*, pp. 18–21; Bowden, *Killing Pablo*, p. 73.
112 McCoy, *The Politics of Heroin*, p. 443.
113 David Bewley-Taylor, *The United States and International Drug Control, 1909–1997* (London, 1999), pp. 188–9.
114 Hargreaves, *Snowfields*, pp. 156–7; Friesendorf, *U.S. Foreign Policy*, pp. 93–6.
115 Hargreaves, *Snowfields*, pp. 152–4.
116 Ibid., pp. 154–5.
117 Friesendorf, *U.S. Foreign Policy*, p. 84.
118 Ibid., p. 85; McCoy, *The Politics of Heroin*, p. 446.
119 McCoy, *The Politics of Heroin*, pp. 487–8.
120 Bowden, *Killing Pablo*, pp. 41–59.
121 Ibid., pp. 60–72.
122 Ibid., pp. 72–80.
123 Ibid., p. 112.
124 Ibid., p. 74.
125 Friesendorf, *U.S. Foreign Policy*, pp. 84–5.
126 Minaudier, *Histoire de la Colombie*, pp. 305–6.
127 Bowden, *Killing Pablo*, p. 125.
128 Ibid., p. 39.
129 Roldán, 'Cocaine and the "Miracle" of Modernity', p. 175.
130 Bowden, *Killing Pablo*, pp. 19–20.
131 Ibid., pp. 125–6.
132 Ibid., pp. 129–31; Minaudier, *Histoire de la Colombie*, pp. 309–10.
133 Bowden, *Killing Pablo*, pp. 108–9.
134 Ibid., pp. 144–5.
135 Ibid., pp. 155–76.
136 Ibid., pp. 109–10.
137 Ibid., pp. 86–8.
138 Ibid., p. 223.
139 Ibid., pp. 232–49.
140 Ibid., pp. 291–7 and 327–31; Friesendorf, *U.S. Foreign Policy*, pp. 85–6.
141 Commission on Narcotic Drugs, *Reports on Sessions*, Forty-third session, 2000, p. 16.
142 Davidde Corran, 'Colombians Grapple with a Big Problem: Wandering Hippos', *Associated Press*, 23 February 2020, accessed on www.apnews.com.
143 UNODC, *Global Illicit Drug Trends*, 1999, p. 42, and 2001, p. 67.
144 Ibid., 1999, p. 43, and 2001, p. 72.
145 Ibid., 2000, p. 6.
146 Ibid., 2001, p. 136.

147 Ibid., 2000, pp. 50–51.

148 Ibid., 1999, p. 45, and 2001, p. 67.

149 McCoy, *The Politics of Heroin*, p. 20.

150 Friesendorf, *u.s. Foreign Policy*, p. 17; UNODC, *Global Illicit Drug Trends*, 1999, p. 15, and 2000, p. 23.

151 John McWilliams, 'Through the Past Darkly: The Politics and Policies of America's Drug War', *Journal of Policy History*, III (1999), pp. 5–41, at p. 27.

152 Ibid., p. 7.

153 McCoy, *The Politics of Heroin*, pp. 449–53; Friesendorf, *u.s. Foreign Policy*, pp. 90–91 and 99–100.

154 Friesendorf, *u.s. Foreign Policy*, pp. 12–13.

155 UNODC, *World Drug Report* (Vienna, 1997–), 2005, vol. I, p. 16.

156 Andreas Siebel, *Drogenstrafrecht in Deutschland und Frankreich* (Frankfurt am Main, 1996), p. 181.

157 Newsday, *The Heroin Trail*, p. xiii.

158 Friesendorf, *u.s. Foreign Policy*, p. 108.

159 Bunker, *Narcos over the Border*, pp. 64–5.

160 Ibid., p. 56; Bergen-Cico, *War and Drugs*, p. 98.

161 Ethan Nadelmann, *Cops across Borders: The Internationalization of u.s. Criminal Law Enforcement* (University Park, PA, 1993), pp. 273–7.

162 Bewley-Taylor, *The United States and International Drug Control*, pp. 202–3.

163 Bunker, *Narcos over the Border*, p. 100.

164 Friesendorf, *u.s. Foreign Policy*, p. 109.

165 Bunker, *Narcos over the Border*, pp. 100–101.

166 Bergen-Cico, *War and Drugs*, p. 64.

167 Bunker, *Narcos over the Border*, pp. 4–6.

168 Hargreaves, *Snowfields*, pp. 61–2.

169 Friesendorf, *u.s. Foreign Policy*, pp. 140–41.

170 Ibid., p. 149.

171 UNODC, *Global Illicit Drug Trends*, 1999, p. 42, and 2001, p. 67.

172 Ibid., 2001, p. 18.

173 Nicholas Parsons, *Meth Mania: A History of Methamphetamine* (Boulder, CO, 2014), pp. 173–9; Commission on Narcotic Drugs, *Reports on Sessions*, Fortieth session, 1997, p. 1.

174 Friesendorf, *u.s. Foreign Policy*, pp. 58–9; Malcolm Beith, *The Last Narco* (London, 2010), pp. 36–7.

175 UNODC, *World Drug Report*, 2017, vol. II, pp. 50–53.

176 Beith, *The Last Narco*, p. 38; Anabel Hernández, *Narcolands: The Mexican Drug Lords and Their Godfathers* (London, 2014), pp. 16–17 and 67–70.

177 Beith, *The Last Narco*, pp. 43–54.

178 Ibid., pp. 73–7; Hernández, *Narcolands*, pp. 39–40.

179 Bergen-Cico, *War and Drugs*, pp. 99–101; Bunker, *Narcos over the Border*, pp. 65–7.

180 Commission on Narcotic Drugs, *Reports on Sessions*, Forty-third session, 2000, p. 16.

181 Bewley-Taylor, *The United States and International Drug Control*, p. 1; 'Secretary-General Calls on All Nations to Say "Yes" to Challenge of Working towards Drug-Free World', 8 June 1998, United Nations, Press Release GA/9411.

182 United Nations/General Assembly/A/RES/S-20/1, f. 2.
183 Ibid., f. 4.

9 THE CONSENSUS CRUMBLES

1 Drug Policy Alliance, 'Public Letter to Kofi Annan', 1 June 1998, f. 1, accessed on www.drugpolicy.org.
2 Ibid., f. 2.
3 Virginia Berridge, *Demons: Our Changing Attitudes to Alcohol, Tobacco, and Drugs* (Oxford, 2013), p. 131.
4 Ibid., pp. 131–2; Virginia Berridge, 'Drugs and Social Policy: The Establishment of Drug Control in Britain, 1900–30', *Addiction*, LXXIX/4 (1984), pp. 17–29, at pp. 26–7; John Strang and Michael Gossop, eds, *Heroin Addiction and the British System* (Milton Park, 2005), p. 13.
5 Berridge, 'Drugs and Social Policy', p. 27; Strang and Gossop, *The British System*, p. 19.
6 David Musto, *The American Disease: Origins of Narcotic Control*, 2nd edn (Oxford, 1987), pp. 97–8 and 167–82.
7 Steven Belenko, ed., *Drugs and Drug Policy in America: A Documentary History* (Westport, CT, 2000), pp. 71–81.
8 Howard Wayne Morgan, *Drugs in America: A Social History, 1800–1980* (Syracuse, NY, 1981), p. 134.
9 Humberto Fernandez and Therissa Libby, *Heroin: Its History, Pharmacology, and Treatment* (Center City, PA, 2011), pp. 91–4.
10 Belenko, *Drugs and Drug Policy in America*, pp. 167–72.
11 William S. Burroughs, *Junky* (London, 2008), pp. 56–7.
12 Musto, *American Disease*, pp. 232–3.
13 David Courtwright, ed., *Addicts Who Survived: An Oral History of Narcotic Use in America before 1965* (Knoxville, TN, 1989), pp. 22–5.
14 Virginia Berridge, 'AIDS, Drugs, and History', in *Drugs and Narcotics in History*, ed. Roy Porter and Mikuláš Teich (Cambridge, 1995), p. 191.
15 Brain Committee Report, *Drug Addiction: Second Report of the Interdepartmental Committee* (London, 1965), p. 3; Berridge, *Demons*, p. 192; Strang and Gossop, *The British System*, pp. 31–3.
16 Brain Committee Report, *Drug Addiction*, pp. 4–5.
17 Strang and Gossop, *The British System*, p. 39; Suzanne MacGregor, ed., *Drugs and British Society: Responses to a Social Problem in the Eighties* (London, 1989), pp. 170–71.
18 MacGregor, *Drugs and British Society*, p. 171.
19 James Inciardi, ed., *The Drug Legalization Debate*, 2nd edn (London, 1999), p. 5; Belenko, *Drugs and Drug Policy in America*, pp. 353–4.
20 Milton Friedman, 'Prohibition and Drugs', *Newsweek*, 1 May 1972, p. 104.
21 Ibid.
22 Thomas Szasz, *Our Right to Drugs: The Case for a Free Market* (New York, 1992), p. xxiv.
23 Ibid., pp. 44–7 and 149.
24 James Ostrowski, 'The Moral and Practical Case for Drug Legalization', *Hofstra Law Review*, XVIII/3 (1990), pp. 607–702, at p. 616.

25 Inciardi, *The Drug Legalization Debate*, p. 35; David Courtwright, 'Drug Legalization, the Drug War, and Drug Treatment in Historical Perspective', *Journal of Policy History*, III (1999), pp. 42–63, at pp. 47–52.

26 Inciardi, *The Drug Legalization Debate*, pp. 5–6 and 17–18; David Bewley-Taylor and Martin Jelsma, 'The UN Drug Control Conventions: The Limits of Latitude', *Transnational Institute Series on Legislative Reform of Drug Policies*, 18 (2012), pp. 1–24, at p. 4.

27 Ethan Nadelmann, 'The Case for Legalization', *Public Interest*, 92 (1988), pp. 3–31, at p. 14.

28 Trebach, 'Rethinking American Policy', in *Policing and Prescribing: The British System of Drug Control*, ed. David Whynes and Philip Bean (Basingstoke, 1991), pp. 268–9.

29 UNODC, *World Drug Report* (Vienna, 1997–), 2019, vol. I, p. 7.

30 Tim Boekhout van Solinge, *Dealing with Drugs in Europe* (The Hague, 2004), p. 5.

31 Belenko, *Drugs and Drug Policy in America*, pp. 353–4.

32 Nadelmann, 'The Case for Legalization', p. 17.

33 Ibid., p. 19.

34 Alyson Martin and Nushin Rashidian, *A New Leaf: The End of Cannabis Prohibition* (New York, 2014), pp. 172–3.

35 Andreas Siebel, *Drogenstrafrecht in Deutschland und Frankreich* (Frankfurt am Main, 1996), pp. 186–7.

36 Ostrowski, 'The Moral and Practical Case for Drug Legalization', pp. 658–63; Nadelmann, 'The Case for Legalization', pp. 15–16.

37 Steven Jonas, 'Why the Drug War Will Never End', in *The Drug Legalization Debate*, ed. Inciardi, pp. 132–4.

38 Jamie Fellner, 'Punishment and Prejudice: Racial Disparities in the War on Drugs', *Human Rights Watch*, 12 (2000), pp. 1–31, at p. 22.

39 Doris Marie Provine, *Unequal under Law: Race in the War on Drugs* (Chicago, IL, 2007), pp. 97–9 and 127–8.

40 Ibid., p. 16.

41 Szasz, *Our Right to Drugs*, pp. 117–24; Steven Jonas, 'Why the Drug War Will Never End', p. 126; Martin, *A New Leaf*, p. 160.

42 James Wilson, 'Against the Legalization of Drugs', *Commentary* (February 1990), accessed on www.commentarymagazine.com.

43 Thomas Babor, ed., *Drug Policy and the Public Good*, 2nd edn (Oxford, 2018), pp. 253–64.

44 Courtwright, 'Drug Legalization', pp. 44–5; Robert MacCoun and Peter Reuter, 'Assessing Drug Prohibition and Its Alternatives: A Guide for Agnostics', *Annual Review of Law and Social Science*, 7 (2011), pp. 61–78, at pp. 72–3. Nadelmann nevertheless wrote that the illicit drugs, unlike alcoholic drugs, did not naturally belong in American culture and would therefore always enjoy limited use: Nadelmann, 'The Case for Legalization', p. 29.

45 Babor, *Drug Policy and the Public Good*, p. 35.

46 Gordon Graham, 'Criminalisation and Control', in *Policing and Prescribing*, ed. Whynes and Bean, pp. 247–52.

47 Alfred McCoy, *The Politics of Heroin: CIA Complicity in the Global Drug Trade* (New York, 1991), pp. 256–8; Norman Zinberg, *Drug, Set, and*

Setting: The Basis for Controlled Intoxicant Use (New Haven, CT, 1984), p. 12; Lee N. Robins, 'Vietnam Veterans' Rapid Recovery from Heroin Addiction: A Fluke or Normal Expectation?', *Addiction*, LXXXVIII/8 (1993), pp. 1041–54, at pp. 1044–5.

48 Substance Abuse and Mental Health Services Administration, *National Household Survey on Drug Abuse: Detailed Tables* (Rockville, 1998–), 1998, Table 104A and Table 105A.

49 Zinberg, *Drug, Set, and Setting*, p. 57.

50 Ibid., p. 157.

51 Ibid., pp. 69–70.

52 Ibid., pp. 194–5.

53 Ibid., pp. 125–6.

54 Ibid., pp. 17–18.

55 Ibid., pp. 154–5.

56 Cited in Mitch Earleywine, *Understanding Marijuana: A New Look at the Scientific Evidence* (Oxford, 2002), p. 32.

57 Babor, *Drug Policy and the Public Good*, p. 40; Dirk Lachenmeier and Jürgen Rehm, 'Comparative Risk Assessment of Alcohol, Tobacco, Cannabis and Other Illicit Drugs Using the Margin of Exposure Approach', *Scientific Reports*, 5 (2015), pp. 1–7.

58 David Nutt et al., 'Development of a Rational Scale to Assess the Harm of Drugs of Potential Misuse', *The Lancet*, CCCLXIX/9566 (2007), pp. 1047–53.

59 Peter Anderson, ed., *New Governance of Addictive Substances and Behaviours* (Oxford, 2017), p. 6.

60 Ibid., pp. 30–32.

61 Fernandez and Libby, *Heroin*, pp. 48–9.

62 Jarred Younger et al., 'Prescription Opioid Analgesics Rapidly Change the Human Brain', *Pain*, CLII/8 (2011), pp. 1803–10, at p. 1803.

63 Nora Volkow et al., 'Neurobiologic Advances from the Brain Disease Model of Addiction', *New England Journal of Medicine*, 28 January 2016, pp. 368–9.

64 National Institute on Drug Abuse, *Drugs, Brain and Behavior: The Science of Addictions*, 5th edn (Bethesda, MD, 2018), p. 22.

65 Interview, Dr Michel Reynaud, 26 April 2018; Nancy Campbell, *Discovering Addiction* (Ann Arbor, MI, 2007), pp. 219–20.

66 Volkow, 'Neurobiologic Advances', p. 364.

67 Ibid., p. 366.

68 Ibid., p. 367.

69 Interview, Dr Michel Reynaud, 26 April 2018.

70 NIDA, *Drugs, Brain and Behavior*, pp. 7–9; Volkow et al., 'Neurobiologic Advances', p. 367.

71 NIDA, *Drugs, Brain and Behavior*, p. 17.

72 Campbell, *Discovering Addiction*, p. 201.

73 David Bewley-Taylor and Christopher Hallam, 'The 2014 Commission on Narcotic Drugs and Its High-Level Segment: Report of Proceedings', *International Drug Policy Consortium* (2014), pp 1–44, at p. 8, accessed on www.idpc.net.

74 See www.drugpolicy.org, consulted on 4 June 2020.

75 See www.beckleyfoundation.org; www.tni.org; and www.release.org.uk, last consulted on 4 June 2020.

76 Sandra Lane et al., 'The Coming of Age of Needle Exchange', in *Harm Reduction: National and International Perspectives*, ed. Lana Harrison and James Inciardi (London, 2000), pp. 49–56; Richard Davenport-Hines, *The Pursuit of Oblivion: A Global History of Narcotics, 1500–2000* (London, 2001), p. 378.

77 Diane Riley and Pat O'Hare, 'Harm Reduction: History, Definition, and Practice', in *Harm Reduction*, ed. Harrison and Inciardi, p. 16; David Bewley-Taylor, *International Drug Control: Consensus Fractured* (Cambridge, 2012), p. 75; interview, Sylvie Reulet, 22 December 2017.

78 Fernandez and Libby, *Heroin*, pp. 110–11; Kathleen Frydl, *The Drug Wars in America, 1940–1973* (New York, 2013), pp. 328–30.

79 Ernest Drucker, 'Maintenance Drugs in the Treatment of Opiate Addiction', in *Harm Reduction*, ed. Harrison and Inciardi, pp. 35–6; Frydl, *The Drug Wars in America*, p. 338.

80 Fernandez and Libby, *Heroin*, p. 116.

81 Ethan Nadelmann, 'Commonsense Drug Policy', in *The Drug Legalization Debate*, ed. Inciardi, p. 164.

82 Riley and O'Hare, 'Harm Reduction', p. 12.

83 Babor, *Drug Policy and the Public Good*, p. 187; interview, Dr Michel Reynaud, 26 April 2018.

84 Strang and Gossop, *Heroin Addiction and the British System*, pp. 140–44.

85 Ibid., pp. 145–51; Riley and O'Hare, 'Harm Reduction', pp. 3–4.

86 Bewley-Taylor, *Consensus Fractured*, pp. 72–3.

87 German Lopez, 'The Case for Prescription Heroin', 12 June 2017, accessed on www.vox.com.

88 Van Solinge, *Dealing with Drugs in Europe*, pp. 122–7; Marcel de Kort, 'The Dutch Cannabis Debate, 1968–1976', *Journal of Drug Issues*, XXIV/3 (1994), pp. 417–27, at pp. 419–26.

89 De Kort, 'The Dutch Cannabis Debate', pp. 425–6; Tom Blickman, 'Cannabis Policy Reform in Europe', *Transnational Institute Series on Legislative Reform of Drug Policies*, 28 (2014), pp. 1–24, at p. 3.

90 Blickman, 'Cannabis Policy Reform in Europe', pp. 3–4.

91 Van Solinge, *Dealing with Drugs in Europe*, p. 139.

92 Caitlin Hughes and Alex Stephens, 'What Can We Learn from the Portuguese Decriminalization of Illicit Drugs?', *British Journal of Criminology*, L/3 (2010), pp. 999–1022, at pp. 1000–1001; Hannah Laqueur, 'Uses and Abuses of Drug Decriminalization in Portugal', *Law and Social Inquiry*, XL/3 (2015), pp. 1–36, at pp. 4–5; Susana Ferreira, 'Portugal's Radical Drugs Policy Is Working', *The Guardian*, 5 December 2017, www.theguardian.com. For Portugal's incidence of opiate use, which Laqueur wrongly describes as low, see UNODC, *Global Illicit Drug Trends* (New York, 1999–2003), 1999, p. 125.

93 Hughes and Stephens, 'Portuguese Decriminalization?', p. 1002; Laqueur, 'Uses and Abuses', p. 7.

94 Alex Reeg, 'Drugs and the Law in Post-Franco Spain', in *Drugs, Law and the State*, ed. Harold H. Traver and Mark S. Gaylord (Hong Kong, 1992), pp. 49–63, at pp. 53–7; European Monitoring Centre for Drugs and Drug Addiction, *Country Drug Reports* (Lisbon, 1996–), Spain 2019, p. 5.

95 Robert MacCoun and Peter Reuter, *Drug War Heresies: Learning from other Vices, Times, and Places* (Cambridge, 2001), pp. 231–3; EMCDDA, *Country Drug Reports*, Italy 2019, p. 5.

96 EMCDDA, *Country Drug Reports*, Estonia 2017, p. 4; EMCDDA, *European Drug Reports*, 2019, accessible on www.emcdda.europa.eu.

97 Riley and O'Hare, 'Harm Reduction', p. 11; Chloé Potier et al., 'Supervised Injection Services: What Has Been Demonstrated?', *Drug and Alcohol Dependence*, 145 (2014), pp. 48–68, at pp. 64–5.

98 Hughes and Stephens, 'What Can We Learn from Portuguese Decriminalization?', pp. 1006–8.

99 UNODC, *World Drug Report*, 2010, pp. 278–95.

100 Hughes and Stephens, 'What Can We Learn from Portuguese Decriminalization?', p. 1006; EMCDDA, *European Drug Reports*, 2019, p. 58.

101 Laqueur, 'Uses and Abuses', pp. 8–9.

102 Hughes and Stephens, 'What Can We Learn from Portuguese Decriminalization?', pp. 1008–10.

103 EMCDDA, *European Drug Reports*, 2019, pp. 41–59.

104 Bewley-Taylor, *Consensus Fractured*, p. 39.

105 Ibid., pp. 60–63.

106 Ibid., pp. 102–27.

107 Commission on Narcotic Drugs, *Reports on Sessions* (New York, 1946–), Forty-third session, 2000, p. 18.

108 Bewley-Taylor and Jelsma, 'The Limits of Latitude', p. 11.

109 Commission on Narcotic Drugs, *Reports on Sessions*, Sixth special session, 1980, pp. 24–5.

110 Thomas Pietschmann, 'A Century of International Drug Control', *Bulletin on Narcotics*, LIX (2007), p. 110.

111 Bewley-Taylor and Jelsma, 'The Limits of Latitude', pp. 11–12.

112 Ibid., pp. 14–15.

113 Zhou Yongming, *Anti-Drug Crusades in Twentieth-Century China: Nationalism, History, and State Building* (Lanham, MD, 1999), pp. 122–4.

114 Dali Yang, 'Illegal Drugs, Policy Change, and State Power: The Case of Contemporary China', *Journal of Contemporary China*, 11/4 (1993), pp. 14–34, at pp. 26–7.

115 Sarah Biddulph and Xie Chuanyu, 'Regulating Drug Dependency in China: The 2008 PRC drug Prohibition Law', *British Journal of Criminology*, LI/6 (2011), pp. 978–96, at p. 979; Bewley-Taylor, *Consensus Fractured*, p. 67; Babor, *Drug Policy and the Public Good*, p. 285.

116 Bewley-Taylor, *Consensus Fractured*, p. 51.

117 UNODC, *World Drug Report*, 2000, p. 87.

118 Bewley-Taylor, *Consensus Fractured*, pp. 176–7.

10 OPIATE OVERDOSE

1 Based on excess death calculations: National Institute on Drug Abuse Online Database, *Number of National Drug Overdose Deaths Involving Select Prescription and Illicit Drugs, 1999–2018*, accessed on www.drugabuse.gov on 22 May 2020.

2 Richard Bonnie, Morgan Ford and Jonathan Phillips, eds, *Pain Management and the Opioid Epidemic* (Washington, DC, 2017), pp. 14–15 and 31.

3 'States Show the Way on the Opioid Epidemic', *New York Times*, 24 August 2018, www.nytimes.com; Paul Blest, 'Delaware's Opioid Crisis', www.theoutline.com, 12 February 2018.

4 Marc Mauer, 'Long-Term Sentences: Time to Reconsider the Scale of Punishment', UMKC *Law Review*, LXXXVII (2018), pp. 113–31, at p. 116; Sari Horwitz, 'Holder Calls for Reduced Sentences for Low-Level Drug Offenders', *Washington Post*, 13 March 2014, www.washingtonpost.com.

5 Chris McGreal, *American Overdose: The Opioid Tragedy in Three Acts* (London, 2018), pp. 14–17 and 27; Sam Quinones, *Dreamland: The True Tale of America's Opiate Epidemic* (New York, 2015), pp. 30–31 and 80.

6 Interview, Dr Garret FitzGerald, 7 December 2018.

7 McGreal, *American Overdose*, pp. 40–43.

8 Ibid., pp. 21–4.

9 Ibid., p. 48; Quinones, *Dreamland*, p. 133.

10 Quinones, *Dreamland*, pp. 126–7.

11 Ibid., pp. 134–5.

12 Subsys only came out in 2012, but Insys had a predecessor: Cephalon, fined $425 million in 2008 for mis-branding its fentanyl pharmaceutical Actiq: Hannah Kuckler, 'Wall Street, Bribery, and an Opioid Epidemic: The Inside Story of a Disgraced Drugmaker', *Financial Times*, 19 June 2020, www.ft.com.

13 Hannah Kuchler, 'Opioid Executive Admits to "No Morals" Ahead of Prison Term', *Financial Times*, 23 January 2020, www.ft.com.

14 Bonnie, Ford and Phillips, *Pain Management*, p. 26.

15 Ibid.; McGreal, *American Overdose*, p. 55.

16 McGreal, *American Overdose*, p. 44.

17 Interview, Dr Garret FitzGerald, 7 December 2018.

18 McGreal, *American Overdose*, p. 232.

19 Quinones, *Dreamland*, p. 190; Bonnie, Ford and Phillips, *Pain Management*, pp. 27–8.

20 Bonnie, Ford and Phillips, *Pain Management*, p. 3.

21 Quinones, *Dreamland*, pp. 81 and 94–108; McGreal, *American Overdose*, pp. 83–5; Bonnie, Ford and Phillips, *Pain Management*, pp. 25–6.

22 Quinones, *Dreamland*, p. 137.

23 Interview, Dr Garret FitzGerald, 7 December 2018; Final Complaint, State of Ohio vs. Purdue Pharma, Teva Pharmaceutical Industries et al., Ross County Common Pleas Court, 31 May 2017, pp. 16–34, accessed on www.ohioattorneygeneral.gov; Thomas Babor, ed., *Drug Policy and the Public Good*, 2nd edn (Oxford, 2018), p. 139.

24 McGreal, *American Overdose*, p. 102.

25 Scott Higham, 'The Drug Industry's Triumph over the DEA', *Washington Post*, 15 October 2017, accessed on www.washingtonpost.com.

26 Beth Mole, 'Drug Companies Submerged WV in Opioids: One Town of 3,000 Got 21 Million Pills', www.arstechnica.com, 30 January 2018.

27 Babor, ed., *Drug Policy and the Public Good*, p. 149.

28 Ben Wiseman, 'The Family that Built an Empire of Pain', *New Yorker*, 23 October 2017, www.newyorker.com.

29 Christopher Glazek, 'The Secretive Family Making Billions from the Opioid Crisis', *Esquire*, 16 October 2017, www.esquire.com.

30 McGreal, *American Overdose*, p. 125.

31 Ibid., p. 281.

32 McGreal, *American Overdose*, pp. 84–90 and 162–4.

33 Ibid., pp. 171–2; Bonnie, Ford and Phillips, *Pain Management*, pp. 36–7.

34 McGreal, *American Overdose*, pp. 204–7.

35 Ibid., pp. 141–2.

36 Higham, 'The Drug Industry's Triumph over the DEA'.

37 Ibid.; McGreal, *American Overdose*, pp. 215–16.

38 McGreal, *American Overdose*, p. 233; Bonnie, Ford and Phillips, *Pain Management*, p. 18.

39 Bonnie, Ford and Phillips, *Pain Management*, pp. 189 and 212–20.

40 Margaret Talbot, 'The Addicts Next Door', *New Yorker*, 28 April 2014, www.newyorker.com; McGreal, *American Overdose*, p. 252.

41 Dan Vergano, 'This Drug Is Cheaper and More Powerful than Heroin – and May Be Killing Way More People', www.buzzfeed.com, 5 June 2017; McGreal, *American Overdose*, p. 260; Bonnie, Ford and Phillips, *Pain Management*, pp. 220–22.

42 Bonnie, Ford and Phillips, *Pain Management*, p. 3.

43 NIDA, *Number of National Drug Overdose Deaths, 1999–2018*.

44 David Crow, 'What Next for the Sacklers: A Pharma Dynasty under Siege', *Financial Times*, 7 September 2018, www.ft.com.

45 Jared Hopkins, 'Wholesalers to Settle Opioid Litigation', *Wall Street Journal*, 14 February 2020, www.wsj.com.

46 Colin Dwyer, 'Your Guide to the Massive (and Massively Complex) Opioid Litigation', *National Public Radio*, 15 October 2019, www.npr.org.

47 Hannah Kuchler, 'Insys Founder Convicted in Opioid Bribery Case', *Financial Times*, 2 May 2019, www.ft.com.

48 Dwyer, 'Your Guide to the Opioid Litigation'; Julia Kollewe, 'OxyContin Maker Purdue Pharma Files for Bankruptcy', *The Guardian*, 16 September 2019; David Crow, 'Billionaire Sackler Family Owns a Second Opioid Drugmaker', *Financial Times*, 9 September 2018, www.ft.com.

49 Bonnie, Ford and Phillips, *Pain Management*, pp. 35–6.

50 Terrence McCoy, 'Inside the Fallout of America's Crackdown on Opioids', *Washington Post*, 1 June 2018, www.washingtonpost.com; Brianna Ehley, 'How the Opioid Crackdown Is Backfiring', www.politico.com, 28 August 2018.

51 'Products: Vital Statistics Rapid Release', www.cdc.gov/nchs/nvss/vsrr/drug-overdose-data.htm, accessed 9 June 2020.

52 Harriet Ryan, Lisa Girion and Scott Glover, 'OxyContin Goes Global', LA *Times*, 18 December 2016, www.latimes.com; interview, Dr Garret FitzGerald, 7 December 2018.

53 Catharine Tunney, 'Canada Has Seen More than 8,000 Apparent Opioid Deaths since 2016', CBC *News*, 18 September 2018, www.cbc.ca. Babor places Canada ahead of the USA in per capita consumption: *Drug Policy and the Public Good*, p. 145, but Van Amsterdam's more precise calculations has it at only about half the U.S. level: Jan van

Amsterdam and Wim van den Brink, 'The Misuse of Prescription Opioids: A Threat for Europe?', *Current Drug Abuse Reviews*, VIII/1 (2015), pp. 3–14, at p. 4.

54 Van Amsterdam and Van den Brink, 'The Misuse of Prescription Opioids', p. 9.

55 UNODC, *World Drug Report* (Vienna, 1997–), 2000, p. 99; European Monitoring Centre for Drugs and Drug Addiction, *Drug Related Deaths and Mortality in Europe* (Lisbon, 2021), p. 7.

56 Babor, *Drug Policy and the Public Good*, p. 140.

57 McGreal, *American Overdose*, p. xii.

58 NIDA, *Number of National Drug Overdose Deaths, 1999–2018*, with 1999 taken as the baseline even though for decades between 1914 and 1995 overdose fatalities can only have been far lower.

59 David Bewley-Taylor, *International Drug Control: Consensus Fractured* (Cambridge, 2012), pp. 158–9.

60 Steven Belenko, ed., *Drugs and Drug Policy in America: A Documentary History* (Westport, CT, 2000), pp. 295–6.

61 Andrew Potter and Daniel Weinstock, eds, *High Time: The Legalization and Regulation of Cannabis in Canada* (Montreal, 2019), p. 17.

62 Belenko, *Drugs and Drug Policy in America*, pp. 297–9.

63 David Musto, *The Quest for Drug Control: Politics and Federal Policy in a Period of Increasing Substance Abuse, 1963–1981* (New Haven, CT, 2002), pp. 113–15.

64 Emily Dufton, *Grassroots: The Rise and Fall and Rise of Marijuana in America* (New York, 2017), p. 36.

65 Ibid., p. 75; Alyson Martin and Nushin Rashidian, *A New Leaf: The End of Cannabis Prohibition* (New York, 2014), p. 48.

66 Musto, *The Quest for Drug Control*, pp. 207–9.

67 Jerome Himmelstein, *The Strange Career of Marihuana* (Westport, CT, 1983), pp. 104–5.

68 Dufton, *Grassroots*, p. 108.

69 Drug Abuse Council, *The Facts about 'Drug Abuse'* (New York, 1980), p. 137; Howard Wayne Morgan, *Drugs in America: A Social History, 1800–1980* (Syracuse, NY, 1981), p. 161.

70 Musto, *Quest for Drug Control*, pp. 230–33; Dufton, *Grassroots*, pp. 89–100.

71 Ibid., p. 123; Martin, *A New Leaf*, p. 54.

72 Dufton, *Grassroots*, p. 70.

73 Martin, *A New Leaf*, p. 16.

74 European Monitoring Centre for Drugs and Drug Addiction, *Medical Use of Cannabis and Cannabinoids* (Luxembourg, 2018), pp. 25–6.

75 James Inciardi, ed., *The Drug Legalization Debate*, 2nd edn (London, 1999), p. 30.

76 Martin, *A New Leaf*, pp. 59–61.

77 Ibid., pp. 62–4.

78 Potter and Weinstock, *High Time*, p. 19. For a critical view, see Patricia Erickson, 'History and Prospects in Canadian Drug Policy', in *Harm Reduction: National and International Perspectives*, ed. Lana Harrison and James Inciardi (London, 2000), pp. 155–69.

79 Potter and Weinstock, *High Time*, p. 20; Martin, *A New Leaf*, p. 208.

80 Jesse Tahirali, '7 in 10 Canadians Support Marijuana Legalization: Nanos Poll', CTV *News*, 30 June 2016, www.ctvmews.ca; Potter and Weinstock, *High Time*, pp. 22–5.

81 SAMHSA, *National Survey on Drug Abuse*, 2016, Table 139BB.

82 Martin, *A New Leaf*, p. 6.

83 Ibid., pp. 160–73.

84 Ibid., pp. 173–80.

85 Ibid., pp. 191–4 and 204.

86 Ibid., p. 216.

87 Dufton, *Grassroots*, p. 228; Nathan Kasai, 'America's Marijuana Evolution', 24 August 2017, www.thirdway.org, accessed on 10 June 2020.

88 Sean Williams, 'These 3 States Will Begin Selling Recreational Marijuana Fairly Soon', *Motley Fool*, 7 September 2019, www.fool.com.

89 Dufton, *Grassroots*, p. 229.

90 Kasai, 'America's Marijuana Evolution'.

91 Dufton, *Grassroots*, pp. 233–5.

92 Ari Rosmarin and Niamh Eastwood, *A Quiet Revolution: Drug Decriminalisation Policies in Practice across the Globe* (London, 2012), p. 35; Guillermo Garat, 'Uruguay: A Way to Regulate the Cannabis Market', in *Drug Policies and the Politics of Drugs in the Americas*, ed. Beatrice Labate, Clancy Cavnar and Thiago Rodrigues (Cham, 2016), pp. 209–19.

93 Garat, 'Uruguay', pp. 218–21; Global Commission on Drug Policy, *Regulation: The Responsible Control of Drugs* (Geneva, 2018), p. 43.

94 Garat, 'Uruguay', p. 222; UNODC, *World Drug Report*, 2019, vol. V, p. 35.

95 Potter and Weinstock, *High Time*, pp. 90–93 and 218; UNODC, *World Drug Report*, 2019, vol. V, pp. 33–4.

96 UNODC, *World Drug Report*, 2019, vol. V, pp. 26–7.

97 Global Commission on Drug Policy, *Enforcement of Drug Laws: Focusing on Organized Crime Elites* (Geneva, 2020), p. 31.

98 Martin, *A New Leaf*, pp. 152–3.

99 Dan Baum, 'Legalize It All', *Harper's Magazine*, 23 April 2018, www.harpers.org.

100 Aurora Cannabis, *2019 Annual Report*, p. 4, www.investor.auroramj.com.

101 Ibid., pp. 9–12.

102 Ibid., pp. 16–19.

103 Ibid., p. 17.

104 Associated Press, 'Jamaica Decriminalises Marijuana', *The Guardian*, 25 February 2015, www.theguardian.com.

105 Global Commission on Drug Policy, *Enforcement of Drug Laws*, p. 28.

106 'NZ Government Needs to be Courageous on Drug Laws – Criminologist', *Radio New Zealand*, 7 November 2020, www.rnz.co.nz.

107 EMCDDA, *Medical Use of Cannabis*, pp. 25–8, pp. 27–8; Jamie Grierson, 'UK Doctors Will Be Able to Prescribe Cannabis Medicine Next Month', 11 October 2018, *The Guardian*, www.theguardian.com.

108 Aurora Cannabis, *2019 Annual Report*, p. 13; Aphria Inc., *2019 Annual Report*, p. 24, accessed on www.aphriainc.com.

109 Tom Blickman, 'Cannabis Policy Reform in Europe', *Transnational Institute Series on Legislative Reform of Drug Policies*, 28 (2014), pp. 1–24, p. 2; interview, Sylvie Reulet, 22 December 2017.

110 Andreas Siebel, *Drogenstrafrecht in Deutschland und Frankreich* (Frankfurt am Main, 1996), p. 237; Rosmarin and Eastwood, *A Quiet Revolution*, p. 24.

111 Blickman, 'Cannabis Policy Reform in Europe', pp. 7–8.

112 Ibid., pp. 8–13.

113 Bewley-Taylor, *Consensus Fractured*, p. 177; David Bewley-Taylor and Martin Jelsma, 'The UN Drug Control Conventions: The Limits of Latitude', *Transnational Institute Series on Legislative Reform of Drug Policies*, 18 (2012), pp. 1–24, pp. 13–14.

114 Bewley-Taylor and Jelsma, 'The Limits of Latitude', pp. 5–7. While the Single Convention merely asks states not to permit unlicensed possession, the 1988 Convention is more aggressive in having as a guideline that it should be a criminal offence.

115 UNODC, *World Drug Report*, 2006, vol. I, pp. 155–6. See also Commission on Narcotic Drugs, *Reports on Sessions* (New York, 1946–), Fifty-first session, 2007–8, p. 39.

116 Alan Feuer, 'El Chapo Found Guilty on All Counts; Faces Life in Prison', *New York Times*, 12 February 2019, www.nytimes.com.

117 Jude Webber, 'After "El Chapo": Mexico's Never-Ending War on Drugs', *Financial Times*, 20 February 2019, www.ft.com; Anabel Hernández, *Narcolands: The Mexican Drug Lords and Their Godfathers* (London, 2014), pp. 225–48; Malcolm Beith, *The Last Narco* (London, 2010), pp. 117–19 and 186–8.

118 Robert Bunker, ed., *Narcos over the Border: Gangs, Cartels, Mercenaries, and the Invasion of America* (London, 2010), pp. 147–8.

119 Ted Galen Carpenter, 'The Drug War's Damaging Impact on Mexico and Its Neighbours', in *New Approaches to Drug Policies*, ed. Marten Brienen and Jonathan Rosen (Basingstoke, 2015), p. 17.

120 Pierre-Arnaud Chouvy, *Opium: Uncovering the Politics of the Poppy* (Cambridge, MA, 2010), pp. 73–5.

121 UNODC, *World Drug Report*, 2017, vol. II, pp. 39–40.

122 Ibid., vol. I, pp. 3–4.

123 Ibid., vol. IV, pp. 13–16.

124 Tom Allard, 'The Hunt for Asia's El Chapo', www.reuters.com, 14 October 2019.

125 Ibid.

126 Jonathan Caulkins and Sarah Chandler, 'Long-Run Trends in Incarceration of Drug Offenders in the U.S.', *Crime and Delinquency*, LII/4 (2006), pp. 1–25, at pp. 7–11.

127 This excludes local jails, unlike the first data set. Paige Harrison and Allen Beck, 'Prisoners in 2005', *Bureau of Justice Statistics*, November 2006, pp. 9–10; Jennifer Bronson and Ann Carson, 'Prisoners in 2017', *Bureau of Justice Statistics*, April 2019, pp. 22–4, both accessed on www.bjs.org.

128 Council of Europe, *Annual Penal Statistics* (Strasbourg, 1998–), 2002, pp. 14 and 26, and 2019, p. 50.

129 These rates are measured as the percentage of firm prison sentences garnered on possession offences actually processed by a court of justice: European Monitoring Centre for Drugs and Drug Addiction, *Drug Offences: Sentencing and Other Outcomes* (Luxembourg, 2009), pp. 10–14.

130 David Bewley-Taylor, Chris Hallam and Rob Allen, 'The Incarceration of Drug Offenders: An Overview', *Beckley Foundation* (2009), pp. 1–18, at p. 8.
131 Sarah Biddulph and Xie Chuanyu, 'Regulating Drug Dependency in China: The 2008 PRC Drug Prohibition Law', *British Journal of Criminology*, LI/6 (2011), pp. 978–96, at pp. 983–92.
132 UNODC, *World Drug Report*, 2006, vol. I, p. 1; see also 2007, p. 1.
133 See Appendix III.
134 Commission on Narcotic Drugs, *Reports on Sessions*, Fifty-fourth session, 2010–11, p. 35.
135 Ibid., Fifty-fifth session, 2011–12, pp. 32–3, Fifty-eighth session, 2014–15, pp. 21–4.
136 Global Commission on Drug Policy, *Enforcement of Drug Laws*, p. 4; www.globalcommissionondrugs.org, accessed on 12 June 2020.
137 Global Commission on Drug Policy, *Enforcement of Drug Laws*, pp. 9–10.
138 Global Commission on Drug Policy, *The Responsible Control of Drugs*, p. 6.
139 Babor, *Drug Policy and the Public Good*, pp. 317–18; Labate, *Drug Policies in the Americas*, p. v.
140 David Bewley-Taylor and Christopher Hallam, 'The 2014 Commission on Narcotic Drugs and Its High-Level Segment: Report of Proceedings', *International Drug Policy Consortium* (2014), pp. 1–44, at pp. 1–15.
141 Ibid., p. 11.
142 Ibid., pp. 1–2.
143 'Resolution adopted by the General Assembly on 19 April 2016', United Nations/General Assembly/A/RES/S-30/1, accessed on www.unodc.org/ungass2016.
144 United Nations/General Assembly/19 April 2016/A/S-30/PV.1, ff. 16–17.
145 Ibid./A/S-30/PV.2, ff. 7–8.
146 Ibid./21 April 2016/A/S-30/PV.5, f. 3.
147 Thomas Pietschmann, 'A Century of International Drug Control', *Bulletin on Narcotics*, LIX (2007), pp. 124–5.
148 Bewley-Taylor and Jelsma, 'The Limits of Latitude', p. 16; Babor, *Drug Policy and the Public Good*, pp. 310–11.
149 Babor, *Drug Policy and the Public Good*, p. 305.
150 Global Commission on Drug Policy, *The Responsible Control of Drugs*, pp. 36–9.
151 UNODC, *World Drug Report*, 2016, vol. I, p. 27.
152 Ibid., 2014, p. iii.
153 Ibid., 2010, p. 4, and 2015, pp. 77–118.
154 Ibid., 2013, p. 33.
155 Ibid., 2019, vol. I, p. 1.
156 Ibid., 2013, pp. xii–xiv. See also the 2011 issue, pp. 26–7.
157 Ibid., 2013, pp. 59 and 108–12.
158 Ibid., 2019, vol. I, pp. 1–12.
159 Ibid., p. 26.
160 Organization of American States, *Scenarios for the Drug Problem in the Americas, 2013–2025* (Washington, DC, 2013), pp. 11–23.

CLOSING OBSERVATIONS

1 Hannes Gatterer et al., 'Mortality in Different Mountain Sports Activities Primarily Practiced in the Summer Season: A Narrative Review', *International Journal of Environmental Research and Public Health*, XVI/20 (2019), www.mdpi.com/journal/ijerph.

2 National Institute on Drug Abuse Online Database, *Number of National Drug Overdose Deaths Involving Select Prescription and Illicit Drugs, 1999–2018*, www.drugabuse.gov; SAMHSA, *Key Substance Use and Mental Health Indicators in the United States: Results from the 2018 National Survey on Drug Use and Health* (Rockville, MD, 2018), p. 14; EMCDDA, *Recent Changes in Europe's Cocaine Market* (Lisbon, 2018), p. 15; UNODC, *World Drug Report* (Vienna, 1997–), 2017, vol. II, p. 48.

3 NIDA, *Number of National Drug Overdose Deaths, 1999–2018*; SAMHSA, *Key Substance Use and Mental Health Indicators*, pp. 14–15.

APPENDIX I: OPIUM SMOKER NUMBERS IN NINETEENTH-CENTURY CHINA

1 'Memorandum on Opium from China', International Opium Commission, *Report of the International Opium Commission, Shanghai China, February 1 to February 26 1909* (Shanghai, 1909), p. 57; R. K. Newman, 'Opium Smoking in Late Imperial China: A Reconsideration', *Modern Asian Studies*, XXIX/4 (1995), pp. 765–94, at pp. 769–74; *China Imperial Maritime Customs Reports on Opium* (Shanghai, 1864–1909), vol. IV, pp. 60–63; *Use of Opium and Traffic Therein: Message from the President of the United States* (Washington, DC, 1906), pp. 167–9; Chantal Descours-Gatin, *Quand l'opium finançait la colonisation en Indochine* (Paris, 1992), p. 210; UNODC, *World Drug Report* (Vienna, 1997–), 2011, p. 46.

APPENDIX II: LEAGUE-ERA OPIUM REGIME STATISTICS

1 League of Nations, Advisory Committee on Traffic in Opium and Other Dangerous Drugs, *Procès Verbal of Sessions* (Geneva, 1921–40); League of Nations, Advisory Committee on Traffic in Opium and Other Dangerous Drugs, *Summary of Annual Reports of Governments* (Geneva, 1926–40); Jacques Dumarest, *Les Monopoles de l'opium et du sel en Indochine* (Lyon, 1938), p. 122.

APPENDIX III: POST-WAR DRUG SEIZURES

1 Commission on Narcotic Drugs, *Summary of Annual Reports of Governments* (Lake Success, NY, 1944–86); International Narcotics Control Board, *Statistics on Narcotic Drugs* (Geneva, 1968–); Commission on Narcotic Drugs, *Reports on Sessions* (New York, 1946–); UNODC, *Global Illicit Drug Trends* (New York, 1999–2003); UNODC, *World Drug Report*, 1997–2019.

FURTHER READING

The literature on drugs and drug prohibition, especially if one includes the medical literature, is effectively infinite, in excess of what an individual could read in a lifetime. The sources referenced in this volume themselves, other than archival, include a large number of books, academic articles and press materials, only a tiny selection of which are discussed below. I have chosen to organize recommended reading thematically. General sources on specific drugs nevertheless include Paul Gootenberg's *Andean Cocaine: The Making of a Global Drug* (Durham, NC, 2008) and Nicolas Rasmussen's *On Speed: The Many Lives of Amphetamine* (New York, 2008). Among archival sources, of particular importance internationally are the various reports by the United Nations agencies and, before them, those of the League of Nations. Few of these are accessible to the general reader, but the full series of UNODC's *World Drug Report* (Vienna, 1997–) are available online, on the agency's website.

CHINA, THE OPIUM WARS AND EARLY ASIA

There exists a rich literature on the Opium Wars, among which the best narrative works, in the English language, are undoubtedly Peter Ward Fay, *The Opium War, 1840–1842* (Durham, NC, 1975) for the First Opium War, and J. Y. Wong, *Deadly Dreams: Opium, Imperialism and the Arrow War* (Cambridge, 1998) for its follow-on. As to their prelude or background, and on opium in Qing China, both David Anthony Bello, *Opium and the Limits of Empire* (Cambridge, MA, 2005), and Stephen Platt, *Imperial Twilight: The Opium War and the End of China's Last Golden Age* (New York, 2018) are excellent works.

The principal challenge to the idea of opium as nineteenth-century drug plague is probably to be found in Frank Dikötter, Lars Laamann and Zhou Xun, *Narcotic Culture: A History of Drugs in China* (London, 2004), whose sometimes over-enthusiastic views are tempered by Melissa Macauley in her remarkable article 'Small Time Crooks: Opium, Migrants, and the War on Drugs in China, 1819–1860', *Late Imperial China*, XXX/1 (2009). For the rest of Asia, the references are more disparate, but it is worth mentioning James Rush, *Opium to Java: Revenue Farming and Chinese Enterprise in Colonial Indonesia, 1860–1910* (Ithaca, NY, 1990).

ADDICTION AND THE ORIGINS OF PROHIBITION

The master work on opium in nineteenth-century Britain and up to the first drugs acts is Virginia Berridge, *Opium and the People*, 2nd edn (London, 1999). On cannabis, a reference is James Mills, *Cannabis Britannica: Empire, Trade, and Prohibition, 1800–1928* (Oxford, 2003). The literature on the United States is notably broad. Steven Belenko's *Drugs and Drug Policy in America: A Documentary History* (New York, 2000) contains and comments on a wealth of extracts from primary sources. Both David Musto, *The American Disease: Origins of Narcotic Control*, 2nd edn (Oxford, 1987) and David Courtwright, *Dark Paradise: A History of Opiate Addiction in America* (Cambridge, MA, 2001) are otherwise key reference works.

Outside the Anglosphere, an important volume is Jean-Jacques Yvorel, *Les Poisons de l'esprit* (Paris, 1992), though it is available only in French. On Mexico, Isaac Campos's *Home Grown: Marijuana and the Origins of Mexico's War on Drugs* (Durham, NC, 2012) is well worth consulting. The book by Kathleen Lodwick, *Crusaders against Opium: Protestant Missionaries in China, 1874–1917* (Lexington, KY, 1996), straddles the United States and China and is an invaluable record of turn-of-the-century anti-opium missionary activity and influence.

On addiction concepts, finally, the most important sources are German, but the classic Eduard Levinstein, *Die Morphiumsucht* (Berlin, 1877) was also published in English as *Morbid Craving for Morphia* (London, 1878). Essential original materials also include, of course, Thomas De Quincey's *Confessions of an English Opium-Eater*, 2nd edn (London, 1856) and Jacques-Joseph Moreau de Tours, *Du Hachisch et de l'aliénation mentale* (Paris, 1845).

THE LEAGUE ERA AND THE UN SYSTEM

The literature on the key period that was the League of Nations era and the early days of the UN remains underdeveloped. Two notable works include Arnold Taylor, *American Diplomacy and the Narcotics Traffic, 1900–1939* (Durham, NC, 1969) and William McAllister, *Drug Diplomacy in the Twentieth Century* (London, 2000), though both tend to take an American more than an international perspective. On the trials and tribulations of oversees drug suppression in the late twentieth century, I otherwise recommend highly both Alfred McCoy, *The Politics of Heroin: CIA Complicity in the Global Drug Trade* (Chicago, IL, 1991) and Cornelius Friesendorf, *U.S. Foreign Policy and the War on Drugs: Displacing the Cocaine and Heroin Industry* (Abingdon, 2007). A dissenting voice highlighting the war on drug's occasional successes, notably, is James Windle's *Suppressing Illicit Opium Production: Successful Intervention in Asia and the Middle East* (London, 2016).

THE HUNT FOR THE DRUG LORDS

A proper account of the French Connection's rise and fall remains to be written, but the contemporary Newsday, *The Heroin Trail* (London, 1975) provides a detailed description of its functioning before it was dismantled. The sources on the main drug lords are likewise surprisingly fragmented, but Mark Bowden's *Killing Pablo*, 2nd edn (New York, 2016) is worthy of mention on Pablo Escobar, and the most information-rich work on Khun Sa is probably Bertil Lintner's

Burma in Revolt: Opium and Insurgency since 1948 (Boulder, CO, 1999). Clare Hargreaves's *Snowfields: The War on Cocaine in the Andes* (New York, 1992), on Bolivia, represents a feat of journalistic reporting.

THE DRUG DEBATE AND
CONTEMPORARY DRUG POLITICS

Time has been lacking for enough works to have appeared on the last two to three decades. An important academic reference is nevertheless James Inciardi, *The Drug Legalization Debate*, 2nd edn (London, 1999). Chris McGreal, *American Overdose: The Opioid Tragedy in Three Acts* (London, 2018) is a noteworthy piece of investigative journalism on the American opioid crisis. Alyson Martin and Nushin Rashidian, *A New Leaf: The End of Cannabis Prohibition* (New York, 2014) offers an equally readable account of marijuana legalization in the USA. Depicting the fraying international consensus, finally, is the invaluable tome by David Bewley-Taylor, *International Drug Control: Consensus Fractured* (Cambridge, 2012).

ACKNOWLEDGEMENTS

My thanks go first to my editor, Michael Leaman, whose enthusiasm and support have steered this book to completion. The Reaktion Books publishing team have likewise supplied multiple comments at the design stage, all of which have been of great worth.

The cliché that this book and its research 'stand on the shoulders of giants' is no less true for being timeworn. Drug history has grown, over the past forty years, into an established discipline thanks to the efforts of a few pioneers, all of whom have become masters in their own speciality and country: Virginia Berridge in Britain, David Courtwright and David Musto in the USA and Jean-Jacques Yvorel in France, for example. Though this book draws from fresh sources and original materials in many areas, it is also a summarizing work, pulling together the observations of these pioneers. They are too numerous all to be named here, but key contributors in the field have also included Alfred McCoy for the boldness of his research on the CIA, James Mills and Isaac Campos for their iconoclastic work on marijuana, James Windle for his probing of early Far Eastern prohibition, and David Bewley-Taylor for his assiduous reporting on contemporary developments.

I am more directly indebted to a number of people for having assisted me in locating or accessing essential primary and statistical sources. The indefatigable Thomas Pietschmann, the principal author of that irreplaceable publication the UNODC's World Drug Report, has very kindly helped me get to the bottom of the data it contains. I would likewise have been unable to orient myself around the archival databases of the United Nations agencies without the help of Petra van den Born from the UNESCO library. I am also thankful to Carol Place, from the American mental-health agency SAMHSA, for her help in accessing and processing its very complete data.

This book makes reference to original and secondary Chinese materials. I would have been able neither to locate nor to decipher these without the assistance of Professor Wang Li from Jiling University, nor that of its star graduate Yang Yizhong. I am equally grateful to my fellow academics Drs Liat Kozma and Haggai Ram for pointing me towards the Ottoman and Egyptian edicts on hashish and for taking the time to discuss them with me. My appreciation goes to Dr Jos ten Berge for very usefully probing the book's premise and causal links. I would also like to thank my Cambridge colleague and friend Sebastian Keibek for his observations and comments on early drug prohibition in France and Germany.

The late Dr Michel Reynaud, who did so much to change perceptions and policies on addiction in France, kindly took time to supply me with essential ideas and information at the beginning of this project. I found it equally useful to be able to discuss drug networks and their policing, and to correct any misconceptions, with Maître Sylvie Reulet. Finally, I would have been unable to discuss the American opioid crisis in these pages with the necessary confidence had it not been for the invaluable help of Dr Garret FitzGerald, from the University of Pennsylvania.

I would lastly like to thank the many friends who, over the years, have expressed their support for this project or, occasionally, volunteered to challenge the ideas it contains. Among them, pride of place goes to Matthew Gertner, Lara Marlowe and Jerry and Anne Toner. My wife, Irena, has once again been of patient support, reviewing early drafts and criticizing them when necessary, and encouraging me along when it was most needed. Special thanks, finally, go to my father René Caquet for his medical wisdom and insights, it being necessary to specify that any errors this book may contain are solely mine.

INDEX